People
in
Peril

PEOPLE
IN
PERIL
And How They Survived

86 True Dramas
From the Pages of the
Reader's Digest

The Reader's Digest Association
Pleasantville, New York
Cape Town, Hong Kong, London, Montreal, Sydney

Library of Congress Catalog Card Number: 82-060965
ISBN 0-89577-154-3
Printed in the United States of America

CONTENTS

Part One

Part Two

Part Three

Part Four

PART

I

Man that is
born of a woman
is of few days,
and full of trouble

Job 14:1

Through sleepless nights
and days of fearful waiting a haunting
inner voice told her

"... Just Be Ready!"

BY ANNETTA HEREFORD BRIDGES

O N WEDNESDAY she first noticed the feeling—a restless something that nagged like a forgotten name. The big man had seemed fretful, and she had suggested a checkup. "Haven't got time," he grunted. "Lab classes today."

That night she had a vivid dream. She was sixteen again, watching in awe as the bronze giant her brother had brought home from college tossed 200-pound bales of hay into the barn loft. Then she looked down to see the same body suddenly lying on the floor at her feet.

She sat up, heart thumping. But the big man beside her was sleeping peacefully.

On Friday—at her insistence—the man was examined and came home with a pleased smile on his face. "See?" he said. "I told you I was fine!"

But in the night a voice wakened her: *"Be ready . . . just be ready!"*

The man beside her stirred. *"Now* what's wrong?"

"Nothing," she whispered.

On Saturday she hid her feelings all day in a frenzy of housework, and on Sunday she suggested the man stay in bed awhile. He surprised her by agreeing, then read the paper, then paced the floor.

That night she counted the hours and dozed fitfully. Monday she moved vaguely through the day, waiting for something definable,

watching for something definite. Another night. She was light-headed now from lack of sleep.

Tuesday dawned clear and beautiful. The calendar said February 3, but the temperature was a mild fifty-five, and on the hill behind the Texas ranch house Spring had already pushed green fingers through the dry grass. Even when the five young adults they had created were not around, there was plenty to do: cattle to feed, the garden to tend, the house closets to finish. And then teaching chores for both of them. Last night they had set the alarm early because the man had a field trip scheduled today for his physics classes.

Six o'clock. *Please stay home,* she said silently. But what reason could she give? She pulled on her clothes and went through the hall toward the kitchen. Then she heard it—an oddly soft sound. And even before she turned, she knew. *"Be ready!"*

At the end of the hall, the big man lay crumpled into a curve on his right side. His feet were in the bedroom, his head wedged against the bathroom door frame, his arms twisted under the hard-muscled, 260-pound body. She raced to his side, but already his face was darkening, and his eyes were rolled back.

Swiftly, fingers to wrist. *No pulse.* She bent her face close to his. *No breath.*

Oh, dear God!

The head was all wrong; the neck was bent too far to allow him air. She clawed at his arms and legs, pulled at his shoulders, hoping to roll the body and straighten the neck. On her knees, she tugged with all her strength. The head was still wedged. She grabbed his feet, catching both under her arms, and pulled toward the open bedroom door. One inch, two. The head rolled; the neck straightened. She pulled at the right arm again, and the shoulder moved slightly to the right as the body's left side settled toward the floor.

The man's face was black now and the eyes were dilated. She laid her left hand over her right on the wide chest and pushed down hard. Up. Down. Her 110 pounds against his 260. She bent her elbows, released the pressure. Again. Up and down.

Bits and pieces of their lives together seemed to float away from the body. *The navy uniform. The babies they'd buried. The giant sons in football games. The lovely, talented daughters. All five in college at once.* Down, two, three, four. Was she going too fast? She watched the procedure from afar now, a spectator viewing actions in slow motion: fifteen, sixteen, up, down.

All five children are about through school now, and maybe we can . . . no. Not if . . . twenty . . . twenty-five . . . *The grandbabies. Such love . . .* thirty . . . thirty-five . . . *So many things . . . like see Alaska.*

Sixty . . . sixty-five . . . seventy . . . eighty. Her arms: They weren't going to make it. . . . *Please, God . . .* eighty-five, eighty-six, eighty-seven. *Squish!* A gurgle!

Oh, God, I'm ready!

A gasp, then the body heaved, and she pumped harder, harder. The heart fluttered, caught, fluttered again. Still she pumped, arms numb, and the big arms started to flail.

The chest rose, throwing her against the wall as the man gasped and struggled for air. The arms waved; the legs bucked. Something heavy crashed into the back of her head. He had kicked the louvered doors of the water-heater closet from their tracks. Knocking aside the doors, she whirled to pull the feet from under the burner, and the man raised himself up on an elbow, mouth open.

A doctor. An ambulance. The phone. Thank God, the extension was just above her head. "Breathe!" she screamed at the man. "Breathe!"

The run of miracles began. For the first time ever, on an eight-party line, she got the operator on the first try. "Hurry! An ambulance!" she shouted. The driver answered—incredible!—after one ring. She yelled directions. "And hurry! *Please* hurry!" But it was at least twenty miles.

More gurgles. But the face was darkening again. She went back to pumping with both hands. The heart fluttered and stopped, fluttered and caught. When the beat had steadied a bit, she ran across the bedroom to open a window. Cold air poured in, and the man opened his mouth and took great gulps. His face turned to gray, then to red.

Long ragged breaths then, and finally he had the strength to gasp for water. She reached a glass on the lavatory through the doorway, gave him a pill the doctor had given him on Friday for "shortness of breath."

Help him breathe, Lord, help him. She propped him against the door and dialed the doctor. Another miracle: She caught him, asked him to meet them at the hospital. Then an eternity until the ambulance came, oxygen was administered, and the long trip to the hospital began.

Through the wide doors of Emergency. Explanations to doctors, nurses, lab technicians. Then blood samples, X rays, electrocardiograms. The man breathed erratically, raggedly, and they took him up to the intensive cardiac-care unit, where they hooked him up to equipment to monitor his pulse and his blood pressure. And no visitors, no matter who.

The woman kept a vigil outside the door, near the nursing station. Once, grabbing a passing nurse, she learned the man was "still breathing; comfortable." The slow hours ticked by. Calls to the children were put through—to Mississippi, to Alaska, to three different universities in Texas. "No, don't come yet," she told them, knowing they'd come anyway. "I'll let you know."

One, two and four o'clock, and through the night. At dawn—splendid and glorious—the man was still alive. They let her see him for five minutes. No talk, but she watched as the lungs drew their ragged breaths, as oxygen gave him life.

The cardiac specialist finally arrived. He shot a needle into a vein, drew blood, did a quick test. "There's no oxygen in his blood! Up that supply! Get that mask on tighter and keep it there!"

A stethoscope probed the massive chest. As the doctor listened, he asked the woman blunt questions. "How long was he not breathing? Skin gray or black? Wet or dry? Fingernails? Eyes?" More listening, then he straightened slowly. "Pulmonary emboli. Multiple," he said. He shook his head. "*More* than multiple."

The cardiologist ordered a computer lung scan. To Radiology. An injection of radioactive technetium, split-second timing, plotting by the scanner. Then back to the heart monitor. She read the answers in the cardiac crew's white faces, in the speed with which they pumped anticoagulants into the body.

"A *very* massive pulmonary embolic phenomenon," the cardiologist dictated. The nurses scribbled, the men conferred. Through the door, the woman strained to see. Finally, the cardiologist came out; the woman caught him by the sleeve. "Please," she said. "The scan. Can't I see it?"

"I don't think you ought to." He looked at her hard, then said gently, "You did bring him back, didn't you? I'll arrange it. Go on down."

The radiologist held the pictures awhile, explaining, preparing her. Looking at them, the woman regretted her request. Instead of two white ovals of lungs, she saw images of two lopsided pieces that looked like Swiss cheese furrowed and chewed into fragments by six black wells of blood clots.

"I've never seen anything like it," said the radiologist. "I understand you saved his life. Are you a nurse?"

"No. A teacher."

"I just don't see how he made it to the hospital. Or how he can poss—"

"He will *live!*" she told the man fiercely, and fled.

Another night, another dawn. Against all odds, the man still breathed. A change came the third day. The racing pulse, nudging 140, gradually slowed to 120 . . . 100 . . . 90. The woman breathed gratitude and allowed herself some questions. Why had this happened to a nonsmoking, nondrinking, active man? Was it a common thing? Could it have been prevented? She cornered the cardiologist.

"Prevent cardiac arrest from pulmonary emboli? Sometimes. But people like this are walking around every day, carrying clots ready to kill them. If only they would cut out the salt, the fats, the sweets. If only they would exercise!"

"But he *did* exercise! Every day."

"Maybe that will save him." The cardiologist paused. "There's been something of a miracle here."

"I know," she said.

Ten days later—a five-minute visit per hour. More days, and to the progressive unit and later to a private room. Then a possibility of going home.

Home: the big brick ranch house they had built themselves; a herd of Black Angus grazing; a shed bursting with its crop of hay. The sons and daughters had come, of course—to return to the man some of the strength he had given them for thirty years. His colleagues came and went. And his students.

His wife? I, too, survived, strengthened by the known, sustained by the unknown.

The big man, by an uncommon clutch of miracles, is alive. We are following the doctor's *don'ts:* Don't cross the legs. Don't fail to wear the support hose. Don't forget the daily anticoagulant. Don't stay too long in one position or forget to exercise or neglect the diet.

Do's? Do resume normal living. Do be grateful you're alive. Do know you're one of the lucky ones.

We've added a *do* of our own: Do know this experience has a purpose. It points to work yet to be done and promises to keep.

"Just be ready!" the voice had said.

We're ready, this man and I. Ready for anything.

To the weather experts, it was "the greatest
recorded storm ever to hit a populated area in the
Western Hemisphere." To the Koshak family of Gulfport,
Mississippi, it brought a night of terror such
as few people have ever experienced

Face to Face
With Hurricane Camille

BY JOSEPH P. BLANK

JOHN KOSHAK, JR., KNEW that hurricane Camille would be bad.
Radio and television warnings had sounded on Sunday, August 17,
1969, as Camille lashed northwestward across the Gulf of Mexico. It
was certain to pummel Gulfport, Mississippi, where the Koshaks
lived. Along the coasts of Louisiana, Mississippi and Alabama,
nearly 150,000 people were fleeing inland to safer ground. But, like
thousands of others in the coastal communities, John was reluctant
to abandon his home unless the family—his wife, Janis, and their
seven children, aged three to eleven—were clearly endangered.

Trying to reason out the best course of action, he talked with his
father and mother, who a month earlier had moved from California
into the ten-room house with the Koshaks. He also consulted Charlie Hill, a longtime friend, who had driven from Las Vegas for a
visit.

John, 37—whose business, Magna Products, was right there in his
home (he designed and developed educational toys and supplies,
and all of the correspondence, engineering drawings and artwork
were there on the first floor)—was familiar with the power of a hurricane. Four years earlier, hurricane Betsy had demolished his former home a few miles west of Gulfport (Koshak had wisely moved
his family to a motel for the night). But that house had stood only a
few feet above sea level. "We're elevated twenty-three feet," he told

his father, "and we're a good two hundred and fifty yards from the sea. The place has been here since 1915, and no hurricane has ever bothered it. We'll probably be as safe here as anyplace else."

The elder Koshak, 67, a gruff, warm-hearted expert machinist, agreed. "We can batten down and ride it out," he said. "If we see signs of danger, we can get out before dark."

The men methodically prepared for the hurricane. Since water mains might be damaged, they filled bathtubs and pails. A power failure was likely, so they checked out batteries for the portable radio and flashlights, and fuel for the lantern. John's father moved a small generator into the downstairs hallway, wired several light bulbs to it and prepared a connection to the refrigerator.

Rain fell steadily that afternoon; gray clouds scudded in from the Gulf on the rising wind. The family had an early supper. A neighbor, whose husband was in Vietnam, asked if she and her two children could sit out the storm with the Koshaks. Another neighbor came by on his way inland—would the Koshaks mind taking care of his dog while he was gone?

It grew dark before seven o'clock. Wind and rain now whipped the house. John sent his oldest son and daughter upstairs to bring down mattresses and pillows for the younger children. He wanted to keep the group together on one floor. "Stay away from the windows," he warned, concerned about shards of glass flying from storm-shattered panes. As the wind mounted to a roar, the house began leaking—the rain seemingly driven right through the walls. With mops, towels, pots and buckets the Koshaks began a struggle against the rapidly spreading water. At 8:30, the power failed, and Pop Koshak turned on the generator.

The roar of the hurricane now was overwhelming. The house shook, and the ceiling in the living room was falling piece by piece. The French doors in an upstairs room blew in with an explosive sound, and the group heard gunlike reports as other upstairs windows disintegrated. Water rose above their ankles.

Then the front door started to break away from its frame. John and Charlie put their shoulders against it, but a blast of water hit the house, flinging open the door and shoving them down the hall. The generator was doused, and the lights went out. Charlie licked his lips and shouted to John, "I think we're in real trouble. That water tasted salty." The sea had reached the house, and the water was rising by the minute!

"Everybody out the back door to the cars!" John yelled. "We'll pass the children along between us. Count them! Nine!"

The children went from adult to adult like buckets in a fire brigade. But the cars wouldn't start; their electrical systems had been killed by water. The wind was too strong and the water too deep to to flee on foot. "Back to the house!" John yelled. "Count the children! Count nine!"

As they scrambled back, John ordered, "Everybody on the stairs!" Frightened, breathless and wet, the group settled on the stairs, which were protected by two interior walls. The children put the cat, Spooky, and a box with her four kittens on the landing. She peered nervously at her litter. The neighbor's dog curled up and went to sleep.

The wind sounded like the roar of a train passing a few yards away. The house shuddered and shifted on its foundations. Water inched its way up the steps as the first-floor outside walls collapsed.

No one spoke. Everyone knew there was no escape: They would live or die in the house.

Charlie Hill had more or less taken on responsibility for the Koshaks' neighbor and her two children. The mother was on the verge of panic. She clutched his arm and kept repeating, "I can't swim. I can't swim."

"You won't have to," he told her, with outward calm. "It's bound to end soon."

Grandmother Koshak reached an arm around her husband's shoulder and put her mouth close to his ear. "Pop," she said, "I love you." He turned his head and answered, "I love you." His voice lacked its usual gruffness.

John watched the water lap at the steps and felt a crushing guilt. He had underestimated the ferocity of Camille. He had assumed that what had never happened could not happen. He held his head between his hands and silently prayed: *Get us through this mess, will You?*

A moment later, the hurricane, in one mighty swipe, lifted the entire roof off the house and skimmed it forty feet through the air. The bottom steps of the staircase broke apart. One wall began crumbling on the marooned group.

Dr. Robert H. Simpson, director of the National Hurricane Center in Miami, Florida, graded hurricane Camille as "the greatest recorded storm ever to hit a populated area in the Western Hemisphere." In its concentrated breadth of some seventy miles it shot out winds of nearly 200 miles per hour and raised tides as much as thirty feet. Along the Gulf coast it devastated everything in its swath: 19,467 homes and 709 small businesses were demolished or severely damaged. It seized a 600,000-gallon Gulfport oil tank and carried it three and a half miles. It tore three large cargo ships from their moorings and beached them. Telephone poles and twenty-inch-thick pines cracked like guns as the winds snapped them.

To the west of Gulfport, the town of Pass Christian was virtually wiped out. Several vacationers at the luxurious Richelieu Apartments there held a hurricane party to watch the storm from their spectacular vantage point. Richelieu Apartments were smashed apart as if by a gigantic fist, and twenty-six people perished.

Seconds after the roof blew off the Koshak house, John yelled, "Up the stairs—into our bedroom! Count the kids." The children huddled in the slashing rain within the circle of adults. Grand-mother Koshak implored, "Children, let's sing!" The children were too frightened to respond. She carried on alone for a few bars; then her voice trailed away.

Debris flew as the living-room fireplace and its chimney collapsed. With two walls in their bedroom sanctuary beginning to disinte-grate, John ordered, "Into the TV room!" This was the room far-thest from the direction of the storm.

For an instant, John put his arm around his wife. Janis under-stood. Shivering from the wind and rain and fear, clutching two of the children to her, she thought, *Dear Lord, give me the strength to endure what I have to.* She felt anger against the hurricane. *We won't let it win.*

Pop Koshak raged silently, frustrated at not being able to *do* any-thing to fight Camille. Without reason, he dragged a cedar chest and a double mattress from a bedroom into the TV room. At that moment, the wind tore out one wall and extinguished their lantern. A second wall moved, wavered. Charlie Hill tried to support it, but it toppled on him, injuring his back. The house, shuddering and rocking, had moved twenty-five feet from its foundations. The world seemed to be breaking apart.

"Let's get that mattress up!" John shouted to his father. "Make it a lean-to against the wind. Get the kids under it. We can prop it up with our heads and shoulders!"

The larger children sprawled on the floor, with the smaller ones in a layer on top of them, and the adults bent over all nine. The floor tilted. The box containing the litter of kittens slid off a shelf and vanished in the wind. Spooky flew off the top of a sliding bookcase and also disappeared. The dog cowered with eyes closed. A third wall gave way. Water lapped across the slanting floor. John grabbed a door that was still hinged to one closet wall. "If the floor goes," he yelled at his father, "let's get the kids on this."

In that moment, the wind slightly diminished, and the water stopped rising. Then the water began receding. The main thrust of Camille had passed. The Koshaks and their friends had survived.

With the dawn, Gulfport people started coming back to their homes. They saw human bodies—more than 130 men, women and children died along the Mississippi coast—and parts of the beach and highway were strewn with dead dogs, cats, cattle. Strips of clothing festooned the standing trees, and blown-

down power lines were coiled like black spaghetti over the roads. None of the returnees moved quickly or spoke loudly; they stood in shock, trying to absorb the shattering scenes. "What do we do?" they asked. "Where do we go?"

By this time, organizations within the area and, in effect, the entire popula- tion of the United States had come to the aid of the devastated coast. Before dawn, the Mississippi National Guard and civil-defense units were moving in to handle traffic, guard property, set up communications centers, help clear away the debris and take the homeless by truck and bus to refugee centers. By ten a.m., the Salvation Army's canteen trucks and Red Cross volunteers and staffers were going wherever possible to distribute hot drinks, food, clothing and bedding.

From hundreds of towns and cities across the country came several million dollars in donations; household and medical supplies streamed in by plane, train, truck and car. The federal government shipped 4,400,000 pounds of food, moved in mobile homes, set up portable classrooms, opened offices to provide low-interest, long-term business loans.

Camille, meanwhile, had headed north from Mississippi. It dumped more than twenty-eight inches of rain into West Virginia and southern Virginia, causing rampaging floods, huge mountain slides and 111 additional deaths be- fore breaking up over the Atlantic Ocean.

Like many other Gulfport families, the Koshaks quickly began reorganizing their lives. John divided his family in the homes of two friends. The neighbor with her two children went to a refugee cen- ter. Charlie Hill found a room for rent. By Tuesday, Charlie's back had improved, and he pitched in with the Seabees in the worst vol- unteer work of all—searching for bodies. Three days after the storm, he decided not to return to Las Vegas, but to "remain in Gulfport and help rebuild the community."

Near the end of the first week, a friend offered the Koshaks his apartment, and the family was reunited. The children appeared to suffer no psychological damage from their experience; they were still awed by the incomprehensible power of the hurricane but enjoyed describing what they had seen and heard on that frightful night. Janis had just one delayed reaction. A few nights after the hurri- cane, she awoke suddenly at two a.m. She quietly got up and went outside. Looking up at the sky and, without knowing she was going to do it, she began to cry softly.

Meanwhile, John, Pop and Charlie were picking through the wreckage of the home. It could have been depressing, but it wasn't:

Each salvaged item represented a little victory over the wrath of the storm. The dog and cat suddenly appeared at the scene, alive and hungry.

But the blues did occasionally afflict all the adults. Once, in a low mood, John said to his parents, "I wanted you here so that we would all be together, so you could enjoy the children, and look what happened."

His father, who had made up his mind to start a welding shop when living was normal again, said, "Let's not cry about what's gone. We'll just start all over."

"You're great," John Koshak said. "And this town has a lot of great people in it. It's going to be better here than it ever was before."

Later, Grandmother Koshak reflected: "We lost practically all our possessions, but the family came through it. When I think of that, I realize we lost nothing important."

The awesome triumph
of a young mother determined
to protect a life more precious
to her than her own

The Courage
of Karla Little

BY JOHN G. HUBBELL

ALL WAS SILENT THOSE LAST, terrible moments in the sky. With engine stopped and power gone, the little plane lost its grip on the turbulent air and began its slide down through the opaque undercast. Below lay the wild, mountainous Pacific Northwest. At the controls, the pilot peered in vain for an opening in the thick gray murk. In the backseat, Karla Little wept soundlessly and clutched her baby daughter tightly to her. Tiny Laurie, bright-eyed, towheaded and full of promise, had been in the world only ten weeks—why did everything have to end so soon for her?

They were down! The plane hit and pounded through an expanse of snow, pitching, bucking, slamming. Karla felt brutal forces trying to wrench her through the seat belt. The aircraft slowed, and for the briefest moment hung on the brink of a steep ravine. Then it plunged downward in a whooshing avalanche of snow toward the final violence.

It had all begun so happily: a golden-wedding celebration for Mable and Ray Erickson of Norwalk, California. From all over the country, five children and fifteen grandchildren were coming—and the first great-grandchild, Laurie. What a party it was going to be!

Their oldest son, Grant Erickson, 49, a radio-supply-company executive in Sioux Falls, South Dakota, borrowed a small plane for the trip: a four-passenger, single-engine Mooney Super 21. With his

wife, Dolly, he flew to Seattle to collect his daughter, Karla, 25, her husband, Loren, and Laurie.

But at the last minute Loren Little could not go. A skilled trumpet player, he had been offered a summer job in a Seattle nightclub. He needed the money to support his family and pay his final year's tuition at the University of Washington Medical School. So, shortly after noon on that twenty-third day of June in 1966, he stood waving as the orange-and-white aircraft, carrying his wife and baby, climbed away from Boeing Field and headed south.

At 4:10 p.m., Boeing Field got word from the Federal Aviation Administration (FAA) that Grant Erickson, who had filed a flight plan to land at Troutdale, Oregon—a Portland suburb—had not arrived. He was two hours overdue. A check showed that he had taken on fuel for four and a half hours' flying. According to the flight plan, he meant to keep an altitude of 5,500 feet. FAA records showed that he was an experienced pilot but not instrument-qualified—and at 2:18 p.m. a special weather report for Portland had indicated a fast-deteriorating weather situation, with thunderstorms forming, winds gusting, icing conditions at 6,000 feet and a total overcast at 2,500 feet.

Erickson had been in radio contact with Troutdale twice. First, he reported that he was thirty miles east of the field. A few minutes later, he reported himself as being twenty miles northwest of Portland, at 8,500 feet, unable to find any break in the clouds below, and having engine trouble. Was he lost? Running out of fuel? Troutdale was unable to reestablish contact. Aeronautic officials in both Oregon and Washington immediately began organizing volunteers for an air search as soon as the storm might lift.

Loren Little was practicing on his trumpet at eleven p.m. when he got the news. Fear quickening in him, he left at once for Portland in his Volkswagen. On the long, dark drive, he prayed and hoped. He told himself that, after all, it had been reported only that the plane was missing. They probably were down safely on some small, unattended emergency airstrip. But what if they weren't? He drove the little car flat out.

Laurie was still in Karla's arms and crying when Karla regained consciousness. The plane lay right side up on a steep slope. In the front seat, Grant Erickson and his wife lay sprawled face down; neither moved when Karla called. There was blood everywhere; it had drenched the seats, clothing and Laurie. Anxiously, Karla examined her baby. There were no wounds, only a bruise on her forehead with the imprint of a button from her mother's coat. Laurie was all right, Karla decided—only hungry. But as she felt the raw, torn places on the right side of her own head, an agonizing, throbbing ache started deep inside her and screamed out in every fiber. As consciousness started to slip away, she exerted a huge effort of will to hang on. She could live with pain, but Laurie could not live without someone there to feed her.

Jars of baby food and fruit juice had been packed in a small suitcase in the luggage compartment directly behind Karla's seat. Holding Laurie in one arm, she strained with the other to reach for the case. She discovered that her legs would not move. From the waist down she was paralyzed. She would worry about that later; she had to feed Laurie now. Karla was thankful she was a nursing mother.

When Laurie, wrapped warmly in a thermal blanket, was asleep, Karla began calling again, softly, to Grant and Dolly. They did not answer. She worked her way forward on her seat, reached down and felt at their faces for a breath of life. But the effort grew too much for her, and slowly, painfully, she moved back again without knowing whether she had felt any breath. She decided that the two were alive and soon would awaken—she *had* to believe that.

Nearly exhausted, Karla looked out her window. All snow out there—but it was June, so she must be high up on a mountain. She hoped a rescue party would arrive soon, because Laurie would be needing that baby food.

The pain subsided a little when she remained still. Night was falling. She slept.

Loren drove straight to the Portland home of a friend. Another friend, a pilot, arrived with maps, and the three men pored over them. Grant Erickson had last reported himself at 8,500 feet; so it seemed likely that something had happened at or near that altitude. In this area, only Mount St. Helens and Mount Hood jutted that high. Loren decided that his family must have crashed against one of the two mountains. All night he paced, hoped, imagined, despaired, prayed.

By seven a.m. he was at the Troutdale airport, talking with search coordinator Pat Mulligan. The weather had not yet cleared the high mountains, but the search was already blanketing the two points where Erickson had last reported himself.

In the air, flying with one of the search pilots, Loren nearly lost heart—it was such an immense country! Awesomely beautiful, but wild, forbidding, full of secrets. The pilot flew low and slow over the great plunge of the Columbia River gorge separating Oregon from Washington. To the north, pilots flew "creeping line" search patterns over heavily forested grid sections thirty miles square. Loren learned that, while hunting for the Mooney, the searchers were also casting about for signs of other missing light aircraft.

Late in the day, when the weather finally lifted from the high mountains, Loren—on his third long search flight—approached 11,000-foot Mount Hood. The pilot began flying a long, slow downward spiral around the mountain. Loren studied every wooded patch, every ledge, every outcropping. There was nothing.

Through that first night, Karla managed. Laurie's stirrings at feeding times awakened her. She would change the baby's diaper, nurse her, then struggle again, against the stabs of excruciating pain, to reach the baby food. It was galling to be able to touch the suitcase and not be able to lift it. She was becoming very thirsty. Karla wanted to scream, to damn the vile circumstances; but that would spend strength and shatter the discipline which, for Laurie's sake, she had to impose on herself. So she kept the baby warm, nursing her until she had enough, then talking and crooning her to sleep again.

She kept trying to find breath in her father and Dolly. She never was sure, but she refused to admit to herself that they were dead.

During the day, in occasional spurts, rocks rolled down the slope and smashed into the aircraft. Most were about fist-size; but some, much larger, dented or even burst holes through the fuselage. A few that rolled by were as big as houses and could have crushed the airplane. Karla was frightened now. And desperately thirsty! She worried that the lack of body fluid would prevent her from nursing.

Suddenly she spied a mining town only a few hundred yards from the aircraft. There would be water there! Somehow she had to drag herself free and get over to that town. Then reason reasserted itself: It was only a bunch of boulders. She would stay here, keep Laurie warm, and wait.

Once she saw aircraft, and wanted to cry with relief that rescuers at last had found her. But the Mooney's white top blended with the snow, and the searchers didn't see it. The planes flew on. But they would come back, Karla knew. She waited. Again night fell. Again she slept.

At Troutdale airport, Loren was sick with uncertainty and suppressed grief. The day's search of the lower areas had been meticulous, thorough. Tomorrow the high mountains would be searched again, all day. It had been planned to search tonight, but a fog was settling in and the pilots were very tired.

The air search could not last indefinitely. After a reasonable period, usually about three days, missing aircraft have to be presumed irretrievably lost and their occupants dead. But Loren knew he would never stop looking for Karla and Laurie. He would walk these mountains until he found them, no matter how long it took.

Sleep came easily after some forty hours without it, but by 5:30 a.m. Loren was heading again for the Troutdale airport. Dawn had broken on a perfect day. The two snowcapped mountains were clearly visible. Loren's attention seemed drawn irresistibly north to Mount St. Helens in Washington. "Do you think Karla is up there?"

he asked. Only God knew—but Loren could not take his eyes off that farther mountain.

Most of the searchers were already in the air. The Washington Civil Air Patrol had dispatched additional light aircraft. So had the Army, from Fort Lewis near Tacoma, along with a half-dozen helicopters. From Portland the Air Force sent big HU-16B planes, each carrying two air rescuemen. By noon, more than forty aircraft were searching.

At Troutdale, Loren paced, waiting. There had been telephone calls from several people in rural areas who had heard an airplane in trouble or seen a possible clue. Each lead was investigated. But for an hour and a half now there had been no word.

Suddenly the phone rang. Pat Mulligan answered it, said hardly a word, and hung up. The Mooney—"the wreckage," he called it— had been found on Mount St. Helens by an army helicopter team. There were survivors—no mention of how many or who they were. They would be brought to Longdale Hospital, near Kelso, Washington, where the northern half of the search was based. It was over! Loren turned away. For the first time he felt tears stinging his face.

Mulligan said, "Let's go to Kelso." The twenty-minute flight seemed interminable. Loren kept his eyes riveted on the mountain, as though he could force it somehow to yield the lives he wanted it to yield.

It was a special moment for Eugene Ingram and Evan Hale. Ingram held a civil-service job; Hale was an auditor for the U. S. National Bank of Oregon; both were pararescuemen in the Air Force Reserve. The moment word came from the helicopter that the Mooney had been found and that there were survivors, Ingram and Hale volunteered to jump in. In years of service they had parachuted to more wrecks that they could remember. But it was a rarity in the wild and rugged Northwest to find any survivors at all.

They landed at the top of the ravine; then the search helicopter picked them up and carried them to within seventy-five yards of the wreck. They floundered through deep snow toward it. They could hardly believe what they found—*a woman, smiling weakly, holding a baby in her arms!*

Ingram took the infant, wrapped her in his flight jacket and carried her to the waiting helicopter. He ducked beneath the thundering rotors and climbed in beside the pilot. Within seconds the chopper was airborne, whirling down over the trees dotting the mountain's flank.

Meanwhile, Evan Hale, helped by a crewman from the helicopter, was gently easing Karla onto a litter. In shock and barely conscious by now, Karla drifted off into a deep sleep as she was lifted aboard a second helicopter.

When she awoke, Loren was with her. "You're alive!" she exclaimed. On that last lonely morning in the plane, she had confused her dead father with Loren.

In addition to deep head cuts and bruises, Karla Little had suffered a concussion, a collapsed lung, a badly smashed vertebra, a ruptured disc and a displaced pelvis. Both legs had frozen, and gangrene had turned her feet black up to the ankles. (They were saved.) The coroner's report showed that the injuries of the two who had died were almost identical to Karla's. Karla believes that she would have died, too, but for Laurie's depending on her for life. Laurie came off the mountain in immaculate condition—not even Karla knows how all the diaper changes were managed—and showed only a loss of a few ounces.

For their rescue operation high on the savage slope of Mount St. Helens, pararescuemen Ingram and Hale both won the Airman's Medal, the only ones awarded to Air Force reservists in 1966.

For thirty terrible minutes,
he drove a potential bomb through
the peaceful countryside

Hans Hugger's
Fiery Ride

BY CURTIS CATE

As Hans Hugger maneuvered his truck into the small town of Teningen in southwestern Germany that September afternoon in 1968, he felt no cause for anxiety. For him it was just another routine assignment. The stocky twenty-eight-year-old was so familiar with his rig—a big Mercedes-Benz tractor pulling a thirty-six-foot tanker—that driving it had become practically second nature to him. His load this trip: more than 6,000 gallons of acetone, a highly flammable liquid even more volatile than gasoline.

When he arrived at his destination, the Tscheulin aluminum factory, Hugger proceeded to pump his cargo into four large underground storage tanks. An hour later, five out of the trailer's six tanks were empty, and the sixth was being drained. It was now 6:15 p.m.

Suddenly, without warning, the air above the trailer's bright aluminum back end turned blue. The next thing Hugger remembers, he was dashing to the rear of his truck, where a five-foot tongue of flame was shooting from the outflow pipe.

The day shift at the factory was just coming off duty. Fearing that if the fire traveled down the hose to the factory's storage tanks it would blow everything sky-high, Hugger plunged his arm into the flames, yanked the master valve shut and then unhitched the hose. In the urgency of the moment, he did not notice his burns.

As the hose end dropped to the ground, the escaping acetone burst into a giant sheet of flame. With an awesome swoosh, it roared up the rear ladder of the trailer, igniting the vapors escaping from the vent of tank No. 6. In seconds, the trailer's entire rear end was ablaze. But Hugger didn't see this. He was already sprinting back to the cab so he could get the burning rig out of there—fast. He swung himself in, started the engine, released the brakes and slammed into low gear. "Send the fire engines after me!" he yelled, and off he roared.

Horn blowing, he crossed the bridge over which he'd driven an hour and a half before. That relieved him, because he remembered that the town of 5,000 inhabitants began to thin out somewhat beyond the bridge. But then he glanced in the rearview mirror, and relief turned to terror. The flames rising behind him were now almost ten feet high!

As the rig picked up speed, Hugger noticed that the flames began to waver and flatten. "I realized," he says, "that speed was my best friend. If I could just keep those flames slipstreamed down until the fire engines caught up, I might be able to avoid an explosion." The area was still too heavily built-up to permit him to abandon his truck; there was nothing to do but keep moving.

But the act of keeping going also held perils. Dead ahead now was a railroad crossing with a passenger train thundering by. As Hugger's wailing fireball roared across the tracks, it missed the train's last car by inches.

Already Hugger's eyes were trained on a T-shaped intersection just 200 feet ahead. Blocking his path was heavy early-evening traffic on a major north-south highway. He applied his brakes, planted his hand on the horn. Though he kept the horn blasting, the traffic would not let him in. To one side was a ditch, to the other a roadside inn. Had he tried backing up, the flames would have been swept forward on his cab. All avenues of escape seemed hopelessly blocked.

Inside the inn, customers could feel the intense heat of the burning truck right through the closed windows. For a full minute and a half they watched in paralyzed terror as the truck stood there, unable to proceed, leaking acetone into a fiery puddle that began to creep forward under the trailer.

Hugger looked in his rearview mirror hoping to see fire engines. There were none in sight; all he could see was a hideous, rising wall of flame.

At last there was a break in the traffic, and Hugger swung into the northbound lane—it seemed to lead more toward open country than the southbound. Soon he had the speedometer up to about thirty-five miles per hour and the flames down again. But traffic was getting heavier.

Amid his doubts about where the unfamiliar highway would take him, there was only one thing of which he was certain: He was determined to cause as little damage to other people and their property as he could.

As he drove north, disregarding speed limits, he prayed that he wouldn't be blocked along the way. Deep ditches bordered both sides of the road; no turn-off into open country was anywhere in sight.

About this time, a driver who saw Hugger's burning truck made a U-turn and raced to notify the nearest fire department. Hans Zuckschwerdt, chief of the Emmendingen unit, moved into action, and by the time his Volkswagen station wagon pulled out, its blue roof-light flashing, two more fire departments had been alerted and the four engines joined the town of Teningen's fire truck, which was already in the chase.

It had begun to rain. Hugger hoped it would help damp the fire, but he also realized that the road was becoming slippery. At last he spotted an autobahn sign for Basel–Karlsruhe. *Here's my chance,* he thought. On the autobahn there would be more space, fewer people. But before he knew it, both turnoffs were behind him and he had to go on. Slamming on his brakes would have thrown him into a skid.

There were several tractors puttering along the road he was on now, but when their drivers saw Hugger's rig coming, they leaped off their machines and made for the fields. Hugger entered a cut, with embankments on either side hemming him in. Past that, he found himself still imprisoned by the road—on his right by a steep slope, on his left by a metal fence.

Worse was yet to come. Dead ahead he saw the village of Bahlingen, with its quaint, gabled houses tucked closely along a winding main street. "That street was a nightmare," recalls Hugger, who normally would have crawled through the town but now charged in, horn blaring. "Narrow, with some really wicked curves. If I'd gone more slowly, the flames behind me would have licked at the gables."

Suddenly, as he barreled past the frightened villagers, another autobahn sign flashed into view. There was still hope—if only he could get out of this deathtrap of a town in one piece! Two more blind turns, a few houses, and he *was* out. Ahead of him lay a long stretch of country road, bordered by trees and ditches but mercifully straight.

Now Hugger was on an overpass and could see the autobahn beneath him. He slowed and turned onto its cloverleaf entry. He was headed north—toward Karlsruhe. Traffic was fortunately light, but, even so, cars began bunching up behind him as if the drivers were mesmerized by the comet's tail of fire. Hans didn't dare pull over to stop on the shoulder: The trailer might blow up just as the bunched-up cars started edging past.

Hugger had covered twelves miles and been at the wheel for almost half an hour. His right hand was cramped from gripping the steering wheel; the fingers of his left hand were numb from pressing the horn. His shirt was soaked with perspiration. Just as he was beginning to lose hope, tiny stabs of bluish light began to flicker in his rearview mirror. At last! It was Zuckschwerdt's station wagon, speeding up the autobahn at eighty miles an hour.

As Emmendingen's fire chief pulled abreast, he signaled Hugger to slow down so that the fire trucks, which he knew were following, could catch up. Soon the two leading engines came along—in the left lane to avoid the rig's flaming tail. The first one overtook him and moved into the right lane ahead of him, and the driver flashed his brake lights. Hugger applied his own brakes. As his rig rocked to a halt, the flames began climbing again. Hans leaped out and cried, "Acetone!" Then he began running. It was the first warning the firemen had of the kind of fire they had to cope with.

But they knew what to do. With fire-fighting powder they attacked the two sources of the blaze—the vent of tank No. 6 and the outflow pipe. Within seconds the blaze itself was out. (It took about twenty minutes of hosing and thousands of gallons of water to cool the red-hot tank so that it could eventually be emptied.) Overtaken by exhaustion from his ordeal, Hugger collapsed and was rushed to a hospital.

While recovering, he was besieged by grateful visitors who wanted to thank him for the selfless way in which he had averted a whole string of potential disasters. His heroism was cited by the German Association of Truckers, and the press presented him with its prized *Kavalier der Strasse* (Knight of the Road) award. One week later, he reported back for trucking duty.

"How would you like to drive your old friend again?" his boss asked, pointing to the completely repaired tank truck. Hugger hesitated for a second, then walked over and, with a grin, heaved himself into the cab. A man who had triumphed over his own fear and a half-hour ride with death wasn't going to let himself be scared by another truckload of acetone.

Stranded on a tiny rock
in a raging river at the bottom
of an 800-foot chasm,
the young hiker saw small chance
of survival.
Then a helicopter
appeared high overhead

Rescue
in the Gorge

BY JOSEPH P. BLANK

THE FOUR-MAN CREW stood wordlessly before Lt. Cmdr. John Morse on the helicopter ramp at Lemoore Naval Air Station, California. It was four a.m. The idling engine of *Angel 4,* a twin-engine UH-1N helicopter of the search-and-rescue unit, seemed to stress the silence that covered the base.

Morse, a veteran helicopter pilot and the father of two young children, wanted his crew to know the worst. "We'll be going into this deep, narrow gorge after a kid who's sitting on a rock in the river," he said. "At least we hope he'll still be there when we arrive.

The situation is very tight; no space to maneuver. Wind and water go down the gorge like coal down a chute. Everything has got to work perfectly, both ship and crew."

He waited. His copilot, Lt. (j.g.) Phil Griesbach, said nothing. The three young enlisted crewmen, Dan Hart, Ted Jones and Sid Chavers, were free to withdraw from any civilian mission. They said nothing.

"Okay," Morse said. "Let's go."

During the one hundred-mile, one-hour flight to Yosemite National Park, Morse mulled over the perils of the mission. On the previous evening, he had talked by telephone with Pete Thompson, the search-and-rescue specialist at Yosemite. Thompson had reported that a young man named Tyler Seal would be spending his second night stranded on a rock in the raging Tuolumne River in Muir Gorge. The gorge was at least 800 feet deep, with almost sheer granite walls that narrowed to a width of about twenty-eight feet at the river. Rescue by winch-equipped helicopter was the only way to save Seal.

"It's a hairy situation," Thompson had said.

Tyler Seal and Rick Yoder, both nineteen, had been close friends for ten years in Modesto, California. Tyler had completed Navy basic training and was home on leave when the two young men decided to take a weekend hiking trip in Yosemite National Park.

They started off on a Saturday, July 7, 1973, and followed mapped trails for ten miles to a site called Ten Lakes. Here they did some climbing, cooked over a campfire, swam and fished.

On Sunday morning, they agreed that it would be more interesting to return to the ranger station where they had parked their car by a different route. They went off-trail to make a one-mile descent to the Tuolumne River, which they intended to follow for two miles before picking up another mapped trail.

For five hours they cautiously worked their way around waterfalls, fallen trees, huge boulders and underbrush. By the time they reached the rushing, rock-strewn river, Tyler's legs were buckling, and he had fallen a few times. The river had no real bank, just a narrow, uneven rock ledge that they carefully walked along for about a mile. Then, at a bend in the river, the ledge dwindled and became sheer granite wall.

By now exhausted and apprehensive, they stared at the impasse. "There's a pool of shallow water down there," Rick said. "I'll jump in with a rope, so you can haul me back up. Maybe I'll be able to see something around the bend."

Tyler wound one end of the rope around his hand. Rick leaped eight feet into the river. As he started wading, his foot slipped on a rock. Fearing that he would pull Tyler in, he instantly let go of the rope.

The gushing waters grabbed him and hurled him downstream. He tumbled through the white, roiling chute, caroming off rocks and frantically flailing his arms and legs to get his head above water. He struck a protruding rock with his shoulder and hugged it. The water tore his hands and arms from the rock and again propelled him down the horrible chute. He surfaced, banged into another rock, grabbed it and held, knowing that the rest of his life might be measured in seconds.

Back on the ledge, Tyler watched in horror as Rick vanished. Then he slipped. He could have regained his footing, but he thought, *I might as well see if I can help,* and jumped in. He landed on a rock, breaking his left ankle. The water whirled him under. Then he hit a projecting rock, and the strength of the current miraculously lifted him on top of it. Rick was about fifteen feet in front of him. "Rick! Rick!" Tyler yelled.

His friend turned his head in amazement. "Tyler, how did you get here?"

"I . . . kind of jumped."

"Tyler, that's stupid. Just stupid! I can't hold on!"

"Get on top of your rock!"

"I can't!"

"You've got to!"

Rick somehow twisted his body. The current hit him broadside, lifting him, enabling him to scratch his way onto the rock. He lay there, half-gasping, half-sobbing, and looked around. Tyler's rock was in the middle of the river; to leave it would be suicide. But Rick saw that the gorge wall was only eight or nine feet from *his* rock. And, halfway to the wall, another rock jutted from the water. A leap to that rock, then to a ledge on the wall, and he would be out. "Stay there!" Rick shouted to Tyler. "I'm going for help."

"It's all up to you, Rick."

Rick reached the gorge wall and began climbing. It was slow and tortuous. To gain footings and handholds, he continually had to work to his right or left; sometimes he found himself totally blocked and had to retreat. He knew that if he slipped he would drop like a stone into the river.

After some 300 yards, the angle of the gorge wall was not as steep. He grimly continued his climb, pushing through thick brush, crawling between enormous boulders, climbing trees to get over small cliffs. The river was now far below him, just a thin white line in the fading light.

At nightfall he slumped down into a patch of weeds. He had to stop. He couldn't take a chance on falling in the darkness. It grew cold, and he shivered in his thin T-shirt. *Poor Tyler,* he thought. *I wonder what he's going through.*

Tyler was also shivering on his three- by four-foot rock. In the darkness, the roar of the river seemed to grow louder and louder, and it made the night seem endless. He tried to find relief from the cold spray by pulling his T-shirt over his head. Periodically, he panicked, screaming and weeping to let out his anguish. He prayed: *Please, God, help me. And help Rick. Don't let him fall. Give him strength to make it.*

Daylight offered no relief. The river, the rocks, the great canyon walls seemed completely indifferent to his terrible plight. He sang songs, told jokes to himself, called out the names of the states. Nothing helped.

He looked at his watch. It was 4:30 in the afternoon. He had been on the rock for twenty-four hours. He decided to remain there until morning. If no help came by dawn, he would slip off the rock and try to make it to the gorge wall. He had no way of knowing that a waterfall, which would surely batter him to death, was just around the bend.

High above Tyler—and now miles away—an exhausted Rick had arrived at the ranger station where Pete Thompson and Richard Smith were on duty. "He did a marvelous job climbing out of that gorge in twenty-four hours," Thompson said later. "Even with my experience and with equipment, I don't think I could have done it in that time."

It was 5:00 p.m. The rangers immediately called for a civilian helicopter. By 6:15, Rick and ranger Smith made the first pass over the gorge. They saw nothing. Tyler, curled on the rock, heard the machine but assumed that his mind was playing tricks. He didn't look up.

The chopper made a second pass. This time Tyler saw it and waved his arms. Rick spotted him and tapped Smith. "There he is!" he yelled.

After the chopper had landed in an open area near the top of the gorge, Smith radioed Tyler's position and predicament to Thompson, describing the difficulties confronting a rescue operation. They agreed that Rick and Smith should climb down into the gorge and spend the night near Tyler to try to bolster his morale. Meanwhile, Thompson would ask the Navy if it could send out a rescue helicopter.

With Rick acting as anchorman on the ropes, Smith eased himself down the gorge wall to within forty-five feet of Tyler. "Can you make it another night?" the ranger called. "We'll have a helicopter with a cable here in the morning."

Oh, God, Tyler thought, *not another night!* Panic seized him at the thought that he might doze and slip off the rock to his death. But he answered, "I think I can."

Angel 4 dipped into Yosemite Valley early the next morning to pick up Pete Thompson. The ranger quickly briefed the crew on the problem, emphasizing that every minute was precious because of steadily increasing wind velocity. Crew chief Hart, 24, looked at twenty-year-old Chavers. "Well, Sid," he said, "you've been waiting to make your first cable rescue. This one's a beauty."

Pilot Morse made one pass over the gorge, then another pass through the gorge at about 400 feet. He quickly weighed all the factors—air temperature, hovering altitude, the gross weight of the helicopter, wind velocity, canyon dimensions—that would affect the operation. Because every extra pound subtracted from flying stability, Pete Thompson was put off on a little plateau about 1,800 feet from Tyler Seal. "Okay," Morse announced finally. "We're going in."

As the helicopter sank into the gorge, each man assumed specific responsibilities. Pilot Morse played the craft's controls against the winds and kept an eye on the south wall. Copilot Griesbach visually measured the distance between the rotor blades and the north wall and at the same time scanned instruments and gauges. If one of the two engines failed, the aircraft might crash in the bare seconds it would take for the other engine to pick up the entire load. Chavers put on his harness and stuffed a second harness into his pocket. Jones reported the movements of the ship's tail.

Crew chief Hart, flat on his belly, his helmeted head sticking out the starboard door, directed Morse to a position seventy-five feet above the stranded hiker. "Forward, Mr. Morse," the crew chief said into his helmet mike. "Ten yards at twelve o'clock . . . easy forward . . . a little more to the left, Mr. Morse."

"I can't."

"You've got to."

Morse inched closer to the north wall.

"Easy . . . easy . . . HOLD! You're right on the money. I'm opening the hoist boom, and Chavers is going out."

Hart used an electrically controlled winch to lower Chavers. "He's halfway down . . . you're drifting, Mr. Morse . . . easy forward and left . . . HOLD! He's three quarters down . . . he's turning . . . he's there!"

Chavers settled on the rock as the thundering river raged by. "You all right?" he asked Tyler.

"Just my ankle."

"You'll be out of here in a couple of minutes. We have to get your arms and legs through this harness. Then I'm going to unbuckle the cable from my harness and attach it to yours. Just take it easy as the crew winches you up."

Hart continued his steady line of chatter, keeping Morse informed of what was happening every second. "The kid is buckled . . . I have a thumbs-up from Chavers . . . the cable is about to pick up the weight—NOW!"

Morse had to be instantly aware of the need to compensate for an additional weight of some 185 pounds imposed on one side of the ship as Tyler started up. Hart moved the winch lever to its top speed. "He's halfway . . . three quarters . . . he's in! I'm sending the cable down for Chavers."

Corpsman Jones peeled off Tyler's clothes and got him into a sleeping bag. Morse said, "The wind is getting stronger." Hart got the message: The pilot was hovering a scant twelve feet from the granite wall; with the rising wind, only a few minutes remained before he would have to pull away from Chavers's position.

The crew chief dropped the cable. To his dismay, it and its two-pound hook were flung about like a kite in a high wind. Hart released more cable—the winch was not unwinding fast enough—until the hook hit the water, then pulled in eight feet of slack with his hands. He swung the cable three times, getting the feel of the weight, then dropped the hook right into Chavers's hands. Chavers hooked up, Hart winched up, and Morse pulled away from the wall while Chavers was still swinging in the air. The entire rescue operation had taken just ten minutes.

Morse clipped through the mounting winds of the gorge to pick up rangers Thompson and Smith and Rick Yoder. As the copter lifted away, Tyler gave Rick a big grin. "Thanks, buddy," he said, then promptly fell asleep. Rick kept shaking the hands of the crew and repeating, "How beautiful. You did it. How beautiful."

Morse was proud of his crew. He also was relieved and exhausted. In 3,500 flight hours including a search-and-rescue tour in Vietnam, he had never flown in a more dangerous mission.

Tyler Seal will never lose his awe of what happened. "I was a stranger to those men in the helicopter crew," he says. "To think that they knowingly risked their lives to save me. Maybe someday I'll understand what makes human beings want to do such things for other human beings."

The wall of water careened
across the Alaskan bay, scouring trees
and topsoil to a height of 1,750 feet.
Squarely in its path bobbed the little
thirty-eight-foot fishing boat

"There's a
Tidal Wave Loose in Here!"

BY LAWRENCE ELLIOTT

ON JULY 9, 1958, Howard G. "Howie" Ulrich, a thirty-two-year-old
commercial fisherman out of Pelican, Alaska, was trolling off the
mouth of Lituya Bay with his seven-year-old son when he picked up
the six p.m. weather report: a possibility of high winds from the
southeast.

Ordinarily Howie would have ignored such a warning, but now
he stepped into the pilothouse of his thirty-eight-foot troller, the
Edrie, and radioed his partner, Julian J. "Stutz" Graham, who was
running a parallel course fifty yards off his port beam. "Stutz," he
said, "since the boy is aboard, I'm going into Lituya for the night."

Howie didn't much like Lituya Bay. Its mouth is constricted to a
very narrow eighty-foot channel by rock; violent tidal currents make
navigating the channel difficult. And there were fishermen around
who remembered that October morning in 1936 when several giant
waves swept across the bay, leaving destruction in their wake.

Still, Lituya was the only natural harbor along one hundred miles
of the Gulf of Alaska coast, and Howie went in.

About ten that night, just before Howie went below to hit the
sack, a second troller put in to Lituya. In the distance it looked to
Howie like Bill and Vivian Swanson's troller, the *Badger.* A few minutes later a third came in and anchored beside the second. But by
that time Howie was sleeping peacefully. There was no wind. The

water was glassy smooth. Small icebergs floated about, sparkling in the deepening twilight.

But one thing was ominously wrong. The gulls and terns that usually screamed above the rocky crags of Cenotaph Island out in the center of the bay were gone. Stutz Graham, who had gone five miles north after leaving Howie, had come upon the birds at Cape Fairweather, and the sight made him uneasy. "I never saw so many of them," he recalled later. "They must have covered twenty acres.

The funny thing was, there wasn't a single one in the air. They were all squatting on the beach like they were waiting for something."

It was still light at 10:17 p.m. when an abrupt and violent shudder brought Howie Ulrich bounding out of his bunk. Not quite awake, he thought, *The anchor must have pulled loose. We've run aground!* The moment he came plunging out on deck, though, he knew the truth.

"It was an earthquake, a bad one," he said. "The water churned, the mountains shook. Those mountains—it was like they were going through some awful torture. Can you imagine what it's like to see a ten-thousand-foot mountain twisting and shaking?"

Clouds of snow and rock went spewing into the sky. Great chunks tore loose from the mountainsides and came avalanching into the bay. Huge pieces of ice came flying off Lituya Glacier, at the head of the bay, like a load of rocks spilling out of a dump truck.

Howie didn't know it, but in Juneau, the capital city, the earthquake jostled people in their beds. Near Cross Sound, octopus, cod and halibut in large numbers were killed by shock waves. The communications cable between Haines and Skagway was severed in four places. In Seattle, the needle of the University of Washington's seismograph jumped completely off its graph. When final readings were correlated, the quake was found to have been one of the most severe in North American history, registering close to eight on the Richter scale. (The San Francisco earthquake of 1906 had registered 8.25.)

As his boat thrashed at anchor, Howie stood transfixed by the spectacle before him. It had a hypnotic, otherworldly quality from which he had to wrench himself free.

His son stood beside him on the deck now, sleepily rubbing his eyes. Howie made a tentative effort to get a life jacket on the boy. He didn't feel any real sense of danger—he was fairly certain the *Edrie* could ride out the quake—but it seemed the thing to do. He didn't bother about a jacket for himself. In fact, a long time would pass before he realized that he was wearing nothing but the shorts in which he had slept. It was seconds shy of 10:20 p.m.

About two and a half minutes after he first felt the shock, Howie heard a gathering, rumbling roar. Soon it filled the hollow of the bay with crashing sound. Howie actually felt its vibrating impact on his bare skin. Along the top of the bay, six and a half miles away, an enormous wedge of mountain and glacier—literally thousands of tons of ice, rock and earth—had heaved, then plunged down into the narrow inlet, causing a cascade of water that now seemed to explode across the bay at an incredible height. Ponderously, inexorably, the wall of water began bearing down on the *Edrie*.

"Get below!" Howie cried to his son. Then, "Wait!" he shouted. "The life jacket!"

Terrified and trembling, the boy stood fast as his father fumbled with the strings on the jacket. Precious seconds fled by. Fragments of panic-flecked thought jarred against Howie's brain: He had to get away from the beach; he had to haul anchor! Then he remembered that Stutz Graham and his seventeen-year-old son, Ken, were only a few miles away at Cape Fairweather. He ran for his radio.

Stutz Graham had just turned out the forecastle light when the *Lumen* pitched forward, then rolled hard to starboard. He and his son bounded onto the deck. The sea was contorted by six-inch waterspouts; waves smashed crazily against one another and churned the water to frenzied white foam. "Start the engine!" Graham commanded. Remembering Howie, he ran to switch on the radio. A babble of excited sounds came over the receiver—shouts, half-sentences, cries of alarm. Then, sharper than the rest: "Mayday! Mayday! This is the *Edrie* in Lituya Bay! There's a tidal wave loose in here! I don't think we've got a chance."

Howie never remembered sending his "Mayday." His recollection was that as the wave tore through the bay, the first thing he did was to start his engine and throw in the full power of his anchor winch.

"I meant to head into it. I felt I had to get into deep water before the wave threw us up on the beach."

But the anchor—a sixty-four-pound Danforth—wouldn't budge. The tortured heaving of the earth had probably opened a crevice that swallowed it. Desperate, Howie let the chain pay out to its full forty-fathom length. Maybe there would be enough slack to permit the *Edrie* to ride up over the wave. Then, with engine and rudder, he began maneuvering the pitching troller about so that she would be faced into the onrushing wall of water.

The water had crested at a height of approximately one hundred feet as it cut a swath through Cenotaph Island. It now stretched from one shore to the other, two and a half miles, breaking sharply as it swept over the north side of the island. And, wherever it struck, it sheared away hundred-year-old timber stands and peeled the earth back to bedrock. Flung into the bay, six-foot spruce trunks were shaved as clean of bark as though they had been sent through a sawmill.

Howie had not quite got the *Edrie's* bow swung into the wave when it hit. He remembered it as "like going up in an elevator. Only there seemed to be no end to it. The half-inch anchor chain snapped off at the winch like a piece of kite string, and the short end came snapping back around the pilothouse and almost took my head off."

The wave lifted the *Edrie* high up over the shoreline. Swooping along above the treetops, Howie abandoned hope. "There was just nothing I could do," he said. "I could see the trees snapping off way below us. I figured we had to be dumped and smashed on the rocks."

Miraculously, the *Edrie* slid over the crest of the wave and was caught by the backwash. Down and down the little troller swept. Howie threw his throttle wide and clung to the wheel in a frantic effort to keep his bow pointed at Cenotaph Island. For the first time, he began to think that he and his son had a chance.

Neither of the other two boats anchored in Lituya Bay lasted so long. On the *Badger,* Vivian Swanson saw the great wave coming and cried out to her husband. "What can we do?" For a moment, Bill Swanson considered following the example of Orville and Mickey Wagner, who had anchored their forty-four-foot *Sunmore* beside them—hauling anchor and making a run for the channel and open water. But he decided that the *Badger* would never make it in time. He moved closer to his wife and just waited. He remembers that the wave was still sweeping them upward when he heard Mickey Wagner's last, plaintive cry on the radio, "Mamaaaaa!" and he saw the sleek new *Sunmore* awash to the pilothouse and heading straight for a sheer cliff.

The Swansons' boat went up like a matchstick and crossed over the 150-yard spit of rock at the mouth of the bay, then down and out into the open sea. "I looked down on rocks as big as houses when we crossed the spit," Bill Swanson says. A quarter of a mile offshore, the boat slammed into the sea, stern first. With the icy gulf waters rising over them through the shattered stern, the Swansons tore frantically at the lines that secured their eight-foot skiff to the pilothouse roof.

The water was at their knees when they shoved off from the stricken troller. Since the oars had been swept away, Bill tore loose one of the skiff's thwarts and began paddling.

By now, radios were crackling all over the area as skippers set out to account for every boat in the little fishing fleet, interdependent in crisis as never before. Racing down from Cape Fairweather at top speed, Stutz Graham kept repeating: "This is the *Lumen* calling the *Edrie*. Howie? Do you read me?"

Howie Ulrich felt that he had been dumped pell-mell into another world. Inside the bay, a stench—"It smelled like an explosion in a root cellar"—hung in the gathering twilight. A strange fog was closing in. He could see water surging up onto the shores, forming lakes hundreds of yards inland and dumping mountains of debris on the beach. But the eeriest sight was the shoreline, thick with timber only moments before, now naked, shorn to glistening rock back to a height of as much as 1,750 feet. In the bay, felled trees were pitching and tossing in unnatural currents and eddies, crisscrossed and upended like jackstraws. Great chunks of glacier ice whirled round and round, grinding against each other.

Nevertheless, Howie decided to have a try at getting out of the bay. Carefully he began threading his way toward the channel.

"I could hardly see a thing by now," Howie said, "not a single landmark. I had to follow a compass course. Maybe the tide would be against me; maybe I'd take a timber through the hull on the way out. But it was still a better gamble than milling around inside until we were crushed. I tucked some seat cushions around Sonny and told him to hang on for dear life."

The *Edrie* hit the channel on the full ebb tide. Howie eased his boat into the swiftly running water, and in moments the *Edrie* was being thrown toward the open sea, pitching under combers that crashed solidly over the wheelhouse. Still, she held steady fore and aft, her snub nose rising stubbornly after each breaker. It seemed to Howie that he hardly breathed until, at last, the stout little troller reached the comparative calm of open water. He began to shake—a delayed reaction to the harrowing moments behind him. Then he went below and dressed.

Bearing southeast at full throttle, Stutz Graham was soon forced to cut his speed, first to five knots, then to two, as the debris flung out of Lituya Bay began spreading up and down the coastline. Ken Graham lay prone across the *Lumen's* bow, playing a flashlight on the dark and littered water, guiding his father port or starboard and sometimes shouting, "Reverse!"

Inexplicably, Stutz Graham cut his engine as he approached Lituya. "There was no reason for me to shut down," he reflected. "Fact is, it was plain dangerous. I couldn't have been in more than five fathoms of water. I might have drifted aground. It was just one of those senseless things you do sometimes. Now, I'm not a religious man, but when something like that happens—when senseless things add up to a purpose that you couldn't possibly know about—then I say that somebody or something higher up is keeping track of things."

The moment Stutz's engine faded, a new sound broke the stillness—a thin, plaintive cry.

"It could have been a bird—it sounded like a bird—but Ken and I kept running from one corner of the boat to another, trying to get a line on where it came from."

But there was only silence, and soon Stutz turned the engine back on. In a little while he felt impelled to turn it off again. Twice more he repeated the process. The fourth time he again heard the weak call for help. Bill Swanson's tiny skiff was almost alongside the *Lumen's* port bow, barely four inches of freeboard remaining. Waist-deep in the fifty-degree water, the Swansons were all but senseless with shock and cold. After nearly two hours of exposure, they were, in fact, only moments from an icy grave.

Stutz and Ken sent out word that the Swansons had been picked up—"Tell 'em to send a plane!"—while he got Bill and Vivian into sleeping bags and heated some coffee for them. Then the *Lumen*, the *Edrie,* and the third boat to arrive, Red Embree's *Theron,* began searching for some trace of the Wagners, whose boat had been anchored beside the Swansons in the bay. Soon after one a.m., Stutz got word that a plane had left Juneau for Dixon Harbor, about forty miles to the southeast; he was to take the Swansons there.

Stutz suggested that Howie follow him to Dixon Harbor. Howie declined. "Suppose they were drifting around in the dark somewhere? It could have been Sonny and me, you know. I felt the least I could do was stick around."

"Howie's kid was just like his old man," Stutz said. "I offered to take him in with me, but he said he guessed he'd stay with his dad."

All night long the two searchers alternately drifted and called, then cruised on to another area and called again. By now the sea was completely littered. Floating clumps of earth, roots and trees, some still standing upright, drifted by like ghostly islands.

It was 5:30, with the morning sun already reddening the sky, when other trollers reached the scene. Howie Ulrich turned to his son. "Well, sport, what do you say to all the excitement?"

"Daddy," the boy replied, "let's go home to Pelican."

Howie hugged the slim shoulders close to him, then turned southeast and increased speed. As he cruised past Dixon Harbor, a boat hailed him. It was the *Lumen*. Stutz Graham had been standing by, waiting for his partner so they could return to Pelican together, as partner boats should. In the full light of the new day the friends made for Cross Sound. It had been a long twenty-four hours.

The search for the Wagners proved futile. Except for a single brightly colored trolling pole, no trace was ever found of them.

In the spring of 1959, the Swansons bought a new boat. A goodly part of its cost was contributed by members of the fishing fleet. As one of the contributors said, "It could have been me, couldn't it?"

And exactly one year and a day after his harrowing experience in Lituya Bay, Howie Ulrich, cruising along through the Gulf of Alaska in the dead of a moonless night, ran the *Edrie* aground, tearing a hole in her starboard bow. Howie managed to beach her and, with a makeshift patch, refloat her when the tide came in. But it was a close call.

Did he think he was jinxed by the ninth and tenth days of July?

"I've got enough real things to worry about without loading myself down with superstitions," he said. Then he grinned. "But check me on July 11, 1960."

Until the
carnage ended,
no one could even
suspect the identity
of the deadly
accurate marksman
firing from the
schoolroom window

"Sniper! Get Down!"

BY GERALD MOORE

J UST BEFORE THREE O'CLOCK that afternoon, maintenance man Earl Metcalf, known as "Slim" to his many friends, finished repairing a broken window in the Olean, New York, high school, an imposing, 1930s-style building on Sullivan Street. It was December 30, a Monday workday squeezed between the last weekend of 1974 and New Year's Eve. School was out in the western New York State community, but the maintenance staff was working.

A lazy holiday mood prevailed as Metcalf reported back to boss Dick Krott in the sub-basement maintenance office. Settling his six-foot-four-inch frame down on a battered couch beside fellow worker Gordie Huff, Metcalf started to read a retirement brochure. In April he would be sixty-two and eligible to retire. After twenty-seven years with the Olean schools, he was looking forward to it.

Suddenly, the three men heard someone yell: "There's a fire on the third floor!"

Huff and Metcalf jumped up and ran for the stairs. Krott, close behind, stopped before they reached the door. "Let's pull the juice," he said. "It may be an electrical fire." Krott and Huff headed for the circuit breakers. Metcalf raced ahead up the stairs.

On a second-floor landing, Metcalf met custodian Joe Kosidlo. Together they ran up the last flight, Metcalf in the lead. On the third floor, outside the student-council room, they saw heavy black smoke and five spent shotgun shells lying near a burned-out smoke bomb. The doorknob was shot away. Alarmed by the sight, Kosidlo hesitated, but Metcalf impulsively burst through the door. A second door, made of frosted glass, barred the way. Through it Kosidlo saw the silhouette of a man with a gun.

"Slim!" Kosidlo shouted. "Get the hell out of there!"

But Metcalf didn't stop. There was a deafening explosion. Glass shattered. Metcalf was driven backward against Kosidlo. Kosidlo recovered his balance, turned and ran. Metcalf did not move. He was dead.

Engine Company No. 1 received the fire alarm. Herbert Elmore had the big yellow pumper, No. 42, out of the station in no time. Riding beside him was Capt. John Snopkowski. Neal Pilon, a fifty-eight-year-old employee of Columbia Gas of New York, Inc., heard the fire siren and followed Engine 42 in his truck. For more than twenty years, Pilon had gone to many of the fires in Olean to shut off the gas supply.

Suddenly, just as Elmore wheeled the pumper into Sullivan Street, a shot rang out. Elmore never heard it; it came through the window and hit him in the head. Shattered glass caught Snopkowski full in the face. The same bullet drove on through the cab and hit George Williams, riding in back. He fell, and Greg Kwiatkowski, his partner, threw himself on top of Williams in an instinctive act of protection.

Immediately there was a second shot, and Pilon, who had crossed the intersection to park beside the school, fell sprawling on the street.

Snopkowski leaned around the cab of Engine 42 and yelled, "Sniper! Get down!" Kwiatkowski helped Williams to his knees. They rolled together off the riders' deck, taking cover behind the truck. Snopkowski ran to join them.

As Bud Fromme brought Engine 41 up Sullivan Street he heard the shots that hit Elmore and Pilon but didn't realize what was happening. Then a bullet smashed through Fromme's cab, neatly splitting his cap and scalp, shattering the back window, and hitting Joseph Snopkowski, Captain Snopkowski's brother, in the stomach.

Unaware of what had just happened to Engine 41 and his brother, Captain Snopkowski spotted a fire-department snorkel truck turning onto Sullivan Street. He waved to them for help, and Frank Ensell, the snorkel driver, hurried on toward Engine 42. He drove right in front of the school before he saw John Snopkowski's bleeding face and knew they were in danger.

Ensell, Lt. John Gibbons and David Nolder tumbled out of the snorkel and took cover. Ensell realized suddenly that the snorkel could be used as a shield between the school and Engine 42. Crawling back to the snorkel door, he slipped the truck in gear. Keeping his head down and exposing only his hand on the steering wheel, he inched the snorkel nearly one hundred feet into a protective position between Engine 42 and the school.

Gibbons saw Pilon lying near the curb and started toward the wounded man. A bullet whined off the street inches from Gibbons. He retreated.

As the firemen tried desperately to invent a way to reach Pilon safely, the wounded gas repairman waved feebly for help. Gibbons, so moved that he was about ready to make another try, flinched as another shot rang out. It hit Pilon in the head. He lay still. Gibbons turned away, sickened by the sight.

Alerted by a phone call, police now ordered the school area sealed off to keep people away. But the order did not come soon enough to save Carmen Wright Drayton.

Mrs. Drayton, twenty-five years old and expecting a child, had promised to take her blind father shopping. On the way to get him, the car stalled. Mrs. Drayton called her sister, Cynthia, and asked her to come help. Carmen Drayton was shivering in the freezing temperature by the time Cynthia arrived half an hour later with their younger brother, Jud. Cynthia said she would drive her sister to get help to fix the car.

Near the high school, Cynthia saw several fire trucks and a police car. As she approached the intersection of Third and Sullivan, she heard a loud explosion. Glass flew everywhere. Cynthia turned to see Jud throw his hands over his bleeding face. Then Carmen slowly slid over in the seat and rested against her.

In the same instant, two more gaping holes appeared in the windshield. Fighting a spray of glass, Cynthia speeded up and headed for the hospital. Jud was taken into surgery to remove the glass from his eyes. Carmen was beyond help.

Seconds later, Wayne Dutton, his wife and three small children approached the same corner in their car. Dutton heard a bang; the engine died and the horn began to blow. It seemed that his car had exploded. His first thought was to get the children out before it caught fire. He leaped out and was knocked flat by a bullet ripping through his arm. Mrs. Dutton shoved her children to the floor of the car and tried to hold them there. The shots and blaring horn terrified the children, and they began to cry. But Robbie, 7, started crawling toward his wounded father.

Jack Marsfelder was walking near the school just as Wayne Dutton was hit. Disregarding his own safety, Marsfelder ran to Dutton, who was bleeding badly from a severed artery, and dropped down beside him. He grabbed Robbie and got him to lie down on the street behind a front wheel. Trained in first aid, Marsfelder ripped up Dutton's shirt and quickly made a pressure bandage for his arm.

Gibbons feared that Herbert Elmore, finally freed from Engine 42's cab by Kwiatkowski and Williams, would die without immediate treatment. But the rifle fire from the student-council room was so accurate that every move on the ground was stopped short by another bullet. Using the radio in the pumper, Gibbons reached ambulance driver Walter Thorpe and briefed him. He told him that Elmore might die anyway and the sniper's aim was sure, but Thorpe did not hesitate. He told Charles Fortuna, riding with him, to duck, then raced down Sullivan across the full field of fire, and stopped beside Engine 42. Sheltered by the engine and the snorkel, Thorpe and Fortuna loaded Elmore in and raced to the hospital.

The Olean police and the state troopers were now in position around the school. There was no chance that anyone could escape, but storming the building without hurting the innocent people inside would not be easy. The police estimated there were at least twelve office and maintenance workers still inside, their whereabouts unknown. As Olean police chief Mike Luty and senior investigator John Stofer, from the New York Bureau of Criminal Investigation, worked out a plan, Lt. Arthur Filjones and patrolman James Tambash arrived in an unmarked police car, roared up to Engine 41 and, under fire, rescued its two wounded.

Just before four o'clock, Luty called for a tank assigned to the Olean National Guard armory. William Foss, the unit's commander, couldn't get a telephone call through to secure the needed authorization from Buffalo or Albany. Foss decided that lives were more important than formalities, and he ordered the tank out.

When the tank lumbered up Sullivan Street, it was carefully placed to screen the Dutton car. Finally released from their ordeal, Mrs. Dutton and the children ran to the cover of the tank. Thorpe and Fortuna, back on the scene now, rushed in and loaded Dutton on a stretcher. The pressure bandage applied earlier had saved him from bleeding to death. Crouching behind the tank as it backed out, the little group trudged to safety.

Luty and Stofer decided to storm the school from the rear. Two police officers armed with shotguns covered the back stairs while four others made their way to the third floor.

The long corridor to the student-council room was quiet. Metcalf's body lay near the burned-out smoke bomb. Carefully, their shotguns ready, the four officers moved forward. On signal, police investigator David O'Brien swung into the vestibule and fired, blasting a second hole in the frosted-glass door, and another officer heaved a tear-gas grenade. After the gas did its work, they rushed into the room. They were hardly prepared for what they found.

An obscenity, the huge letters still damp and dripping, had been spray-painted on one wall. The floor was littered with brass cartridge cases and empty shotgun shells. Behind an overturned desk, O'Brien spotted a figure dressed in camouflage pants and jacket sprawled on the floor. His face was hidden by a gas mask. Near his head a tape machine was playing rock music. O'Brien pulled the mask away and saw the face of a boy.

O'Brien quickly determined that his prisoner, though unconscious, was unhurt. The gas mask was improperly fitted and had leaked. The boy was loaded onto a stretcher and strapped down. Mike Barbaro, the school security officer, pushed in to see who was on the stretcher. "My God!" he stammered, his face twisted with disbelief. "That's my nephew! Why would he do it? *Why?*"

The sniper carried out of the student-council room that terrible Monday was Anthony Barbaro, a seventeen-year-old honor student, the kind of boy who, until that day, would make any community proud. Only weeks before, Tony had been awarded a state regents scholarship. He ranked eighth—with an average of 96—in a class of 290. He did not smoke, drink or use drugs. He was an altar boy, and a member of the National Honor Society. He was also the third-best marksman on the high-school rifle team.

The Barbaro family had been in Olean for three generations. Tony's father had entered Olean High School in the same year as the slain Earl Metcalf. Almost everyone in town knew some member of the Barbaro family and seemed to understand immediately that Tony's parents were victims of the tragedy, too. The Barbaro home was flooded with calls of sympathy from people who understood how terrible the experience was for Tony's parents. And, for their part, Mr. and Mrs. Barbaro, racked with shame and anguish, later called on the family of each victim to express their sorrow.

Tony, a small but muscular boy, had been the oldest of four children. One classmate recalled him as a "nice guy, always ready to help others."

But a fellow member of the rifle team said that Tony sometimes spoke of "ripping through town" on a National Guard tank or holing up for a standoff gunfight. And among Tony's possessions was found a diary in which he had considered the best place for a shooting spree, even mentioning the high school.

Tony's room, too, had been filled with rifles and shotguns—including the scope-sighted .30-06 that he had bought from a local gun store with his mother's permission and that he was to use in the sniping attack, a gun powerful enough to kill a deer at 600 yards. According to friends, he had once spoken of "how strange it must feel to be a sniper holding people off."

Tony Barbaro was charged with the murder of three people. He pleaded "not guilty by reason of insanity," then committed suicide shortly after his trial began.

As the town of Olean recovered from these shocks, the community did not turn to hatred or recrimination but to helping those who suffered. Olean literally surrounded its wounded and mourning with aid and support.

Luty took it upon himself to research all the financial aid that might be available to those who were wounded or lost a member of their family. Members of the police and fire departments visited the wounded and offered help with such simple things as seeing that firewood was kept in supply at their homes and that families had adequate transportation. Friends and strangers alike brought food and sympathy to the widows. And the Masonic Lodge staged the largest memorial service ever seen in Olean for Earl Metcalf.

When Herbert Elmore recovered sufficiently to come home from the hospital in Buffalo, he was greeted by a giant motorcade. The high-school band marched in front of the ambulance carrying the still partially paralyzed Elmore. Main Street was lined with well-wishers, shouting, "Welcome home, Herbie!" Elmore, in an act of will that seemed to personify Olean's spirit, raised himself slowly, painfully, into a sitting position in the ambulance. He smiled broadly and began waving back.

One man, watching Elmore wave, seemed to sum it all up: "It's too bad it had to happen," he said. "But when the chips are down, people in Olean—just ordinary people—will show you that they are made of something pretty special."

On a fateful summer day,
in a tide rip off
the Australian coast,
a father discovers
the strength and courage
of his three young sons

"My Sons Are Drowning!"

BY BRIAN DAVIES

IF IT HADN'T BEEN for my little daughter, we would never have gone to the beach on Christmas Day, 1976. It had been a hot, windless holiday. In the late afternoon, I decided to take four-year-old Sarah to the local pool for a swim. The boys—Ben, 15, Luke, 14, and Felix, 12—declined the invitation to join us. They loved the water. But go swimming on holiday with your old man and little sister? No way!

When Sarah and I found the pool closed, I elected on the spur of the moment to drive eight miles to Mona Vale, one of Sydney's popular surfing beaches. And I had another inspiration: I would dig those lazy boys out of their Christmas-afternoon torpor and make them come with us.

To be completely honest, this was something of a paternal power play. My sons had been getting above themselves recently. When I herded them into the car, only Felix was enthusiastic. Luke was resigned, Ben mutinous.

To celebrate Dad's "victory" over his recalcitrant sons, I donned a huge and ridiculously beaten-up straw hat. The boys groaned and averted their eyes. But my wife, Joan, grinned as she settled back for the drive. She was anticipating coolness at Mona Vale and the joy of watching Sarah splashing in the water.

When we reached the beach, around six-thirty p.m., about a dozen people, mostly kids, were still swimming and surfing at the far end. There was no sign of a beach patrol or lifeguards.

While Joan relaxed on the sand and I splashed in a rock pool with Sarah, the boys beat a hasty retreat. After a perfunctory swim far enough along the beach to conceal from their contemporaries the fact that they were in the company of their parents, they tried out their jointly owned surf board.

Ben and Luke were strong swimmers, and I had given up on the repetitive warnings they had suffered as preteenagers about staying between the flags that marked the swimming area, watching out for rips and undertow, and not going out too far. These days, I nagged about fitness. I told them that their habit of lying around on the sand rippling their muscles for admiring girl friends did not make for swimming stamina.

Deciding that the surf was all wrong, the older boys condescended to give Felix sole use of the board. They settled down glumly on the sand to await release, watching their brother's ineffectual attempts at surfing with the amusement the vast difference in their ages conferred on them. Felix was still learning to handle the board and the big offshore waves. He had yet to summon the courage to venture beyond the beachside breakers.

For me, this was an idyllic end to Christmas Day: my daughter dog-paddling happily in the pool; my older boys relaxed and happy beneath their resentful pose; Felix gaining confidence on the board;

my amiable fool of a dog tumbling around my wife's legs. The sun was an orange ball, dazzling our eyes and bequeathing long, fantastic shadows to the beach. Nearby, two men my age—give or take a couple of years either side of forty—and four children between the ages of eight and twelve were wading and diving into the first line of breakers.

It was a scene of near perfection, a greeting-card illustration of Early Evening, Christmas Day, Australia.

Leaving Sarah with her mother, I plunged in for a last roll in the surf before going home. Beyond the first breakers, I caught sight of the bobbing heads of the family group of two men and four children. They were bunched together in a curious way, and suddenly I felt a chill of fear. *They're okay,* I tried to reassure myself, *or else they would be calling out to me.*

I edged obliquely toward them and realized that they were drifting farther away. Now I could read anxiety in their faces and see the straining in their bodies. I called out: "Are you all right?" And prayed they would answer yes. But the reply I dreaded came back across the waves: *"No, we're not!"*

The two adults were on the seaward side of the children, trying to usher them toward the shore. Although they were swimming desperately, they were making no headway. And there was panic in the children's swimming.

Reluctantly, I started toward them. My God! What could I do to bring two adults and four children back to the beach? At my best, I could barely manage a hundred yards in the town pool. Fear and reflex kept me going. And then I felt the rip.

An unbelievable surge of power tore at my body and sucked me out toward the struggling family. Amid the shouting and confusion, I managed to snatch the arm of the small girl who was closest to me. Somehow, with strength born of desperation, I managed to flounder out of the rip's awesome grasp.

As I stumbled back into the shallows with the little girl, an unthinkable thought crossed my mind: *Abandon the others; forget it. There's nothing more you can do.*

Felix, unaware of the building drama, was still messing about with the board. *The board!* Of course. I shouted to him above the roar of the surf, "Bring the board! The board, Felix!"

On the beach, Ben and Luke cringed. Dad's going to have a go on the board, they imagined—or so I was told later.

But Felix had awakened to what was happening and, instead of bringing me the board, shot through the breakers himself, paddling furiously. I screamed at him to come back; then, frozen with terror, watched him pierce wave after wave as he angled toward the bobbing heads.

When he vanished behind the waves, I started to swim toward him. Suddenly, two slim, tanned bodies flashed by me. Ben and Luke speared into the waves, strong young arms thrashing. My idyllic Christmas evening had disintegrated.

Then, astonishingly, a surfboard fin sliced the crest of a wave. Felix was coming back. Two children were on the board in front of him, and my baby boy was paddling for dear life. I joined him, and together we maneuvered the board into shallow water and hustled the children ashore.

But *my* children, Ben and Luke, were still out there! Surfboards were the answer; I must get more surfboards. I started running toward a few distant surfers.

Then another panicky thought hit me. *Felix.* But already he was on the board, heading out through the surf again. (Later, he told me, "I didn't want to go, Dad. But my brothers were calling me to bring the board out.")

I ran uselessly back the way I had come. I was winded, slow, almost hysterical. My three sons would drown. I could see them all, my boys and the other family, tossing in a trough between the ominous waves.

One of the men called in a panic-fighting voice: "Help! Help!"

Back into the surf I plunged, but I could not force myself into the rip. One figure—no, two—came toward me. It was Ben, towing a young boy. He pushed the child in my direction and without a word turned back. All the children were safe now—except mine.

I had never felt so useless. Through a break in the surf I could see Luke, Felix and one adult clinging to the board as it yawed across each outgoing swell. Ben and the other man were struggling in the water nearby.

I imagined Felix's tense little face as he gripped the board, and my fear brought me to tears. Ben might make it back to the beach, but Luke and Felix never. I would have to go into the rip. Reason no longer counted.

Suddenly, two young men of twenty or so raced past me. They leaned their boards gracefully into the surf and flew through the breakers. Without my realizing it, Joan had completed my unfinished quest along the beach. She had reached the surfers and brought them running.

Moments later, Felix was back, perched beneath one rider, shaken but grinning like a monkey over the longest surf ride he had ever had. Then Luke was there with our board, helping to guide the two adults to safety. And then Ben. He was swimming back without a board, determined to finish on his own, and in the end almost too exhausted to crawl up the beach.

Nobody talked much. Not us, not the family whose lives had been saved, not the two young men who had come to our aid at the crucial moment. I settled Ben, Luke and Felix, hooded and wrapped up in Christmas-present beach towels and shivering despite the heat, in the back of our car.

Then, during the drive home, we started to talk about it—over and over.

And soon my own perspective on the afternoon's events began to take shape. Ben, Luke and Felix had done this fine thing by themselves, without any urging or supervision from me. They had acted together on their own initiative, drawing on their own strength and courage. And now, blessedly, I was reunited with my sons, my boys—my splendid young men.

Before you offer a ride
to that next unknown hitchhiker,
consider this young couple's
harrowing experience

A Stranger
in the Car

BY JOHN P. DAVIS
Detective, Kansas City, Missouri, Police

AUGUST 16, 1957, dawned hot in Kansas City. I was a traffic officer then, and I went on duty at 7:00 a.m. At 9:30 I had parked my three-wheeled motorcycle at Fifth Street and Grand Avenue in the welcome shade of a building as I watched the flow of traffic through the intersection. Suddenly a man got out of a car and came running toward me.

"Officer," he shouted excitedly, "there's a cream-and-green Pontiac westbound on Fifth with a hand sticking out of the trunk! The car has an Indiana license."

Here are the events that led to that moment—as they happened.

Earlier that day, at 2:30 a.m., twenty-one-year-old Airman Carl A. Wagner and his eighteen-year-old wife, Molly Sue, were driving west on Highway 40 from Kingdom City, Missouri. Wagner had been home in Indiana on a fifteen-day leave and was returning to duty at Schilling Air Force Base, Salina, Kansas. Just west of Kingdom City, where highways 40 and 54 intersect, he noticed a young-looking hitchhiker, dressed neatly in a checkered sports shirt and gray slacks. "Shall we give him a lift, honey?" Wagner asked his wife.

"I don't know, Carl. It might be all right," she replied.

"He looks okay," said Wagner reassuringly. "He might be another serviceman." He stopped the car and shouted, "How far are you going, buddy?"

"Denver," the man answered.

"We can take you as far as Salina, Kansas," said Wagner. "That's over halfway."

"Yeah," the man answered laconically, climbing into the backseat of the two-door Pontiac sedan.

Wagner's attempts to start a conversation with the hitchhiker failed, and as time passed, he remembered things he had read about hitchhikers and began to worry a bit. He could see that Molly Sue, who was expecting their first child, was worried, too.

But as the miles rolled by and nothing happened, Carl and his wife began to relax. The man in the backseat, who looked older than he had first appeared to be, had fallen asleep. Had the Wagners known that they were befriending a convicted killer, they would not have been so complacent as they drove through the night toward Kansas City.

The man they had picked up, James Richard Esson, 36, had a record that showed that he had been released from an Ohio reformatory in 1943 after serving a three-year sentence. In 1944 he began a one- to five-year penitentiary term in Michigan. In 1948, convicted of first-degree murder in Cleveland, he started a life sentence in the Ohio State Penitentiary at Columbus and was later transferred to a prison farm. He had escaped from there on May 27, 1956.

At 4:30 a.m., Wagner passed a road sign: KANSAS CITY—65 MILES." He nudged the accelerator gently.

Suddenly, without warning, the hood of the car flew up in front of the windshield. Wagner jammed on the brakes and brought the car to a quick stop.

The man in the backseat sat upright. "What happened?" he asked.

Wagner was getting out. "The hood came unlatched," he replied. "It's a good thing there's no traffic tonight."

As Carl walked to the front of the car, Molly Sue felt something press against her shoulder. She turned and saw that it was a pistol in the hitchhiker's hand. She was terrified.

Carl slammed the hood down and got back into the car. As he reached for the ignition key, Esson hit him on the side of the head with the pistol. Carl felt a searing pain, and blood started running down his neck.

"Do exactly as I say or I'll kill you both," Esson snarled, his pistol at Wagner's head. "Drive on down the highway."

At the intersection of a small country road Esson ordered Carl to turn. Then, after they had gone a couple of hundred yards, he said, "Stop. Both of you get out."

Molly Sue was crying as she and her husband stood in the road with their hands up. Esson again struck Carl with the pistol, knocking him to the ground. Blood streamed from another head wound. The escaped lifer kicked Wagner in the side, saying, "Get up and open the trunk." Carl dragged himself to his feet and did as he was told.

"Now get in." Esson slammed the lid.

"Please," Molly Sue pleaded. "Just leave us here and take the car."

Now the pistol was pointed at her. "Get in front."

Esson drove a short distance back toward the highway and stopped. Molly Sue screamed as he slid over and pulled at her maternity blouse. Now she became hysterical and pleaded with him to release her husband. Esson ordered her out of the car.

"Okay, you want to be with your husband, so get in with him," he said, opening the trunk. The lid slammed shut. Soon the car began to move.

Carl and Molly Sue could scarcely breathe in their cramped positions. After what seemed an eternity the car stopped again. The trunk lid opened, and Esson told them to get out. After tying their hands and gagging them with strips torn from clothing he found in the car, he pushed them back into the trunk. With gags cutting at their mouths, the young couple struggled for every breath.

Five more times during the night Esson stopped the car. Twice he pistol-whipped Carl; twice he pointed the gun at him and snapped the trigger. Each time the gun failed to fire. The last stop Esson made was for gas, after warning the Wagners that he would kill them and the filling-station attendant if they made a sound.

As Esson drove on again, Carl managed to free his hands and untie Molly Sue. He tried to force the lock on the trunk, but it wouldn't move. Finally, he pried open one corner of the trunk lid with a tire tool. They breathed deeply of the fresh air.

It was daylight now, and they began to hear the sounds of traffic.

"We must be in Kansas City. There are cars all around us," Carl whispered. He pried frantically at the trunk lid.

"Maybe if we drop some things out of the trunk we'll attract attention," said Molly Sue.

They dropped the strips of cloth they had been bound with; they dropped small hand tools—anything that would go through the opening. Their efforts went unnoticed. In desperation, Carl forced his blood-drenched hand through the opening and began to wave. It was then that the man saw Carl's hand and alerted me.

I started my motorcycle, snapped on the radio transmitter and swerved into the westbound lane. After weaving my way around cars for about a block I spotted the Pontiac. The sight of a bloody hand waving from the trunk caused my pulse to quicken as I reached for the microphone in front of me. "Five-two-one to headquarters—emergency."

The dispatcher answered almost immediately. "All cars stand by. Come in, five-two-one, with the emergency."

I gave my location, direction of travel and a description of the car I was following. As he called other units to assist me and gave their locations, I realized that there were no other units in the vicinity. I was on my own.

At Washington Avenue, Fifth Street makes a forty-five-degree turn to join with the Sixth Street Freeway. If the driver of the Pontiac reached the freeway, he could easily outrun my three-wheeler and escape into Kansas. It was now or never.

As I crossed Washington, I turned on my red lights and stepped on the siren. Traffic slowed, came to a stop. The Pontiac was sandwiched between two other cars. I was off the motorcycle and moving toward the left rear of the Pontiac almost before the driver had it stopped. There were screams from the trunk of the car.

Through the left rear window I saw the driver of the Pontiac grab a pistol on the seat and start to turn as I leveled my revolver.

"Don't do it, fellow. One quick move and I'll shoot," I warned.

He hesitated. Self-preservation told me to play it safe and pull the trigger. But the thought of taking a human life—any human life—held me back. I could see the hatred in his eyes as he slowly made his decision. Finally, deliberately, he laid the pistol on the seat and raised his hands.

With a deep feeling of relief I ordered him to step out of the car. I handcuffed his hands behind him. The key to the trunk was in his pocket. Now other officers were arriving to assist me. I took the key and unlocked the trunk.

Bloody, dirty, soaked with perspiration and weakened from their ordeal, the Wagners were immediately taken to a hospital. Esson was taken to police headquarters. Later he pleaded guilty to a charge of first-degree robbery and was sentenced to prison in the Missouri State Penitentiary. He was eventually returned to Ohio to continue his sentence there for the earlier convictions in that state. He died in 1977 while still in prison in Ohio.

Carl and Molly Sue Wagner had a fine baby son. But perhaps their harrowing experience with a hitchhiker will be a warning to others who are tempted to offer a ride to a stranger at the side of the road.

The girls lay pinned
under the wreckage of the smashed railroad cars,
while two hundred rescuers began the desperate,
delicate job of freeing them

"Do You Think We're Alive?"

BY JOSEPH P. BLANK

THE ENGINEER OF Illinois Central Gulf commuter train No. 720 slammed open the door of his compartment and dashed out, yelling, "We're going to crash!"

In the first seat, directly behind his compartment, Lisa Tuttle stared at him; her next words to her seatmate, Patricia Wysmierski, froze in her mouth. Pat saw part of the train's interior coming at her as she tried to hide her face in Lisa's shoulder. Then—nothing.

The accident, the worst railway disaster in Chicago's history, occurred at 7:35 a.m., October 30, 1972. Local train No. 416 had inadvertently eased past its stop at Twenty-seventh Street on the South Side and halted several hundred feet beyond the station, tripping a signal that gave oncoming express No. 720 a yellow caution light to proceed at a maximum of thirty miles per hour. The local then began backing up to discharge its passengers. This action flashed a red stop signal four city blocks behind. But the express had already passed this signal, and the motorman's distant view of the local was blocked by a curve in the tracks and by the station building.*

The onrushing express and the slowly backing local collided with an impact estimated at 66.7 million foot-pounds of energy, the heavy steel express mashing through half the length of the crowded local's rear double-decker car.

The result was carnage. Dead, injured and dazed were tossed into piles like so many dolls. Many passengers were trapped in a vise of mangled steel, while others with fractures, cuts, whiplash injuries and broken teeth staggered in all directions. Forty-five died; 332 were injured.

At the bottom of the tons of twisted, crushed steel lay Lisa and Pat, side by side. The girls, seventeen-year-old high-school seniors, had been commuting to part-time office jobs in a school work-study program. Drifting back to consciousness at about the same time, they awakened to a strange, incomprehensible world. Their car tilted at a forty-five-degree angle above them. Only their heads protruded from the wreckage. They couldn't move. Pat heard the death gurgle of a woman to her right. Lisa was aware of a body on her left, and shouts and screams. Both felt pain in their heads and legs; then the pain in their legs began to turn to numbness.

Pat spoke weakly. "Are you okay? What happened?"

"I don't know," Lisa moaned. "Do you think we're alive?"

---

* According to the findings of the National Transportation Safety Board, which conducted the official investigation of the accident, the lead train, before reversing, should have sent a crewman back down the track to flag the oncoming train and warn it of a problem ahead. The engineer of the following train was found to have failed, while operating faster than the prescribed speed, to perceive the train ahead in time to avoid a collision.

They cried, screamed. Lisa, her hands at her sides, pushed against the wreckage like an ant trying to shove aside a mountain. Then a voice suddenly said, "My God, there are two girls alive here!"

A face peered down at them. It was Capt. John Windle, a twenty-four-year veteran of the fire department and commander of Snorkel Squad No. 1, the special rescue unit. "Are you in pain?" he asked. They said, "Yes."

About six inches of space separated the torsos of the girls from the wreckage. Windle reached in and pulled out their schoolbooks to give them more breathing room. Then he carefully extricated Lisa's arms. He knew that any kind of freedom would reduce their panic. Lisa grabbed his wrist with a strength he didn't expect. Her eyes appealed to him.

"We're going to get you out in fine shape," he said gently. "I'll send someone to stay with you."

Windle and Chief Fire Marshal Curtis Volkamer agreed that the two girls had to be the last persons freed from the wreckage. They were at the bottom of a mountain of steel. If cranes were used to lift the mangled metal, the lifting movement could further injure all those trapped above them. The metal had to be cut and peeled away like lettuce leaves until only the girls were left.

Windle also knew that the girls had to be continually reassured and kept alert. Doctors had to know their feelings and their pain. If the girls were allowed to dwell on their terrifying circumstances, they might panic and try to move. This would produce bleeding, which could lead to shock and possible death. Windle quickly decided that the best man for the job of reassuring them and diverting their attention was fire fighter William Nolan, 37, the father of seven children and a spontaneously friendly man. Windle briefed him succinctly. "Keep 'em calm, Billy. We don't want to lose them."

Nolan knelt by the girls. "I'll be with you every second until you're out of this little mess," he explained.

Dr. Joseph Cari, the fire department's medical doctor, leaned over the girls and asked, "How much can you feel?" Both girls said that they had feeling to their knees.

"Move your legs."

Pat could move one leg a little. Lisa couldn't budge either leg, and she thought of her father who had recently had to have a leg amputated. She felt a sickening flush of fear. "Can you put us to sleep?" she asked.

"No, it's best if you stay awake. But I'm going to give you something to make you feel more comfortable." He injected morphine and marked the dosage on their foreheads with a felt-tipped pen.

As Nolan began talking to the girls, Windle brought over an asbestos tarpaulin and covered the trio. "This tarp is to protect us from sparks," Nolan explained. "Hear those whooshing sounds? Those are acetylene torches cutting metal. We have power spreaders that can separate pieces of metal with five tons of pressure. That'll make creaking and screeching noises. We'll hear winches and chains and cables and cranes. Nothing to worry about. My buddies have to use that equipment to get through all this junk."

Nolan kept up a steady line of chatter, asking the girls about their parents, their boyfriends, their plans for Thanksgiving, and the upcoming presidential election. Dr. Cari regularly checked them and kept them sedated. They showed no signs of shock, and their pulses were steady, which meant they weren't hemorrhaging.

Dr. Cari was greatly concerned, however, by Lisa's repetition of "I can't feel my legs." He discussed the problem with Volkamer: The steel crushing the girls' legs or feet probably was acting as a tourniquet. Partial removal of the pressure would allow possibly fatal hemorrhaging. Pressure had to be relieved totally and surely in one movement so that emergency medical teams could begin immediate assistance.

Some 200 fire fighters and technicians, sometimes laboring suspended head down or at precarious, off-balance angles, were now carefully cutting, peeling and snipping through the jungle of steel. In effect, they were disassembling a jigsaw puzzle, removing one piece at a time without disturbing the scores of other pieces. The implications of each act had to be appraised. Every piece undergoing work had to be shored, jacked and wedged to avoid unwanted movement and pressures.

The victims and the flammable materials in the smashed cars had to be protected from the sparks created by the acetylene torches and the power saw. Since metal transmits heat and the injured were gripped by metal, the rescuers kept wetting the steel. At the bottom of the wreckage, water puddled around the girls and soaked them.

Lisa remembered a health class where she had learned that if circulation is cut off from a limb, gangrene sets in. She shuddered and tried to block out the thought.

The two girls were clasping hands when Lisa felt her friend's grip relax. Pat had slipped into a doze. Nolan gently touched her forehead, saying, "Are you still there?"

"Yes, I'm still here." She wondered what her parents were doing and thought of her boyfriend. "Will our legs be all right?" she asked Nolan.

"Don't worry. You'll be dancing in a couple of days."

By now it was about noon, four and a half hours after the crash. Nolan kept saying to Lisa and Pat, "You've done great so far. You deserve a medal for courage. We'll have you out in no time." Although he sounded casual, he ached to help the girls. He wanted them out from under the wreckage. He wanted them warm and dry and safe.

Father Matthew McDonald, the fire department chaplain, stuck his head under the tarp, introduced himself and assured the girls that they were going to be all right. He said a brief prayer and left.

They began crying. "Isn't that what they do when a person is dying?" Pat sobbed.

"Oh, come on," Nolan scoffed. "Prayers are part of a chaplain's job. He's just keeping in practice." He was aware that the girls had been staring, off and on, at one of the train's loosened advertising cards reading, "The Lord Will Save." They were looking at it now. "Don't think that's a sign over the gateway to heaven," Nolan added. "You'd better think about what you have to do in school this afternoon."

The girls were shaking from the cold and their wet clothes. They could see showers of sparks from the blazing acetylene torches. Lisa worried about the sparks hitting her hair.

The girls had now been pinned under the wreckage for about five and a half hours. All the others who had been trapped—eighteen men and women—had been safely removed. Windle and Snorkel Squad No. 1 were working feverishly to reach the girls. Lisa and Pat could feel the heat from the tools, and smoke seeped under the tarp, making it difficult to breathe.

To make as quick work as possible of the thick steel door frame and bulkhead that held them, a 150-ton railroad-car crane was finally brought in. Volkamer directed the lifting inch by inch. No loose steel could be allowed to fall or shift.

"We're going to get you out now," Dr. Cari told the girls. "Tell me everything you feel."

"Take Pat out first," said Lisa.

"No, Lisa first," Pat answered.

"We have to move Lisa first," Dr. Cari told Pat. "Her legs are on top of yours."

As the pressure lifted, Lisa said, "I feel something warm along my legs." Dr. Cari knew that it was blood flowing. Then both girls screamed in pain. A dozen hands worked frantically around them.

Lisa was moved, hands holding her nearly-severed feet. A medical team ran her on a stretcher to a waiting helicopter. In four minutes she was in a hospital emergency room, where surgeons began reattaching her feet to her legs.

Pat was moved seconds later. She tried to raise her shoulders to look at her feet. Hands pushed her back, but she glimpsed the heel of one foot where her toes should be. She, too, was rushed off by helicopter, and surgeons immediately went to work on her foot and her fractured left thigh bone.

The rescue of Lisa and Pat had taken six hours of skilled, brutally difficult work. The rescuers returned to their stations exhausted by their efforts and subdued by the tragedy. "In fire fighting and rescue work, our men sometimes risk their lives," reflected Captain Windle. "There are also periods of boredom. Innumerable false alarms. Heat and subzero cold and smoke and falling walls. But the really important thing is what we were able to do for Lisa and Pat and eighteen others. That's where the reward is."

Lisa returned to high school six months later, although her ankles were still weak. Pat's right foot also mended slowly, but with home tutoring, both she and Lisa graduated with their high school class in June 1973.

Saint-Jean-Vianney was a proud,
prosperous little town.
Then one night the earth opened up
—and it began to melt away

The Town That Disappeared

BY JOSEPH P. BLANK

*T*HE DOGS OF SAINT-JEAN-VIANNEY *were the first to recognize the signs of oncoming disaster.*

Eleven-year-old Marcel Riverin had never seen his pet in such a frantic state—scurrying about, barking, yelping. Mrs. Jacques Tremblay's toy Pomeranian was also unusually nervous. "He yapped to go out and yapped to come in," she recalls. "Finally I slapped him."

Laval Blackburn, building superintendent at the local college, followed his father's dog outside and watched him dash around in circles, sniffing the ground. Blackburn was baffled. He returned to the TV (most of the men in Saint-Jean-Vianney that night were absorbed in the Stanley Cup hockey play-off between Montreal and Chicago). But the dog drowned out the announcer's voice.

No one in town realized what the dogs were trying to say.

Saint-Jean-Vianney was a well-kept, prosperous community of 1,308, located 135 miles north of the city of Quebec. Once farmland, the town had bloomed with houses in the last decade. Most of the men worked as skilled laborers or technicians for the nearby aluminum plant or the paper mill. Their homes were impeccably maintained, and both husbands and wives spent much of their leisure time making improvements. It was a young town and a proud one. "A good place in which to live and raise children," Harold Simard liked to say.

No one knew—and the knowledge probably would not have disturbed any-one—that the town had been built on the site of a gigantic landslide that oc-curred some 500 years ago. That slide didn't pour down the side of a mountain. It happened on relatively flat land. Beneath the crust of topsoil, the earth in this part of the Province of Quebec is generally composed of clay with pockets of sand. One particular quality of this clay, which runs about one hundred feet deep, frequently causes slides. When the sand pockets become over-saturated with moisture, the pressure against the clay causes it to dissolve and simply flow away.

Several things occurred in Saint-Jean-Vianney before the disaster that might, collectively, have represented a warning. A few cracks appeared in the asphalt of two streets. Two driveways settled about five inches. One man painted the exposed portion of his house foundation; the following spring the earth around the foundation settled about eight inches, and neighbors kidded him about the unpainted margin. And sometimes the power pole outside the house of Gilles Bourgeois swayed when there was no wind.

On the night of April 23, 1971, many residents heard a loud thump that seemed to come from under their houses. People checked their basements and peered out windows but could detect

The people, places and events in this story are real, but some of the names have been changed at the request of the individuals involved.

nothing. On the following day Pitre Blackburn drove out to the far eastern corner of his farm to work. At that location stood a forty-foot hill that blocked the view from Saint-Jean-Vianney of the big town of Chicoutimi, six miles away. "When I drove around the hill I saw that the back half of it had disappeared," Blackburn said. "In its place was a great hole, a V-shaped thing, maybe eighty feet deep, two hundred feet wide, and five hundred feet long. Many people from town came to look at it."

A week later Mrs. Robert Paquette was visiting her neighbor, Mrs. Patrick Gagnon. "I don't know what's happening around here," she complained. "I hear water flowing under our house, but my husband tells me I'm crazy."

Since the rains had been heavy during April and an abrupt rise in temperature was producing a fast thaw, Mrs. Gagnon thought it might just be a natural spring phenomenon. No one realized that all the rain was not running off, that it was seeping slowly into the soil and slowly liquefying the substratum of clay.

The clay began moving on Tuesday evening, May 4, a gray, rainy day. At 10:45, Mrs. Paul Laval telephoned her close friend, Marcelline Fillion, six houses away. "Something strange is going on," she announced, her voice tight. "The Blackburn hill is no longer there. I can see the lights of Chicoutimi." Then she hung up.

Mrs. Fillion turned to her husband and said, "It's getting scary around here." He nodded absently, his eyes riveted to the television screen. A few minutes later the lights flashed out and the screen went black. "A car must have hit a power pole," he remarked.

Fillion told his wife to light candles and went outside to investigate. He heard shouting on the east edge of town. In the street he could make out a bus, headlights burning, angled into a hole. Beyond that he could see only a black void where the Laval house had stood. He sprinted back inside. "Marcelline!" he shouted, "the Laval house is gone! Get our boy. We must leave. NOW!"

The slide had begun at or near the Blackburn hill and swiftly moved westward toward the homes on the east side of town. The earth simply dissolved to a depth of nearly one hundred feet; in the canyon thus formed, a river of liquefied clay—sometimes as deep as sixty feet—flowed at a rate of sixteen miles per hour toward the Saguenay River, two miles away. At its widest, the canyon was half a mile across, and it extended for approximately one mile.

When the slide reached the Laval house, everything—house, car, tricycles—plunged like a fast-moving elevator into the river of clay. Laval, his wife and three young children found themselves on a large cake of slippery clay. Waves of melted clay battered them. The children disappeared, one by one. Then Mrs. Laval went down. Laval himself was smashed against the roots of a standing tree. He grabbed them and pulled himself to solid ground. Stripped of all clothing, shocked, dazed and unbelieving, he staggered along the edge of the crater until the police found him and rushed him to a hospital.

Next door to the Lavals, Robert Paquette was in his basement playroom when the lights went out. He walked to the street to find out about the trouble. His wife and five children remained in the house.

He heard excited voices up the street, so he quickly walked about 200 feet to join the group. As he reached them, Patrick Gagnon gasped, "Look!" Paquette turned toward his house. He saw it swivel a little, tilt, then slide from sight. He began running toward the hole, but Gagnon grabbed him. "I don't understand," Paquette sobbed. "I don't understand."

Huguette Couture lived next to the Paquettes. About eleven that evening she heard a cracking noise and felt the house shake. Alone with her three children (her husband worked the four p.m. to midnight shift at the aluminum plant), she was terrified. From the kitchen window she saw a nearby house, lights still on, disappear from view. She ran to pick up three-year-old Benoit, screaming to her girls, "Let's get out! It's the end of the world!"

She jerked open the front door but saw only blackness. The concrete steps had disappeared. She ran back to the kitchen door. It was jammed. She flung open the window. Martine, 13, clambered out. Mrs. Couture shoved her younger daughter, eleven-year-old Kathleen, through the window just as a five-foot crack opened alongside the house. The girl fell into it, then scrambled out. The house moved and Martine yelled, "The foundation is going! The hole is getting bigger!"

Mrs. Couture pressed the boy to her breast, sat on the window and fell backwards into the hole. Holding the boy with one arm, she raised the other for help. Martine, with a strength beyond herself, pulled her mother and brother out of the hole. As they raced up Stanley Street to safety, Benoit, who was facing the rear in his mother's arms, said, "Mommy, our house has melted."

Jules Girard, who operated a bus service for employees at the aluminum plant, was driving his bus across a crack in the road when the front end of the vehicle sank into the earth. Through his windshield he saw the whole road ahead sinking. "Everybody out the back door!" he shouted. "Quick!"

The last man out, Girard fell into a hole and clawed his way up. He and several passengers ran up the street, throwing stones at houses and yelling warnings. When he looked back, he could see only the red roof lights of his bus. For a few seconds he watched in horror as a car came racing down Harvey Street on the far side of the crater. Then the headlights disappeared into the hole.

As the alarm spread, Georges Vatcher grabbed his high-powered battery lantern and cautiously approached the crater. Several men joined him. "The beam of light showed only the edge of the hole," he described. "It couldn't penetrate enough to show the size or depth. I heard screams for help from below. There was a kind of muffled, liquidy, sucking noise from the hole. Then the cries grew fainter and stopped, as if they were coming from a boat moving down the river."

Throughout the east side of town the slide caused panic, shock and disbelief. People didn't know which way to run or drive. In fleeing their homes, several women took only their wigs. An eighteen-year-old girl couldn't make up her mind what was most precious to her, so she grabbed a worn doll from her childhood. One man, leaving his sinking house, told his wife, "I forgot to lock the door." "You can do it later," she answered.

By midnight the sliding and liquefying of earth had stopped. Thirty-one men, women and children had perished; thirty-eight houses had disappeared from the town. The surrounding communities and the Quebec provincial government reacted quickly to the emergency. A relief mission was established at the Kenogami Memorial Hall, and the government began moving 131 mobile homes into the area.

Six days after the slide Mrs. Jacques Tremblay and her family climbed down into the crater to look at their house. It was one of the last to sink. Except for the foundation, the house was intact. Their glassware was unbroken and their little turtle still crawled around in its bowl. Mrs. Tremblay spent two hours in the house that she knew the government would have to burn. She dusted about, made up the beds and wept.

Twenty-three days after the slide the Quebec government declared Saint-Jean-Vianney unsafe for habitation. Before the year was out, it was totally evacuated.

The survivors examined several sites for a new community; ninety percent of them eventually chose a tract of land in nearby Arvida. The government replaced the homes destroyed by the slide and moved the undamaged homes to the new community. A fund of $850,000, privately contributed by Canadians, enabled families to replace their household effects.

Saint-Jean-Vianney soon was empty and desolate. Weeds and wild undergrowth began to camouflage the house foundations. The curious came to stare at the enormous crater, which grew shallower year by year as the rains carried earth into it. The name of the town, deleted from atlases and road maps, will live on only in the memories of those who lived there.

What happened seemed unreal to most families on that terrible night and even more unreal today. "Sometimes it all seems like a dream," said Leo Bourgeois, who lost his son, his daughter-in-law and his grandchild. "I find myself asking, 'Did the earth really open up and swallow those people? Did that actually happen?'"

How, in a raging gale and thirty-foot seas,
could the Coast Guard cutter save the sixty-nine
persons trapped in the foundering seaplane?

The Rescue
on Station Charlie

BY CAPTAIN PAUL B. CRONK
of the U. S. Coast Guard weather ship George M. Bibb

AT 3:40 ON MONDAY *afternoon, October 13, 1947, the giant American sea-plane* Bermuda Sky Queen *took off from Foynes, Ireland, for Gander, New-foundland. Aboard were a crew of seven and sixty-two passengers—the largest group that had ever been booked for a transatlantic flight—thirty men, twenty women and twelve children.*

At 2:32 a.m., somewhat later than scheduled, the Queen *passed Ocean Station Charlie, a weather post in the mid-Atlantic where the U. S. Coast Guard cutter* George M. Bibb *was keeping her vigil.*

It had turned into a wild, windy night and the sky was overcast, but the crew of the Bermuda Sky Queen *reported that they were satisfied with the progress of the flight and expected no difficulty. Shortly after they left Station Charlie, they passed the point of no return. There was no longer enough fuel left to get back to Ireland.*

At five o'clock the overcast cleared, and celestial navigation was possible. A check revealed the awful truth: their ground speed had been reduced during the night to sixty-eight miles per hour by head winds of gale force.

This meant that now there was insufficient fuel to reach either Newfound-land or Ireland.

The pilot, Charles Martin, a twenty-six-year-old ex-naval aviator, was faced with a decision that could cost the lives of all aboard. The instinct to continue west toward the nearest land must have been strong. It was lucky for all those on the plane that Martin had nerve enough to put about, home in on

Station Charlie's radio beacon, and attempt to set down on the open sea near the Coast Guard cutter.

At 6:47 a.m., the Bibb *received a message: "Aircraft King Fox George going to make emergency landing at Station Charlie at approximately zero eight hundred." Naturally, a message of this nature must be reported to the captain at once.*

Because of a series of emergencies I had not, except for a catnap or two, slept for seventy-two hours prior to climbing into my hammock at five a.m. Now, less than two hours later, my sleep was interrupted by a quartermaster shaking me. "Sir, an airplane is going to land near the ship at zero eight hundred. Shall I call you at seven-thirty?"

"Aye, aye; do that. Tell the Officer of the Deck to have the rescue gear broken out, and tell my steward to make some coffee."

I turned over with a sigh, and then he was back. "Sir, it is zero seven-thirty, and we have the plane on the radiophone. There are sixty-nine persons on board."

"All right! Man the rescue stations."

I stood in the cabin, numb with shock. Transatlantic planes carried twenty-one passengers—the big ones, forty-two. Who ever heard of a plane moseying around in the middle of the ocean with sixty-nine people aboard? I went on deck and found that a fresh gale had whipped up short, steep, angry cross-seas—the most dangerous situation possible for an attempted landing.

All the *Bibb's* crew not on watch were topside—more than a hundred of them. All eyes were turned westward, searching. Scramble nets were over the sides. Boat crews stood by their craft. Swimmers in rubber suits were ready to go overboard.

And then the forty-two-ton plane hove in sight. How big she was! My mouth was full of the dust of horror. In my mind's eye I saw that flying eggshell collapse as it smashed against the thirty-foot waves; saw the wings wrenched off; heard the screams of the passengers as the sea poured in upon them. *Oh, God, grant that I do not have to stand here helpless. Help me save them.*

I called pilot Martin on the radio, and gave him the direction of the swells and the length of the waves. As the plane circled, everyone held his breath and watched with horrified fascination as it slanted toward the sea. It was almost too much to bear. Not only could we imagine the crushed plane awash, but we all knew it was too rough

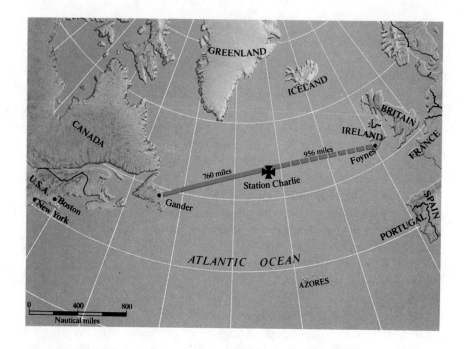

for lifeboats. And how, with the ship rolling forty degrees, could we maneuver alongside the plane without beating it to death?

And then the plane was down. There are spots where the different wave systems oppose each other and create a comparatively smooth sea. Martin had found one. Flying very slowly against the wind, he had plunked into a big wave just back of the crest. The *Queen* seemed to disappear completely in a great wash of white water; then, miraculously, she reappeared like a huge whale and wallowed toward the rolling *Bibb*.

Pilot Martin thought it would be possible to hook up a towline from the cutter to the seaplane while some method of transferring the passengers was being worked out. The *Queen* revved up all four engines and began plunging toward our lee side. This seemed to be working out well until, on the top of a huge wave, the plane was caught in our lee and whirled out of control. Martin cut his engines, but it was too late. Deprived of the braking effect of the wind, the plane sailed into the cutter's steel side. The *Queen* took the impact squarely on the nose.

It was a sickening business, and it looked like the end. Rising on a swell, the seaplane's number-three engine struck the top of a boat hanging in its davits, twenty-five feet above the waterline, driving it inboard. The boat crew had evacuated so quickly that no one remembered seeing them do it. The next roll of the ship found the starboard wingtips smashing the cutter's catwalk, aft, and the next found the port wingtip crashing against the bow. The ship's engines, meanwhile, had been going full astern. After an eternity the screws bit into the water, and the cutter pulled away from the foundering seaplane.

We lowered a ten-oared surfboat; it was wild work. In the boat were lines to pass to the plane to be attached to injured persons so that they could be tossed overboard and hauled into the boat—a desperate expedient but the only one available.

Then we lay to windward pumping oil on the seas to smooth them down. This was not too effective because we were also drifting out of the slick at the rate of three knots, and the plane was blowing downwind at five knots. (It drifted one hundred miles during the twenty-four-hour rescue operation.)

Since there were no injured to be removed, the small boat reconnoitered about the plane. The boat crew saw the passengers peering through the windows. The boat dared not approach the plane from any quarter—both craft were alternately climbing the crests of the waves and dropping dizzily into their troughs.

Because the sea was running steep and short, the plane plunged violently many times each minute. It reminded me of a giant swing at Coney Island, and I felt sick as I realized the suffering and danger of those in the plane, tossed about like dice in a cup.

After an hour, the order was passed by walkie-talkie for the boat to stand by to be picked up. The crew were by now exhausted. Hoisting a boat by a ship rolling over forty degrees from side to side offers some difficulty, but it was finally hooked on. Just as the boat reached the davit heads, the sea rose up, unhooked the forward lines and spilled the crew out of the boat. But the crew was well drilled; each man had a grip on the dangling lifelines and now scrambled on board.

Martin, alarmed by the damage the collision had done to the plane, said that perhaps they had better abandon the plane in their "ten-person" life rafts, but he was told to hang on unless the plane opened up. The capacity of the life rafts was based on three people in each raft and seven in the water hanging on to grab lines. The sea temperature was 50°F. The weather forecast promised a cold front and a new gale from the northwest for the next day. That could mean that the current gale would move away with a short lull before the next one struck.

If Charles Martin had to abandon the plane, his people could take to their rafts or jump into the sea, and we would try to fish them out. But it was asking a good deal to tell them to stand such a beating indefinitely, waiting for the storm's abatement, which might not come or might come too late. Yet we felt certain that hasty action might save some but hardly all.

We suggested that the plane launch a rubber raft on a line and see what happened to it. The small raft flew like a kite or spun about crazily in the wind.

Then we launched one of our fifteen-person abandon-ship-type rubber rafts, which did a little better; but even when it stayed right side up, the motion was so violent that it was evident that its use would be a desperate measure.

At 3:30 Martin reported that the plane was taking on water and the tail section was coming loose. "Skipper, will you try to get us off, some way, before dark?" he asked. The chips were down. Sunset was due at 5:32.

I instructed Martin to obtain volunteers from among the strongest men and get them into a raft somehow. If the test we were about to make failed, these men would have a better chance of surviving in the cold water until the cutter could drift down and pick them up. If the raft behaved well, it was to be cast adrift; otherwise the men were to be hauled back on board.

At first the operation went badly. The raft did not seem to be sufficiently inflated, and when a second flash of compressed carbon dioxide gas was fed to it, it burst. Martin inflated a second raft. When launched, it rode like a chip on the ocean with three of the plane's passengers crowded into it. The cutter drifted down upon it. The bullhorn blared admonitions not to stand or reach out until each man received a bowline from the cutter and passed it around his body. In a few minutes they were hauled on board. While adrift it was touch and go as to whether they would make it, and the experiment demonstrated the impracticality of effecting the rescue by means of the small rafts. We decided to use the cutter's large fifteen-person rubber rafts.

With darkness approaching, the action became fast and furious. In no time at all, one large raft was leaking to the point where it was useless; the second had been tossed by the sea into the ship's lacerating propeller; the third and last was beating itself to pieces alongside the ship.

It was clear that towing this raft on shuttle trips was going to be impractical. A huddle on the bridge produced the plan of launching our heavy motor surfboat, towing the raft to the plane, and mooring it there as a loading platform.

The Coast Guard twenty-six-foot self-bailing surfboat is the finest all-round rescue craft in existence. Girdled with flotation tanks and filled beneath the entire deck with air cells, it sheds water like a duck. But it was designed for use at surf stations, where it is put into the water from a special launchway.

Launching the 5,800-pound boat from a rolling ship is another matter. In less than a minute the ship had swung the boat afoul of the cradle and torn off the rudder shoe. It was a race against darkness to repair the damage, with the heavy motorboat trying to brain the launching crew. Finally it was launched and away from the ship, towing the big rubber raft downwind.

It was not easy going. The light towline broke repeatedly, resulting in a chase each time, and a heavier line could not be used for fear of tearing the raft's thin walls of duck and rubber. They finally made it, however, and at 5:30 p.m., two minutes before sunset, the raft began receiving passengers from the plane. The traditional priority of "women and children first" was put aside in favor of "families will not be separated."

The first family to leave consisted of an eighteen-month-old baby held in her father's arms, a five-year-old boy clinging to his mother, and their nine-year-old boy who was put in the care of another woman. The raft was hauled as close to the bow of the plane as could be done without getting it caught underneath. First, a man made the leap successfully. His assignment was to catch those who followed and keep them from being washed away. The father came

next, the baby in his arms; then the mother, holding her five-year-old son.

The plane in calm water was twenty feet high; when a trough of the sea passed, the raft would be thirty to forty feet below the exit hatch. Sometime during this downward plunge the nine-year-old boy jumped and landed in the sea. As he was hauled aboard the raft, he complained, "I'm ruining my good suit." Other passengers landed squarely in the raft.

The ticklish business of the transfer to the motor surfboat followed. This was necessary because the raft was not staunch enough to be towed and the surfboat could not lay alongside the plane for fear of puncturing it. When the surfboat came alongside the cutter's landing nets, its passengers were to be hauled on board by lines secured under their arms.

On board the cutter, excitement was at a high pitch. The boat crashed against the cutter's side as the wind pressed the ship down upon it, tossing it wildly up to the rail, then down out of sight into the darkness, flayed by the wind and spray—and, in the midst of it all, a baby held aloft! Eager hands reached out for it. A woman in the boat, hysterically resisting attempts to place a line about her, screamed, "Save my baby! Save my baby!"

So anxious was everyone to get the baby quickly on board that men got in each other's way. A burly man shouted, "Let go, you stupid bastard! Are you trying to drown that baby?" He was sobbing. The baby was snatched up by those on the nets and passed up to the deck. Finally, all the passengers from the raft were safely aboard and carried to the *Bibb's* sick bay.

At 6:10 p.m., a group of ten were hauled up the nets and, at 6:34

p.m., eleven more. During this third trip the gale reached forty-five knots. As we watched the plane careening dizzily in the beam of the searchlight, disaster seemed to be at hand.

The raft was being battered by the seas. As the motor surfboat lay alongside, it was repeatedly submerged or slammed into the side of the ship, and it began to show signs of premature old age.

The boat rode too deep in the water as it again set out for the plane—the air tanks were filling up. I judged that this would be its last trip.

In the meantime, the plane had drifted too far away for comfort, and the raft had broken away from the plane. When, after a desperate search in the darkness, Lieutenant Hall, the surfboat's coxswain, finally found it, it was already deflating.

This time there were sixteen passengers in the raft—too many. Their legs and arms were so entangled that no one could be swept away by the sea.

It was sink or swim together. They were all yanked into the surfboat; but what with the overload and the leaky tanks, that boat, too, began to sink. However, Hall had no trouble persuading three of the passengers to go back into the rubber outfit with three of the boat crew.

The raft was held alongside the surfboat by hand. The signal light was sought in order to call the ship for help. It could not be found in the tangle of humanity.

Just then the propeller fouled some of the stray lines of the raft. The gear case flew to pieces, the engine housing was smashed by a wave, and the tail shaft and propeller disappeared. The boat broached broadside to the sea as wave after wave washed over it. Boat and raft were kept right side up by delicate balancing by the crew.

With the searchlights playing on the scene, I could see people changing places between raft and boat. Both craft seemed too deep in the water, but if they were in trouble they should have signaled with their light. If I should drift down on them before they had completed their transfer, someone might get hurt. On the other hand, if the boat had lost too much buoyancy . . .

I eased the ship nearer and called them on the bullhorn. "Are you all right? Acknowledge with your light." There was no answering flash. They shouted something no one could understand. I worked the ship upwind and drifted down on them.

The boat crew and the passengers were by turns in the boat, in the raft and in the sea. Some of the crew were trying to get lines around the passengers; others were grabbing someone out of the water. Suddenly I saw a person washed out of the raft and whisked aft into the darkness. Someone leaned far over from the bow of the surfboat. One hand held the gunwale, the other darted down into the sea. A collar with a head sticking out appeared grasped by the outstretched hand and I heard a triumphant "Got him!"

All those who were washed out of the boat were saved. What we did was to bend a line around a seaman's chest and send him over the side with a line to tie around a passenger. Both lines were tended on deck by a group. Teams formed all along the ship, and somewhere along the line the drifters were latched on to. It was pretty rugged for those men dangling from lines, dunked in the cold sea as the ship rolled, but they were so excited that not one I questioned noticed the cold.

In less time than it takes to tell it, these passengers were out of the sea and safe on board. Mike Hall was the last up. He tottered up to me, saluted, and said, "Sir, permission to take another boat over and get the rest of them?"

My reply was, "I think you've had enough. Anyhow, go below and get some dry clothes on. First go to the sick bay and get a snort."

The loss of the motor surfboat dimmed the prospects of completing the rescue. A pulling boat could not tow the raft fast enough to catch the drifting plane, which was moving at four to five knots. But if the boat and raft were to be dropped downwind of the plane in line with the plane's drift, it might be possible to close in quickly as the plane blew down and pass a line to it from the raft.

I sent for Ensign Macdonald. "Mr. Macdonald, do you think, if we put you near the plane, that you can take six volunteers, row over and pass a line to the plane with a shoulder gun?"

Macdonald had seen what had happened to the strong motor surfboat; he was shivering with excitement. "I'll do my best, sir!" He called over the public address system for volunteers. Immediately there was the sound of running feet from all directions. I cannot say how many volunteered, but it seemed to be everybody.

They were out there from 9:39 until 10:45 in the darkness, in a gale with only six oars. Sometimes we caught them with the searchlight on a crest, but mostly we could not see them. A whitecap and a white boat are hard to tell apart at half a mile—and that was as near as we dared to get.

They passed the lines from the raft to the plane—a wonderful bit of boat work. I would not have given a plugged nickel for their chances. I just hoped. Then they waited an hour for people to appear in the raft, and nothing happened. They conceded failure on the walkie-talkie.

We got them back on board with their boat. They were used up. But the plane did have the raft.

I called the officers about me. "Shall we take a chance on the plane's staying afloat until daylight? If it does we can most likely get every last one of them off. Or should we save all we can now?"

Various opinions were voiced, but the one that seemed to make the most sense to all present was: "We've used up all our luck tonight. We came awful close to disaster that last trip. Let's not push our luck too far."

If the plane should show sudden signs of sinking, the twenty-two people on board could go for the raft—some would be on it, others in the water hanging on to the grab lines. I was confident I could drift the ship down on them within a few minutes. Anyhow, Pilot Martin would have to make the decision.

The plane's radio was dead and we had not had good results with blinker, so I took the ship close to him and used the bullhorn. "How do you feel about spending the night on the plane?" It seems an absurd question to have asked, but the plane's landing lights flashed a dot followed by a dash, meaning "Affirmative." Then complete darkness again; not a light anywhere on the plane. We settled down to watch our charge for seven anxious hours.

With the plane spotted in the searchlight, I toured the ship. All hands had been broken out at seven a.m. and had been strenuously engaged since. Half the crew were told they could hit the sack until called for. The others assisted with the survivors and tended the engineering plant.

At 6:45 a.m., sunrise, the wind was no more than a fresh breeze. A treacherous swell was running but, compared with the night before, conditions were mild. The captain's gig was lowered to transfer the remaining passengers; soon it was back with eight survivors.

The gig shoved off again, got near enough to the raft to take off two passengers, then had engine trouble and drifted away. A pulling boat was launched and took off six more.

One more trip and total success would be ours—something I had not dared to hope for. I was taut as a violin string, fearing some last-minute mishap. But the pulling boat came back with the last survivors, and the noble raft was cut adrift, its work finished. The crew of the gig finally got its motor running. It pulled up alongside, and at 8:33 a.m., the last passenger climbed over the rail.

As for Pilot Martin, his was the triumph. Triumph over the sea and the air. Triumph over himself. His nerve in turning back, his incomparable landing and his fortitude in keeping his plane under control after landing had made this rescue possible.

We could not start for port just yet; not with the big seaplane wallowing on the surface, a menace to navigation. Word came that the operators agreed to destroying it, and I hastened to do so before they changed their minds. I did not care to risk lives in a hopeless salvage attempt.

We poured explosive and tracer bullets into the *Queen*. There was not enough gas left to make a belch of flame, but the oil tanks for each of the engines burned fiercely, and eventually some gas tanks caught fire. The giant tail dropped off, the wings drooped, and the *Bermuda Sky Queen* gave up the ghost. She was a staunch old girl, though. She kept alive until all her people were saved. Then, down she went in a blaze of glory.

Forced off the road,
his car plunged down a cliff
and crashed to a halt, straddling a railroad track.
In minutes a huge freight train
would come roaring around the curve

Car on the Track!

BY EVAN McLEOD WYLIE

"I'LL BE HOME before dark," Max Lindner had told his wife ten minutes earlier. It was about three-fifteen p.m. on the first day of March
1978. Snow lay deep in the Green Mountains of southern Vermont,
and the temperature was well below freezing.

Max Lindner was a meticulous man, proud of his "retirement
car," and he tinkered with it continually to keep the engine in perfect running order. Not satisfied with the results of a radiator check,
he had decided to go to a service station in nearby Pownal. He drove
along a farm lane until he merged onto Route 7, the main highway
for north–south traffic in western New England.

Heavily traveled, Route 7 was clear of snow and ice. Swinging south, Lindner started down a long, descending curve that overlooks a deep valley. The sinking sun was shining into the traffic in the other lane. Max noticed the sun glinting on the windshield of a big truck as it roared uphill toward him. As the truck came closer, he was alarmed to see that it was edging over into his lane, heading straight for him.

Veering as far to the right as he dared, Max drove on the shoulder of the highway. He could go no farther—to his right was a steep drop to the railroad tracks. In a split second the truck blasted past, missing him by inches. But it was too late for Max to recover. He hurtled over the embankment and nose-dived crazily down the cliff. Fighting to keep the bucking, twisting car from overturning, Max wrenched the steering wheel so hard that it snapped off in his hands. His head went forward, smashing his face into the steering post and the side window.

Earlier that day, *New England One* had left Portland, Maine, with eighty boxcars loaded with paper, chemicals and food products. After stopping in Fitchburg, Massachusetts, to beef up its power with two extra engines, the big freight rambled westward. Near the town of Zoar, it entered the Hoosac Tunnel. Emerging through immense barnlike doors designed to keep snow out of the tunnel, *New England One* swept down into North Adams, Massachusetts. In a few minutes, it would cut across the southwestern tip of Vermont into New York. The time was 3:30 p.m.

Max Lindner, several of his teeth shattered, his nose and mouth bleeding profusely, slumped behind the broken steering wheel. Fighting to stay conscious, Max found his car upright but—and now fear stabbed at him—squarely in the center of the track. "I knew there was a freight due any moment," he recalled later. "I *had* to get out, but I couldn't move." His seat belt had held him in during the plunge down the cliff, but now he couldn't loosen it—and his door was jammed shut.

Terror gripped him. The railroad hugged the curve in a sharp bend, and by the time the engineer saw his car, the train would be only a few yards away. *I'm done for,* he thought.

At the service station around the curve at the bottom of the hill, Leo Pambianchi, 66, had fixed a balky crank on his car window and was relaxing with a bottle of soda. A woman pulled in. "I think I just saw a car on the track when I came down the hill," she called. Pambianchi stared at her in disbelief. "Is anybody in the car?" he asked. "I don't know," the woman replied, and drove off.

Leo notified the Pownal rescue squad and the police. But he doubted the story because traffic on the hill seemed normal. *Well, I'll go up and see.* The time was 3:35 p.m.

Driving slowly up the hill, Leo glanced across the road and down at the tracks. He saw nothing, and soon the cliff dropped so sharply that the tracks were not visible. Leo turned around and started back. The woman could have been mistaken.

Then he saw it. Braking to a stop, Leo leaped out, slid down the cliff and peered into the wreck. A man was in the driver's seat, drenched in blood, calling feebly to him. Leo jerked at the jammed driver's door, then ran around and yanked open the other door.

"Crawl out this way," he cried. Max Lindner shook his head, and Leo realized the man could not move.

Thinking only about a man bleeding to death, Leo debated what to do. The man was big and bulky. It would take a lot to move him. It might be best to wait for help. Overhead, cars whizzed along Route 7, but no one stopped.

"Help me!" Lindner gasped. "Help me!"

A soft-spoken man, not given to panic, Leo replied, "I'll get you out." He crawled into the car and managed to free the seat belt. "Now can you move?" he asked.

"Can't," gasped Max. "I'm stuck."

Leo reached in, seized Max's right leg and pulled at it until he had propped it on the front seat. Then he got the other leg and foot away from the brake pedal and gearshift.

Although Leo didn't know it, *New England One* had passed through Williamstown, Massachusetts, and was hammering up the westbound track. The eighty-three-car freight sped rocking and swaying into Pownal. The time was now 3:42.

Pulling hard, Leo dragged on Max's legs until they dangled out the door. He leaned in, got his arm around Max and pulled him out, supporting him on his shoulder. Resting from the effort, he leaned against the car with Max draped over him, wondering what to do next. He couldn't carry Max up the cliff, and there was only a narrow space between the track and the side of the embankment. Taking Max's weight, he backed away from the car to get off the tracks.

Then, without having heard its roar, he felt the ground shake beneath the onrushing freight train. And suddenly he saw it coming round the bend—yellow headlights and a giant blue engine, looming head-on just a few yards away. Reacting instantaneously, Leo spun Lindner around, flung him into the side of the cliff and sprawled beside him.

"Don't move an inch!" he shouted. "Stick your face in the dirt! Hang on!"

With a monstrous roar, the train was upon them. There was a fearful shriek of metal as the first engine struck the car, then raced by, carrying the wreckage with it. In its wake came a shock wave and a great blast of wind. Amid the noise of air brakes, showers of sparks and flying metal, Leo and Max felt the suction of the train. It seemed to be reaching out to drag them beneath the wheels of the freight cars that swayed by only inches away.

Locked in a desperate embrace, blinded by a storm of cinders, sparks, stones and bits of burning brake drums, the two men dug their fingers into the embankment.

Wheels grinding, boxcars jolting and shuddering, *New England One* finally ground to a halt. Slowly Leo picked himself up. Through the cloud of smoke and dust, he saw the train crew running toward them and heard the sirens of the approaching rescue truck. The time was 3:45 p.m.

Police and rescue-squad medics slid down the cliff with a stretcher. A nurse, seeing Max clutching at his throat, realized he couldn't breathe. Reaching down his throat, she removed a mass of broken teeth and blood clots. In a few minutes, he had been hoisted up the cliff and sped to the hospital in Bennington, Vermont. "He'll be okay," somebody told Leo. "He'll make it."

When it was all over, Leo drove up the road and watched as a wrecker hoisted up the mass of metal that had been Max Lindner's retirement car. The aftereffects of the incident swept over him in a wave of weakness. "It had been quite a day," he said afterward. "I thought I'd better go home and lie down."

For his heroism, Leo Pambianchi received a citation from the Vermont Department of Public Safety and, in March 1979, the Carnegie Medal, the highest civilian award for bravery in the United States.

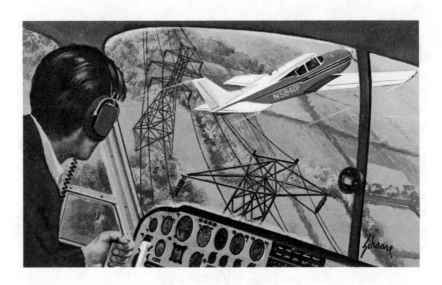

An untrained woman was at the controls
and one of the most hair-raising episodes in the history of
light-plane flying had just begun

"Our Pilot
Has Fainted!"

BY SCOTT AND KATHLEEN SEEGERS

"**M**AYDAY! MAYDAY!" Edged with panic, the clear feminine voice re-sounded in the radar room serving the Atlantic City, New Jersey, airport.

"Aircraft on Mayday, are you out of Atlantic City?" asked air-traffic controller Thomas Van Swearingen.

"This is Comanche N-five-eight-four-one Pop, off Ocean City, New Jersey," responded the woman. "Our pilot has fainted! Can somebody help me?"

Van Swearingen again: "Five-eight-four-one Pop, can you fly that aircraft? Repeat, can you fly the aircraft?"

"I can fly it in the air, but I cannot land it."

That day, June 15, 1974, had begun as a pleasant Saturday outing for Bill and Martha Waite and their Rockville, Maryland, neighbors, Dwain and Mary Ballew. With Bill Waite, 52, at the controls of the four-seat Comanche airplane, they had made an easy one-hour flight from Montgomery County's Free State Aviation Park to the airport at Ocean City, New Jersey. After a swim and lunch, they took off for home at 3:46 p.m., into thickening overcast.

A few seconds after takeoff—before the plane had reached an altitude of 500 feet—Martha felt Bill's weight suddenly lean against her. "At first I thought he was reaching for something between the seats," she recalls. "But he didn't straighten up, and then I saw that we weren't climbing. I shook him, but he didn't react. I thought he had fainted. So I grabbed the wheel in front of me and eased it back to gain a little altitude."

Martha Waite, slim, attractive, 42, had worked as an airline stewardess, and so had some experience in the air. In addition, her husband—a marine engineer-naval architect and retired Naval Reserve Commander—had taught her to read the instruments showing airspeed, altitude, rate of climb and descent, the compass and the artificial horizon that indicates which way and how much a plane is tilting. And on several occasions he had let her hold the control wheel in level flight for a few minutes at a time. "But all that's easy," experienced pilots say. "Landing is something else."

"The odds were astronomical against Mrs. Waite being able to land that plane safely," sums up Atlantic City chief controller Martin Sonnett.

From the back seat, Dwain Ballew wrestled Bill Waite's inert body off Martha and slapped him. "Bill, wake up!" he urged. As Martha leaned across Bill to reach the microphone beside the pilot's seat, Dwain tried mouth-to-mouth resuscitation. "I felt for his pulse, but there was none," he said later. "I knew then that Bill was dead."

"Mayday, Mayday!" Martha screamed into the mike.

The plane climbed through a thick layer of clouds that began at 2,000 feet, and when it came out into brilliant sunshine at 3,400 feet, Martha had no idea where they were. But she knew that she *had* to get that plane down so that Bill could get to a doctor. She thought, too, of her fifteen-year-old son and of the Ballews' two small children at home.

Meanwhile, Van Swearingen had located the Comanche on the Atlantic City radarscope. "Five-eight-four-one Pop, *reverse course!* Fly heading two hundred to Atlantic City airport. Can you descend to one thousand five hundred feet, ma'am?"

Slowly, fearfully, Martha eased the Comanche around in a wide, wobbling turn. "I am now on heading two-zero-zero. But I don't know how to throttle this thing back."

While the tense drama developed in the air, a thirty-seven-year-old furniture manufacturer named Robert Corson was paying his airplane parking fee at nearby Bader Field, outside Atlantic City. Overhearing Martha's exchange with Van Swearingen on the radio, he climbed into his fast, twin-engine Bonanza, 4954B. A pilot since the age of sixteen, Corson had once owned a Comanche and was familiar with its controls. Maybe he could help, he thought as he took off. "Atlantic City Departure Control, this is four-niner-five-four Bravo. Where's this bird that's lost?"

Van Swearingen: "Five-four Bravo, aircraft is now five miles northeast of Atlantic City airport. Are you familiar with the Comanche?"

Corson: "Affirmative. Now, how about pointing me in the right direction?"

Martha, urgently: "Do you have any instructions for me? Do you have me in radar control?"

Van Swearingen: "Affirmative. I have you in radar control." Then, to Corson: "Fifty-four Bravo, turn left, heading two-six-zero."

Corson: "Okay, left two-sixty. What's her gas situation?"

Van Swearingen: "Three hours of fuel. The problem seems to be that she can't fly the aircraft."

The air-traffic controller, now tensely on his feet, watched as the two blips came closer together on the radarscope. Suddenly, Corson's voice rose jubilantly: "Atlantic City Approach, I got my target at twelve o'clock. . . . Forty-one Pop, this is fifty-four Bravo. Do you read me, honey? I'm about two miles right behind you. I'll come up beside you so you can see what I look like."

A moment later, Corson was there. "Okay, honey, here we are. Do you see me off your right wing?"

Martha: "Boy, do you look good!"

Corson: "What's your airspeed?"

Martha: "One-four-zero."

Corson: "Okay, fine. I'm gonna slow down to one forty. You just fly with me."

At this point, the weather suddenly closed in over Atlantic City airport, and clouds began forming in front of the two planes.

Corson: "Atlantic City Approach, this is fifty-four Bravo. How about a heading toward Millville?"

Van Swearingen: "Roger, fifty-four Bravo. Heading two-seven-zero."

Corson: "Now, forty-one Pop, how about pushing that throttle in a little bit and pulling back on the wheel because we want to stay above the clouds. Just fly with me."

Martha: "I'm with you."

As cool as ice, Corson began giving Martha a remote-control flying lesson. "Okay, ma'am, we're going to go through how to land. Have you ever landed an airplane before?"

Martha: "No."

Corson: "Okay, fine. Let's go over a couple of things. Do you see the landing-gear switch?"

Martha: "Yes."

Corson: "Okay, now, I want you to put the gear down. Just pull the switch down and see how it feels."

Martha pulled the switch, and the landing wheels slowly unfolded.

Corson: "Okay, you see how it feels, right? Now, put the gear up again and push the throttle in. Let's get above these clouds."

Suddenly, the Comanche vanished into a cloudbank.

Corson: "Atlantic City, this is fifty-four Bravo. I've lost my bird."

Van Swearingen: "She's off to your left a mile to the southwest, at ten o'clock southbound. Suggest you go west. We have reports of much better weather to the west."

A few minutes later, Corson sighted the Comanche clear of the clouds ahead of him. "Stay where you are," he instructed Martha. "I'm coming up on your right again. We're going west to get clear weather. Start turning."

Martha: "Here goes."

Corson: "Keep turning. . . . Okay, just hold it right there. You fly that thing pretty good."

Martha: "Thanks, pal. But I wish I knew a little bit more than I do."

By the time the two aircraft arrived over Millville airport, the

weather there had also worsened so that a long descent would have
to be made through heavy clouds. Van Swearingen told Corson that
visibility was better to the north, at McGuire Air Force Base.

Corson: "Forty-one Pop, we're going to McGuire Air Force Base. I
want you to stay above those clouds, though, so I don't lose you."

Martha: "Airspeed is one-thirty. Okay?"

Corson: "One-thirty is real nice. Are you comfortable?"

Martha: "Well, under the circumstances, I guess."

Corson, gently: "Everything is going to be all right. I want you to
hold one-thirty airspeed and let the plane descend. Pull the throttle
back, and you'll feel it descend."

Van Swearingen: "McGuire airport is twelve o'clock to you now at
six miles. You are cleared to land on any runway."

Below, McGuire officials had marshaled ambulances, fire-fighting
gear—a full complement of crash equipment. Automatic warning
lights flashed; sirens wailed.

Corson: "Tell you what we're going to do. We're going to fly
around this airport once. See that big, long runway down there?"

At this crucial moment, the Bonanza vanished from Martha's vision. "I've lost you!" she cried.

"Okay, hold on," Corson said calmly. He called Atlantic City.
But both airplanes were now beyond Atlantic City's radar range,
and Van Swearingen could no longer help them. "Talk to McGuire
Approach Control," Van Swearingen advised. "They understand
the situation."

In the McGuire radar room, Tech Sergeant Philip A. Smith swallowed hard and took charge of the two meandering blips.

Smith: "Fifty-four Bravo, we have radar contact on the lost aircraft. She's off to your right about two o'clock and three and a half
miles."

Martha, lost and headed east toward the Atlantic: "My altitude is one
thousand. My airspeed is one-forty."

Corson: "Okay, honey. We lost you, but we'll . . . *we got you now!* I
want you to pull that throttle back. Do not descend. Pull the throttle
and the wheel back at the same time so we don't lose more altitude."

Martha: "Okay. My airspeed is one-twenty."

Corson: "Fine. Now we're going to make a right-hand turn here
and make a big, big circle around the field. Then I want you to put

your gear down. When the gear comes down, you may notice the nose wants to drop a bit. If it drops, pull back and give it a little power. Make sure you go one hundred and twenty miles per hour."

Martha: "Gear down and locked. Airspeed one-twenty. Altitude nine hundred."

Corson: "Fine. You're right behind me now. I'm going to slow down. Come up beside me on my right, okay?"

Corson knew that the moment of truth had arrived. Any misunderstanding of his words, any lag in executing his instructions, could result in fiery death for the four frightened people in the Comanche. "I'll do all the talking from here on in," he said to Martha. "You just listen. Your gear is down and you're all set to land. You see that runway ahead?"

Martha: "We see the airfield."

Corson: "Okay, aim for the middle of that runway. We'll fly a little way over it before we decide to land. You lined up on the runway?"

Martha, alarmed: "I don't see you!"

Corson: "Just fly straight. That's the girl . . . now hold it . . . I want you to cut the throttle about . . . *now!* Not too much! Not too much! Now—all the way!"

The Comanche headed for the runway at a steep angle—steep enough to guarantee a fatal crash. "No!" Corson yelled. "Push the throttle all the way in! Get all the way up!" The Comanche pulled out and climbed steeply.

Corson to Sergeant Smith: "We're going to have to try this a couple of times, I'm afraid." *Then to Martha:* "Relax, honey. You had that landing practically perfect except you were a little too high. So we're going to come in a little lower, and I want you to maintain your altitude with that throttle. Understand?"

Martha: "Yes."

Corson, as the Comanche completed its circle and sidled uncertainly back into position: "Okay, you're lined up on that runway. Keep your altitude exactly the way it is."

But the wide swing around the airport for the second pass had headed the fliers for a new and deadly hazard: Taking his eyes off the Comanche for an instant, Corson saw a web of high-tension power cables directly across their line of flight only a quarter-mile ahead.

"There's wires in front of us!" he said quietly. "Keep it up! Push the throttle in!" Martha did, and the wires whipped past only seventy-five feet below.

Corson: "Okay, you're doing fine now. Get the nose down. Cut the throttle back a bit. Throttle back . . . throttle back . . . throttle back. All right, give it some gas, give it gas now, *now!* Just enough to get you over the runway. That's it."

Corson led Martha down to one hundred feet and then zoomed up in a climbing turn. "How does she look?" he asked Smith. "I lost her."

Smith: "Looks like she's almost over the end of the runway."

Corson: "Okay, honey, you've got it made. Now cut the throttle."

The Comanche hit hard, and bounced. When it hit again, the landing gear collapsed and the propeller dug into the concrete with a screech of metal and a shower of sparks. The plane slid to a jolting stop, smoke boiling up from the mutilated tires. Fearing fire, Martha threw open the door and yelled, "Get out of this airplane!" Ballew dragged Bill's body onto the wing and into the hands of the crew of an ambulance that had already appeared alongside.

Corson landed on another runway and called Smith, who told him: "Yep, she's right down the runway. She's okay!"

Corson to Martha: "You did a great job, honey!" Then, as if he himself had done nothing, he took off and headed north to continue his interrupted business flight.

They had been flying for one hour and twenty minutes. Fifteen minutes after they landed, McGuire Air Force Base was socked in, visibility zero.

The hospital at nearby Fort Dix subsequently confirmed what Dwain Ballew had known during the first ten minutes of flight: Bill Waite had died instantly. The cause: a blood clot in his aorta.

"I guess I suspected it all along," Martha said later. "But I wouldn't let myself think about it. I had to concentrate on flying. Then, after we came out above the clouds, I had the strangest feeling that Bill was right there watching me, helping me fly the plane. I still think he was."

Something had gone terribly wrong
in the small California town:
A school bus, its driver and twenty-six children had vanished.
Why them? Why there? And who—or what—was responsible?

Kidnapped!
The Ordeal That Shook Chowchilla

BY JOSEPH P. BLANK

CAROL MARSHALL SUDDENLY grew restless and uneasy. It was five o'clock in the afternoon of July 15, 1976, and Mike, her fourteen-year-old son, should have been home from summer sessions at the Dairyland Elementary School, located in flat farmland about seven miles south of Chowchilla, California.

At 5:50 she telephoned the office of school superintendent Lee Roy Tatom and learned from a secretary that Mike had indeed taken the regular school bus. "Well," Carol said, "he isn't home yet. What time should I expect him?"

"We've kind of lost the bus," the secretary said in a seemingly casual tone. "But don't worry. It's probably a mechanical failure. We have people checking the route and as soon as we locate it I'll call you."

As Carol hung up she sensed that something was seriously wrong. She knew that Mike would have called her about this long a delay in reaching home. Could there have been an accident?

She paced through the house a few times, then grabbed her handbag, hurried out the door and climbed into her pickup truck to search for her son.

Just about the time that Carol turned onto Road 16 to make the ten-mile drive to the Dairyland School, Madera County Sheriff Ed Bates put out a county-wide all-points bulletin for the bus. He wasn't alarmed. A late-bus episode on a rural route was not that unusual. It was a hot day; the bus could have had radiator or water-hose trouble. Maybe a flat tire. If the bus remained missing after another half-hour, Bates decided, he'd make the fifteen-mile drive to Chowchilla and look into the problem himself.

By now, phone calls from parents of the children on the bus were clogging the lines to the Chowchilla police station, the sheriff's office and the home and office of Superintendent Tatom. Many cars and pickups were moving slowly along the roads around town as drivers peered about, hoping to glimpse the bus or the children.

Then a young pilot telephoned Tatom and, with some astonishment, reported seeing a school bus in Berenda Slough, a dry creek about five miles southwest of town. Sheriff Bates raced to the spot.

He found an empty bus that had been driven seventy-five feet off the road. The depth of the slough and a fifteen-foot-high stand of bamboo had effectively concealed the vehicle; law officers, uneasy parents and others had driven past the spot innumerable times.

Bates walked carefully through the bus, picking up a few children's bathing suits, a towel and some books and notebooks. There was no sign of a struggle. Outside, he couldn't find a single child's shoeprint. He did note two sets of tire tracks that did not belong to the bus.

Bates learned that the bus carried twenty-six children—nineteen girls and seven boys, ranging from five to fourteen years old. He also ascertained that no one related to the children was famous or "had money." The driver, fifty-five-year-old Edward Ray, had an un-blemished record for honesty and reliability. In addition to driving the bus, he farmed thirty-three acres of cotton and corn. His wife worked in a bank.

Bates realized that the children must have been forcibly removed. But why was this California town of 4,550 mostly middle-income people selected for such an act? Why these children? And who was responsible for their disappearance?

Bates drove to the Chowchilla police station and called the FBI.

Hours earlier, at 3:50 that afternoon, thirty-one children, some still in bathing suits from an earlier swim in the municipal pool, had climbed into Ray's bus at the Dairyland School.

About twenty minutes later, after dropping off five children, Ray turned onto Avenue 21 and saw, several hundred yards ahead of him, a parked white van, its open driver's door extending across the white divider line. He made a slow approach, intending to swing around the door if there was no oncoming traffic.

As he neared the van, a man, wearing a stocking mask and carry-ing a pistol in one hand and a sawed-off shotgun in the other, sprang out of the driver's seat and blocked the path of the bus. Shocked and disbelieving, Ray braked to a stop. The masked man stepped quickly to his window and told him to open the door. Ray promptly obeyed. Two other stocking-masked men bounded out of the van and followed the gunman aboard the bus.

The children stared at the intruders. The gunman told Ray, "Get in the back of the bus," then directed the children up front to follow him.

An accomplice wearing white gloves slid into the driver's seat. The bus, followed by the white van, moved about a half-mile along the road, then swayed down a rough incline into Berenda Slough. As the bus stopped, Ray saw a green van parked in the slough.

The white van, its rear doors opened, backed to the door of the bus. The gunman told the children to move directly from the bus steps into the van. Larry Park, a fearless child of six, protested: "My Aunt Sylvia is picking us up at four-thirty and if we're not there she's gonna get mad and come looking for us and she's really gonna give it to you!" The gunman told him to move on.

Slight, five-year-old Monica Ardery looked at the stocking leg hanging from the gunman's head and innocently asked, "Are you the Easter Bunny?"

"Are you going to hurt us?" another child asked.

"No one is going to get hurt. Just be quiet."

Twelve children were loaded into the white van. After the rear doors were locked, it pulled away and was replaced by the green van. The gunman motioned for Ray and the other fourteen youngsters to move into it.

As the vans rolled toward their destination, the younger among the crowded, terrified children sobbed and screamed for their mothers. The interiors of the vans were pitch black. The windows in the cargo sections had been blacked out with paint. Plywood partitions prevented the captives from seeing the driver's section and the road. The interiors became hot and stifling. As the hours passed, a few girls fainted for brief periods.

Ray was heartbroken by the cries of the children with him. They kept asking, "Edward, why are they doing this to us?" and he had no answer. He kept repeating, "Everything will be all right. You'll be home soon." He didn't believe his own assurances. He was frightened for them and anxiety-stricken about the plans of their captors.

At times, the older girls tried to get the others to sing. One girl made an attempt at "If you're happy and you know it, clap your hands." Only Robert Gonzalez, 10, a boy with unfailing good humor, clapped. The others cried. Then the girl tried, "If you're sad and you know it, clap your hands." Everybody clapped.

By nine o'clock that night, the captives were begging for water and the use of a toilet, but there was no response from the front. The vans stopped twice en route. The clink of metal could be heard, then came the sound of gasoline being poured into the tanks. The children assumed that the stops had been made at service stations. They yelled and cried for water and the use of toilets. The only answer was, "Be quiet in there!" The kidnappers probably had carried cans of fuel in the front of the van.

By midnight, most of the children were sleeping, despite the heat and stench. Ray remained awake, two youngsters using his thighs as pillows. Around 1:30 a.m., he felt the van leave paved road and bounce and sway as it moved along at reduced speed. He heard brush dragging under the chassis. Then the vehicle stopped.

Some time passed, and then he heard a voice call, "Hey, bus driver! Out first."

The rear doors of the green van opened. Edward Ray stepped down to the ground, blinking in the glare of a flashlight beam. It seemed to him that he was in a kind of tent-like structure, obviously erected to conceal the kidnappers' lights and activities. A masked man asked for his name and age and told him to remove his pants and boots. He was handed a flashlight and two spare batteries and then directed to climb down into a manhole-size opening with a few feet of a ladder sticking out of it. He cautiously climbed down about eight feet until his feet hit a floor. He glanced at his watch. It was 3:30.

One of the kidnappers said, "You guys! Out of the van, one at a time." The two vans slowly emptied. Each child was asked his or her name and age, and an article of clothing or other possession was taken from most of them before they were directed to descend the ladder. Some were crying and asking what was going to happen to them and why they couldn't go home.

After the children had climbed down the ladder into their prison, the kidnappers handed down a roll of toilet paper and pulled up the ladder. Ray heard a metallic sound as the access hole was covered. Larry Park again shouted to the kidnappers that they could expect a good what-for from his Aunt Sylvia. But there was no response—only silence.

Edward Ray slowly moved the beam of the flashlight around the prison. It looked like the interior of a trailer, about twenty-seven feet long, eight feet wide and eight feet high. Wire mesh covered the ceiling and sides. Against one wall stood a small pile of food—boxes of dry cereal, loaves of bread, bags of potato chips, a jar of peanut butter and about a dozen large plastic jugs of water. Mattresses and box springs occupied most of the floor space. Two toilets had been improvised over the wheel wells. Two flexible pipes projected a few inches through the roof. Ray felt air coming through one of them and heard the sound of a fan at its far end.

The children gulped the water, used the toilets and tore into the food. Some of the younger ones persisted in crying for their mothers, and Ray tried to soothe them. Little Monica Ardery asked him, "Why did the men bury us?" He had no answer.

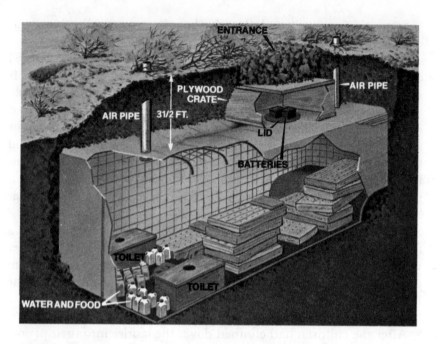

The child then turned to Jeffrey Brown, 10, and climbed into his lap. The boy assured her, "I'm gonna make sure you get home all right. I'm gonna hand you right over to your father." Monica soon was calling him "Uncle Jeff" and snuggling in his arms.

Sometimes Ray was overwhelmed by the desperate plight of the children and himself. He felt an unreasonable responsibility for what had happened. Why did he decide to stop for the gunman? He should have stepped on the accelerator, plowed over him and speeded away. He knew, however, that such an instantaneous reaction would have depended on his being alert to the possibility of kidnapping. After twenty-three years of uneventful bus-driving, how could he have imagined such a possibility?

A pattern soon developed in the hole. Ray and the older children were occupied trying to pacify the younger ones. Irene Carrejo, 12, looked after Barbara Parker, 8. As it grew hotter, Barbara had difficulty in breathing. The word "die" never occurred to the child, but it was translated into a shivering fear that she would never again see her mother and father.

Within an hour, the food was gone. After twelve hours, only three containers of water remained. When they were emptied, the children would begin to dehydrate.

Mike Marshall, at fourteen the oldest child, also was considering their terrifying predicament. He could hear the roof of the trailer creaking under the weight above it. It already had begun to cave in and a little dirt had sprinkled the captives.

The next day, Friday the sixteenth, FBI agents telephoned the parents and asked them to bring in photographs of the children and a few articles of their clothing. Jim Estabrook told his wife, "I'll do it." He walked slowly into the bedroom of their eight-year-old son Johnny. A few pieces of the boy's clothing were strewn about. He stood still for a few moments, then stuffed the items into a paper bag. He knew they were for dogs, to pick up a scent and—and what? Find the body? He felt sick.

As the parents sat in the courtroom waiting to be interviewed by the agents, a few were crying. Several couples held onto each other. Others sat stiffly, with grim, shocked expressions on their faces.

At the command post set up in the police-and-fire station, some 300 residents and newspeople were standing about, talking and waiting. Chowchillans wanted to help. They prepared and brought in food. They volunteered to drive the parents of the kidnapped children who were too nervous to drive. They offered to house relatives of these families. Farnesi's Restaurant, the largest in town, kept sending in boxes of food. And a youth named George appeared, handed Sheriff Bates a white box and said, "For you and your men." Inside was a large, untouched cake inscribed, "Happy 16th Birthday, George."

Meanwhile, in the buried trailer Mike Marshall worked his way around to Ray and asked, "Do you think we should try to get out of here?"

"I've been thinking about it." He wondered if one or more of the kidnappers were stationed on guard above them. If so, what would be done to the captives if they tried to escape and failed? Yet he knew that the children couldn't take much more of this imprisonment.

The kidnappers had placed a piece of metal over the entrance hole. It was shortly after four o'clock in the afternoon when Ray finally said to Mike, "All right, let's try to get out. We'll pile up enough mattresses to reach the roof and see what we can do with that plate over the hole."

Standing on this rocking and dipping platform, first Ray, then Mike, then Ray and Mike together tried to push open the metal hatch but couldn't budge it. They kept at it until they were drenched in sweat. Then, in the dying glow of the flashlight, Ray noticed a piece of wood wedged between the side and the roof of the van. He pulled it loose and with great effort forced it between the lid and the hole. Slowly, he widened the space enough to insert his fingers and pulled the lid open a few more inches. A heavy weight apparently was on top of the lid. He squeezed an arm through and touched two objects. His fingers told him they were rectangular with a series of knobs on top—truck batteries.

Ray managed to push back the lid far enough to grasp a battery—it weighed more than fifty pounds—and to pull it toward him. With Mike's help, he lowered first one, then the other to the floor of the trailer. He shoved the hatchback halfway across the hole. The faint beam of the flashlight revealed the interior of a plywood crate about three feet square that had been placed over the hatch. Ray could not budge it. He needed tools. Several children jumped on the edges of a box spring until the slats broke. Then they tore open a side. Pieces of the slats were used by Ray, Mike and Robert Gonzalez to pound a corner of the box. They finally broke a small opening and some dirt spilled through.

By now, though, Ray was exhausted. The effort seemed almost futile to him. He slid off the platform, poured water over his head and lay panting on a mattress. But after a few minutes, Ray got up. He returned to the platform where he, with Mike and Robert, continued to dig into the dirt, letting it fall into the trailer, until, finally, a wonderful beam of daylight could be seen through the top of box. Cries came from the children below—this time, cries of triumph. Then the workers heaved themselves against the nailed top of the box and broke it loose.

They looked around. Except for the opening, the entire trailer was buried under dirt, with dead shrubs stuck into it for camouflage. Trees partially surrounded them. The terrain was hilly, and a few parked trucks could be seen in the distance. It was a little after seven o'clock in the evening.

Ray dropped back to the trailer floor and handed the children, the youngest ones first, up to Mike and Robert. The last one to emerge, Ray saw that they were in an enormous stone quarry. A few hundred yards away stood a large construction shack where a welder was working on some equipment. Ray ran toward him and shouted, "Hello!" The welder turned slowly, lifted his face guard and stared at the bus driver, shoeless, standing in his undershorts, hair matted, face streaked with dirt, leading a bunch of filthy, scared-looking children.

"We're the school-busload of people that were taken away," Ray announced. "We were buried out in your yard. Please help us."

"Come on into the shack," the startled welder said.

"Where are we?"

"Livermore." The city was ninety-five miles northwest of Chowchilla—the kidnappers had obviously prolonged the two-and-a-half-hour drive from Chowchilla to confuse their victims and to await the dead of night.

Within ten minutes, several police cars and a sheriff's department bus arrived at the quarry. The children and Ray were taken to the county's Santa Rita Rehabilitation Center, where they were checked by a physician, fed, and questioned by the FBI.

It was nearly four a.m. on Saturday when the chartered bus carrying the children and Ray swung off the highway, moved down Chowchilla's Robertson Boulevard and made a left turn to the police-station parking lot. A welcoming crowd of several hundred let out a long cheer.

Carol Marshall and most of the other parents wept as the bus doors opened and the sleepy, dirty children, some wrapped in blankets, tentatively stepped down. Mike was the last one out. As he and his mother embraced, he said, "Let's go home. I want to go to bed."

The kidnapping of the children—probably the most bizarre and incredible nonpolitical kidnapping in history—had quickly spurred the widest manhunt ever mounted in California. The Alameda County Sheriff's Department exhumed the prison that held the victims in the quarry of the California Rock and Gravel Company. It turned out to be a moving van, readily traceable to a firm in Palo Alto. Company records showed that it had been sold for cash on November 20, 1975, to a Fred Woods of Portola Valley, a wealthy community south of San Francisco. Woods's father owned California Rock and Gravel. The records of the security guards at the quarry showed that Woods and two other men had spent considerable time there at night in November and December of 1975. During this period a guard also noted three men digging a large hole with a bulldozer.

The sheriff's department obtained a warrant to search the sprawling family estate on which Woods lived in a private cottage. There the sheriff's deputies found the draft of a ransom note demanding five million dollars, with instructions for air-dropping it in a mountainous area south of San Francisco. They also discovered a paper bag listing Ray and the children in the order in which they had descended to the buried moving van. Other material led them to a San Jose warehouse, where space rented in Woods's name contained the two kidnap vans.

Further discoveries caused the Alameda County sheriff's office to conclude that James Schoenfeld, 24, and his brother Richard, 22, sons of a Menlo Park podiatrist, were connected with the crime.

On July 22, a week after the kidnapping, an all-points bulletin for the three suspects was distributed. The next day, Richard Schoenfeld, accompanied by his father and his lawyer, surrendered to authorities in Oakland. On July 29, his brother James was arrested while driving through Menlo Park.

On that same morning, the FBI informed the Canadian police that Woods probably would visit the main post office in Vancouver to pick up a package. Later that day he was arrested at the post office, escorted to the border and turned over to U. S. authorities.

On arraignment, the three suspects entered pleas of not guilty to kidnapping charges related to the abduction of the twenty-six schoolchildren. They later changed their pleas to guilty and were each sentenced to life imprisonment.

The backgrounds and personalities of the criminals did not reveal anything that might have led anyone to suspect they were capable of plotting and carrying out such an infamous deed. Aside from joining together in one misdemeanor—using a car without the owner's permission—the three had no record of crime. Woods was a member of a wealthy and respected family. Known as a "loner," in high school he was shy and rarely mingled with any group. His one consuming interest was motor vehicles, and he and James Schoenfeld were partners in a successful automobile restoration business. The Schoenfeld brothers had never caused any trouble nor had they attracted any special attention.

With the lives of twenty-six children at stake, there seems little question that the kidnappers would have obtained their ransom from governmental or private sources. According to a plan found in Woods's cottage, they apparently intended to keep one million dollars each, then fly to Argentina. The rest of the money was to be given away to the poor.

Why Chowchilla? Some investigators believe that several small towns in central California had been selected as likely prospects for such a kidnapping. Ray's bus was chosen because it was in the right place at the right time.

To the world outside Chowchilla, the kidnapping had a happy ending. The children and the bus driver returned with no obvious physical injuries. The suspects were caught. But the emotional upheaval caused by the crime did not end as quickly.

The kidnapping preyed on Carol Marshall's mind for many months. When her husband was away, she nervously fretted between calls. If a child was not home by an agreed time, she was seized with panic.

"A lot of the worry that I and other parents feel must come from a new awareness of what we have," Carol told me. "We want to protect it—perhaps too much. My son was taken from me. My son was returned. And while he was gone I realized more than ever in my life how precious a child is."

Vern Bagley
may not have
looked like a hero,
but in those harrowing
minutes above the
raging Bay of Fundy
he proved
that he *was* one

Up
the Cliff

BY DAVID MACDONALD

THE CALL FOR HELP came at 12:30 a.m. It was an icy night, February 26, 1963, and a gale was howling across the Bay of Fundy. The Seal Cove telephone operator first roused a dozen ablebodied fishermen. As an afterthought she rang Vernon Bagley, a bandy-legged little man of forty-six who doubled as game warden and village wag.

Bagley stumbled sleepily to his phone. The operator's words shook him awake: "Someone's over the cliff at South West Head!"

Bagley shuddered. Like most folks on Grand Manan, a small Canadian island just off the coast where Maine meets New Brunswick, he knew that rugged, rocky precipice well. It towered 200 feet above the sea, and on this savage night he could almost feel the fury of the wind and waves that were lashing at it.

"Wal," he drawled, "I'd best get crackin'." As Bagley dressed, his wife tucked a spare pair of mittens into his hip pocket. Then he slid into his beat-up car and set out for South West Head, six miles away. The twisty road was slippery, swirling with snow. Bagley, a former fisherman who'd been glad to take a job ashore, drove carefully: no sense taking unnecessary risks.

The night's events, shaped by the raw forces of nature and human need, had actually begun the morning before. Fifteen miles across the bay, at Haycock Harbor, Maine, two men had cast off in a leaky motorboat. Billy Jones, 42, and his brother Floyd, 36, who eked out a living from odd jobs, were hoping to gather periwinkles to feed their families. But a gale struck from the north, the boat's engine failed, and for twelve hours, in thrashing seas, both men bailed, retched and prayed. After dark, the storm drove them toward a winking lighthouse on the southern tip of Grand Manan, then flung them aground below towering South West Head. There the brothers managed to drag themselves up beyond the surf. Floyd, numb with cold, could go no farther. Billy started climbing up the cliff. "I'll make for that light," he yelled. Floyd didn't answer.

Three hours later, lightkeeper Ottawa Benson and his wife heard a thump at their door. Mrs. Benson opened it—and shrank back. Crouched on hands and knees, covered with snow, a man stared up at her with half-crazed eyes. "My brother . . ." he stammered. "Me and my brother's been blown ashore. I got up the bank, but he's still down there."

Benson was dumbfounded: He knew it was next to impossible to scale that almost vertical cliff. He quickly rang the telephone operator at Seal Cove, the nearest of the island's seven fishing villages.

On Grand Manan, a close-knit seafaring community of 2,500, any cry for help is a command. Soon the Seal Cove men began arriving, seventeen in all, including Vern Bagley. They conferred briefly with Benson, then trudged through the blizzard to the place where Billy Jones had come up the cliff and begun crawling to the light—a mile away. Far below, roaring breakers slammed at the ink-black bluff, hurling spray high into the night. Searchers yelled Floyd's name, but the fifty-mile-an-hour gale drowned out their words.

"It's murder to send anyone down there now," one man shouted. There was a rumble of agreement. "Let's wait till daylight."

"No!" came a firm protest. "That'll be too late." Out of the crowd stepped Vern Bagley, his face grave, his manner untypically determined. "Tie a line on me."

The others stared in surprise. Vern Bagley was regarded as the local "character," always joking and good for a laugh. "That Vern," islanders often observed, "he'd poke fun at his own grandmother."

But tonight Vern was deadly serious. He secured a nylon line around his waist, took a flashlight, and began inching down toward Hog's Back, a ridge of loose rock sloping sharply to the sea. He'd gone only a few yards when the rocks began sliding and tumbling out from under him down the bank. In panic, Bagley clambered back to the top. "No use," he panted. "I can't do it."

With the line still knotted at his waist, he walked slowly away. Sensing his embarrassment, the others quietly resumed debating what to do. And then a strange thing happened. Bagley suddenly looked up. "Yessir," he said aloud—though no one had spoken—"I sure would!" He went straight to the brink of the bluff. "I've got to go down again."

This time Bagley swung wide of treacherous Hog's Back. Beside it ran a steep gully, the quickest way down—for him, or for a rockslide. Edging across the top of the gully, he vanished behind another almost perpendicular ridge, hesitated, then began to feel his way down the cliff's jagged face. Some 150 feet down the crag, he paused on a flat rock and flashed a light to either side—no sign of Jones—and then up the bluff. High above, to his horror, he saw that his lifeline had hooked over the gnarled root of a fallen tree. Instead of running straight down, it ran horizontally across the gully to the snag, and then down, in the shape of a figure 7. If he moved any farther, his weight could unsnag the line from the root, and the sudden slack would drop him to the cliff's bottom.

Frozen with fear, Bagley pondered his precarious position. His only hope, he saw, was to flick the rope free, so that the resulting slack could be noticed and pulled in. "More line!" he yelled. But it remained taut. "More line!" In the thunder of wind and sea, no one above could hear him.

Somebody else did, however. From off to Bagley's left, beyond Hog's Back, came a feeble cry: "Over here!" Floyd Jones was alive.

Bagley now faced an agonizing choice. If he continued his descent to save Jones, his rope could pull loose at any second. Yet if he held back, Jones would surely die. "Oh, God!"—Floyd's wail was weaker now—"Help me!"

Up on the cliff, a bonfire cast an eerie glow on the weathered faces of the men handling the ropes. Bagley's cousin Horace lay at the very edge of the precipice, "reading" the line. It quivered in his hands, and he saw a flash of light far below. "Pay out more line," he called. "Vern's going into the gully!"

Bagley had made his choice. Crossing the gully, he slipped on ice-crusted snow. But the lifeline—his sole hope and greatest fear—held fast. To keep his mind off it, Bagley concentrated on Floyd Jones as he crept up the rocky flank of Hog's Back. Atop the ridge, he lay flat and shone his light over the other side.

About twenty-five feet below, just out of reach of the surging sea, Floyd Jones knelt on a narrow ledge, arms and face pressed into a crevice. His clothes were stiff with ice. Only his blond hair moved in the wind. Now Bagley completely forgot his own predicament. While the men above felt his motions and released more rope, he backed over the edge. Hanging over the sea, arms and legs straight out from the rough rock, he made his way downward.

Suddenly, atop the cliff, Horace felt the line go limp. "We've lost him!" he screamed. Frantic, he hauled in the rope—thirty, fifty, seventy feet of it. Then, just as suddenly, he again felt his cousin's weight and a reassuring yank on the line.

Far below, Bagley crouched beside Jones, trembling. He had just been brushed by death. At the very instant that he stepped onto the ledge, his slender lifeline had finally jerked loose from the snag. Over and over he told himself, *I'm alive!*

But Floyd Jones appeared to be dead. Bagley removed a glove and touched the man's frigid, uncovered head. "Can't move," came a hoarse rasp. "I'm froze from the belt down."

"Don't worry now," Bagley replied. "We'll get you up in no time."

Brave words. For the problems ahead were as large as the cliff itself. The semiconscious Jones couldn't be hauled up alone; the savage winds would batter him against the rock. There was only one possibility. With the rope still tied to himself, Bagley got Jones to his feet and eased his hands into the extra mittens his wife had given him an eternity ago. Then he wrapped Floyd's arms around his own waist, from behind, jammed them under the rope, and tightened it securely. "Hang on!" he shouted.

After three sharp tugs—the haul-up signal—the lifeline strained. The two men dangled in space, then began to rise. Jones, a 180-pounder, clung to his rescuer with the strength of desperation. For Bagley, the ascent was agony. The rope tightened around him so terribly he thought he was being cut in two.

As he neared Hog's Back, Bagley felt Jones slipping. He caught him by the neck and wrestled him over the hump. There they lay; Jones was unconscious, Bagley gasping for breath and trying to figure out his next move.

Vern was now too tired to make a wide detour, the way he'd come down. And on Hog's Back itself were tons of loose rocks, flung down by an earlier landslide; one false step there could be fatal. That left only the steep gully, where the lifeline might dislodge stones and start an avalanche.

Bagley retied his line around Jones and signaled to the men at the top of the cliff. Buckling under the inert body's weight, he descended into the gully and began the long climb. Clinging to the rope with one arm, using the other to protect Jones, he pushed and pulled to make headway up the slope. At times, he had to lift Jones over fallen trees. Other times, he straddled and dragged him.

About twenty-five feet from safety, Bagley's legs gave out. Wedging the unconscious Jones behind a boulder, he crept on up the rope alone. Ninety minutes after he'd left on his impulsive mission of mercy, Bagley was hauled back over the edge at the top. "He's just below," he gasped to the waiting men. "But I'm all done in."

Assistant lightkeeper Sid Guptill went down on another line while Bagley dropped into a snowbank and lay there, waiting. Within half an hour, Floyd Jones was pulled up, still alive. Quickly, he was covered with coats and rushed to the hospital.

Exhausted, aching in every fiber, Vern Bagley stood at the cliff's edge and gazed down in silent disbelief, a man tested and proved strong. As he turned and trudged away, two fishermen linked their arms through his, supporting him. "We're mighty proud of you, Vern," said one.

Next day, at the hospital, the Jones brothers tearfully thanked the man who had risked his life in their behalf. Billy couldn't remember how he'd scaled the cliff, except that the wind at his back had helped to keep him from falling. All that Floyd recalled of his rescue was the touch of Bagley's hand waking him. "It felt," he said, "like a hot flatiron." Doctors doubted that Floyd could have survived another fifteen minutes of his ordeal. Though both men suffered from exposure, they quickly recovered. As Bagley phrased it, "Them two's tougher'n tripe."

A year later, 300 islanders packed the Grand Manan high-school gym to see Vern Bagley awarded the Carnegie Silver Medal for heroism. After the ceremony, Bagley was asked about the strange remark he'd made—"Yessir, I sure would!"—before he went to Floyd Jones's rescue.

"Wal," Bagley replied, "I'd been tellin' myself all the reasons why I couldn't go back over that cliff. But then this idea hit me: *Would you go if it was your own brother?* That's when I talked out loud, I guess. 'Cause, when you get right down to it, we're *all* supposed to be brothers."

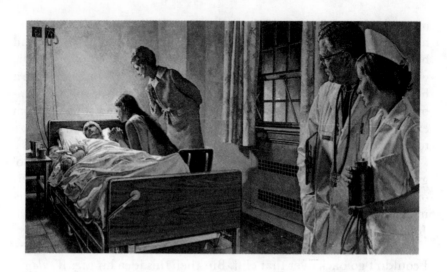

"He was hurt so cruelly,"
his doctor recalls, "that life became unbearable."
Then, slowly, a miracle began to unfold

The Long Return
of Warrant Officer Meade

BY JOSEPH P. BLANK

YOU OUGHT TO GO HOME," the army neurosurgeon told Kathy Meade. "There's no point in your continuing to live here at the hospital. If your husband ever wakes from his coma—and there's no sign that he will—I doubt that he'll ever be able to function as a human being."

The doctor's frank appraisal stunned the young wife. She returned in a daze to the intensive-care room at Madigan General Hospital, Tacoma, Washington, where her husband, CWO James P. Meade, Jr., 20, lay dying. One cast covered his entire trunk and his badly fractured, deeply infected left leg; another covered his fractured right ankle. One side of his head was indented from loss of bone and showed two burr holes where army surgeons in South Vietnam had drilled exploratively. His weight had plunged from 145 pounds to an emaciated 80.

To Kathy, it seemed impossible that this pathetic figure was her husband. Only sixteen weeks earlier, he had been in perfect health—and eager to reach Vietnam. The son of a career sergeant major in the Army, he had enlisted after a year at the University of Oregon, where he had been a brilliant student and president of the freshman honor society.

"I can't go on with school while men are dying out there," he had told Kathy in their frequent talks about the war. "I've got to do something to save lives, and the best way is for me to become a helicopter pilot."

Jim and Kathy were married shortly before he went to South Vietnam, where he immediately saw combat. He flew day and night, and in less than four months was shot down three times. On the third crash he had turned his falling ship into trees at an angle that exposed him to the greatest danger and his three crewmen to the least. At impact, the broken but still-spinning rotor blades smashed through the cockpit, tore his helmet to bits, gouged out part of his skull and battered his brain. He was the only one injured.

Fifteen days after the crash Jim was wheeled into Madigan General, where a medical team headed by Maj. George Palmer quickly went to work. They made repairs on his battered body, fed him nutrients intravenously and got his blood chemistry into balance. But they could do nothing about the brain damage that caused his strange coma. After a few days his eyes opened, but they remained unfocused and expressionless. Frenetically active, he had to be tied to the bed with towels. Incomprehensible animal sounds came from his throat.

Kathy and Jim's mother were at his bedside throughout the day, trying to break through the coma by giving him every possible expression of love. Periodically, they removed his arm restraints. And

---

The people, places and events in the story of Warrant Officer Meade are real, but some names have been changed at the request of the individuals involved.

each time he tried to throw himself out of bed, biting, snarling, growling. Unable to express himself like a human being, he behaved like a trapped animal.

Major Palmer could offer no hope. "We were losing him," he recalls, "and I had the feeling that he wanted to go. He was hurt so cruelly that life became unbearable."

Jim's mother, a surgery-room nurse in a civilian hospital, also recognized that her son was sinking. "You and I know that he is dying," she told Major Palmer. "Can't you try something else?"

The major had concluded that Jim remained alive only because of the loving attention of his wife and mother. What might help to lift the coma, he thought, would be the additional care and concern of others. Perhaps the answer could be found in the hospital's orthopedic ward, 13, which housed some of the Vietnam war's most seriously disabled amputees.

"Ward 13 had a fine spirit," Major Palmer later explained. "The men there, having fought depression and emotional withdrawal, were more capable of helping Jim than all the hospital's doctors and nurses. Ward 13 was his only chance, although a remote one."

First Lt. Carole Burke, head nurse on the ward, told its occupants only that a young chopper pilot with a head injury, who could neither talk nor respond, was being admitted. She asked nothing of them. She knew they had a great respect for these pilots; each, in fact, had been carried from the battlefield to a hospital by an army helicopter.

The men glanced up casually as Jim was wheeled into the ward. Two nurses removed the towel restraints from his raw wrists, then posted themselves on either side of his bed. In a few minutes a patient in a cast hobbled over. "I'll stay with him," he said. Soon two other patients drifted by and began a conversation; although Jim seemed oblivious to it, he was included. During the next twenty-four hours the men lounged around Jim's bed, spoon-fed him meals, played the radio, bantered, kidded with the nurses. All the while Jim was treated as if he were "there"—aware, participating.

After a few days, Jim's hyperactivity—the biting and writhing—subsided. He took long naps, curled up in a fetal position. It may have been that he was preparing to be "born" again, Major Palmer surmised, as hitherto unused cells in the right side of the brain were being activated to take over the functions of the destroyed cells in the left side.

When he grew restless in bed, nurses and patients moved him into a wheelchair and pushed him into the semicircle of amputees around the television set. "Want to watch a ball game, Jim?" one asked. No response. "Want some ice cream, Jim?" No response.

One day, when nurse Burke was helping him into a wheelchair, Jim swung his forearm sharply against her head. It seemed a deliberate movement, perhaps to express impatience. "Jim," she said, "we're trying to understand you. Help us." No response.

More than a month went by while the men eagerly watched Jim for any sign of change. Then one day a veteran told nurse Burke, "I think he looked at me. For just a flash."

Gradually Jim's eyes began to focus, to look at things, at people. And now, as he began emerging from his coma, puzzlement replaced the empty, unseeing expression. Neither he nor the doctors realized at this time that the chopper blades had destroyed a portion of his brain's memory cells. Like an infant, Jim was looking at a world he couldn't recognize.

Actually, he was more helpless than an infant. He couldn't talk, laugh or cry. The pain in his left leg was deep and searing, but he had no way to tell anyone about it. As the days passed, and a part of his intelligence returned, he became convinced that his inability to communicate meant he was dying. He sank into a state of deep depression.

But Ward 13 would have none of it. Prodding, cajoling, they forced him into action. He learned to nod or shake his head in answer to questions. He learned to eat on his own power—by reaching erratically for the food and throwing it toward his mouth. He wanted to talk. He worked his mouth, grimaced, pushed, fought. But the words simply would not come out.

Then, early one Monday, it happened. Nurse Burke entered Ward 13 with a cheery "Good morning, gentlemen." As she passed Jim's wheelchair she thought she heard him answer, "Goo' moorn'." Was it wishful hearing? His eyes told her that he *had* made the sounds.

That same day, he greeted Kathy with three barely understandable and obviously rehearsed words. "I—love—you," he said.

Her heart jumped. She repeated the words to him. Then she pointed to her expanding middle. "Baby," she said. He tried furiously to say the word. He couldn't. He tried other words. But they wouldn't come either. Then he went limp, as if to say, "Why try? It's hopeless."

Kathy leaned over him. "You can't give up," she whispered. "We need you. You're going to make it." Then she excused herself, went to the ladies' room and cried, out of hope and fear, and sympathy for her husband in his terrible struggle.

Nothing came easy to Jim as he fought to "grow up again." To read, he first had to relearn his ABCs. Then he progressed to children's books of the "Look, Jane, see Spot" variety. His greatest problem was making his legs, hands and voice respond to his brain's commands. It took him nearly a year to go from scattering food across the table to cutting his meat and bringing it accurately to his mouth.

Writing, even simple words like *cat,* was an ordeal. He would forget how to spell the word or how to print the letters. He couldn't write in a straight line, make the letters the same size or keep one from overlapping another. But, finally, there it was—a legible *C A T.*

It took Jim nearly three years of sweat, strain and determination to walk without supports. From a wheelchair, still wearing a leg cast, he moved to crutches. One afternoon he joined other disabled veterans who were bouncing a ball off a handball wall. He laid down his crutches to see if he could maintain his balance and move just a little. He reached for the ball—and fell. Choking back tears of frustration, he picked up his crutches, went around to the back of the gym and pounded his head against the wall.

His father understood his feelings. "Jim," he told him, "you've done a lot of things that most people thought you'd never be able to do. I know you can learn to walk. Let's get to work on it." At his father's home, where Jim now spent periodic leaves, the elder Meade built a thirty-foot-long wood platform with hip-high parallel railings. Using the railings for support, Jim tried to walk. He fell, got up, fell—and kept falling until, exhausted, he could no longer pull himself up.

Undaunted, he crawled up and down the platform, trying to coordinate the movements of his legs and arms. He performed these exercises for weeks until he could crawl as well as a normal year-old infant. Back to the rails, and now he was able to take some steps without falling. "I've got to make it," he told himself. "I've got to." And his father, beside him every minute, assured him, "You will, you will."

From the parallel bars he went to canes, walking, weaving, staggering, falling. Slowly, over the months, he learned to maintain his balance, to walk in a straight line, to maneuver over street curbs. In February 1970, he walked into Ward 13 with a big grin on his face—and no canes. Thirty months after one authority had labeled him a "hopeless vegetable," Jim Meade was clearly making it.

In September 1969 he had taken another long step, enrolling in the two-year Mt. Hood Community College on the outskirts of Portland. It was tough. He was self-conscious about his limping gait and occasionally slurred speech. He couldn't take notes fast enough. Homework took him three times longer than the average student.

"I felt so dumb, so worthless," Jim recalled later. "Why, I even had to learn to add, subtract and multiply. It was terrible not to be able to keep up."

He became despondent. "Then he remembered what people had done for him," recalls his college counselor, psychologist Patrick Loughary. "He developed an ambition to help others as he had been helped. His determination returned, and he changed remarkably. In eight months he rose from a D to a B student."

Jim received his diploma from Mt. Hood in June 1970 and began working toward a degree in psychology at Portland State University. "I want to get into work where I can use what I've learned to help people," Jim explained. "A person who is deeply hurt feels very lonely. It's hard to survive this feeling. But love can make the difference. Even in my coma I must have felt the love of my family and wardmates, and felt my love for them. If I hadn't, there would have been no reason to go on. Surely I would have died."

A Dime
of Pure Gold

BY STEPHEN G. FREEMAN

The three crewmen of the hijacked *Kamalii*
concluded that just three questions faced them:
Where, how and when would they die?

THE SEVENTY-FIVE-FOOT KETCH *Kamalii* lay at her berth in Honolulu's Ali Wai Yacht Harbor. She had competed recently in the Transpacific Yacht Race and was now provisioned for the return to her home port in California.

It was eleven p.m., August 6, 1971. The *Kamalii's* three crewmen were aboard and asleep. Mate Frank Power, 47, awoke abruptly in his after cabin. He heard footsteps on the main deck. *Why would anyone be boarding the* Kamalii *at this hour?* He looked out a small porthole at deck level and saw legs passing, moving forward. Power got up, mounted the steps to the bridge—and almost walked into a pistol pointed at his stomach!

Power saw that three men were standing on the bridge, all with pistols drawn and ammunition belts across their chests and around their waists. Two of the three also held knives in their left hands.

When Robert Waschkeit, 49, the *Kamalii's* captain, and John

Freitas, 52, the cook and able-bodied seaman, also appeared, the three crewmen were ordered to lie down on the deck of the saloon. Their wrists were handcuffed behind their backs, their ankles roped, then drawn up behind and tied to the handcuffs.

At first, skipper Waschkeit thought it was a holdup and was thankful that little cash was aboard. But when the gunmen left the saloon and returned with three duffel bags and a roll of charts, he was not so sure. Then they freed Waschkeit's ankles and ordered him to the engine room, where they had him explain details of *Kamalii's* operation. Brought back to the saloon, he was again trussed, and all three crewmen were gagged—their mouths stuffed with absorbent cotton and their lips sealed with surgical tape. Each was carried sack-of-potatoes fashion and dumped into the forecastle, where one gunman stood over them. "Make any noise," this man said in a high-pitched, uneven voice, his gun quivering in his hand, "and I'll *kill* you." He would, they knew.

Now the *Kamalii* was backing out of the slip. Waschkeit winced as a piling was hit hard, then scraped. He soon realized that they were heading out to sea. Moreover, he knew that no one would impute any significance to the *Kamalii's* departure, since they had been preparing for a voyage. Only if owner E. L. "Larry" Doheny III, now enjoying his island home on Oahu's south shore, appeared at the slip to find the *Kamalii* gone would an alarm be raised—and it could be days before such an appearance.

The three gunmen, all in their twenties, were slender, cleanshaven, with short hair. They were obviously longtime acquaintances. Their names, unknown then to the *Kamalii's* crew, were Kerry D. Bryant, Mark E. Maynard and Michael R. Melton. Melton had been in the Coast Guard, and Bryant and Maynard had been together in the Marine Corps in Vietnam and, later, in communes in California and Hawaii. Their conversation, their captives soon discovered, verged on preoccupation with things paradisal— Bryant's in particular. He seemed obsessed with the "groovy commune" they would establish "out there"—a world of peace somewhere in the South Pacific. "Like with Gauguin," Maynard added.

Bryant, the one whom the prisoners would come to refer to as The Slapper—he continually slapped the flat side of his bared knife into the palm of his left hand in a slow *plat . . . plat . . . plat*—told them, "We're going to make it easier for you. No one could hear you now if you did holler." The gags were removed and the behind-the-back trussings released. Wrists were handcuffed in front, but the ankles were still lashed, and the ankle ropes tied to their wrists. Waschkeit was moved to a single cabin amidships; the other two were put in the double cabin aft.

It's piracy! Power thought as he lay helpless on his bunk. *Unbelievable!* No matter what plan the hijackers had in mind, each member of the *Kamalii's* crew had by now concluded that the young men would ultimately have to get rid of them.

For a while, they'll need us to run the boat, Waschkeit thought. *They don't know much about navigation.* (Melton had toyed with the ship's sextant, but finally tossed it aside, apparently finding it incomprehensible.) *And the way they're gunning the engine she'll be out of fuel after 800 miles—which leaves them nowhere. To proceed under sail, they'll need us.*

Power found hope in the thought that they might be put off on an uninhabited island. And Freitas, who as a young man had fought forty-six professional boxing bouts, kept thinking about how to wrest a gun away from the hijackers.

August 7—morning. The weather was sunny and warm, the sea flat. The hijackers were steering an erratic course on a generally southwesterly heading. At noon, Power estimated their position 120 miles off Honolulu on a bearing of 230 degrees.

At 3:00 p.m., Power asked if his cramped legs might be freed so he could walk a bit on deck. At 5:30, Waschkeit was taken from his cabin and escorted topside, his legs released. Watching, Power assumed that the captors had decided to allow them, singly, a turn or two.

But no. Within the next few minutes, Power and Freitas were brought on deck; their handcuffs were removed—and all three men were abruptly ordered to jump overboard! *Without life jackets!* they remember thinking. *In these shark-infested waters!*

Waschkeit pleaded for a life raft. Maynard seemed hardly attentive, but finally motioned to The Slapper, and the two joined Melton at the wheel. They conferred for some time.

Maynard returned to Waschkeit. "Okay," he said. "You'll get a life raft. But first the three of you go overboard in life jackets. We'll turn the ship around, come back and toss over the raft."

Why not put the raft over now? Waschkeit was thinking—but he had already answered his own question. *They probably have no intention of letting us have a raft. They'll simply sail off.*

The men got into the life jackets. "Let's go," Maynard said.

Slowly they stepped over the guardrail, their hands holding to its top strand behind them, feet on the gunwale. The boat's speed had been reduced.

"Jump!" Maynard ordered. No one did. Power found himself thinking of Neil Armstrong's "giant leap."

"You first," Maynard said, poking his gun into Waschkeit's back. Waschkeit let go. The others followed.

The men surfaced and held hands, a small triangle in the sea. The boat was moving away, fast. Would the hijackers come back to drop the life raft?

From sea level, distance assumes a different dimension. The *Kamalii*—the trio in the water could still see the gilded name on her transom—was diminishing rapidly.

Then she turned.

She was alongside. The rubber raft was put over and inflated.

Maynard stood over the trio as they climbed in. "We were undecided whether to let you have a raft or not," he said, "so we finally tossed a coin." He reached into a pocket. "You were lucky." The *Kamalii's* propeller was churning; she was beginning to move away. "Here," he said—and he threw a dime into the raft.

It was 6:30 p.m. The *Kamalii* was gone, over the horizon. The raft's position was roughly 140 miles southwest of Honolulu. Power and Waschkeit, both former merchant mariners, had been moodily silent. They knew that their position put them in waters as desolate and untraveled as any in the Pacific. Commerce between Asia and the Americas passes far north of Hawaii, and even ships calling at Honolulu use the Kaiwi Channel to the north. Furthermore, the raft was not provisioned for prolonged survival. Among its supplies were two parachute distress signals, three small hand flares, eight pints of fresh water—but no rations.

The three men were already fatigued. Waschkeit took the first watch; Power and Freitas fell asleep immediately.

The night was clear, calm and moonless. Waschkeit, having difficulty staying awake, decided he'd stand and identify as many stars as he could. He'd raise an arm, point at a star, name it aloud. His words were slurring; his arm was dropping. He felt himself rocking, dozing—or perhaps hallucinating. He was afraid he might pitch over the side. He kneeled, then sat.

Two lights! He saw two lights. *Was* he hallucinating? Confused, he cried, "Land!" and shook Power and Freitas awake.

The lights were real; the range lights of a ship—five or six miles off. "We've *got* to get her," Waschkeit muttered. He sent one of the two big parachute flares arcing into the night sky. Seeing no change in the ship's course, he lit one of the small flares and held it aloft. Again, no response. Soon the ship would be broadside, and then moving away.

Waschkeit sent up their last parachute flare. It arced into the sky, then dropped softly into the sea—and the night became much darker.

Nothing.

Then, very slowly—imperceptibly at first, yet gradually, steadily—the ship turned toward them. Suddenly, the three of them were sobbing.

Soon the ship, at dead slow, was almost on them. From high on its bridge, its searchlight swept back and forth across the open sea until it found the men on the raft.

At 9:40 p.m., the three men were safely aboard the freighter *Benadir*. They would accompany her to Yokohama, where she was bound with a cargo of bananas. Those of the *Benadir's* men who were not on watch began questioning the survivors.

After the *Kamalii's* crewmen had told their story, Waschkeit asked the *Benadir's* Captain DiDomenico how it was that his ship was in these waters, some 1,300 miles south of the summer shipping lanes.

The captain laughed and explained that the *Benadir's* engines had broken down twice shortly after they had left Ecuador. He therefore had changed his course in order to pass closer to ports where repairs could be made en route to Yokohama.

"You can thank this man here for your rescue," he said, jovially gesturing toward the *Benadir's* chief engineer. The *Benadir* was a German-built ship, newly acquired by Italian owners. All the instructions for running its complex engines were in German and had not yet been fully mastered by its new crew.

The engineer smiled. "From the bad sometimes comes the good—eh?"

Simultaneously a thought occurred to each of the men from the *Kamalii*. They looked at one another for a moment, then nodded. Bob Waschkeit spoke: "We would like to give something to you, Captain DiDomenico." And from a pocket he withdrew their lucky dime.

The Benadir *radioed news of the stolen yacht to the Coast Guard at Honolulu, where a search was organized. The next day, Air Force and Coast Guard planes spotted the* Kamalii, *and a day later, two Coast Guard cutters intercepted her. Bryant, Maynard and Melton were taken into custody and brought to trial in Honolulu. For their parts in the crimes, Bryant and Maynard were each sentenced to ten years in prison. Melton received a five-year suspended sentence.*

Without warning,
visibility on the turnpike dropped to zero.
In the burning wreckage,
one man's heroism stood out like a beacon

Trooper Plebani
and the Killer Smog

BY PETER MICHELMORE

NEW JERSEY STATE TROOPER Cornel Plebani, a hard-muscled man with a handsome face and short-cropped dark hair, had occasion to take stock of himself as he drove to work the night of October 23, 1973. It was his twenty-sixth birthday, and he was content. He had survived two years as a marine in Vietnam, then returned to realize his boyhood dream of becoming a trooper, married the prettiest blonde in his hometown and already had a fine son. Never again would he have to take the sort of chances he had taken in Vietnam, wriggling on his belly through enemy-held territory, calling in strikes over his own position.

It was cold and clear when Plebani signed in for the eleven p.m. to seven a.m. shift. He was responsible for patrolling thirty miles of the New Jersey Turnpike north of Newark, a segment that leads to two major access routes into New York City. Unknown to him and his partner, Tony Simonetti, a lean trooper in his early thirties, the night was to become the most disastrous in the history of the turnpike. Dawn would see more than sixty vehicles destroyed, nine men killed, thirty-seven persons injured.

The first accident that night was harrowing enough. Three cars and four trucks, speeding south, smashed into one another in a patch of fog. In the middle of the pileup, eighteen-year-old Robert Musto was trapped in his car. Plebani broke a window and crawled inside to warm the dying Musto with blankets and to hold him still. It was twenty minutes before ambulance crews arrived, and all that time Plebani would not budge, even though gasoline from ruptured tanks washed under the car. "Holy hell!" an ambulance man declared. "One spark and you'd have gone!"

Fog continued to move in as the temperature dropped. Back at Troop D headquarters, Sgt. Gary Buriello ordered the highway warning lights lit: REDUCE SPEED. FOG AHEAD. What Buriello did not know was that a garbage-dump fire near the scene of the accident was pumping thick smoke into the gathering fog, creating an enormous black cloud. Unseen in the night, this cloud had drifted upward, flattened against a lid of warmer air above, and was now slowly billowing back down toward the roadway.

At 1:50 a.m., with the fog worsening, Buriello ordered his troopers to block traffic from entering the Newark section of the turnpike. Still, the sergeant had to sweat out the safety of the hundreds of drivers already past the barriers, roaring along unaware of the danger ahead. For the southbound travelers, fate was good. In the thickening fog, drivers had their windshield wipers going, and were just creeping along. For the northbound drivers, however, coming from higher ground, there would be no warning fog at all.

Emory Burton, 34, a husky Virginian hauling a flat-bed stacked with newsprint rolls, saw the traffic warning lights a few miles past Newark and tried, unsuccessfully, to get some information about the weather ahead on his citizen's-band radio. Burton's partner, thin, bespectacled James Wagner, followed with a second load of newsprint. Leading both, Bill Diegel of Baltimore was at the wheel of a giant rig loaded with bottled whiskey. Two heavy tankers of hot asphalt lumbered along in the right-hand lane. Wesley East, a Philadelphian driving a van of mail, kept pace behind a station wagon driven by forty-four-year-old New Yorker Casper La Marca.

Down into this northbound convoy of traffic thundered a total of forty cars and trucks, most doing about fifty miles an hour. Directly in front of them, second by second, the great blanket of smog was dropping lower and lower. Thirty feet above the road, then twenty feet—down came the enormous blanket of black.

The reflector at Milepost 110 glittered back at the onrushing vehicles' headlights, then suddenly vanished. For hundreds of feet, the turnpike was plunged into a terrifying blackness. As the inky curtain dropped, trucks and cars slammed together in a series of deafening crashes. Vehicles twisted, spun, rolled over, spewing cargo, glass and tires everywhere.

Casper La Marca, conscious of a hulk careening across his path, swung the wheel of his station wagon wildly, bounced off a truck and stopped dead. Lunging out the door, he was hit by flying debris that knocked him under a moving trailer. With incredible presence of mind, he rolled to the center of the hulk above to escape the rear tires. Then, catching a glimpse of the white guardrail, he was over it and down into a marsh in an instant.

Wesley East was not so lucky. The entire top part of his mail-van cab sheared away in the collision, and he died at the wheel. Behind him, Bill Diegel's rig buckled at impact, tossing Diegel lifeless to the road. Also killed were Dick Zimmerman and John Mott in the asphalt tankers, which split like melons and gushed hot tar across the highway. Sparks from the grinding metal and electrical shorts ignited the diesel fuel and gasoline that flowed everywhere, and soon the tar and spilled whiskey created an inferno. Several men would remember nothing of the crash from that point on.

Outside that black envelope of death, nobody knew what was happening for many minutes. A fuel truck driver, caught in a standstill traffic jam in the southbound lanes, finally radioed Newark on his citizen's-band radio that he thought he saw an explosion in the fog ahead. Simonetti and Plebani, listening in, gunned their car toward the scene, hit the southward traffic clog, then barreled down the shoulder with lights flashing and siren screaming. Drivers who had abandoned their vehicles rushed toward them, arms waving. "Tanker on fire!" they shouted. "Everything's exploding!"

Simonetti had barely braked the car to a halt at the head of the column before Plebani was off and running, his leg brushing against the guardrail for guidance in the gloom. He heard shouts and moans, and the whoosh of flash fires, but saw nothing until an air current lifted the blackness and then dumped it down again. Right before him, and into the distance, he glimpsed flaming wreckage and shadowy, lost figures.

He grabbed his radio. "We got one hell of a mess, Tony," he reported back to his partner. "Newark," he barked, "I need heavy-duty rescues. I got a tractor-trailer jackknifed, and I got a tanker with oil spilling out on the roadway with its tractor demolished. At least three other rigs are smashed. We're all engulfed in smoke here. We can't see six inches."

With that, Trooper Plebani was off again. Stumbling into a wreck, he found a trucker twisted down on the seat, his chest and face bloodied. Crawling over the cab's snubbed nose, the trooper hefted the driver free through the shattered window and carried him back to the patrol car. The man was shivering and regaining consciousness. The trooper tucked his own blue jacket around him before he left.

Plebani found the mail van next, with Wesley East dead in the cab. A trailer to the left was ablaze, and the van could go up at any second. Nevertheless, Plebani grabbed East under the arms and dragged his body free.

In the fiery interior of the pileup, Plebani heard a shout for help. "Keep yelling so I can find you," the trooper called into the darkness. He heard the cry of distress again, and this time he could tell where it came from—behind a trailer wrapped in flames. Without stopping to figure the odds, Plebani dropped to his hands and knees and scuttled under the blazing trailer. On the other side, a roofless cab, torn away from its trailer, was surrounded by a ring of fire— and inside the cab was the driver who had been calling for help.

"Are you a doctor?" the man cried. "Will you help me?"

"We're gonna get you out of here," replied Plebani, climbing through the top of the cab. He seized the man, pulled him up and over to the hood, and together they slithered across the fender to the ground. The trucker tried to stand up, yelped with agony, and passed out.

Minutes had gone by. The escape route under the trailer was nearly closed. Burning timbers were dropping from the truck floor, and the entire rig threatened to collapse in one fiery heap at any moment. Plebani backed under the truck on his knees, tugging the man along behind. He could feel his hair being singed, his face scorched. Two yards, three yards. Suddenly he was out and standing, snatching the trucker free at the instant the trailer tumbled to the road.

When he emerged, Plebani saw Simonetti laboring with the injured who were making it out of the chain collision on their own. Simonetti's supply of oxygen and bandages was exhausted—and there was no sign of ambulances. "God knows when they will get through," Simonetti said. "Visibility is zero."

Plebani plunged back into the conflagration. Jammed doors defeated him at one cab; fire drove him from another. Then, inside a pool of spilled tar on the fringe of the flames, he discovered the body of Bill Diegel in a pile of debris. He was staggering clear with the 210-pound load over his shoulder when a flying chunk of tire from an exploding trailer hit him in the back. As he sprawled over the body, Plebani was overcome with fatigue and fear. *Hit the deck and stay there.* That was the rule in war when the barrage started. *Not here, Plebani.* The trooper got unsteadily to his feet, seized Diegel's collar and forced himself on.

By now, Engine Company 2 of nearby Kearny, New Jersey, had arrived on the scene, and the firemen raced to help. Capt. Stanley Paradowski grabbed Plebani's arm. "Take it easy," he said gently. "You're hurt. We'll get you to an ambulance." Paradowski could see that the young man's shirt was soaked with blood, his hair singed into ashen tufts, his face scorched a bright red.

"No, no," Plebani said. "I still got men trapped."

Impatience flashed in Paradowski's eyes. "Who are you?" he asked.

"Trooper Plebani, sir."

Paradowski snapped a half-salute in respect. "Right, troop," he said. "Show us the way."

Right through till dawn and beyond, Plebani worked with the fire crews, rescuing more truckers from the inferno. He broke away once to inhale oxygen; then it was back into the fight again until, finally, Buriello ordered him back to his car to rest.

A few weeks later, Sgt. Frank Maggion, of Troop D, compiled a report. "Trooper Plebani," he wrote, "went far beyond the fine line that separates general duty and heroism in a police officer. He is recommended for commendation commensurate with his stalwart performance of duty."

It would be more weeks before Plebani's wife, Sharyn, read that report and finally knew the full story. All through the day of October 24 she had waited for her husband to come home and take her and Cornel, Jr., to a Halloween parade. She couldn't reach Plebani. The Newark station would say only that he was still investigating the accident.

Sharyn and Cornel, Jr., went to the parade without him. When they came in at 10:30 that night, he was freshly showered and dressed and sitting at the breakfast table sipping coffee. She saw the singed hair, the red face. Her heart jumped as she bent to kiss him.

"You okay?" she asked.

"Pretty good," he said huskily. "Just a long day."

How the flood that couldn't happen
brought death and destruction
down from the Black Hills

Night of Terror
in Rapid City

BY JAMES H. WINCHESTER

IT WAS ONE OF THE WORST *flood disasters in our nation's history. Starting early on Friday evening, June 9, 1972, and continuing through most of the night, an unpredicted and unprecedented ten to fourteen inches of rain poured down onto one small area of western South Dakota where normally only fourteen inches of rain fall in an entire year. The steep, rocky, 4,000-foot-high Black Hills could not absorb the downpour. Starting near the foot of Mount Rushmore, the torrential runoff picked up force as it funneled through narrow canyons and headed toward the grasslands to the east. Thundering against the back door* *of Rapid City, a community of 43,000 people, the flash flood crumpled a thirty-four-year-old earthen dam, unleashing a rampaging five-foot-high wall of water that went straight through the heart of town.*

Before the rains stopped and the flood dissipated early the next morning, 237 people had died, 5 were missing and 5,000 had been left homeless in a thirty-mile-long, half-mile-wide path of sudden destruction. Dozens of bridges were destroyed; 5,000 cars were demolished or damaged; 1,200 homes and about a hundred business buildings had vanished.

The cause of this night of terror in Rapid City was a freakish coincidence of weather conditions. Although the official forecast for the day had been "partly cloudy with scattered thundershowers, some possibly reaching severe proportions," there was no evidence to suggest an exceptional rainfall. In fact, a local technological institute had continued its aerial cloud-seeding experiments throughout the afternoon (meteorologists say those experiments had nothing to do with the deluge). But in the late afternoon a strong breeze blowing from the southeast carried a supply of unusually moist air to the eastern side of the Black Hills. Here the steep slopes forced the incoming air upward, causing great amounts of moisture to accumulate over the hills. Normally, high-level winds would carry much of this moisture away—but on this day, the upper-air circulation came to a near standstill. The damp accumulation hovered, almost motionless, and the rains began to fall.

The first inkling of the flood that couldn't happen came just before six o'clock that Friday evening. South Dakota highway patrolman Clyde McCue, driving in the Black Hills forty miles northwest of Rapid City, radioed the police department in Deadwood that a local stream was dumping a foot of water across the road in the area.

Ten minutes later, another highway patrolman reported a cloudburst on Highway 40, ten miles west of Rapid City. As the storm drifted eastward, it began to rain in Rapid City, but no one was overly concerned. At the new Stevens High School a sell-out audience filled the auditorium to hear a visiting band from West Germany. The local dog-racing track was open, and the town's summer theater was preparing for a new production—*You Know I Can't Hear You When the Water's Running.*

Meanwhile, in the Black Hills area, rain and runoff were suddenly turning small streams wild, washing away cars, campers, homes, bridges, roads. Six miles northwest of Rapid City, the waters in Box Elder Creek reached flood proportions. Ron Rathman, a twenty-seven-year-old father of three, started off in his pickup truck to help an elderly couple who, he knew, lived in the path of the rampaging creek. Before he could reach them, an eight-foot wall of water roared down from the hills and Ron and the truck were swept away. His body was never found.

Just a few miles from Mount Rushmore, waters in Battle Creek rose eight feet in minutes, sweeping down through the old gold-mining town of Keystone. Nine tourists camped on the banks of the stream, some of them already in their sleeping bags, were drowned.

A dozen miles southwest of Rapid City, on Sheridan Lake Road, a young National Guardsman stepped out of his stalled truck into water up to his armpits and was sucked off his feet into a water-filled culvert running thirty feet under the submerged highway. He shot out the other end like a bullet, only to be swept over what had become a raging, fifteen-foot-high waterfall and into the churning wreckage at its bottom. Carried some 200 yards downstream, he finally managed to grab a tree and hang on until he was rescued.

In Rapid City, most people remained buttoned up inside their homes against the driving rain, largely unaware of danger. Regular radio and TV programs continued, broken from time to time by short bulletins about still-vague events dozens of miles away, in the Black Hills. If there was no alarm in Rapid City, however, there was already trouble. Water was now pouring down Rapid Creek into Canyon Lake, a forty-acre man-made lake in a west-side residential area that was normally from three to fifteen feet deep. The water was rising at an alarming rate—at least 30,000 cubic feet per second—against the lake's twenty-foot-high earthen dam, built by the WPA in 1938. About eight-thirty p.m., spillways were opened to relieve pressure on the dam. Even so, water later began cascading over the top of the structure and on down Rapid Creek, which curves through town from one end to the other.

Rapid City's twenty-nine-year-old mayor, Don Barnett, and Leonard Swanson, city engineer, inspected the Canyon Lake dam and left the area about ten p.m. Firemen and policemen warned residents around Canyon Lake and the area along Rapid Creek below the lake to seek higher ground. The reaction was all very low-key, and only a handful of people left their homes.

Actually, the crisis was already full blown. Streets were now rush-

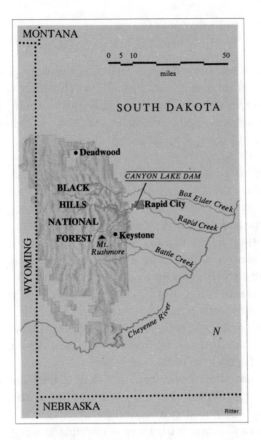

ing rivers. Three city firemen were knocked from their feet and were drowned in the maelstrom as they tried to evacuate people from houses and cars. Wayne Granum, another city fireman, sought refuge inside an empty house but quickly realized that the house was creaking and shifting. Removing the fire gear that was weighing him down, he broke a window with his bare hands, cutting himself badly, and climbed to the roof. Minutes later, the house was swept downstream. It struck a utility pole, which crashed down on the roof a few feet away from him before the house was caught for a moment on a wooden bridge. Then the house suddenly broke away, leaving behind only the section of roof that Granum was clinging to. Spinning crazily, the roof section then was swept across Canyon Lake to the opposite side, where it lodged in some trees on top of the dam. Granum grabbed a stout branch to hang on to if the roof went over the dam. "I'll never live to see another day," he thought. "No way!"

Although many people had already been killed in the flood, radio station KOTA's ten p.m. news, which devoted only part of its time to the growing emergency, announced: "At this hour we have no reports of serious injuries." Then, at 10:30, an unidentified caller in the Black Hills reached Mayor Barnett with a terrifying message: A wall of water, at least four feet high, was sweeping down Rapid Creek toward the city.

Mayor Barnett now gave a definitive warning. At 10:39, relaying his call to radio and TV stations from a police car, he ordered: "If you have property anywhere adjacent to Rapid Creek, get out!"

It was too late. Those who heard him didn't have time to react. Only minutes later, at about 10:45, the dam crumpled like a washed-over sand castle before the force of the flood. Fireman Granum, still on the roof section and clinging to the branch, remembers: "It was like pulling the plug in a bathtub." As the water subsided and the roof section rapidly settled on top of the dam, Granum jumped down to safety. After a stop at the hospital, where thirty stitches were needed to sew up his injured hands, he insisted on rejoining fellow firemen to help save others.

When the dam was ripped from its roots, a five-foot-high wall of water and debris poured down on Rapid City with the roar of a freight train. Homes and stores along Rapid Creek were upended and washed away, many with their occupants inside. Utility poles, torn from concrete bases, speared floating trailer homes like giant harpoons. Cars, tossed about like toys, wrapped themselves around power pylons like crushed tinfoil. One survivor remembers: "A thirty-foot-long mobile home went by me riding a wave like a surfboard. Just behind was a Volkswagen with people hanging onto it and screaming for help."

Dorrance Dusek, a furniture-firm representative, fought his way through the roaring water to a stalled car that held a double amputee and his terrified wife. Dusek managed to get the man out before the car and the woman in it were swept away. With the legless man clutching him around the neck, he half-swam to a nearby house. "We were still in the front room when one entire side of the house broke away," Dusek later told the Omaha *World-Herald*. "The amputee went with it. Then the whole house gave way. Two blocks downstream, I grabbed some telephone wires that were attached to a house and kicked against the boards until a man inside heard me.

When he appeared at the door, I let go of the wires. As I floated by, he grabbed me."

As the disaster developed, acts of life-saving heroism became almost routine. Kerry Conner, a twenty-five-year-old garage mechanic, drove in the direction of the dam to see if he could help. On the way, he spotted an aluminum rowboat on the lawn of a house and loaded it on his truck. He then picked up well-driller Stan Bice, who had been evacuating his neighbors. In the Canyon Lake area, they launched the purloined boat and pulled a young couple and their baby from the floating debris. While Stan headed for the hospital with them, Kerry took the boat and joined several firemen who were desperately fighting to reach other stranded victims of the flood. Before the night was over, he had helped in the rescue of more than two dozen people. Conner, who couldn't swim, had to be rescued himself after the boat overturned and was demolished by the force of the water and hurtling debris.

Patrolman Sam Roach called police headquarters from his radio car: "The back wall of the Mountain View Nursing Home has collapsed." Seven of the forty-eight aged patients were spilled into the water-filled basement. Roach, joined by the Reverend Charles Russell, education director of the Sioux Baptist Chapel, tied some sheets together, threw one end down to an elderly woman holding on to her mattress in the water, and pulled her to safety. As the building threatened to collapse around them, Roach and Russell, helped first by two nurses and a nurse's aide, then by others, carried the surviving patients, most of them still in their beds, to safety. Three elderly people had drowned—one when she went back into the building for her glasses.

William Medley and his wife, Joy, both majors in the Salvation Army, were driving some girls to a Salvation Army camp in the Black Hills when they were turned back by National Guardsmen. William said to his wife, "We'd better see if we can help." They stopped first at their home in Rapid City, and Joy made coffee and sandwiches. Then they drove downtown to the Salvation Army Citadel, where William kissed his wife and said, "Honey, I'm going out to help evacuate people." She never heard from him again. His body was found the next day.

The high water and heavy debris destroyed the main electrical transmission lines, blacking out the city. Natural gas spewed out of dozens of broken mains and, as it escaped, some of the still-live downed power lines ignited it. The towering torches of flame turned the rain-filled skies above them into a hazy red mist.

Shortly after midnight, the waters below Canyon Lake began to recede. Everywhere along the flood path there were cries for help, and more than a thousand people were stranded in trees or on roof-tops. Four National Guardsmen spotted a submerged car in mid-stream. Thinking someone might still be in it, they tried to reach it by forming a human chain, with one of them holding tight to a small tree on shore. The tree broke. All were swept away. Two of them drowned.

Trapped in her flooded bedroom, a young mother held an infant daughter on top of her head for four hours, with water lapping at her shoulders, until someone heard her shouts.

A frail seventy-one-year-old woman, Gertrude Lux, was rescued after standing for five hours in neck-deep water balancing her six-teen-year-old granddaughter—who was both physically and men-tally handicapped—on a floating foam-rubber mattress.

Below the broken dam, near dawn, rescuers reached the Reverend Ronald Masters, his wife and two young daughters, who huddled on top of the submerged roof of their four-wheel-drive utility vehicle. As the basement of their home had filled with water about ten-thirty p.m., the thirty-six-year-old Masters had put his wife and five chil-dren into the car and started for high ground. They were a quarter of a mile below the dam when it broke and a solid wall of water hit the side of the vehicle. "All four wheels were lifted off the road, and we started spinning downstream, like a record on a turntable," the minister said later. "Then we were jammed between the upper trunks of two big cottonwood trees."

As the water rose within and his family began to pray aloud, Masters braced himself against the steering wheel and tried desper-ately to kick open one of the doors. Finally, he kicked a window open about ten inches, and pulled himself to the roof. Reaching back, waving his hand back and forth inside the water-filled vehicle, he caught an arm and pulled his wife head first through the narrow slot. He pushed her into the branches of a small tree growing near the cottonwoods. Then, reaching inside again, he caught a foot. It was his daughter Karen's, and he pulled her through the opening feet first. Her two-and-a-half-year-old brother was in her arms as she slid out, but the current tore him from her grasp. His body was found three weeks later.

By this time, the water was high over the roof of the vehicle, and it was impossible for Masters to reach down through the window again to his eight- and twelve-year-old sons and ten-year-old daughter still inside. For more than two hours, Masters clung to the trees on top of the car with his wife and daughter Karen. The roar of the rushing water was stunning. The torrential, bone-chilling rain seemed unending. Dead bodies swept past. Finally, the flood level began to recede, and Masters was startled by a voice in the darkness. Groping again inside the vehicle, he grabbed a moving wrist. It was his daughter JoAnn! She had survived by holding her head in a small air pocket. Her two brothers were not so fortunate. They were dead.

In the drizzly, gray light of Saturday morning, as the floodwaters ebbed across the plains, Rapid City started fighting back. Amid a nauseating odor of gas and acrid smoke, the desperate search for the living still trapped or marooned went on. The dead were everywhere. More than eighty-five bodies, washed downstream, were discovered in one ten-block area alone. By midmorning, the local Civil Defense had established its headquarters in the basement of the county courthouse.

There was no shortage of helping hands. Joy Medley, her husband dead, got the first relief station organized and operating, working steadily for forty-eight hours. An Associated Press reporter marveled: "The first sandwiches she made in her kitchen Friday night multiplied like the loaves and the fishes to more than twenty thousand meals a day."

Gary Pedersen, an ex-navy medical corpsman who had lost an arm in Vietnam, helped in the inoculation of more than 20,000 residents and relief workers with typhoid and tetanus shots.

To help get the water system working again, Paul Harper, a twenty-nine-year-old doctor from Conway, New Hampshire, assigned at the time to Ellsworth Air Force Base, and his wife, a registered nurse, donned their scuba-diving gear and worked underwater to clean out the intake pipes to the treatment plant.

Using heavy equipment, much of it from contractors who sent their trucks and cranes and bulldozers from hundreds of miles away without any expectation of profit, some 3,000 workers began clearing away 275 truckloads of debris every hour. Another 2,000 National Guardsmen and volunteers searched for bodies, a grisly task complicated by the danger of live rattlesnakes washed down in the floodwaters.

From all over the nation came an outpouring of generosity for the stricken city. Cash gifts from individuals and companies mounted to more than a million dollars. A huge hangar at Ellsworth Air Force Base was quickly filled with 120 tons of donated food and clothing. One chicken farmer sent thousands of hens. Carloads of boys and girls came from as far away as New England, offering to do anything that needed to be done. Many were put to work hunting for bodies; others worked for the Red Cross or Salvation Army, or stood for hours on street corners directing traffic, in red dust so thick they had to wear face masks. Civil Defense authorities called the kids' work "magnificent." Noting that the community effort showed how life might always be, but isn't, the Rapid City *Journal* said, "Goodwill was born of tragedy in a shining example of sharing and caring."

It is, indeed, the strength and unselfishness of man that will remain in memory long after the physical scars of the Rapid City disaster are erased. "When I think of how people responded when needed," sums up Rapid City's Mayor Barnett, "I am the proudest man in America."

For the young family from Montana
what began as a beauty-filled hike on a well-traveled
Canadian National Park trail quickly turned into a morning
of terror and a never-to-be-forgotten struggle for survival

Grizzly
on the Nature Trail!

BY JOHN AND FRANKIE O'REAR

OUTDOOR ENTHUSIASTS Al and Nancy Auseklis had worked out a pretty good life for themselves. Former competitors on the national ski-racing circuit, they both had coaching jobs with the junior racers in Kalispell, Montana, their hometown, and this helped augment their income from a small-engine sales business. In September 1972, after several weeks of hard training to get in shape for the coming ski season, they decided to take a break. With their two children—Alex, 3½, and Anna, 2½—they headed up to Jasper National Park, high in the Canadian Rockies, for a hiking holiday.

On arriving at Jasper, Al and Nancy consulted a park map and chose a short, not-too-steep nature trail suitable for the children. Alex immediately forged ahead, with his sister skipping along behind, her blonde ponytail flying. After about an hour of hiking, the children tired and asked to ride in their parents' backpacks. This may have saved their lives, for no sooner were they happily underway again—Alex in Al's pack and Anna in Nancy's—than a paralyzing roar knifed through the silence of the dark pines around them.

Nancy was the first to see the grizzly bear. Her heart all but stopped as she instantly recognized the dark, silver-tipped coat, the unmistakable hump between the shoulder blades, the sheer bulk of the awesome beast. Al and Alex were just ahead, out of Nancy's sight over a slight rise, and the grizzly was charging in their direction. From the corner of her eye, Nancy also saw a bear cub, running away in the opposite direction.

One horror-filled moment after the grizzly disappeared from sight, Nancy heard what she later described as a "shattering roar and then what sounded like a pack of angry dogs fighting, only much worse." But "above that terrifying clatter"—and worst of all, she remembers—"came the ear-piercing screams of my son, Alex."

Shocked into action, and recalling that grizzlies are unable to climb trees, Nancy sought safety in a nearby pine. But, with thirty-pound Anna in her backpack, she was unable to get off the ground.

"It was then that an instinctive rage coursed through me," she says now. "I had to do *something*. I had to try to save all that was dear to me in life." Fighting off feelings of helplessness, she hunted for weapons—a tree branch, rocks, anything.

Warned by the grizzly's roars, Al had wheeled about just in time to see the bear "charging at us like a freight train." He tried frantically to pull up a young lodgepole pine, but the roots refused to let go and there was no time to struggle with it. At the last instant, he jumped to one side, and the grizzly charged past. She turned immediately, however, and charged again—this time from behind Al, making straight for his back, where Alex was strapped in the pack. Al pivoted fast to protect the screaming child. This time the bear plowed headlong into Al, knocking him to the ground and pinning Alex beneath him.

Snarling with rage, the grizzly pounced on the fallen father and son. Al could feel his flesh tearing as the bear shook his left leg in her jaws. In desperation, Al kicked the bear on her sensitive nose with his free foot. The grizzly suddenly let go and headed toward Nancy. But when Al managed to struggle up onto his good leg, the grizzly charged back at him. Knocking Al to the ground again, she started chewing and tearing his right leg. Cursing the pain, Al kicked the bear's face with his injured leg. Once more the mother grizzly let go and charged toward Nancy.

Meanwhile, Nancy had scavenged a long pine pole and anchored it under her arm. Now she came running down the trail toward Al. When she caught sight of the onrushing bear, she ducked into a clump of pine saplings and, with Al shouting orders to poke and jab

at the grizzly, backed up to a tree to protect Anna. Then, like a knight of old, she jousted with the panting grizzly—driving the pole into her shoulder each time she lunged at them. All this time, not a sound came from little Anna: The child was frozen in shock.

Suddenly, unaccountably, the frenzied mother grizzly turned away and lumbered off down the trail that the Auseklis family had been following so happily only minutes earlier. In the eerie silence after the bear's departure, Nancy felt a new flood of terror gripping her. Not daring to think about what she would find, she ran toward Al. He was struggling to get up, she remembers, and "swearing in anger that this could have happened. Somehow his cursing was a tremendous relief to me." Alex was trembling and crying in Al's backpack but, miraculously, was unharmed.

Both of Al's legs were brutally mangled, with gaping holes where chunks of flesh had been torn away. As Nancy ripped up her wind-breaker to make pressure bandages, questions raced through her mind: *Should I leave Al and go for help? Could I find him again? Will he bleed to death? What if the bear comes back?* A whimper from Alex inter-rupted her jumbled thoughts. "Are we going to die, Mama?" he asked. "Is Daddy going to die?"

That was enough for Al. "Let's get out of here!" he said, strug-gling up with Nancy's help. In terrible pain, fighting shock, getting weaker every minute, Al dragged himself along on crutches that they improvised from tree branches. Nancy carried Alex in her backpack and cradled Anna in her arms—sixty-five pounds in all.

"It was essential, at this point," says Nancy, "to appear light-hearted and unafraid, for there is nothing more terrifying for a child than to realize that his parents are hurt and unsure of what to do. Anna still had not said one word, and I was really beginning to worry about her."

Since the grizzly had headed down the trail in the direction they had been following, Al and Nancy bushwhacked through the thick brush in another direction that they hoped would lead them out. They finally came upon what they thought was another hiking trail—but after following it for about an hour, they came to a dead-end. Arguing over which direction to take, they finally stumbled upon a clearing. From it, they could see, at the base of a long slope, the Athabasca River. They felt they had no choice but to head to-ward the river and trust it to lead them back to civilization.

A steep cliff blocked their way, but they found a game trail zig-zagging down through a wooded ravine—the only passable route. Nancy remembers that she was "near collapse from the weight of the children and my constant fear that Al would pass out." She per-suaded Alex to get out of her pack and hike on his own.

To this day she's not sure how Al made it down the ravine, "unless it was his hard training for the ski season that pulled him through." Al says simply that he knew he had to have medical attention fast, and so he literally crawled down on his belly, using the stick crutches when he could and sliding his legs behind him.

At the bottom they came upon railroad tracks and, with over-whelming relief, heard the throb of machinery from a nearby oil-pumping station. Knowing that help was near, Al gave in to a state of semiconsciousness. The children stayed with him while Nancy ran to the station and flung open the door. She shouted for help above the noise of the pumps. No answer. She finally found and pushed open a door marked EMPLOYEES ONLY. Five men were seated inside, eating lunch. "Thank God!" she said to herself, and then, "Please help! My husband has been attacked by a grizzly!"

While one man telephoned the park warden and Seton General Hospital in Jasper, others grabbed up a big first-aid box and headed for Al. He was fully conscious when they reached him, though his face was white with shock. They were treating his wounds as best they could when another of the men drove his car up. After Al had been stretched across the backseat, the rest of the Auseklis family climbed in and the car sped off to the hospital.

It took about two hours for a waiting team of doctors to sew up Al's wounds. He had been lucky on three counts: Although both legs were horribly torn, all the vital tendons were intact; nerves and muscles were damaged, but not irreparably; most important, no main arteries had been severed.

Leaving Al at the hospital, Nancy described the incident to the park warden, who immediately closed all trails in the attack area while a search—unsuccessful—was made for the grizzly. When the warden dropped Nancy off at the Auseklises' car, she "felt uneasy just walking from the warden's truck to our car—one of those ridiculous reactions that you laugh at later."

After two months of slow, painful convalescence, Al was up on his feet, eager to get back into training. By midwinter he was skiing as usual, with nothing to show for his ordeal but some scars and a bit of numbness in one leg. The children, too, have bounced back. "They still ask questions about the attack," says Nancy. "But we have tried to make them understand that the grizzly wasn't simply vicious. We had walked into her house and got too close to her baby, and in that sense the attack was our fault."

Speaking of the ordeal, Nancy says, "In our family we love animals, and we want to keep it that way. Even now, we feel no real malice toward that grizzly. It was a mother's instinct that provoked her attack, and a mother's instinct that drove me to courage I never knew I had. She was protecting her cubs; I was protecting mine."

Life is infinitely stranger
than anything
which the mind of man
could invent

Sir Arthur Conan Doyle
"A CASE OF IDENTITY"

The "impossible" experience
of an RAF tail gunner in World War II
—and its amazing proof!

I Fell
18,000 Feet and Lived

BY NICHOLAS STEPHEN ALKEMADE
ex-Warrant Officer, Royal Air Force

At 21,000 FEET THE REAR TURRET of a Lancaster bomber is a cold and lonely place, separated from the rest of the crew by two sets of doors and twelve yards of fuselage. It's a cramped space, being little more than a shell for the body of the gunner, outfitted in his bulky flying clothes. There is not even room for him to wear a parachute—only the harness; his chute pack is stowed in the main fuselage, a few feet inside the second door, and separate from the other crewmen's packs. In an emergency the gunner has to leave his turret, get his chute pack and hook it onto the harness, then bail out, hoping that the trailing radio aerial will not cut him in two. Being a "Tail-End Charlie" gunner was rated by the RAF as a "hazardous occupation."

As our Lancaster neared Berlin on the night of March 24–25, 1944, we could see the long fingers of searchlight beams probing the sky. Closing in, we spotted the sparkling red and green markers laid down for us by our pathfinder aircraft ahead of us. Plane after plane made its bombing run, and fireworks erupted below us: golden incendiary fires, brilliant white and red explosions and the orange flashes of ack-ack guns. Then . . .

Bombs away! Our own 4,000-pound "cookie" and three tons of incendiaries hurtled downward. Through weaving searchlight beams we turned for home, keeping a sharp watch for German night fighters. I could see them at work in the distance. A flash of white light would burst into a great red-and-orange ball of fire, then arc across the sky toward the black earth below. Some poor "Lanc" had got it, and some of my buddies would not return to base.

We were somewhere over the Ruhr when suddenly a series of shuddering crashes raked our aircraft from nose to tail, then two terrific thunderclaps as two cannon shells exploded on my turret ring mounting. The Plexiglas blister shattered and vanished—one large fragment slicing into my right leg.

Luckily my turret had been facing astern. I quickly depressed my guns and stared out. Not more than fifty yards from me was the shadowy outline of a Junkers 88 fighter, his leading edge a line of brilliant white flashes as he blazed away at our wounded ship. I aimed point-blank and squeezed the trigger of my four 303 Brownings. They fired simultaneously and the Junkers was transfixed by four streams of fiery tracers. He peeled away, his port engine trailing flame. I did not watch to see his fate; I was too concerned about my own.

Flaming fuel from our tanks was streaking past me. On the intercom I started to report to the captain that the tail was on fire, but he cut me short with, "I can't hold her for long, lads. You'll have to jump. Bail out! Bail out!"

Flicking the turret doors behind me open with my elbows, I turned and opened the fuselage door beyond—and stared for a horrified instant into a giant blowtorch. Flame and smoke swept toward me. I recoiled, choking and blinded, into my turret. *But I had to get my chute!* I opened the doors again and lunged for the pack.

Too late! The case had burned off and the tightly-packed silk was springing out, fold after fold, and vanishing in puffs of flame.

In the turret I took stock. Here I was, only twenty-one years old, and this was the end of the road. Already oil from the turret's hydraulic system was afire and flames seared my face and hands. At any moment the doomed aircraft might explode. Should I endure this roasting hell or should I jump? If I was to die, better a quick, painless end by diving into the ground. . . .

Quickly I hand-rotated my turret abeam, flipped the doors open and, in an agony of despair, somersaulted backward into the night.

Oh, the blessed relief of being away from that shriveling heat!

A body falling freely in the vacuum of space, with no air resistance, would drop sixteen feet the first second, forty-eight feet during the next, eighty feet in the third, etc. Falling from 18,000 feet, therefore, it would attain a final speed of 730 miles per hour before crashing to the earth.

A body falling through the atmosphere, however, is retarded by the resistance of the air. Because of this, Sergeant Alkemade's "terminal" speed has been estimated by the Aero Medical Laboratory at Wright Air Development Center at approximately 122 miles per hour. His incredible survival can be attributed only to the fact that the final stage of his fall was cushioned, first by the thickly interlaced branches of fir trees, and further by the heavy, snow-covered brush on which he landed.

Gratefully I felt the cold air against my face. I had no sensation of falling. It was more like being at rest on an airy cloud. Looking down, I saw the stars beneath my feet.

"Must be falling head first," I thought.

If this was dying it was nothing to be afraid of. I only regretted that I should go without saying good-bye to my friends. I would never again see Pearl, my sweetheart back home in Loughborough. And I'd been due to go on leave the following Sunday.

Then—nothing. I must have blacked out.

In slow stages my senses returned. First there was an awareness of light above me, which gradually became a patch of starlit sky. The sky was framed in an irregular opening that finally materialized as a hole in thickly interlaced boughs of some fir trees. I seemed to be lying in a deep mound of underbrush heavily blanketed with snow.

It was bitterly cold. My head throbbed and there was a terrible pain in my back. I felt all over my body. I found I could move my legs. I was all in one piece! A prayer of thanksgiving and utter wonderment came to my lips.

"Thank you, God!" I said.

I tried to sit up—but it hurt too much. Craning my neck, I could see that my flying boots were gone and my clothes scorched and tattered. I began to be afraid of freezing to death. In the pocket of my tunic I found the flat tin, badly bent, in which I kept my cigarettes and my lighter. The cigarettes were unharmed; I lit up. My watch, I found, was still ticking. The luminous hands showed 3:20; it had been close to midnight when our aircraft was hit.

Attached to my collar was the whistle for use in case of ditching at sea to keep crew members in contact with one another.

"Here is one man happy to become a prisoner of war," I said to myself. From time to time I blew on the whistle. It seemed hours later that I heard a far-off "Hulloo!"

I kept whistling, and the answering shouts grew closer. At last I could see flashlights approaching. Then some men and boys were standing over me. After relieving me of my cigarettes they growled, *"Heraus!"* ("Get up!") When they saw I couldn't, they put a tarpaulin under me and dragged me across a frozen pasture to a cottage. There an old lady with a gnarled but kindly face gave me the finest eggnog I have ever tasted.

As I lay on the floor I heard a car pull up outside. Two men in civilian clothes stomped into the room. They looked me over carefully. Then, quite indifferent to my pain, they yanked me to my feet and bundled me out to their car. We seemed to hit all the bumps on our way to a hospital.

I was a long time in the operating room. Only later did I learn the sum of my injuries: burned legs, twisted right knee, a deep splinter wound in my thigh, strained back, slight concussion and a deep scalp wound; first-, second- and third-degree burns on face and hands. Most of this damage I had sustained before jumping.

Finally, cleaned up and with most of the Plexiglas fragments picked out of me, I was installed in a clean bed—but not to sleep! In came a tall, pompous character in a *Wehrmacht* uniform, thin as a hatchet in the face and wearing rimless glasses. Through an interpreter, a young convalescent soldier, he asked me the usual probing questions: What targets did you attack? Where is your base? How many aircraft are there at your base? . . . and many others. I stated my name, rank and serial number. To the other questions I could only reply, "I am not allowed to answer."

Then they began asking about my parachute. "Where did you hide it? Did you bury it?" (Spies dropping into enemy territory commonly concealed their parachutes; airmen falling out of a sky battle did not.)

"Parachute?" I said. "I didn't use one!"

I thought Hatchet-Face would burst with rage. He let out a stream of oaths, then turned on his heel and stalked out. For three days the questioning was repeated. Finally I was left alone.

After three weeks, when my wounds were fairly well healed, I was whisked off to Dulag Luft near Frankfurt and put into solitary confinement. The time gave me the opportunity to think out how I might convince my interrogators that my incredible story was true.

So I was ready when a week later a young *Luftwaffe* lieutenant led me into the office of the *Kommandant* of Dulag Luft. On the *Kommandant's* desk I was amused to see a pack of Players cigarettes and a bar of chocolate.

"We have to congratulate you, I understand, Sergeant," the *Kommandant* said dryly, in excellent English. "Would you tell me all about your remarkable escape yourself, please? I have only a garbled account from the *Leutnant*. I gather you claim to have jumped from a blazing bomber at a height of six thousand meters without a parachute—a very tall story, Sergeant, *nicht wahr?*"

He could prove the story if he cared to, I told him. Hadn't a wrecked Lancaster fallen in the area the night of March 24–25? If so, that would be the plane I had jumped from. The burned remnants of my parachute pack could be found just forward of the rear fuselage door. Also, he could examine my parachute harness—to see for himself that *it had never been used.*

The *Kommandant* listened to me in silence. "A really remarkable story," he said, "and I hear many!"

He fired some rapid German at the lieutenant, who saluted and left. The *Kommandant* handed me a cigarette, and we chatted pleasantly for the next quarter hour. Then the lieutenant, waving my parachute harness, burst into the office with three other officers, all shouting excitedly in German.

The lieutenant flung the harness onto the desk, pointed to the snap-hooks that were still in their clips and the lift webs still fastened down on the chest straps. The *Kommandant* soberly took in these facts, then leaned back in his chair and thoughtfully studied each of us in turn. I'll never forget his next words; he spoke in English:

"Gentlemen! A miracle—no less!"

He arose, came round his desk and offered me his hand. I took it. "Congratulations, my boy, on being alive! What a story to tell your grandchildren!"

Then I was assailed with slaps on the back, handshaking and vociferous good wishes. The *Kommandant* dismissed me with, "Tomorrow, I promise, your comrades will be told about how you became a P.O.W."

In the *Kommandant's* office next morning I saw that the *Luftwaffe* authorities had been busy. On his desk lay some pieces of scorched metal, including the D-handle of a parachute ripcord and a piece of wire that would be the ripcord itself.

"The remains of your parachute pack," the *Kommandant* explained. "We found it precisely where you said it would be. To us it is the final proof."

The wrecked Lancaster lay about eight miles from where I had landed, I was told. Four crew members had burned to death and had been buried in a military cemetery near Meschede with full military honors. From their names and numbers I realized that only "Ginger" Cleary, our navigator; Geof Burwell, the radio operator; and myself were left. (They had been blown clear in the final explosion, I learned later.)

A German flying officer and two noncoms marched me into the compound, where some 200 captured Allied fliers were assembled. I was directed to stand on a bench. Then the *Luftwaffe* officer recounted my story to the incredulous airmen.

There was pandemonium. Nationalities were forgotten. I was mobbed by French, German, British and Yank, shaking my hand, shouting questions, forcing upon me gifts of a cigarette or a square of chocolate. Then I was presented with a paper, signed by the senior British officer at the demonstration, who had taken down the German authentication in writing and had it witnessed by the two senior British NCO's. It is only a faded scrap of paper, but it will always be the proudest thing I own:

Dulag Luft

It has been investigated and corroborated by the German authorities that the claim made by Sgt. Alkemade, 1431537 R.A.F., is true in all respects, namely, that he made a descent from 18,000 feet without a parachute and made a safe landing without injury, his parachute having been on fire in the aircraft. He landed in deep snow among fir trees.

Corroboration witnessed by

F/Lt. H. J. Moore
Senior British Officer
F/Sgt. R. R. Lamb 1339582
F/Sgt. T. A. Jones 411
Senior British N/C/O's
Date: 25/4/44

After liberation came in May 1945, RAF intelligence checked the records at Dulag Luft, found the reports of my strange adventure to be true and included them in the official records of the Royal Air Force.

As I write this, Pearl and I are living happily in Loughborough, in the English Midlands, where I am a buyer in a department store. (Geof Burwell was best man at our wedding.) I have taken the first important steps toward following the *Kommandant's* advice—to tell my story to my grandchildren. I'll have to wait, though, till little Valerie and Nicholas provide me with grandchildren to hear it. In the meantime, I can only wonder why such a marvelous thing should have happened to a man as ordinary as myself.

We used to think of it as "our" river,
a member of the family—
until the day it reached out for our lives

Death and
the Friendly River

BY SCOTT SEEGERS

FOR SEVERAL WINTERS my wife, Katie, and I had promised ourselves that the next time there was a really good snow on the ground
we would row out to the big rock near the far side of the Potomac
River and take some pictures of our house. The site is spectacular.
The heavily forested Virginia shore at that point rises almost as
steeply as a cliff, and our house is perched on a hilltop high above.
From the rock, the turbulence of Yellow Falls just downstream
would make a dramatic foreground; by combining it with the snow-
covered hillside reaching up to the house, we hoped to produce a
stunning photograph.

On February 8, 1967, a foot of new snow glistened in the brilliant
sunlight. It was bitter cold but achingly beautiful. "We'll never have
a better day for it," I said. "Let's go."

We were on good terms with this stretch of the Potomac, located a
few miles above Washington. It was like a member of the family, the
place where our kids had learned to swim and on whose sun-

drenched rocks we had picnicked for years. But this amiable river, *our* river, taught us a lesson that day that we will never forget.

The roundabout track down to the river had once been a wagon road leading to a small gold mine, now long abandoned. Although decades of spring rains had dotted it with deep holes, our jeep would take us to the river's edge and back, except that in two places on the return trip I would have to hook a cable to a tree and use our power winch to drag us over obstructions.

Through the woods and down the steep hill we went, our eight-foot aluminum skiff sliding behind us as gaily as a sleigh. At the shore, I carefully loaded my cameras into the skiff. Bundled into layers of heavy clothes, booted and gloved, we clumsily got aboard and shoved off.

The river was high and the current swift, but I launched the skiff well upstream of the big rock. It was no problem to row across, then drift down upon the rock. As we swept past, I grabbed a little scrub maple and pulled us ashore. I had done it many, many times before.

I tied up the skiff, brushed the snow from the rock, and carefully climbed to its top. The view of the house *was* magnificent. In the foreground, the falls leaped like molten sapphires in the intense sunlight. One at a time, Katie handed up the cameras, some with normal, others with telephoto lenses. To be sure of getting just the photos I wanted, I took several shots with each.

Carefully, Katie stowed the cameras and sat down in the stern of the skiff. I climbed aboard and set the oars in the oarlocks. But, still bemused by the beauty of the scene, I pushed away from the rock while still standing, instead of sitting down and being ready to row the moment I cast off. Before I could sit down, the current had caught the skiff and whirled it past the rock. The falls were not more than forty feet away.

I dropped to the seat and pulled as powerfully as I could on the oars. The skiff hesitated an instant as the blades bit into the water. We would have escaped the pull of the falls if one oar had not hit a barely submerged rock and jumped from the oarlock. The lopsided thrust threw the boat crosswise to the current, and we raced toward the falls.

At this particular spot, the falls are in three steps, the last and largest a drop of about two feet into a deep, swirling pool. The skiff bounced gently as it went sidewise over the first step. I got the oar back in the oarlock and straightened the boat out as we dropped over the second step in a welter of foam. There was no chance of getting upstream now, but no water had yet come aboard. I had an instant's wild hope that we might also get through the last drop. "Hold tight," I said to Katie. "Here we go." The skiff bucked like a wild stallion—and the world exploded.

I came to the surface clutching at the overturned skiff. Katie was beside me, also holding on. The paralyzing cold squeezed my chest with steel bands. I could hardly breathe. In a voice that sounded like a run-down Victrola, I said, "Hang on to the boat. Kick and paddle toward shore."

We were in the main branch of the river, about 250 feet from the Virginia shore and our waiting jeep. Although we kicked and paddled mightily, our booted legs and gloved hands were heavy and nearly useless, and the current carried us rapidly downstream. I spared a few seconds to watch the fine black leather case containing my new Graflex disappear in the water.

Suddenly, with a crash, the current brought the skiff up against a large boulder. As if in slow motion, we struggled onto the rock and took stock. The oars were gone. Although I managed somehow to turn the boat over, it remained half under water, riveted against the rock by the current. I tugged at the skiff for almost ten minutes, but I could not drag it high enough up the rock to bail. "We'll have to leave the boat," I said.

We took off our boots and heavy outer clothing. With fingers as numb as sticks, I removed the skiff's mooring line and tied one end to Katie's wrist. Holding on to the other end, I started wading out on a submerged bar. "I'm going to try to get to that rock," I told her, pointing to a boulder a little way out in the racing channel between us and shore. "If the rope reaches, I'll pull you over. If it isn't long enough, jump in the instant it tightens."

The savage cold hurt like an enormous toothache. (The water temperature was 35°F., the air temperature 20°F., we learned later.) But we were not frightened, simply because we had not realized how desperate our plight was. We couldn't swim in our remaining clothes, but we knew that by keeping our feet down when we went under we would soon hit a shallow or a rock on which to push to the surface for another breath. And if we consistently pushed toward shore, we could make it. Then it would be only a matter of walking back through the forest to the jeep, getting home, and building a fire. Or so we thought.

I launched myself into deep water and plummeted to the bottom. The current whirled me along, banging my legs against underwater rocks. Finally, I got my feet under me, kicked hard against the bottom, and sailed toward daylight. Too soon, I opened my mouth to breathe—and got instead a big swallow of Potomac. I felt surprised and indignant. "Our" river was trying to drown me!

I missed the rock I was aiming for, but fetched up on another one downstream. Katie had hit the water the instant the rope tightened, and a moment later she was beside me. I don't know how many similar rock-to-rock traverses we made, but we finally stumbled ashore about 400 yards downstream from the jeep. "The worst is over," I said to Katie. I was wrong.

The shore rose above us in a steep bank some eight feet high. Katie could not make the climb even on her hands and knees. Hanging on to each other, we floundered along through the ice and tangled roots at the water's edge until the bank leveled off. Katie fell frequently, and each time she fell she pulled me down with her. Within a few minutes I no longer had the strength to pull her to her feet.

We began progressing by trees. We would stumble a few steps, then fall. I would scramble to my feet and try to pull Katie along until we reached a tree. Using the tree as a prop, we would get her upright and aimed for another tree. Then the next tree, one at a time.

With the soft gray fuzz of oblivion lapping at the edges of our consciousness, we tottered and crawled through a little clearing from which we could look up at our home. It sat less than 500 feet away, straight up the hill. But it might as well have been on the moon for any chance we had of climbing that precipitous slope.

About 150 yards from the jeep, Katie fell for the last time. "I can't go any farther," she mumbled, lying face down in the snow. I shook her. "You've got to keep moving," I said. She did not respond.

"I'll go get the jeep and come back for you," I said. She never heard me. I staggered toward the jeep. Suddenly the trees went into a wild dance, and the ground rose and hit me in the face. I fell every time my numb feet hit a stone. With about seventy-five yards to go, I could not get up again. I crawled to the nearest tree, pulled and shoved myself upright. Through lips too stiff to form the words properly, a voice groaned, "I'll be damned if I'll freeze to death this close."

I shoved myself away from the tree, staggered a dozen steps, fell, and crawled to the next tree. I no longer felt cold. There was room in my mind for only one thought. *Jeep.* The world was a red jeep.

Suddenly I was there, groping at the door, dragging myself into the seat. With the concentration of a chess master, I stared at the instrument panel. The ignition lock swam into focus. I fumbled the key into it. *Choke.* When the motor was cold, I knew that the jeep wouldn't start unless I used the choke. My useless fingers slipped off the choke knob. I used both hands, and both slipped off. The choke was the center of the universe. *Pull the choke out.* A partly opened wrench lay on the floor. I slid the jaws over the choke shaft, got my hands behind the wrench and pulled. The choke came out. I could not turn the ignition key. I used the wrench again. The motor sputtered into life.

I pawed at the steering wheel for a precious minute before realizing that my hands would not grip it. I hooked my wrists over the spokes, then cautiously piloted the jeep across the rocks to where Katie lay. I do not remember rousing her and cannot imagine how she got into the jeep. With the glimmer of consciousness left to me, I gave myself step-by-step instructions.

I must remember not to turn around here because the trees are too close. Back up. I poked a few times at the gearshift, and it finally slid into reverse. The jeep backed erratically to a more open spot. I turned it around and put the accelerator to the floor. Weaving crazily, I watched the forest fly past on both sides.

I must not try the road we came down because I cannot handle the winch and cable. Try the track up the other side of the valley.

Roaring wide open in four-wheel drive, the jeep plowed along the twisting track up the ridge. It came out on top at the home of a neighbor. He must have seen us coming because he opened his door instantly. Faces floated before me. They got Katie out of the jeep.

My memories of the rest are confused. Someone gave me brandy. Someone else dabbed at my face with a cloth, and I realized that saliva was streaming out of both corners of my mouth. I was lying on the floor before a big fire, shaking uncontrollably and making strange involuntary noises. Through the fog came Katie's voice: "Darling, are you all right?" "No," I mumbled ungraciously, "I'm cold."

I passed out then, and was roused by a squirt of oxygen administered by the local Rescue Squad. They took us to a hospital, packed a score of gorgeous hot-water bags around each of us, and gave us typhoid and tetanus shots. From the waist down, our bodies were a mosaic of bruises and cuts from being banged against rocks, but nothing was broken.

They took our temperatures. Katie's was 92° F. This was about two hours after we had arrived at the neighbor's house. I learned later from cold-weather-survival specialists that it is very difficult to recover from a drop in body temperature of ten degrees or more below normal. Katie must have been very close to the edge.

During the years that Katie and I have been married we have tried to live each day aware of the beauty around us, taking joy and strength from it. We continue to live that way. Still, the brush with death has cleared away a lot of cobwebs, and things that once were great problems now seem not so important.

We still love the river. When summer came again and our grown children visited us, we jeeped back down to it for a picnic, and afterward we all romped and tumbled in the falls as we had done so many times before.

But we will never again think of the river as one of the family. It is a body of moving water, beautiful with its still pools, its swiftly running channels and its foam spraying over the rocks below our house. But it is without a conscience. If you forget that it obeys only the law of gravity, it can quite easily kill you.

He had it all carefully plotted:
guns, handcuffs, hideout, ransom note
—but then came a hitch in the timing

The Princess
and the Kidnapper

BY PETER BROWNE

JUST AFTER 7:30 P.M. on Wednesday, March 20, 1974, Britain's Princess Anne and her husband, Capt. Mark Phillips, emerged from a charity film show in London and settled in the back of their maroon limousine waiting near St. Paul's Cathedral. As the limousine slid away, no one really noticed a white Ford Escort edge out from a nearby curb and start to follow.

At the wheel of the rented Ford was a gaunt twenty-six-year-old man, Peter Sydney Ball—or Ian Ball, as he called himself. Ball intended to kidnap the Queen's only daughter and hold her for a ransom of three million pounds—almost seven million dollars at the time. He had been planning the crime for three years. The previous

December, Ball had flown to Spain and obtained two pistols from a Madrid shop: a five-shot .38 and an eleven-shot .22. Smuggled into Britain, the guns, now loaded, were stowed in his car, along with four sets of handcuffs—two of them linked to form leg shackles. And tucked inside his jacket was a typed letter addressed to Queen Elizabeth.

Inside the limousine, the Princess and her husband chatted with lady-in-waiting Rowena Brassey. Like the other royal cars, NGN 1 had neither bulletproof windows nor an emergency radio. Such things were considered unsightly; besides, the Queen did not like a fuss made over security.

NGN 1 went through Admiralty Arch into The Mall, the broad processional route that runs along St. James's Park to Buckingham Palace. Beside the chauffeur sat Inspector James Beaton, 31, Princess Anne's appointed "personal police officer." In the holster beneath his suit jacket was a Walther PP automatic—the only weapon in the car.

It seems unlikely that Ian Ball had planned to kidnap the Princess in the heart of London. Instead, he had apparently planned to wait for a suitable moment in the Surrey countryside, near her home at the Royal Military Academy of Sandhurst, where her husband was a staff instructor. Ball had been shadowing her every movement for seven days, awaiting his opportunity.

But something had gone amiss. That Wednesday morning, parked near the rear gate of the Royal Military Academy, his white car had caught the eye of a police officer who was investigating a local burglary. When questioned, Ball produced a license in the name of John Williams, an alias. His car was searched. Since nothing was found, there was no reason to detain him.

Badly shaken by the experience, Ball realized that he could not delay much longer. By telephoning the press office at Buckingham Palace, he had learned that Princess Anne would be going to Germany in five days. He followed the Princess to London that evening, drawn as by a magnet to any chance of watching her.

As he drove along The Mall behind the royal car and saw Buckingham Palace looming some 500 yards ahead, he realized that within thirty seconds Princess Anne would once more be out of reach. Already it was dusk, with pools of heavy shadow between the

Victorian lamps lining The Mall. Suddenly, he cast aside all caution: He would wait no longer.

Ball accelerated and swept past the royal limousine, then swerved his Ford in front of the limousine and stopped. The chauffeur of the royal car braked hard to avoid a collision.

When the Princess's bodyguard, James Beaton, saw what he took to be an irate motorist leave the Ford and hurry back toward the chauffeur, he got out and started around the back of the limousine to see what was wrong. Ball reached the right front window with his .38 in his hand. "Switch off the ignition," he ordered the chauffeur. Then he went to the rear window and said to Princess Anne: "Come with me. I only want you for two days."

The hideout was ready: a house five miles from Anne's home at Sandhurst. Ball, giving his name then as Jason Van der Sluis, had signed a six-month lease, commenting that he looked forward to moving in shortly with his wife. He had equipped it for the Princess with brand-new bedding, towels, an alarm clock, even a toothbrush—all bought at stores like Woolworth's to make the purchases untraceable. There was enough food for two people for a week.

On a rented Olivetti typewriter he had composed his ransom letter to the Queen: "Your daughter has been kidnapped. A ransom of three million pounds is to be paid in five-pound notes. They are to be used, unmarked, not sprayed with any chemical substance and unconsecutively numbered." Describing how the ransom money, in unlocked suitcases, was to be loaded into a plane that would later fly to Zurich, Ball instructed: "A police car is to meet Anne and myself at the roundabout just before entering the tunnel into London Heathrow airport, at seven a.m. It is to escort our car to the aircraft."

Ball pledged that once he was safely in Zurich and assured of immunity from the Swiss police, Princess Anne would be released. But he demanded documents guaranteeing a pardon covering the kidnapping and all crimes connected with it—including "the murder of any police officers."

ROUNDING THE REAR of the royal car, Inspector Beaton came face to face with a tall, thin figure leveling a revolver at him. Ball fired twice. One bullet scuffed Beaton's jacket; the other smashed into his shoulder and pierced a lung. Beaton realized he had been hit only when, drawing his gun, he felt the strength drain from his arm. His first shot missed Ball. He tried again, using both hands to steady the Walther. The gun jammed.

As Beaton stepped back, working to clear the Walther, chauffeur Alec Callender came up behind Ball and tried to grab his gun. "I'll shoot you," said Ball, and he fired at point-blank range. The chauffeur reeled back into the driver's seat, a bullet in his chest.

Meanwhile, Rowena Brassey was scrambling out the left rear door to make room for Princess Anne to escape. But Ball had caught the Princess by the forearm, commanding, "Please get out." To the bodyguard, now on the far side of the car, he shouted, "Drop that gun, or I'll shoot her!"

Beaton had no choice. He put his jammed automatic on the ground.

A bizarre tug-of-war developed, Ian Ball pulling at the Princess with one hand while her husband, Mark Phillips, held her round the waist and leaned across her trying to shut the door. Beaton had climbed into the car, intending to place himself between Anne and her would-be kidnapper. The Princess coolly asked Ball why he wanted to take her and was told: "I'll get a couple of million."

As Beaton edged forward, Mark Phillips managed to close the door. "Open it," Ball shouted, "or I'll shoot!"

Beaton put his hand up directly in front of the muzzle. The bullet shattered the window and lodged in his palm. Twice wounded, he kicked the door open, hoping to knock Ball off balance. But the ruse failed. And now, for the third time, Ball shot James Beaton—this time in the stomach. Stumbling out, through yellow roses scattered from Princess Anne's bouquet, the inspector collapsed on the pavement.

Perhaps ninety seconds had passed since Ian Ball had swung his Ford in front of the royal limousine. Passersby were gawking, and a tangle of horn-blowing traffic was building up along The Mall. From a hundred yards away, Police Constable Michael Hills heard what sounded like an engine backfiring. He saw a knot of cars. As he got closer, he recognized the big maroon limousine and radioed the Cannon Row police station that a royal car seemed to have been in an accident. Dodging the traffic, Hills crossed the road. He saw that the limousine's right rear window was shattered, and a man was leaning inside. Someone shouted to Hills, "Get away, you bloody fool. He's got a gun." But the constable stepped forward, gripped the gunman's elbow, and said, "What's going on?" Ball spun around and shot him in the stomach.

Ball had emptied the .38. It was a .22 bullet that clipped the policeman's whistle chain, plowed through a pocket diary, and settled just outside his liver. To Hills, it felt like a hard punch. Ducking behind the royal car, he radioed to Cannon Row: "I have been shot. Royal car is involved. There is a man with a gun. Urgent assistance is required."

AT THE AGE OF NINETEEN, Ian Ball had begun to question his own behavior. Fearing persecution, suicidal, hearing "voices," he sought psychiatric help, and became one of the 150,000 people in Britain diagnosed as schizophrenic. But he refused full-time treatment. He drifted through a succession of menial jobs, turned to petty crime and soon had a record. He dreamed of the perfect crime that would make him a millionaire playboy and a success with women.

As his illness progressed, he became more secretive. In September 1972, he was certified to be suffering from a nervous debility and psychiatric depression, and he abandoned his last job to draw twelve pounds (about thirty dollars) a week in social security benefits. Living alone in a furnished room in Bayswater, rarely going out, never speaking to anyone, he began to plot the kidnapping.

ON THE MALL, Glanmore Martin, a chauffeur driving a privately owned Jaguar, backed his car against the Ford's front bumper to block any escape. Courageously he approached Ian Ball, who stuck a gun in his ribs and snapped, "Clear off!" As Martin turned, he saw the dazed Constable Hills, who had picked up the bodyguard's jammed automatic. As Hills swayed, trying to steady his aim at Ball, Martin led him to the sidewalk, where he collapsed.

Another passerby, journalist Brian McConnell, leaped from a taxi to challenge Ball. Ball swung around and warned, "Keep out of this." McConnell took two steps forward and was shot in the chest.

A third unarmed member of the public, Ronald Russell, a burly six-foot businessman, now left his car and dashed across The Mall.

The kidnapper was hammering at the limousine's door with the butt of his gun. Russell punched him on the side of the head. Ball fired at him and missed. Russell ran to the other side of the car, where the chauffeur of the Jaguar was tending wounded Constable Hills. "Give me his truncheon," said Russell. Two more shots sounded, and without waiting for the truncheon, Russell doubled back to find that Ball had forced the door and was again trying to pull Princess Anne from the car. With his gun pointed at the Princess, Ball said: "Come on, Anne. You know you've got to come."

"Why don't you go away?" said the Princess, calmly. "What good is all this going to do?"

Like a child given an unexpected scolding, Ball stared at her, momentarily irresolute. Princess Anne seized her chance. She broke free from his grip, moved over and began to climb out the other side of the car. But then, as Ball came round the front of the car, Mark Phillips promptly pulled his wife back. The burly Russell, standing in front of her as a shield, met the oncoming Ball and punched him twice—delivering the last blow with such force that Ball lost his balance and fell headlong.

As he picked himself up, he heard the sirens of approaching police cars. He turned and ran.

Jumping out of a police car, trainee detective Peter Edmonds heard Princess Anne call, "Get him!" He spotted Ball, gun in hand, running. He gave chase and brought him down with a flying tackle. A moment later, five more policemen threw themselves on top of Ian Ball, one knocking the revolver—which still held five cartridges— from his hand.

It was just seven minutes since the kidnap attempt had begun.

A woman from one of the stalled cars walked over to the royal limousine and saw that Mark Phillips still had a protective arm around his wife. "Are you all right, love?" the woman asked. The royal couple looked up and smiled at her. "Yes, thank you," said Princess Anne. "I'm fine."

On May 22, Ian Ball pleaded guilty to two charges of attempted murder, two of wounding, and one of "attempting to steal and carry away Her Royal Highness, Princess Anne." The trial was brief. A Home Office psychiatrist testified that Ball was suffering from a severe personality disorder. Lord Chief Justice Widgery ordered that he be detained "without limit of time," and he was placed in a top-security hospital.

In November, the Queen held an investiture at Buckingham Palace. James Beaton was awarded the George Cross, Britain's highest honor for peacetime gallantry. The George Medal went to Ronald Russell and Michael Hills. The Queen's Gallantry Medal was presented to Alec Callender, Peter Edmonds and Brian McConnell. Glanmore Martin received the Queen's Commendation for Brave Conduct.

In those violent seven minutes in The Mall, Ian Ball brought about something no one else had been able to achieve. Since then, there has been a tightening of royal security. As he told detectives: "There's one good thing coming out of this—you'll have to improve Princess Anne's protection." In that, at least, he was right.

The turbulent river had
seemingly swallowed young Chuck Warnock alive.
As the hours ticked past, hope vanished

"A Very Lucky Individual"

BY SEAMUS McGRADY

EARLY ONE SUNDAY MORNING in June 1977, Charles Warnock and his family left their home in Bremerton, Washington, for an outing at nearby Olympic National Park. The two Warnock boys—Chuck, 18, and Donny, 16—planned to swim down Staircase Rapids, a fast and turbulent chute of water they hoped would be ideal for their favorite sport, which combines the thrills of body surfing and river rafting.

The Warnocks left their car near the park ranger station, then hiked the mile up to the head of the rapids, arriving shortly after noon. It was a hot, sunny day, and Chuck, wearing his wet-suit jacket and gloves, quickly slipped into a quiet pool. When the shock of the icy water wore off, he relaxed and, feet first, let the current carry him downstream. Nearing the white water, he whooped with expectation.

Standing on a boulder overlooking the pool, Donny watched his brother approach a small waterfall. Suddenly, noticing some large rocks at the bottom of the falls, he yelled, "Stop! It's too dangerous!"

Chuck tried to brace his wiry five-foot-eight, 120-pound frame against the flow, but his shoes skidded on the slick pebbles. He made an attempt to grab onto a rock, but his gloves slipped off the wet moss and he shot head over heels down the cascading white water.

Donny scrambled off his perch and checked below the falls.

178

"Dad!" he shouted. "Chuck went under and hasn't come up yet."

When he heard Donny call, Charles Warnock left his wife, Carol, and rushed to the riverbank. He remembers thinking: *He probably just stayed under longer than expected. He'll turn up farther down the river.* Then, about fifteen yards upstream, he saw Chuck's glove pop to the surface. *He must be caught under a rock. How else would he lose his glove?* "Donny," he called, "run to the ranger station and get help."

Leaping from rock to rock, the distraught father tried to race straight up the river to the waterfall about a hundred feet away. *How long could Chuck last? A minute? Two?* The water became deeper and swifter. Making his way to a huge boulder in the middle of the river, he tried to probe beneath the boiling rapids with a long stick. He found nothing. Minutes sped by. A hiker on the trail gave Carol Warnock a twenty-five-foot rope, which she threw out to her husband. Warnock lassoed a log caught between two rocks at the head of the waterfall and wrapped the other end around his hand.

Slowly, he inched his way down the left side of the boulder. *If he's down there—and conscious—he might try to grab my leg. I could pull him out.* He worked his way down to the end of the rope. There was no sign of Chuck.

Next he went down the right side of the boulder. When he came to the end of the rope this time, the force of the river made him lose his footing. He held on with both hands. He thought: *He has to be right down there, and I can't even reach him. I could let go, but it wouldn't help—there would be two dead instead of one.* It took all his strength for Warnock to work his way to the top again.

Carol Warnock called out to her husband: "Do you see him?"

"No. But stay away! The river's too fast here."

Carol felt her stomach tighten. *There must be something he doesn't want me to see,* she thought. *Something terrible.*

At 12:55, the park rangers arrived and, despite the fact that Chuck had been missing since 12:15, they initiated a "hasty search," a method for covering an area as rapidly as possible in the hope of finding a person instead of a body.

Ranger Andy Cohen tied two climbing ropes around his waist and quickly entered the water where Warnock had been looking. He realized that chances of finding Chuck alive were "slim to none," but hurried from pool to pool anyway, crossing and recrossing the churning river. Cohen used his hands and feet and short sticks to search around and beneath rocks and overhanging ledges. Behind the largest boulders, the suction was so great that he had to be hauled out bodily by the rangers at the ends of his ropes. After forty-five minutes, Cohen struggled ashore and nearly collapsed. The rangers called off the hasty search.

Meanwhile, after his tumble down the cascade, Chuck had surfaced inside a cavelike air pocket beneath a huge boulder at the foot of the falls. He felt all right—at least nothing was broken—and he had air to breathe. When his eyes adjusted to the darkness, he could see that his little chamber was about three feet wide and six feet long. He saw no escape route other than leaving the way he had come in, which meant going up an almost vertical chimney of churning water. To get a better grip, he took off his gloves and stuck them inside his jacket. One of them fell out. Standing on tiptoe on a small rock, he grabbed a ledge near the opening and tried to pull himself up. The frothing cataract pushed him down and back into the hollow. He hit his head on the way in. "God damn it," he muttered. *No, God. I didn't mean that. Please, please help me get out of here!*

He paused to catch his breath before making a second attempt. Getting out, he realized, would be more difficult than he had imagined. *If only I can get up high enough to yell, somebody might hear and come take me out.* He pulled himself up as high as he could, but he discov-

ered he could not breathe, much less shout. Worn out, he let the swirling water carry him to the rear of the cave. There was no light back there and no evidence of an exit.

He rested and tried to think clearly. He knew he had strength left for only one more try. Perhaps if he reduced the resistance of his body to the water flow, he could make it. He took off his wet-suit jacket and set it on a log. Shivering, he swam quickly to the entrance, grabbed the ledge and heaved. Once again he was forced back into his cell.

Chuck managed to get back into his jacket, but it brought no warmth. Its buoyancy, however, helped him stay afloat. He draped his arms over a log and locked his fingers together. The light seemed to grow dimmer, the air heavier. He fell asleep.

After resting, ranger Cohen had reentered the river for the "thorough search" phase of the operation. Wearing a wet suit and face mask, he worked carefully and slowly, reaching as far as he could into each crevice and under every rock. Despite the face mask, the visibility was poor. The afternoon sun had melted the snow in the mountains, and the river was higher and more turbulent than it had been. Cohen wondered how the parents would react when they saw their son's body—the white face; the blank, staring eyes.

Soon the sun dipped beneath the park's towering fir and cedar trees, and the air grew chilly. Head ranger George Bowen had stationed observers along the banks of the river, hoping that the afternoon's rising water level would dislodge the body from its hiding place. Now, back at the ranger station, he began planning for the next day's search. At daybreak, there would be fresh men in complete scuba gear ready to go down into the deepest pools. *If necessary, we'll turn over every damn rock in the river. But we* will *find him.* He told the Warnocks his men would soon have to give up the search for the day.

"No matter how long it takes," Warnock told his wife, "I can't leave here until he's found."

"Neither can I," she said.

When Chuck opened his eyes, the cave was pitch black. The water swirling at the entrance now came up to his chin. The air seemed dense, and it was hard to breathe. He was cold and, despite his nap, exhausted.

Knowing it would be useless to try to pull himself up the waterfall again, he began exploring every inch of the cave. Finally, near the back, he felt an indentation he had not noticed before. Was this a chink in the stony armor of his monolithic prison? He stuck his leg in as far as he could and met no resistance. *It could be a way out. Or I could get stuck in there. But I can't hold out much longer here.*

He took a deep breath and squeezed down into the opening. Immediately, the current forced him through and out into the river. He shot to the surface, to the light and the sweet, fresh air. Alive and free, Chuck could not remember ever being so happy. He swam to a rock and clung to it.

Andy Cohen, resting on the bank after fighting the river for almost three hours, wondered if he should go in for one more try. He told Cal Early, a ranger who had been pulling him out of the water all afternoon, "It would be different if we were looking for somebody alive. But for a body . . ."

Early interrupted, pointing out at the river, "Who's that?"

Cohen saw someone in the middle of the river crouching on a boulder. *Oh, no. That's all we need—some overzealous bystander trying to help.* "What are you doing out there?" he demanded. Then he looked again, remembering a photo Charles Warnock had shown him. "It's him! It's him!" he yelled.

Cohen and Early hit the water at the same time. Cohen grabbed Chuck and tied a rope around his waist. Early climbed up the boulder and slowly hauled Chuck to the top. Cohen, an emergency medical technician, joined them and examined Chuck. "How do you feel?" he asked.

"Hungry," Chuck said. Then he fainted.

In the ranger station, a quiet voice came over the radio: "We found him . . ." There was a pause, then, triumphantly, . . . "And *he's alive!*"

Carol Warnock felt tears roll down her cheeks. "Thank God," she murmured. "Oh, thank You, God." She put her arms around her husband, and they both wept.

Cohen was afraid they might yet lose Chuck. The youth's pupils were fixed and dilated, his skin was bluish, his pulse weak and his breathing shallow. Cohen and Early carried Chuck to the riverbank, lay down beside him and hugged him to keep him warm. Whenever

Chuck was conscious, Cohen tried to feed him hot coffee and chocolate, but his patient had difficulty keeping the food down. Not until emergency equipment—warm clothing, blankets, a stretcher and oxygen—arrived from the ranger station, and the youth was breathing the pure oxygen, did Cohen know the worst was over.

Despite the difficulty of carrying Chuck by stretcher through trailless woods to the ranger station, Cohen recalls it as the "most joyous hike" he had ever been on. When the Warnocks finally met their son and the rangers about a quarter of a mile from the station, there was not a dry eye among them. But they were also smiling and joking. Carrying the stretcher and still in his wet suit, Cohen inquired, "Who's going to sign for this package?"

At 6:05, Chuck and his mother were flown by a rescue helicopter to the Naval Regional Medical Center at Bremerton, where Chuck spent the night. He was released the next afternoon.

Although Chuck has gained a healthy respect for the dangers of swimming down rapids, he won't give up his favorite sport. "The Staircase Rapids is too rocky and too fast," he said afterwards. "I won't do that one again. But you don't give up driving a car because you've had one accident, do you?"

Perhaps the last word belongs to ranger Bowen, who concluded his report with this simple observation: "A very lucky individual."

The airliner's wing
was a hurricane of flames.
A jet engine had melted off and plummeted to earth.
There was one hope . . .

Ordeal
in Whiskey-Echo

BY RICHARD HAMOND

UNTIL THAT SERENE AND cloudless afternoon high above London's
Heathrow Airport, I had never known the true meaning of fear. My
work as a marine zoologist had brought me a knowledge of life in
some of its strangest forms; now it was to bring me uncomfortably
close to a firsthand knowledge of death, yet provide a unique
glimpse of human courage.

Although there was nobody to see me off, my spirits were buoyant
that April day in 1968 as I boarded BOAC's flight 712 for Zurich on

the first leg of a long journey to Australia. There I was to take up an appointment with the Commonwealth Scientific and Industrial Research Organization.

As I entered the plane I could feel that others were as excited as I was as we settled down for the trip. A flight attendant helped an elderly crippled lady into her seat; a small, fair-haired girl bubbled with happiness as she chattered to her two brothers. Apart from the many emigrant families, the passengers were an everyday mix from several countries—here and there an Indian traveling to Bombay, some Americans visiting the Middle East, one or two Chinese going on to Singapore.

When I had found my own seat, I felt a twinge of disappointment. I was placed right alongside the trailing edge of a wing, which almost obscured my view of the ground. Photography is not only a necessity in my work but my hobby as well, and here I was, my faithful Exa II 35-mm camera ready and loaded with color film, but all chances for decent pictures gone.

Our Boeing 707, improbably named "Whiskey-Echo," taxied toward the runway. A cheerful flight attendant checked our safety belts, then demonstrated the emergency routines. Before booking the flight my mind had kept turning to a recent airplane accident in which two of my family's oldest friends were killed. Now, as I watched the flight attendant calmly going about her preflight duties, all qualms vanished. If she and her companions could choose to face the dangers of air travel as part of their daily lives, what reason had I to be anxious on this one rare trip?

Certainly none of the other passengers seemed worried. Beside me sat two brothers, aged perhaps eight and ten, bright, intelligent lads, obviously longing for the journey to start. At last the plane was rumbling off down the runway and as the fierce acceleration suddenly thrust us back into our seats I could see their faces light up with excitement; I was delighted to be sharing their adventure. At 4:27 we were airborne and Whiskey-Echo was soaring swiftly and smoothly into the sky. I watched the houses dwindle to toys, to matchboxes, to sugar lumps.

The photograph on the opposite page was one of those actually taken by the author as he watched the airplane's wing burn.

It is still difficult for me to believe that the events that followed lasted no more than four minutes. Even for a scientist, accustomed to precise measurements of intervals, time has a subjective quality. We were still less than half a minute out of Heathrow when, suddenly, the plane lurched. Air turbulence, perhaps? A moment later, staring vaguely at the jet's port wing, I saw it—a long, straight spurt of yellow flame, like that from a blowtorch, streaming astern a few feet below the wing, apparently from the inboard engine.

At first I felt no alarm. Obviously it was some kind of booster to speed the heavy plane's ascent, or excess fuel being harmlessly discharged. But within a few seconds it had grown bigger, and a wisp of orange flame about the size of a man's hand appeared slowly and unmistakably over the leading edge of the wing.

The chief flight attendant, who had been sitting across the aisle, now shot off to the pilot's cabin. In the first-class section, the flight attendants began briskly taking back the drinks they had been serving and checking that all other loose equipment and baggage were properly stowed.

But some scientific reflex overcame the fears rising within me. *Photograph it!* I told myself. *Photograph it!* Quickly I took an exposure reading. Then I aimed my Exa camera carefully through the window at the blazing wing, focused on the sharp trailing flames, and pressed the shutter.

By this time everyone else in the plane had seen the fire. Conversation had died down to subdued whispers. Several people had turned around to gaze at the hideous spectacle while a young couple opposite stared straight ahead, their hands clutched tight in a mute gesture of support. I gave the two boys beside me what I hope was a reassuring smile. Whatever their inward feelings, they appeared rigidly calm.

When I looked through my window again, fresh tongues of flame were bursting up through the wing itself, coalescing with those above and below. Before long the outer part of the wing was lost to view behind a roaring wall of yellow fire.

As I prepared to take a second photograph, I could see the paint at the edge of the flame curling up and breaking off, flying away in a shower of sparks.

The captain and his crew had one hope: to land Whiskey-Echo

before the 6,000 gallons of jet fuel on board exploded. Already the giant Boeing had started a tight left turn above the sunlit Thames. I calculated they had about two minutes. I looked at my watch: 4:29. As the second hand eased its way round the dial, I timed the progress of the fire along the wing. The rivets, I guessed, were four inches apart. The flame was advancing toward us at about one foot every three seconds. *We'll never make it,* I thought. As I took my second photograph, I could already feel the heat—like that from a roaring bonfire—through the window.

As the plane wheeled, the near engine that had started the fire tore through its melting supports and plummeted earthward; by a fantastic stroke of luck, the blazing missile missed houses and shops in the town of Staines and plunged harmlessly into a water-filled gravel pit.

Inside, the plane was lit as if by flickering stage lights. Passengers eyed the window, their anxious faces jerkily illuminated by the flames racing past.

The chief flight attendant returned, his face wan but his voice admirably steady. "We are going to make an emergency landing. Please don't be alarmed. Get your heads down in your laps and keep your safety belts tight."

Our flight attendant came by, no longer laughing but still managing a brave smile. She checked our belts again, gave the two boys beside me a comforting hug and gently eased their heads down closer to their knees. Then she was gone.

I couldn't resist the urge to take one more look. Advancing the film, I raised my head to the window. Through three thicknesses of Plexiglas the heat struck me so savagely that I felt as if hot metal had been drawn across my face. I wiped away the pouring sweat, screwed up my eyes against the blinding light, and held my exposure meter toward the flames. The needle almost shot off the dial. Somehow I managed a third photograph, aiming the camera through the window while turning my head away.

Aghast, I shielded my face and stared through the window again. The sight, at once utterly terrible and beautiful, transfixed me. The whole universe was on fire. Whiskey-Echo's wing was visible only as the white-hot floor of an inferno. The blinding, incandescent vapor was shot through with sparks and flares and yellow firebrands. Now, one by one, the outer windows of the Boeing began to melt, crack and bubble.

But even more unnerving than the pyrotechnic destruction of the aircraft was the reaction inside the cabin. Apart from a baby whimpering softly in his mother's arms, all the passengers were in the grip of a shocked, leaden silence.

Face in my lap, I waited for the end—and found myself shaking uncontrollably. *We can never survive,* I thought. And through my fear came other emotions—frustration, anger, a bitter sense of unfairness, waste. I had worked hard to get my doctorate from London University and find the job I wanted, and just when I was making a new life, I was to be cheated of the rewards. What a stupid way to have to die!

By now the greedy roar of the blaze was audible above the noise of the engines, and increasing steadily. I hoped the plane would smash into the ground and end everything quickly. That would be better than if it split open and spilled us out—better than being burned alive.

Ever since my schooldays I had been the organist at our ancient church of All Saints in the quiet village of Morston, Norfolk. Now, even with all thoughts of the village, the sea, the fields and the church blotted out by fear, some remnant of this experience came to my aid. I prayed aloud.

Our Father . . .

My voice shook. My head was in my lap.

Hallowed be thy name. . . .

The engines droned. Outside, the fiery hurricane roared louder than ever.

And forgive us our trespasses . . .

At the word "trespasses" there was a tearing jolt. The wheels had struck the runway. This was followed at once by the tremendous shuddering of powerful brakes savagely applied. The remaining engines bellowed triumphantly in reverse thrust. And then, marvelously, the plane had stopped.

We filed out. There was no panic—but no loitering. "Right! Come along please. Move along!" A flight attendant was coaxing, persuading and pushing travelers down an escape slide at the rear, but I was already being carried along in the stream of people to the front of the craft. Behind me, a man trod on my heels and his nose rubbed my neck as he muttered to himself in some incomprehensible tongue. In front, a girl gasped as she fought to keep herself from hysteria. A few small children were crying. For the rest, the prospect of action quelled most of our fears.

With the plane stationary, the fire gave full vent to its fury, tongues of reddish flame licking at the outside of the windows. A ceiling of heavy fumes began to thicken at the back of the cabin. As we pressed slowly forward, with some twenty tons of fuel boiling in tanks just a few feet away, there were three heavy, muffled thuds. The wing tanks had exploded, sending large chunks of Whiskey-Echo high into the air.

Then suddenly we were down the escape slide and standing in the blessed fresh air. Sirens screamed as fire engines, police cars and ambulances came racing toward us. Airline staff shouted to us to get clear before the plane blew up, and those who couldn't run, walk or limp away were carried to safety. From a safe distance I turned to look back and, guessing at the exposure, I took two more camera shots.

A gigantic ball of black smoke, shot through with reddish-yellow flame, blotted out the sun. At its base lay the remains of Whiskey-Echo in her final agony—her spine broken, her tail vanishing amid the smoke and fire, her oxygen tanks exploding. Already, the seats we had occupied barely a minute before were being consumed by the fire.

For several minutes many of the passengers were unable to tear themselves away from the ugly, hectic scene. Airport personnel were passing out paper cups of tea, and we heard that one of the flight attendants was still inside the plane and that a small fair-haired girl was also missing. I watched the firemen in breathing apparatus hurry toward the plane—and suddenly I wanted to get as far away from Whiskey-Echo as I could.

Of the 116 passengers and eleven crew members, all but five had survived, somehow getting out of the aircraft in the fifty-five seconds between its coming to a halt and its final incineration. Thirty-eight passengers were injured.

My photographs, I was told, provided valuable evidence in establishing the cause of the fire. While revolving at full power during takeoff, an engine's compressor wheels had snapped and the blades had flown in all directions, severing the fuel lines, electric circuits and fire extinguisher pipes.

Two weeks later I was on my way to Australia again, first class, courtesy of BOAC, with a perfect view of land and sea. It was many months, however, before I was fully able to grasp how much I and others owed to the crew of Whiskey-Echo.

Captain Charles Taylor, the brilliant New Zealand-born pilot, was later awarded the gold medal of the British Airline Pilots' Association for an epic feat of airmanship. With one engine lost and another beginning to fail, he had nursed the blazing, crippled and lopsided aircraft down for a perfect landing. And Neville Davis-Gordon, the chief flight attendant, was given the British Empire Medal for Gallantry for the cool efficiency with which he led the evacuation of the plane.

But it was Barbara Harrison, the small, cheerful flight attendant that had welcomed the passengers aboard at Heathrow, who paid the highest price. After the rear escape chute had collapsed with the heat, she had shepherded passengers to the front of the craft. Although she could easily have made good her own escape, she insisted on going back once more. She knew that somewhere in the smoke at the back of the plane were two women who had become rigid with fear, an elderly lady who had difficulty in walking and a little girl crying for her mother. For her courage, she was awarded the George Cross—Britain's highest civilian honor for gallantry. "Barbara Harrison," said the official citation, "was a very brave young lady who gave her life in her utter devotion to duty."

Nearly a mile deep,
surrounded by lethal smoke and carbon-monoxide gas,
two men fought to stay alive for seven days

Fire in the
Sunshine Silver Mine

BY TREVOR ARMBRISTER

NO ONE KNOWS HOW the fire began, deep in an abandoned section of the Sunshine Silver Mine near Kellogg, Idaho. But shortly before noon on Tuesday, May 2, 1972, it erupted with a fury, feeding on scrap timber and timber supports. Escape routes were soon engulfed with smoke and carbon monoxide.

The order went out to evacuate the mine, and eighty men were lifted to safety. Then deadly fumes struck down the operators of the hoists, or elevators. Ninety-three men were trapped somewhere in a hundred miles of underground passageways.

Nearly a mile beneath the earth's surface sounded the terrifying cry: "Fire! Fire on the upper levels!" Ron Flory, 28, and his partner Tom Wilkenson, 29, boarded a battery-powered locomotive and drove west along Syndicate Drift, the mile-long tunnel where they were working, to alert two other miners. They all returned together to a tiny shed called "the station" at the vertical No. 10 shaft. Snatching emergency respirators, the four men pinched rubber clamps over their noses, stuck the tubes in their mouths and activated chemicals to neutralize any carbon monoxide. Soon five other miners joined them. But the cage that was supposed to take them to safety never appeared.

Smoke swept in around the station. They moved a hundred yards back to the motorbarn. At five-minute intervals two of the men

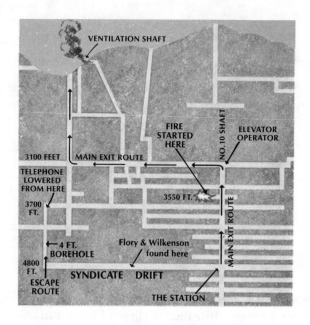

VENTILATION SHAFT

FIRE STARTED HERE

NO. 10 SHAFT

ELEVATOR OPERATOR

3100 FEET — MAIN EXIT ROUTE

TELEPHONE LOWERED FROM HERE

3700 FT.

3550 FT.

MAIN EXIT ROUTE

4 FT. BOREHOLE

Flory & Wilkenson found here

4800 FT.

ESCAPE ROUTE

SYNDICATE DRIFT

THE STATION

would walk to the station, check for the cage and try the telephone there. No luck.

Soon the motorbarn too was flooded with smoke. Wilkenson's respirator slipped off. Turning to Dick Allison, he said, "I'm going out," then lapsed into unconsciousness.

Flory ran to the station and yanked the emergency cord. Then, dizzy themselves, he and Allison laid Wilkenson on top of the locomotive and drove westward again. Once clear of the smoke area, they leaned their friend against the side of the tunnel, then returned to urge the other miners to join them.

"Let's check the station just one more time," someone said. "We can phone up and say where we'll be."

The other miners took another locomotive and drove toward the station. But Flory, weak and nauseated, decided to walk back to his partner. He felt sure that rescue was imminent. With a piece of chalk he scribbled a message on the side of the passageway: RON FLORY WAS HERE. MAY 2 TO—?

In Coeur d'Alene, forty-five miles away, Marvin C. Chase, vice president and general manager of the Sunshine Mining Company, was addressing the annual stockholders' meeting. He had good news: In 1971, Sunshine had produced seven million ounces of silver—one sixth of the total silver production of the United States—and 1972's figures should surpass even those. After his speech, Chase called the mine. A switchboard operator told him that a fire had started underground. Fires in hard-rock mines aren't always serious, and this one didn't sound bad. But Chase drove over immediately.

Arriving at 1:25, he saw smoke billowing up from the mine's main ventilation shaft, and he knew at once that the fire was serious. Sunshine had long prided itself on its modern ventilation system: Huge fans pushed thousands of cubic feet of air per second into the mine's depths and pulled stale air out. Now those fans were circulating smoke and the odorless, colorless fumes of deadly carbon monoxide.

If they had known where the fire had started, and where the miners were in the mine, fans and bulkheads could have been used to confine the blaze. "The men who have the answers—our key foremen and shift bosses—are trapped," said Chase in frustration. "If we cut off a fan somewhere, we might make matters worse."

Myrna Flory was just sitting down to lunch when her sister arrived with the news. Myrna headed for the mine. Other wives were already there, some upset and crying. She spotted miner Dennis Clapp. "Ron could have got out," he told her. "But he went back to help Tom Wilkenson." Suddenly, Myrna Flory felt ill. Frances Wilkenson heard the news on the radio. "How much can rocks burn?" she thought as she drove to the mine. She was surprised to see so many police and rescue workers. "A couple of hours," she told herself. "They'll come out, take their baths, and go home okay."

Through the shifting haze of smoke, Ron Flory became aware of a headlight a hundred yards away. It was the locomotive the other miners had taken an hour and a half ago. He yelled; no one answered. He walked toward it cautiously—and recoiled at what he saw. In the driver's seat, slumped over, was Allison. Three men were sprawled nearby. Apparently they hadn't been using their respirators, and carbon-monoxide fumes had killed them. Flory felt spooked. He ran back and got his partner.

With their respirators securely in place, Flory and Wilkenson pulled Allison out of the smoke. They felt for his pulse. Then Wilkenson put his ear to his chest. "It's no good, Ron," he said.

The two survivors now weighed their predicament. They had no food or means of communication; they didn't know where the fire was raging. When the batteries on their cap lamps and the locomotive's headlight failed, they would be in total darkness. Still, the water line to their level was intact and fresh air was flowing from a four-foot circular borehole that had recently been drilled down from the 3,700-foot level. As long as smoke didn't enter the borehole . . .

Tuesday evening they drove farther westward along the passageway. At the borehole opening Flory noticed a green canvas bag that had been dropped from the 3,700-foot level. It contained a field telephone. He unzipped the bag, picked up the receiver and turned the crank excitedly. "Hello, hello!" But no reply. A jagged rock inside the borehole had severed one of the phone's lines, rendering it inoperable.

They spent an uncomfortable night. The possibility of death underground, particularly a slow death caused by starvation, was a new idea to them. Flory thought about his two-year-old son. *Who's going to teach him to fish and hunt if I'm not there?*

Wilkenson couldn't relax. "Talk to me, Ron," he said. "Are they going to get us out? What are they doing up there—playing pinochle?"

Maybe they should walk back to the station. Maybe they should climb the wooden escape ladders that paralleled the No. 10 shaft—up to the 4,600-foot level, then the 4,400-foot level. . . .

"We can't use the ladders now," Flory insisted. "There may be smoke up there. At least down here we have fresh air."

"But we've got to let 'em know we're still alive!" Wilkenson exclaimed. "We can tell 'em to come down the borehole and get us out that way."

Minutes later, Flory started walking toward the station. His respirator wasn't functioning well, and he soon felt dizzy. Reaching the point where the bodies lay, he stopped just long enough to remove some cigarettes from the dead miners' caps, then stumbled back to the borehole. Later that evening, he thought he heard voices—one of them Allison's. But that couldn't be. He had seen the body himself.

Miners' families were waiting in a cordoned-off area by the main mine entrance. Red Cross volunteers passed out name tags to the families, but Frances Wilkenson declined. "I don't need one," she said. "My husband is going to walk out alive."

Once, a clergyman notifying the victims' relatives tapped Frances on the shoulder. She spun around, her large brown eyes widening with fright. "Oh," the pastor said, "I'm sorry. You're not the one I was looking for."

Rescuers worked around the clock. On Wednesday evening, they found four more bodies.

Wilkenson and Flory talked about fishing, the fun they'd had, the trout they'd catch next time. But such talk always led to a discussion of food. They hadn't eaten since Tuesday morning.

Wilkenson was still impatient; he wanted to go to the station right away. Reluctantly, Flory agreed. Placing soaked T-shirts over their mouths and noses, they headed east. They passed the four bodies and soon discovered a fifth. But the smoke was just too thick to go farther. They had to turn back.

Flory remembered how his wife had often complained that she had no pictures of him. If he survived, the first thing he planned to do was pose for a family photograph.

Rescue efforts were centering on the No. 10 shaft. By Thursday noon an eighty-man crew was using giant exhaust fans to clear the smoke away from the shaft head, 3,100 feet underground. Once they reached it, they'd send an elevator down deeper to measure the smoke at the lower levels. Then just before midnight, a temporary bulkhead keeping the smoke away from them developed a leak. Workmen scurried to shore it up, but it would be a six-hour job.

Chase decided now to begin a secondary rescue effort via an existing borehole that descended from the 3,700-foot level, using the U. S. Bureau of Mines rescue team. The Atomic Energy Commission promised to provide, from its Nevada test site, torpedolike capsules that could carry two men. To see if the rough, narrow hole could accommodate a capsule, a television camera was lowered into the opening.

Confident until now, Frances Wilkenson felt her spirits sagging. Her twelve-year-old Eileen and three-year-old Tommy kept asking when Daddy would appear. She couldn't tell them. She was sure the men's cap lamps had burned out long ago. *In total darkness,* she thought, *something may snap in their minds.*

At five p.m. Friday, Flory noticed that water was just trickling out of the water line—the pressure was almost gone. Without water, they knew, they couldn't survive long. Now they *had* to get to the station.

Because he had the brighter lamp, Wilkenson set the pace. The smoke was thinner now, and they didn't have to stop so often to catch their breath. Finally, they reached the station. Stacked nearby were the lunch pails of their dead co-workers, containing sandwiches, a can of sausages, cold coffee and candy bars. They hesitated momentarily, then started eating.

On Saturday morning, Flory started to sing. The only tune whose words he could remember was "The Old Rugged Cross." Then he began banging his wrench against the water pipe. Echoes vanished in the darkness.

"That won't do any good," Wilkenson chided.

"Maybe not," Flory replied. "But it sure makes me feel better."

On Sunday afternoon, it rained. Frances and Myrna walked together, oblivious of the rain, clinging to slender hopes. One wife whose husband was still underground gazed up at the slate-gray sky and said, "The whole world is crying for us."

Sunday evening, Flory and Wilkenson found two more bodies at the station. One man had collapsed in the station shed, with the telephone in his hand. But the area seemed clear of smoke. Perhaps they could try the escape ladders now.

Suddenly, they sensed a new, eerie stillness. The fans had stopped. "What are they *doing* up there?" Wilkenson asked. "They know we need air." Without fresh air circulating, it would be foolish to try the ladders.

Hot, moist, steamlike air moved closer to them now that the fans had been cut off. Flory and Wilkenson watched, terrified. For all they knew, it was smoke. They stuffed food in their lunch buckets and stumbled along the passageway. Then the steam enveloped them. To their relief, they found they could still breathe normally.

RESCUE HOPES DIMMER, said the Kellogg *Evening News* headline on Monday, after nearly a week's efforts. About nine o'clock that evening, a two-man crew entered a torpedo capsule on the 3,700-foot level and started down the borehole. So jagged was it, so busy were the men removing loose rock from its sides, that by three a.m. Tuesday they had progressed only 450 feet.

Flory and Wilkenson had just about given up hope. Their cap lamps were dim, and without light they couldn't climb the escape ladders. Only the can of sausages was left to eat. The two men walked again to the station and tugged forlornly on the emergency cord. There was no reply.

At noon Tuesday a fresh crew went down the borehole, and this time reached the 4,800-foot level without difficulty. They spotted footprints near the borehole opening—and saw the green telephone bag, unzipped! Excitedly, the rescuers searched a thousand feet into the tunnel toward the No. 10 shaft. Finding nothing, they returned to the surface. Another descent was scheduled for later that afternoon.

Flory checked his calendar watch. The light was so dim now that he had to squint. It was 5:30 p.m. on Tuesday, May 9—his eighth day underground. Suddenly he saw a flash. "Tom!" he shouted. "There's a light—down by the borehole!"

"Baloney," Wilkenson said.

Flory grabbed his wrench and swung it against the water pipe. He saw the light again. Wilkenson began blinking the weak locomotive beam. "Over here!" he yelled.

"Stay right there!" the rescue workers shouted.

As he watched them approach, Wilkenson tried to smile—but he was crying instead. "Thank God!" he said. "Thank God you've come!"

The capsule inched up the borehole to the 3,700-foot level, carrying one of the rescuers and Ron Flory. A doctor examined him and asked if he wanted to ride to the surface immediately. "No," he said. "Tom and I were down there together. We'll go out together."

At 8:20 that evening—177 hours after their ordeal began—they stepped through the portal, the only survivors out of the ninety-three trapped men. Blinking in the glare of television lights, the two haggard, bearded miners fell into the arms of their waiting wives. Frances Wilkenson kept hugging and kissing her husband. "*Now* we're going home," she cried. "*Now* we're going home!"

When they pulled Warren Churchill
from the icy Wisconsin lake,
his blood pressure was zero, he wasn't breathing,
and his body temperature
was dropping toward a record low

The Coldest
Man Alive

BY LOUIS A. GOTH

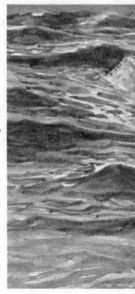

SPRING CAN BE DECEPTIVE in Wisconsin. It can beguile the eye with clear skies and brilliant sun while whipping the body with icy winds. April 5, 1973, was that kind of day. Out on Lake Wingra, a 345-acre lake in downtown Madison, were Warren Churchill, 57, Thomas Kuczynski, 29, and Tom Waters, 23, three scientists from the Department of Natural Resources. Working on a research project to determine the number, growth and mortality rate of fish in the lake, they were making their daily inspection of nets they had placed at various points.

By midafternoon the sun had raised the temperature into the fifties, but a twenty-mile-an-hour wind, with much higher gusts, churned the lake's surface into angry whitecaps. A team of botanists, unable to hold their boat in position, had given up before noon. Churchill, Kuczynski and Waters, however, were experienced boatmen. So, despite the conditions, they checked their nets on the south shore, then started across the lake to their next station. That boat ride would carry them into medical history.

Their sixteen-foot aluminum scow was flat-bottomed, squared off

at bow and stern. Kuczynski and Waters sat on the front seat, while Churchill steered the outboard motor from the rear. The wide bow slapped and pounded the waves. They had hammered their way to the middle of the lake, perhaps a quarter of a mile from shore, when a pair of huge waves broke over them. Seconds later the boat was floating bottom up, barely two inches out of the water, with the three men clinging to it in forty-one-degree water.

Luckily, all three men were wearing some rubberized clothing. For the first few minutes in the water, they were not terribly worried. After all, Lake Wingra is only a dozen blocks from the state capitol and even closer to the University of Wisconsin. More than 175,000 people surrounded them.

Three fourths of Wingra's shoreline, however, is covered by the university's arboretum, a near wilderness area. The other fourth is divided between Edgewood College, which is screened from the lake by tall pines, and Vilas Park, a zoological garden. This early in the spring, the lakefront was deserted.

The boat had swamped at three-fifteen. By three-thirty, Kuczynski was becoming numb. To stay by the boat seemed pointless. Even one man's full weight would sink it, so it was useless as a raft. Moreover, Wingra is twice as long as it is wide and the wind was pushing them the lake's length. He decided to free himself from his clothes so that he could swim for help. But when he tried to roll off his hip boots, he quickly realized that an unclothed swimmer couldn't survive for a hundred yards in such cold water, and the shore was a quarter of a mile off. Clinging to the capsized boat was their only hope.

By four o'clock, Churchill was having trouble. Time and again the waves broke his grip. He seemed unable to keep water out of his mouth. He coughed and sputtered and appeared to be losing consciousness. The gas tank, tethered to the engine by its hose, bobbed near him, and Kuczynski and Waters slid it along the bottom of the boat and told Churchill to pull himself onto it. Both were relieved when he smiled and responded.

But Churchill's condition steadily worsened. Waters, his own position precarious, struggled close enough to Churchill to help him cling to the gas tank. By this time, they had been in the frigid water, beaten by wind and waves, for an hour. Kuczynski and Waters were shivering so badly that often one of them would have to release the boat until a spasm passed or he would have shaken the others off. Thoughts of death entered their minds. Churchill, in fact, was certain that he would never make it to shore.

By four-thirty, Churchill was unconscious, though his eyes remained open, a fact that first misled and then frightened his companions. The gas tank slipped from his grasp, and Kuczynski and Waters pushed him up onto the bottom of the boat. It faced into the wind, bucking and twisting, water smashing over it until it threatened to escape them. By leaning on their side, Kuczynski and Waters were able to raise the far side enough to break the worst impact of the waves. There was no conversation. Actions were instinctive. They didn't know how long they could hold Churchill on the trembling platform. But they knew their lives and his had become one.

At that same time, four-thirty, Julie Bauhs and Diane Montalto, both nineteen, were walking through Vilas Park. Looking out over the turbulent waters, they spotted the boat pitching near the middle of the lake and ran to Julie's house nearby to call the police.

The police dispatcher logged the call at 4:39, and he relayed the report to officers Richard Hyland and Ire Rees, who were in their patrol car not more than half a mile from the stranded men. In minutes they launched the rescue boat that is maintained on the lake. Once on that rough water themselves, they were unable to spot the overturned craft, but their siren had attracted a number of spectators who guided the officers with shouts and gestures. While Hyland fought to maneuver as close as possible, Rees threw Kuczynski a line. Kuczynski tried to grab it, but he could barely move his arms away from his body. Rees had to jump in the water to get the three men into the boat.

As the police boat sped to shore, the officers draped their coats over Churchill's limp body. There was no pulse, and they feared he was dead. Meanwhile, a fire-department ambulance was on the way.

Richard Lindauer and Ralph Chamberlain, two firemen who soon arrived at the boat landing, had the same initial reaction—that Churchill was dead. He was cyanotic (blue in color), and he wasn't breathing. But they administered oxygen, and Churchill began to breathe. Even so, he had a very faint heartbeat, his body temperature was obviously way down, and his blood pressure was zero. "Believe me, he was cold," recalls Lindauer. "Just holding him sent a chill through me."

When the ambulance delivered Churchill to University Hospitals at 5:02, attendants were unable to obtain his pulse and blood-pressure readings. His heart was beating at only half its normal rate and was irregular. His breathing was very slow and deep. Worse still, a rectal thermometer showed his body temperature to be 65 ° F. Within the next hour Churchill's rectal temperature would sink to 61 ° F—the lowest ever recorded for an adult patient who survived.*

Dr. Marvin Birnbaum assumed command of a twelve-member team of physicians, technicians and nurses to revive a man who should already have been dead. Churchill was shivering so badly

---

* According to the *Guinness Book of World Records,* there are two recorded cases of female patients surviving body temperatures as low as 60.8 ° F. They were Dorothy Mae Stevens, who was discovered in an alley in Chicago in February 1951 and Vickie Mary Davis, two years old, of Milwaukee, who was found unconscious in January 1956 on the floor of an unheated house in which the air temperature had dropped to −24 ° F.

that now that it was impossible even to assist his breathing. Birnbaum ordered an injection of curare (a drug used on the poison darts of South American aborigines) to paralyze Churchill and break the chills. A machine was used to help him breathe.

The major problem was how to warm him up. The standard method is to immerse the patient in a warm bath. But with this method, it would have been difficult for the physicians to keep a check on his irregular heartbeat. Had Churchill experienced cardiac arrest while in the bath, the team would have lost precious time getting him out of the tub and drying him before countermeasures could be taken. Another method is to remove the blood, warm it, and pump it back in, but the doctors were afraid this might warm him too fast or not fast enough, either of which could be fatal. So Birnbaum decided to use thermal blankets, something that had never been done before. Instead of wires, these blankets have tiny tubes in them through which a special fluid is pumped from a machine that can warm the solution precisely. Churchill was laid between two such blankets and their temperature was raised to 104°F.

Meanwhile, Kuczynski and Waters had been taken to Madison General Hospital. Kuczynski's temperature had dropped to 91°F. and Waters's to 94°F.—cold, but within acceptable limits. With blankets and massage both men returned to normal, and were released early that evening.

When Churchill came to, he could not move or even open his eyes. He could hear people talking and feel them working on him. Slowly it dawned on him that he was in a hospital. "I heard someone mention curare," he remembers. "I knew what that was, and it explained why I couldn't open my eyes. Then I heard someone mention that the two boys were all right. That's what I wanted to hear. Somehow I was sure that I was going to be okay, too."

At ten p.m., Churchill's body temperature reached 90°F. By two a.m., the curare had worn off and his temperature was back to normal. Wrapped in the thermal blankets that had saved his life, he slept peacefully through the rest of the night.

Recovery was smooth. "I worked a lot of math in my head that next week to assure myself that my brain hadn't been damaged by lack of oxygen," Churchill said later. It hadn't. The only serious injury was to his muscles. "Shivering is some of the hardest work you can do," says Birnbaum. "Muscles can be strained and torn." Three months after the accident, Churchill was still sore from head to foot.

On Good Friday, fifteen days after he had been pulled from the icy water, Churchill left the hospital to recuperate at home. When he returned to work, aching muscles confined him to a desk, and not until July was he able to rejoin the two young men with whom he had shared so much. As they toured the net sites, almost retracing their path on the day of the accident, the lake hardly seemed to be the same one. The water that had been raging and freezing was now glass-smooth and warm. This was the Lake Wingra most Madisonians know. At the police dock where the firemen had strained to hear a faint heartbeat, an old man and two small boys fished for bluegills. The boat livery nearby swarmed with teenagers. Shouting children frolicked at Vilas Park beach.

There was a time when Warren Churchill might have preferred the quiet of a wilderness pond. On this occasion, he found in the clamoring life around him an echo of his own joy.

What are the secret qualities
of heart and mind that
enable a man to defeat death?

The Incredible Survival
of Demi McClure

BY LIEUTENANT COLONEL DAVID G. SIMONS (MC), USAF
with Don A. Schanche

In 1955 WHEN WORK began on Operation Man High, the U.S. Air Force's high altitude manned balloon research project, the purpose was largely academic—to study cosmic rays. There were no *Sputniks, Vanguards, Explorers* or *Pioneers* in space then. But when *Sputnik I* was launched two years later, a new and urgent question arose: How soon could the United States put a man into space?

To find at least part of the answer became the responsibility of Operation Man High when Brig. Gen. Donald D. Flickinger, chief of human-factors research for the Air Research and Development Command, ordered the high-altitude balloon research to continue. We already knew something of the mental pressures that might perplex and frighten a man in space. How he reacted to them was vital, for no amount of engineering skill on the ground could change the fact that he alone was commander of his destiny. The technological miracles protecting him could be destroyed by a single instant of thoughtlessness, a single unforeseen hazard, or—even more frightening—a single subconscious act that he might not even recognize, much less control. We had to find the sort of man who could meet this challenge.

Three Air Force captains and a first lieutenant were put through a procedure that later was followed in selecting the *Mercury* astronauts. The lieutenant, jet-pilot Clifton "Demi" McClure, a tall, muscular, dark-haired, twenty-five-year-old South Carolinian, won out. Trained as a ceramic engineer, Demi had a broad interest in many sciences, including astronomy. Though he was both intellectually and physically restless, he could also be remarkably calm. He would push his mind at full bore when there was something to do, but he would also take every chance to relax and conserve energy that might be needed later.

On the night of October 7, 1958, we were ready for the ascent from Holloman Air Force Base in the Tularosa Valley of New Mexico. By one a.m., the narrow capsule was sealed, with Demi buckled into the seat inside. The electrodes and thermistors hooked up to his body would keep those of us who were following his flight by radio informed about his skin resistance, heartbeat and respiration. These, in turn, would reveal his state of mind. But they could not predict how he would react to an emergency brought on by some accidental upset in our careful plans.

In the capsule, McClure soon faced his first emergency. As he turned to look at the pressure gauge, his wrist brushed against the emergency chest parachute on a hook in front of him and dislodged the stay pins; one hundred yards of billowing nylon was spilling down in his lap and over his legs.

It was one-fifteen a.m. This parachute, made for high-altitude emergency use, was built to open automatically in case its wearer was unconscious and unable to pull the rip cord. There was not another one like it at Holloman. If he reported the accident, the capsule would have to be opened, the chute repacked and the launching canceled. Or he could say nothing and attempt the incredibly difficult task of repacking the chute within the narrow confines of his capsule. McClure began the repacking. As he worked, he described each stage of the process to his tape recorder, stopping frequently to answer routine check-out questions from the unsuspecting technical experts outside.

The chute folded, he struggled to force the stubborn, springy material neatly into the parachute pack and fit the stay pins into place. By three-thirty, the job was finished. Then his heart sank: He had inserted the pins backward. Already tired and perspiring, McClure popped the pack open again and grimly, prayerfully, repeated the closure. At five a.m., it was perfect.

Lt. Col. Simons was a doctor in the U.S. Air Force Medical Corps at the time of Operation Man High and received the Distinguished Flying Cross for a record-breaking 102,000-foot balloon flight in 1957.

Outside, our ground crew began inflating the balloon with compressed helium. By seven a.m., capsule and balloon were airborne, rising straight overhead and climbing rapidly toward the stratosphere. Demi was on his lonely way. A panel of specialists, to whom he would report on weather patterns, sky brightness and relative distances of the stars, gathered together in a communications van. In case the balloon moved away from us too fast, a C-47 transport plane had been rigged as an emergency conference room and was ready for takeoff.

Demi's first report, radioed from 24,000 feet, was routine until he reached the cabin temperature: eighty-nine degrees! We checked the capsule's design charts and discovered with relief that the temperature gauge had been incorrectly installed on top of the air-regeneration system; what we were getting was the temperature of that equipment. This reassuring information was relayed to Demi.

At 35,000 feet, Demi reported passing through the tropopause—the band of extreme cold and wind at the top of the troposphere. At 90,000 feet, he called again, this time to me. "I see the most fantastic thing—the sky that you described. It's blacker than black but saturated with blue. I can almost *feel* it."

At 99,700 feet, the balloon leveled off and began moving rapidly to the northwest, too fast for us to follow over the rough terrain in the van. We transferred to the C-47.

On his next report, Demi's voice sounded sluggish. The temperature gauge now read 118 degrees, as high as it would go. Even allowing for the faulty data from the gauge, that was alarming.

Capt. Eli Beeding, our physiological expert, called for Demi's rectal temperature. There was a pause. "It's one-oh-one point four," McClure reported.

As flight surgeon, I knew he couldn't possibly survive that kind of heat for the rest of the day. Laboratory experiments had indicated that the point of collapse is near when the body temperature starts to go up that high. I told him to sit back and relax and not try to do anything else. "Roger, Colonel," he replied. "I don't think it's bad enough to worry about yet. I don't want to come down. Repeat. I don't want to come down."

I remembered myself at a much lower temperature, still cocky and confident, rating myself high on my efficiency chart. I was the last to know how exhausted I was and how marginal my ability to act intelligently had become because I failed to recognize the effects of fatigue, heat and the awful isolation of space on my judgment.

It was only one o'clock in the afternoon now. The capsule was going to get a lot hotter in the late afternoon. Sunset was six hours away, and it would be a good three hours after that before the capsule started cooling. I decided to abort the flight then and there and get him down. Demi protested, pointing out how much he could get done if he stayed up. But I was adamant. From now on it was simply a question of whether we would recover him dead or alive.

Reluctantly, Demi began the descent. We asked him to valve in repeated short bursts to keep the balloon from falling too rapidly, but by three p.m. he had dropped only a few thousand feet from his peak of 99,700. Beeding asked for another rectal-temperature reading, and Demi reported 104.1; his body temperature was rising steadily at about one degree an hour. Capt. George Ruff, our psychiatrist, was certain he would lose consciousness at 106—and maybe, under these conditions, at even less. We asked him to valve again to speed the descent. Now, apparently beginning to understand the desperate emergency for the first time, Demi complied, responding in a voice so slowed and thickened that it was difficult to understand.

In the capsule, McClure tripped the valve switch, opening two big holes for gas to escape from the apex of the balloon. Hammering at his dimming consciousness was a feeling of urgency. The metal top of his radio transmitter was hot enough to blister a finger. Where was the heat coming from?

He forced himself to think back over each move since the parachute spilled at his feet, until he found the answer—an astonishing accomplishment for a man in his condition. Repacking the chute had made him produce more body heat than the air-regenerating system was designed to take; an excess of sweat had overburdened the potassium-hydroxide absorbent in the system and caused the chemical to heat up like charcoal on an open burner; then the air blower circulated the heat in the capsule. Around and around went the ever-hotter air, boosting itself and him to a temperature more nearly fatal each time.

Through dimming senses, Demi remembered a moment of panic years before when he had got caught in the surf in an overpowering undertow. Flailing against the powerful rip tide had got him nowhere. He relaxed, then started swimming at an angle to the current then resting, and he was soon out of it.

Now he made himself relax under the tight restraint of his shoulder harness to conserve what little energy he had for the critical moments ahead. Even that motion took its toll: His vision flickered with unreal color, as if he were seeing things through the glass walls of an aquarium.

In the old C-47 circling far below the capsule, we anxiously considered the drastic solution of cutting McClure's capsule loose from the balloon. But he might land anywhere from a 10,000-foot mountain peak down to a level spot on the desert. In a parachute landing the capsule would hit at a speed of about twenty miles per hour. If he was unconscious and unable to release the parachute from the capsule, it could billow with the ground wind and drag the capsule. Even if he was not crushed, the caustic chemicals in the air-regeneration system might leak out, drip over his body and burn it.

Time for the five o'clock report. With effort, McClure made his eyes focus on the body-temperature gauge; clumsily, he pressed his foot on the microphone switch. "Rectal . . . now reads . . . one-oh-six point six degrees." Steadily and surely the heat was killing him. At 60,000 feet he had at least two hours to go. With a powerful mental effort, he vowed that he would not give in.

He saw the gun-shaped spot photometer sway against its rack. Must stow it on the floor, *he thought. Reaching out, his fingers grasped the instrument's handle, then trembled and opened; the photometer fell and the tube-shaped lens of the instrument slid neatly between the radio foot switch and the floor. The switch was jammed.*

Unable to raise McClure, we landed the C-47. It might be that our own radios, rather than Demi's, had cut out. But I could still check his heart rate: just over 180, almost three times normal; his respiration was sixty, five times higher than that of a normal, relaxed man. He was still alive, but was he conscious?

All of us strained to sight the shimmering disk of the balloon far above us. Now at 40,000 feet, it was about to enter the tropopause; in the next 10,000 feet it would double its speed downward. Suddenly at 38,000 feet a black object fell away from the now visible capsule, then stopped short under a billowing, small parachute! When most people would have been in a coma or suffering hallucinations, McClure had been able to read his rate of descent, decide that it was too fast and trip a switch to release ballast.

Then, as the sun began to set, the capsule's flashing red beacon light came on.

"He's still alive and thinking!" I called exultantly.

George Ruff climbed into a tracking helicopter. As the doctor most familiar with the effects of tremendous stresses, he would be the best man to have on the scene when the capsule struck.

At 21,000 feet, McClure stirred in his seat. Slowly, deliberately, he shut down the air-regeneration system, closed the valves against caustic chemical leakage in case the capsule crashed, checked the electrical switches: radio, off; air blower, off; emergency batteries, on. Then he thought of something else. "All future flights," he dictated into his tape recorder, "should have some provision for dumping the liquid oxygen overboard before landing. It creates a fire hazard."

He sat back again, exhausted.

At 13,000 feet, he aimed the small panel light directly on the altimeter and directed the beam of a second light on two switches, each covered by a safety guard. Carefully he lifted the guards and eased two fingers over the switches. When the gondola struck the ground, he would pull the switches to release the balloon. If he was out when he hit, the impact would jerk his fingers down over the switches to cut the balloon free.

The altimeter spun on: 12,200 . . . 8,000 . . . 4,700 . . . WHAM! The capsule struck and tipped crazily to one side; McClure's fingers tugged the release switches and the balloon drifted free, leaving the capsule standing upright on the desert sand.

As Ruff rushed from the helicopter to the capsule, its top hemisphere fell away. Demi had pushed it off. Now he stood there, smiling. "We'll have a stretcher in a second," said Ruff soothingly as he helped him down.

"A stretcher?" Demi said. "I've come down almost a hundred thousand feet by myself. I can make the last few feet on my own, thanks." He walked to the helicopter, climbed in and stretched out on his back. His body temperature was 108.5 degrees.

The day after the flight, McClure showed no signs, beyond a slight weakness in arms and legs, of his incredible body temperature. He was as energetic and animated as ever. "But I didn't get to see the stars," he said.

The aborted ascent, Ruff concluded, had become a much more important experiment than if it had gone off routinely. It made abundantly clear an esssential quality that we must look for in any future candidate for space travel. When most pilots would have been out like a light, McClure not only continued to function efficiently but actually found the energy within himself to think creatively, as he had when he recorded his suggestion about dumping liquid oxygen in future flights. How had he been able to carry on under such extreme conditions?

The answer was evident. McClure possessed to a high degree a quality which, until now, we had failed to rate candidates on: psychophysiological stamina, a combination of deep physical reserves plus the all-important emotional determination to use them. Drawing on this quality, he had been able to surmount the stresses of the emergency and carry out the mission, not as planned, but as it had not been planned.

And the source of this stamina? Demi gave us the clue when he discussed his motivation for entering these experiments: "The underlying desire is to do something with my life, to leave the world better because I was here. Not that I expect to do anything earthshaking, but I want at least to accomplish something; and because a man can accomplish most in areas where he is most interested, I prefer to do a job connected with flight and science. The biggest dream, of course, lies in using the basic scientific tools in space to unlock some of the wonderful secrets that are held there."

This is the kind of motivation our astronauts and our nation must have in order to extend the frontiers of human knowledge. The great challenge of our time remains essentially the same as it was when Columbus sailed for the west almost five centuries ago: discovery and an unrelenting search for truth.

The saga of three men
and a girl struck by lightning
on a storm-racked mountain peak

Lightning Strikes
on Bugaboo Spire

BY COLIN FLETCHER

THEY HAD JUST SCALED precipitous Bugaboo Spire, a sharp, 10,400-foot granite peak in British Columbia's Purcell Mountains, when the sudden storm forced them to take shelter in a shallow cave near the summit. As the three men and a young woman tried to eat lunch, sleet and snow drove them back against the wall. Now bolts of lightning began striking the peak barely one hundred feet above them, with deafening thunderclaps following almost instantly.

Silently, that August noon in 1948, they sat contemplating a truth that haunts every experienced mountain climber: A lightning strike is one hazard about which you can do little. If the storm gives

211

enough warning, you can get off peaks and ridges. But once lightning strikes, the rest is luck. Of two people side by side, one may be unharmed, the other killed.

The three younger climbers were uneasy; their leader, forty-one-year-old Rolf Pundt, reassured them with a confidence that he probably did not feel. Then, when fifteen minutes had passed without damage, they began to relax.

Ian Mackinlay, 21, an architecture student at the University of California, sat with his back to the wall of the sloping cave, eating a piece of salami. Beside him sat pretty, eighteen-year-old Ann "Cricket" Strong, a Stanford University freshman. To her left sat Bob Becker, 21, also from the University of California. Rolf Pundt squatted near the mouth of the cave.

Cricket was just lifting a handful of raisins to her mouth when the lightning bolt struck. (Later, neither she nor Ian had any recollection of the flash.) Ian regained consciousness first, probably in seconds. He felt as if he were rolling over and over in midair, though actually he was lying flat on his back looking up at the rough granite of the cave's roof.

He tried to sit up but could not; he was paralyzed from the neck down. Cricket and Bob were beside him, both unconscious. Out in front of the cave, in the full fury of the storm, lay Rolf Pundt, writhing about on the steeply sloping rock. His head was bloody, and his legs jerked in convulsive spasms. Each spasm was carrying him closer to the 2,000-foot precipice.

Ian managed to shout, "Rolf, lie still! Lie still!"

Pundt, clawing at the rock, didn't seem to hear. At the brink of the precipice, a spasm twisted his body once again—and sent him plunging over.

Ian let his head fall back on the rock. Slowly, sensation was returning to his extremities. He managed to sit up, then struggled to his feet. Cricket, stirring now, watched him as he bent over Bob, who was still sitting with his back against the wall, as he had been when the lightning struck. He was mentally confused, and his legs seemed badly burned. With Cricket's help, Ian tried to make him comfortable. Bob mumbled, "The fog's coming in," then lapsed into a coma.

Ian took stock of the situation. Obviously, he and Cricket would never be able to get Bob Becker down off Bugaboo Spire—they would be lucky to make it themselves. Ian's left arm hung limp and useless. Cricket, though seemingly uninjured, was still dazed. Somehow the two of them would have to get help from the base camp of an eighteen-man expedition 4,000 feet below.

To prevent the unconscious Becker from sliding down the sloping floor of the cave, Ian and Cricket roped him securely to a knob of rock. Then they put all the remaining food beside him and began to coil two nylon climbing ropes. "I knew it would have to be a team effort," Ian said afterward. "Neither of us could possibly make it down without the other."

Both sides of Bugaboo Spire dropped straight down about 2,000 feet to a glacier field. The only route to the glacier was down a jagged, knife-edge ridge and across a steep slope of ice. Unhurt, and in fine weather, the two might have reached the camp in three hours. Now the chances were against their reaching it at all.

Ian and Cricket were experienced climbers—they had trained hard on California's highest peaks—and they were in excellent shape. Ian's six-foot-four-inch frame carried a spare 180 pounds of bone and sinew. Cricket was lithe and superbly coordinated; she climbed like a monkey. Now they would need all their skill and experience—and luck as well.

They had their first stroke of luck right away. Fifty feet down the ridge, where one of Bugaboo's terrifying faces fell away to a tiny ledge eighty feet below, then almost 2,000 feet to the glacier, they found a rope sling looped over a point of rock.

The sling showed them that this was the way they had to go: Three members of an expedition climbing Bugaboo the day before had left it there. Cricket threaded one of their two 120-foot climbing ropes through the sling, knotted it to the other rope, then lowered both free ends over the precipice.

Ian went first. He straddled the rope and tried to place it in the rappel position by picking it up from behind, then passing it diagonally across his chest and back over his right shoulder. But his left arm still hung useless. Cricket, realizing for the first time that he was injured, lifted the rope over his shoulder.

By now Ian was gaining some control over the fingers of his left hand. He grasped the rope behind him and leaned back so that it was pulled tightly around his body. He smiled at Cricket, then stepped back over the precipice.

Facing the rock and standing far out from it, he began to let himself down, paying out the rope inch by inch at first. As he gained confidence in his fingers, he moved foot by foot. At last his feet touched the ledge. He planted them firmly and slacked off the rope. Then, laboriously, he worked at the rope until it fell free from his body. He looked up, took a deep breath and shouted to Cricket.

Hearing the cry, Cricket fastened the second rope about her and took the first step backward over the rock face. Soon she was standing beside Ian. Silently, he pointed southward. A black line of storm cloud was racing toward them. From its base, lightning flickered.

New urgency swept through them. Hurriedly coiling their ropes, they started along the ledge. Above them towered the blank rock wall. Below yawned immense space. The ledge grew narrower until, at one point, it was barely a foot wide. Then, quite suddenly, they were out on the knife-edge.

Almost at once the new storm burst upon them. Wind tore at their clothes; sleet stung their faces, pounded their backs. Lightning stabbed down around them, and thunderclaps hammered at their eardrums. Now the whole ridge became a bizarre electrical display; once when Ian spread his right hand, blue flashes crackled out from the fingertips.

But what he noticed most was the odor. "Mainly it was ozone," he said afterward, "sharp and acrid, like smelling salts."

Cricket smelled the ozone, too; but it was the electricity that she recalled most vividly. "There was a slow, inevitable rhythm about it," she says. "After each strike we moved in silence for a while, with only the tearing wind and slashing rain. Then the rocks would begin a shrill humming, each on a slightly different note. The humming grew louder and louder. You could feel a charge building up in your body. Our hair stood on end. The charge increased, and the humming swelled, until everything reached an unbearable climax. Then the lightning would strike again—with a crack like a gigantic rifle shot. The strike broke the tension. For a while we would grope forward in silence. Then the humming would begin again."

Suddenly the ridge dropped away in front of them. With Ian's arm still hanging useless, Cricket fixed the rope. As she followed Ian down it, she felt electric charges humming along the wet nylon. But below, the storm was less violent and, as fast as they dared, they worked their way downward. Finally, the knife-edge blunted, and the route grew easier.

Occasionally a deep weariness overcame Cricket, and she sat down. Ian urged her on. Several times his own coordination failed, and he fell.

They made two more rope descents, slowly and laboriously. Then, on the last, the ropes jammed above them. Ian's heart sank. They were safely down the ridge now, but they would need the rope for the ice work. Again and again they heaved on the dangling ends. Nothing gave. At last they abandoned the rope and strapped on their crampons (steel-spiked climbing irons) and crunched out onto the snow and ice. For the first time, Ian believed they would really make it. Only the lack of rope worried him: the glacier was seamed with crevasses.

They hadn't gone fifty feet before Cricket fell. The first thing she knew, she was flat on her back and hurtling down the glacier. A well-trained mountaineer, she rolled over and dug down with her ice-ax point. The action slowed her momentarily. Then the ax wrenched both mitts from her weakened hands, tore the wrist strap free and spun away.

"Suddenly, rocks and silt and muddy water began thundering down around me," she says. "I found myself thinking in a matter-of-fact way, 'Well, this is the end.' Yet I wasn't thinking about the *bergschrund.*"

To Ian, still standing above, the gaping *bergschrund,* the glacier's topmost crevasse, was a terrifying reality. Blue and cold and deep, it crossed Cricket's path. As she went hurtling down at forty miles per hour, half-hidden in an avalanche of rocks and silt, Ian watched helplessly. He knew that nothing could stop her.

And then, unbelievably, she was beyond the *bergschrund.* Miraculously, she had crossed a partly hidden snowbridge. But she was still falling as fast as ever, wrapping and unwrapping herself around rocks in a peculiarly relaxed way, heading straight for a line of huge boulders. Then she stopped just short of the boulders 400 feet below him—and lay still. Rocks from the last of the avalanche rained around her.

"Get out of there!" Ian yelled frantically.

Dimly, Cricket heard him. Fighting an almost overwhelming weariness, she crawled off to one side of the chute and escaped the crashing rocks. When Ian reached her, he found her sitting up and smiling as if nothing had happened. Her face was covered with blood; but when he mopped it with snow, he found only superficial cuts. He helped her up and gave her his ice ax and spare gloves. Then, arm in arm, they started down the glacier.

As daylight began to fade, they came off the end of the glacier and crossed a final boulder slope. Soon they walked into camp. It was seven hours since the lightning bolt had struck on Bugaboo Spire.

Almost at once, despite the still-raging storm, two climbers in camp left with food, a sleeping bag, and medicines for Bob Becker. The others tended Ian and Cricket. And for the first time they discovered what the lightning had done to them.

The left side of Cricket's long underwear was charred away. Underneath, her left leg had been severely burned. Coins in Ian's pocked had fused. His jacket zipper was welded fast. His jacket had only a few dime-size holes; but his water-soaked sweater and shirt were burned and tattered. When his companions took them off, the front of his cotton T shirt fell away. The back had charred into his flesh. The expedition's first-aid expert said later, "It was as if somebody had been at Ian's back with an arc welder."

For two days the weather drove back each attempt to reach Bob Becker. On the third day, a daring climb took two men up to the cave. Becker was dead. He sat exactly as Ian and Cricket had left him. The food they had left behind had not been touched; it seemed unlikely that Bob had ever regained consciousness. When they cut the ropes holding him, his body slid through their hands and over the precipice. Neither his nor Rolf Pundt's body was ever found.

Down at camp, Cricket's companions discovered that she no longer remembered that Rolf Pundt had been on the climb. By the time she and Ian reached a doctor five days later, however, her memory had returned, and so had the feeling in Ian's arm.

The question of whether they ever fully recovered from their ordeal is easily answered. You have only to meet Ian and Cricket Mackinlay today. Or, better still, watch them skiing expertly down California mountain slopes, perhaps with one of their five children.

As the enormous lion bit down hard,
Tony Fitzjohn felt sure he had only a minute to live.
Then he realized that another lion
was entering the fray

Locked
in the Lion's Jaws

BY ARNOLD SHAPIRO

THE EIGHTEEN-MONTH-OLD lion cub, already bigger than a Great Dane, leaped out of the thick underbrush, put his furry front paws up on Tony Fitzjohn's broad shoulders and rubbed heads joyously with his friend. It was Thursday, June 12, 1975, and in lion fashion Freddie was welcoming Tony back to Kora Camp from a two-day supply trip.

Kora Camp is an isolated huddle of tents protected by a high wire fence in northern Kenya, where naturalist George Adamson rehabilitates lions in a unique conservation project. Orphaned cubs or young zoo lions—lions that would otherwise remain in captivity—grow up, reproduce and live free in an area the Kenya government has designated a national game reserve.

Conditions at the camp are rugged: intense heat and biting tsetse flies, no electricity or plumbing, and a six-hour drive to the nearest settlement. But thirty-one-year-old, English-born Fitzjohn had read *Born Free* as a teenager and been captivated by the story of Joy and George Adamson raising the orphaned lioness, Elsa. Living in Africa and working with Adamson for the past three years had been a dream come true for Tony.

One of his regular jobs was a monthly trip by Land Rover to buy supplies at the tiny outpost of Garissa. This morning, before his return, he had stopped to see the district game warden and thank him

for evicting a gang of armed poachers who had been leaving poison traps for rhinos inside the reserve.

The warden had asked about Freddie, the abandoned lion cub he had found in the bush some seventeen months earlier and turned over to Tony. "That was the first cub I'd known," Tony recalls. He had taken the frail, fluffy animal in his arms, driven him home to Kora and given him the name Freddie.

Later, three more cubs were brought from zoos. But Freddie always held a special place with Tony. Freddie was not only unusually good-natured, he was also the bravest of the cubs, scrappier and more inclined to take liberties with the fully grown wild lions that prowled around the fence.

After two days of rough driving, Tony was exhausted and glad to be back at Kora. He was dressed only in shorts and sandals, his tanned skin glistening with perspiration in the ninety-seven-degree heat. It was time to gather the cubs—the other three had joined Freddie now in welcoming Tony—and take them inside the fence for the night. To calm the frisky Freddie, Tony sat down, his arms clasped around his knees, his back to the underbrush a few yards away, and began talking quietly. One rule in the bush is never to *sit* on the ground outside camp, because of the possibility of an unexpected confrontation with the animals. But Tony felt safe within shouting distance of the tents.

It was 5:10 p.m. The camp, fifty yards away, was quiet. Then, without warning, Tony felt a giant creature pounce on him from behind. He crashed forward to the ground and momentarily lost consciousness. When he came to, it was with the terrifying awareness that his head was locked between the jaws of an enormous lion.

The attacker clamped down hard, then released the headlock. It began a barrage of biting and clawing—sharp bites to the neck and head, deep bites to the shoulders, slashing claws to back and legs.

To Tony this horror was a "series of jerky slides separated by periods of blackout." His glasses were smashed and he saw flashes of the camp he had thought close by; it seemed to be moving farther and farther away, getting smaller and smaller. Which lion was attacking him? One of George's? He only knew that the beast was fully grown and powerful—about 400 pounds and eight feet long.

Tony didn't have a chance. He covered his genitals and closed his eyes. More blows from the mighty paws struck his head; more deep gashes from razor-sharp claws opened his face. Because he was in shock and had suffered a concussion, he felt no pain and heard no sounds. Paralyzed by his injuries and bewilderment, he was experiencing his own death as he would a silent movie.

Now the lion grabbed Tony's neck and bit down. Tony couldn't breathe through his nose and couldn't open his mouth. He remembered that lions often kill by strangulation, holding their victims in a viselike grip until breathing stops. It takes no more than a minute.

During this minute, Tony suddenly realized that there were two lions in the battle. As he forced his bloody eyelids open, he saw Freddie charging toward him. *Oh, no, not Freddie, too!* he thought.

But little Freddie wasn't attacking Tony; he was after the mighty lion, four times his size. Proper behavior calls for young lions to submit to adult lions; to attack an enraged full-grown lion was suicide.

Freddie kept charging, however—snapping and snarling and biting at the flanks of the lion who stood astride Tony's torso. And for an instant it worked. The lion released his grip on Tony's neck and charged after Freddie, who ran for his life. Tony lay in a pool of blood, gasping for air. The attacker could have caught Freddie and torn him apart on the spot. But he stopped his pursuit and ran back to Tony. Again, he clamped down on his neck in the fatal strangulation hold. *God, I'm dying! I can feel it,* Tony thought. In seconds, he lost consciousness again.

But Freddie returned to the fray and bit the surprised beast's rear, then circled with snarls and yelps, bold charges and nips. Freddie withdrew only when the bigger animal swiped at him with his powerful paw. But he could not stop the foe.

Throughout the attack, Tony was a silent victim and the lion a silent killer. The only sounds were Freddie's unrelenting growls and piercing yelps that Tony could not hear.

But Freddie's shrill cries *were* heard by Erigumsa, the compound's cook. At first, he thought two cubs were fighting, but Freddie's distant cries sounded too desperate. The cook ran to the gate—and saw Tony being mauled to death. Erigumsa raced toward the dining tent, seventy-five feet away, where Adamson was having tea.

"Simba ame kamata Tony inje! Anataka kuua yeye!" he cried in Swahili. ("The lion has caught Tony outside! He's trying to kill him!")

George believed the cubs' playfulness had unintentionally got too rough. So he took only a walking stick, bypassing a loaded rifle, when he ran from the tent.

Outside the gate, George saw Tony's neck locked between the jaws of a full-grown lion. There was no time to return for the rifle—he had to act instantly. Without a second thought, he charged the lion, frantically yelling and waving the walking stick.

Now George was vulnerable to attack. But the beast released Tony and retreated to stare at George. The lion prepared to spring, but George kept moving forward, shouting and brandishing the stick.

It worked! The lion hesitated, then slunk off into the bush, splotched with Tony's blood.

The next thing Tony realized, he was stumbling back to camp, supported by George.

"George, I think I'm dying. Whatever you do," Tony pleaded, "don't shoot the lion. My fault . . . caught unaware . . . shouldn't have happened . . ."

The minute he got Tony into his tent, George rushed to the short-wave radio to call the Flying Doctor Service in Nairobi. It was too late—the 135-mile flight would take an hour and a quarter, and regulations firmly prohibited landing on a bush strip after dark, even for a critical emergency.

The nurse assured George that the plane would come first thing in the morning and advised him on first-aid treatment for Tony's many deep wounds. George signed off, staring at the setting sun. Could Tony possibly make it through the long night ahead?

Drifting in and out of consciousness, Tony fought for breath—and life. At dawn, outside camp, George and Erigumsa managed smiles; thirteen hours after his mauling, Tony was still alive.

The first one out of the Flying Doctor aircraft when it touched down was Tony's girl friend, Lindsay Bell, who lived in Nairobi. George had radioed her the night before about Tony's condition. "I was expecting bad wounds, but not all over his head," she recalled later. "He could hardly breathe. The right side of his neck was completely open and his wounds were oozing. It was horrible." During the flight back to Nairobi with Tony, Lindsay broke down and wept. "I knew how much he loved his work," she said. "If he lived, would he ever want to return to the lions?"

Tony spent two hours in surgery when they got him to the hospital. There were three dozen wounds—some so deep and dangerous they couldn't be stitched at that time. His trachea had been squeezed but not broken. Miraculously, the lion's teeth had not severed any nerves, arteries or veins. Tony would be one of the few people ever to survive such an attack by a lion.

The day after the attack, a large lion appeared outside Kora with dried blood on his chest and muzzle. It was a two-and-a-half-year-old wild lion George had known since infancy, a creature so placid that he'd been named Shyman.

Now the cubs wouldn't go near Shyman, and he, uncharacteristically, began growling menacingly at them. George drove outside the compound and positioned the Land Rover between Shyman and the frightened cubs. Then he observed Shyman carefully. His movements were erratic. The once-gentle lion had probably eaten from a poisoned carcass left by the rhino poachers. Since he had attacked once, he could do it again. Their lives and the lives of the animals in the reserve were in jeopardy. After an hour of watching Shyman's behavior, George sadly raised his rifle and put a bullet into the lion's brain.

Such a mauling as Tony had received would make even the bravest soul reevaluate the risks of working in the bush. He had been literally eaten by a lion—the flesh had been chewed off his face and neck—and the scars will be with him always. But Tony remembered that a lion cub he loved had tried to save him.

Two months after the incident, Tony returned to Kora, wondering what kind of greeting, if any, he'd receive after his absence. As he reached the camp, he saw the cubs on top of a large rock. And when they saw him, they rushed toward him, Freddie in the lead, making woofing sounds all the way. Typical lion greetings last less than a minute; this one lasted close to ten—the excited cubs leaping all over Tony.

"I never had any thoughts about not going back," Tony told me when I visited him. "We're creating an animal reserve. People from all over the world can eventually come and see our lions, and the lions can live free and unmolested in nature. I belong here."

He was a stranger in their midst,
but the entire island rallied to his rescue

"We Cannot
Let Him Die!"

BY RONALD SCHILLER

It WAS PAST MIDNIGHT on the Mediterranean islet of San Pietro, a few miles off the southwest coast of Sardinia. Bundled up against the wind, eyes turned skyward, the islanders waited tensely for a rescue helicopter. Lips moved in silent prayer for the stranger none of them knew, a German, who at that moment was about half a mile offshore, fighting for his life in the depths of the wild sea.

Ulrich Neuffer, 35, a mechanic from Limburgerhof, had been camping on the island with his pretty blonde wife, Hannelore, and their eleven-year-old son, Thomas. The Neuffers spoke no Italian, but on the ferry to San Pietro they had met a young German airman, Werner Schatz, who spoke the language fluently. He shared Ulrich's passion for scuba diving and, as luck would have it, was also spending his vacation at the same campground. Before the half-hour crossing was over, Uli and Werner were fast friends. At the campsite, Werner introduced them to other diving enthusiasts—forty-year-old

M. Sgt. Antonio "Tonino" Alagna, of the Italian air force, and forty-three-year-old Daverio Giovannetti. Uli joined the team.

The days that followed, that summer of 1969, were idyllic. Every morning, the four men shoved off for a jutting rock four miles from the beach, where they wriggled into their wet suits and Aqua-lungs and spent hours exploring the fantastic undersea caverns, harpooning edible fish and photographing brilliantly colored ones.

But scuba diving is by no means all carefree fun. The problem is nitrogen, which composes almost eighty percent of the air we breathe. At sea level or above, most of the nitrogen we breathe is eliminated by the body. But as the diver descends and the pressure increases, the nitrogen dissolves, instead, in his blood. This does no harm so long as a diver remains where he is, and no harm when he comes up *if* he ascends slowly enough to permit the dissolved nitrogen to be "bubbled off" in his lungs. But if he shoots to the surface too quickly, the nitrogen forms millions of bubbles throughout his blood vessels. These may coalesce into "air embolisms" that cut off the circulation of oxygen through the body and result in permanent paralysis or agonizing death. Uli was well aware of this phenomenon, known familiarly as *the bends*. But it did not worry him. He knew the safe rate of ascent exactly.

On Friday, August 22, Uli was on a ledge some 110 feet below the surface, harpooning bream. His air gauge showed that his tanks still held almost half their original air pressure, but suddenly he found himself gasping for breath. Uli detached the gauge and knocked it against his weight belt, then screwed it back on the air tank. To his horror, the needle fell to zero—enough air for five minutes at most, instead of the fourteen minutes he needed for decompression while surfacing from that depth! Keeping his cool, Uli rose as slowly as the remaining air allowed.

As he took off his gear in the boat, Uli said nothing about his mishap to Tonino, who was in the boat with him. But later as he sat warming himself in the sun he suddenly experienced severe stomach cramps. Then his chest began to feel as if it were encased in iron bands. Through gestures, he made Tonino understand what had happened. Tonino, who had once watched a coral fisherman die of the bends, knew that the only thing that could save Uli now was to get him back into the water to decompress. Snatching up another

Aqua-lung, he strapped it to Uli's back, then put on his own; without waiting to put on their wet suits the two descended to a sixty-five-foot depth.

The moment he reached deep water—where the nitrogen again dissolved—Uli's pains disappeared. After taking eighteen minutes to surface, the two climbed back in the boat. Other than being chilled to the bone, Uli felt fine. But when they reached the beach, his legs felt stiff and tingled as though they had fallen asleep. This sensation, known as "diver's fleas," is an unmistakable warning of too-rapid decompression. Werner relayed the symptom to Tonino, whose orders were curt: "We're going out again."

This time they took thirty-one minutes to come up, far longer than normally required. Again Uli's symptoms disappeared and again he felt fine, though very tired. But a short time later, back in camp, the prickling numbness returned and grew rapidly worse. Grimly, Uli's companions decided that the only hope was to get their friend to the decompression chamber in Sardinia's capital, Cagliari, about seventy miles away.

Uli's friends helped him to the car—for by now he was almost completely paralyzed from the waist down. "No need to worry," they reassured his frightened wife and son. "We'll have him in Cagliari in three hours and he'll be back diving tomorrow."

They raced to the ferry slip, honking their way to the head of the line, where Tonino ran to the phone to alert the hospital in Cagliari. Moments later he was back with the bad news: The decompression chamber there was out of order; the nearest available unit was in Rome, an impossible 310 miles away.

News spreads unbelievably fast in San Pietro, and a crowd had already gathered. Carlo Biggio, mayor of Carloforte, San Pietro's chief port, and Matteo Malgioglio, commander of the island's six-man police force, had also arrived. A call was put through to the Italian naval base at La Maddalena, on the northern tip of Sardinia. "Put the man back in the water and keep him there until he can be flown to a decompression chamber," the naval surgeon advised. "But, frankly, his chances are slim. Even if you manage to fly him to the mainland for treatment, the low pressure at the higher altitude will quickly finish him off."

The odds against Ulrich Neuffer's survival were long, indeed.

Rocky little San Pietro had no landing field. He could be taken to Cagliari only by helicopter, then by plane to Rome. The Cagliari police had a short-range helicopter that could take care of the first part of the trip. But for the 240-mile flight to Rome another plane was needed, and snarls of red tape would have to be unraveled before one could be found.

However, Carlo Biggio is a very stubborn man. In words that became a rallying cry and quickly spread throughout the island, he declared: "The German is our guest. We cannot let him die!" From seven that evening until past midnight, he and police commander Malgioglio kept the telephone wires busy—to the prefect of Cagliari, to the Canadian, German and Italian commandants of the NATO air base on Sardinia, to the Italian air force, to police headquarters in Rome—forty calls in all.

In the meantime, Uli's friends weren't sure he could take much more underwater punishment. But he, realizing the seriousness of his case, readily agreed to dive for the fourth time that day. A thirty-knot wind whipped the bay to a frenzy. The water was cold below the surface, with currents so strong that Uli had to cling to the anchor rope to keep from being swept away. But he was never alone—Tonino, Werner and others carrying waterproof flashlights descended in relays to signal encouragement, pat his back and massage his freezing limbs.

Throughout the long ordeal, Uli's wife, Hannelore, and son, Thomas, kept a vigil on shore. At one point, the telephone operator from a waterfront hotel ran to the beach and announced that a helicopter was about to land there. Fifteen minutes later the girl came back to tell them it was a false alarm. Four more times the arrival of the helicopter was announced, then retracted.

It was past midnight when the last snarl of red tape was finally unraveled, and Mayor Biggio relayed the news that the police helicopter, manned by air force pilots and a doctor, was on its way.

Signal rockets were fired to recall the divers' boat. They came in the nick of time, for Uli, at the limit of his endurance after four and a half hours underwater, felt himself slipping into unconsciousness. The first things he saw as he surfaced were the flares in the sky. On the shore, Hannelore clutched Thomas in her arms and, for the first time that day, wept.

In Carloforte the problem was where the helicopter was going to land at night, particularly with the strong wind. The only flat area large enough was the football field, but the pilot could never find it in the dark. "Round up some cars and send them to light up the field with their headlights," the mayor instructed an aide. Within minutes, practically every car on the island was climbing the hill to the field, which was soon ablaze with light.

The helicopter and the divers arrived at the football field almost simultaneously. Uli, whose paralysis had returned almost as soon as he was out of the water, was put on a stretcher in the helicopter. On doctor's orders, the pilot flew as low as possible despite the winds that bounced the flimsy craft up and down like a yo-yo.

At the Cagliari airport Uli was transferred to a waiting air force plane that flew to Rome at just 650 feet. By two-thirty in the morning—eighteen hours after he had first set out in the boat with Tonino—he was at last under oxygen in the decompression chamber of the Polyclinic Hospital in Rome, very sick but safe at last.

The encouraging news set off a wild celebration in the camp at San Pietro the next day. Daverio organized a feast; music blared and a lamb was roasted on a spit. The citizens of San Pietro clearly considered the Neuffers one of them, their troubles to be shared by all.

When I met Uli in Limburgerhof six months later, he was almost fully recovered. He had spent only six days in the Rome hospital and was miraculously back at work within three weeks of his return home. His legs still tingled and turned numb on cold days, and he could not run as fast as he used to, but he was improving steadily. The doctors at the University of Heidelberg, where he underwent therapy, attributed his remarkable recovery partly to the decompression dives Tonino and his friends forced on him, and partly to Uli's own courage and physical stamina.

But Uli has an additional explanation: "I would have quit a dozen times during those hours in the water, were it not for the knowledge that so many people who didn't know me were risking their own lives to save mine. I couldn't disappoint them."

None but I knew the secret
as we passed through the valley of the shadow.
I had to act—not to save *my* life, for that was doomed—
but to save the lives of the others

The Night
My Number Came Up

BY AIR MARSHAL SIR VICTOR GODDARD
Royal New Zealand Air Force

I HAD BEEN A PROFESSIONAL aviator since 1915, and though I had experienced disaster by air, I was not given to premonitions of mishap. Yet as we were about to take off from Shanghai for Tokyo I was depressed.

After two years in command of the Royal New Zealand Air Force in the Pacific and two more administering British air forces in Burma and Malaya I was on my way home via Tokyo to say farewell to General MacArthur and other Americans with whom I had worked during the war. Admiral Mountbatten had loaned me his own plane, the *Sister Ann,* and her crew, both the embodiment of reliability.

My depression was due to a foreboding that I was about to carry into mortal danger all who flew with me and the knowledge that I could not, for want of justification, bid my passengers remain behind. As an air marshal, how could I possibly say that I'd been warned supernaturally?

It had happened at a party the previous evening in Shanghai. I was talking with my old friend Brig. Gen. John McConnell, USAF, when I heard two Englishmen behind me begin a conversation that caught my attention at once:

"Wasn't this party to welcome Air Marshal Goddard?"

"It certainly was. Why?"

"He's dead! Died last night in a crash."

The man spoke with a disconcerting tone of authority. I turned around. The man, a British naval commander, glanced quickly at my face and started as though I had hit him.

"My God!" he exclaimed with a gasp. "I'm terribly sorry! I mean I'm terribly glad—that is—how extraordinary! I do apologize! You see, I had a dream last night. It seemed so true."

I smiled. "I'm not dead yet, Commander. What did you dream? Where did it happen?"

"On a rocky, shingly shore, in the evening, in a snowstorm. It was in China or Japan. You'd been over the mountains in a cloud. Up a long time . . . I watched it all happen."

"What sort of plane was I in?"

"An ordinary sort of transport. Possibly a Dakota." (The *Sister Ann* was a Dakota.)

"What about the crew in your dream—all killed too?"

"It was a shocking awful crash," he replied.

I was about to leave the commander when I decided to test him further on facts. What he had said about geography and terrain seemed to fit too well.

"Did your dream show you what sort of people I was traveling with?"

"Yes," he said, a little slowly. "An ordinary service crew and three civilians. Two men and a woman. All English."

"Thanks very much. That's quite a relief. I'm carrying no one but a service crew. No civilians. By the way, I don't know your name."

"Oh, I'm Dewing, from the *Crécy*. I'm in harbor here."

We chatted awhile and moved apart. I never saw him again.

A few minutes later Seymour Berry of the London *Daily Telegraph* drifted up alongside me and said, "I'm anxious to get home and would like to cadge a lift to Tokyo with you. Your pilot said it will be okay by him. Do you mind?"

With a feeling of shock, I replied, "Not at all. Plenty of room. I'm leaving at half past six in the morning." But in my heart I feared this acceptance of Berry as a passenger.

That same evening, George Alwyne Ogden, the British consul general, gave a dinner party for me. Ogden was questioning me about my journey when his Chinese butler handed him a radio message. Ogden passed it to me, saying, "I am sorry to impose upon you, but I wonder if you can possibly take me with you tomorrow?"

How could I refuse? The message was from the Foreign Office; it was imperative that the consul general visit the British high commissioner in Tokyo as soon as possible.

I reflected: *That makes two civilians. Englishmen. But there's no woman. Anyway, what bosh, worrying about a stranger's nightmare.*

Before the meal was over, the butler again presented an envelope. Another radio message. Ogden said, "You'd better read it. It's from Gardiner, our representative in Tokyo."

". . . I have no reliable conference stenographer," I read. "Most grateful if you could loan one for a few weeks."

"Are you going to be able to help me on this too?" asked Ogden.

"I guess I can take him," I replied reluctantly. "That is, if he's a man!"

"Does that make a difficulty? He's bound to be a girl, I'm afraid."

Three civilians, one of them a woman.

That was a cheerless dawn at the Shanghai Airport. Consul General Ogden had brought Dorita Breakspear, a tall, fair girl about twenty, who told me she had never flown before. "But I expect I shall survive," she said. Her trusting remark stabbed me, and I shivered in the chill breeze off the runways.

Squadron leader Don Campbell, our captain, didn't look particularly cheerful.

"Morning, Campbell. Got a good weather forecast?"

"Not too bad, sir. About a hundred miles from Tokyo there may be a good deal of high cumulus—something like a front, perhaps. Should be about six hours' flight."

With that we went aboard, and shortly afterward, the *Sister Ann* soared away over the sprawling city, set on her course for Tokyo or—perish the thought! Dewing had said this thing would be in the evening in a snowstorm. We should be in Tokyo soon after lunch. I was dog-tired. After a while I fell asleep.

I could not have slept long when the bumpiness of cloud flying awakened me. I was breathing rather fast. We must be high. The starboard wing was searing through the mist; gray fragments seemed to be breaking away from the leading edge and flying away aft. Ice was beginning to form on the wings!

Dorita and Seymour were asleep. Consul General Ogden seemed distressed with his breathing: said he had a rotten cold in the head. Soon the light grew brighter. We were soaring blithely in blinding sunlight. But there, clinging to the shining metal of the great, flexing wings, I could see a thin layer of ice.

Campbell came aft and spoke to me in a low voice. "We shall have to keep above it. If we go through we shall get heavily iced again."

"Yes," I said. "I noticed that. We must be pretty high now."

"Seventeen thousand."

"No oxygen aboard?"

"No."

After a while Campbell came aft again. "We shall have to have another shot at going through it, sir. The cloud tops are still higher, and we are now at about eighteen thousand. I expect it will be a bit bumpy."

In we went—into that swirling, darkening mist—and down.

Campbell throttled back a bit. Then I heard the *Crack! Thud!* of broken ice against the cabin—ice chunks flung off the propeller blades. It grew darker. My watch said 11:20. That would be only 12:20 Tokyo time. And that wasn't evening! But how long before the ice would cease to snap away and, instead, suddenly build up a great solid shroud?

But there was no snow. Surely Dewing had said there would be snow?

Once again those enveloping gray mists were suddenly flung aside. As if hurtling over a chasm, the *Sister Ann* flashed into the dazzling blue among the towering, billowing cloud tops.

The pressure on our ears and our quickened breathing told us we had climbed again to heights where oxygen is rare. The consul general and Dorita were ill and faint from lack of oxygen. They could hardly carry on much longer at that height.

Campbell came aft again, a little gray in the face from fatigue and anxiety, but carrying a smile and an air of quiet confidence.

"Aren't we above the maximum ceiling for a Dakota?" I asked. "Couldn't we let down a bit steeper now to get to warmer layers? We must be getting light in fuel by now. That should lower the stalling speed if the ice keeps off. But you do it your own way,

Campbell. I guess we shall come through all right." *Unless,* I thought to myself, *we hit that rocky seashore and shingle.*

Campbell smiled and said he would give it a go.

We started down. Once more began that plunging, jolting, heaving that was to continue unabated for yet another four long hours. We bumped our way down, down, into the wet, cold base of those towering clouds. How dark it grew! Then I heard that vicious *crack-crack* on the metal flanks of the *Sister Ann.* Ice. Ice on the props again.

Then suddenly we were out of it—but nearly into something else! Those yellow lumps heaving there below were waves of the sea.

And now it's snowing hard! What's the time? Three-thirty.

Sea and snow. That was what Dewing had said it would be. Below us we saw the blackness of a snow-flecked cliff, with broken waves lashing angrily at its feet.

The turbulence was the worst in my experience. We followed the shore and after a while came over a bay. There, beside a rocky, shingly shore, lay a snow-covered fishing village. The beach was less than 300 yards of sloping shingle interspersed with rocks and bounded at each end by black crags. No fit place to land.

We swung out again to follow cliffs and breakers in a shallow, horizontal chasm of driven gray snow between the clouds and the surging sea. My watch, now at Tokyo time, said five past four. At that latitude it would be dark soon after five on a day like this.

Then we lost the cliff. Fearing to butt into another headland, Campbell held away for a while, then edged in again.

So it went. We lost the cliff. Found it again. Never a break. Never even a stretch of shore on which to attempt a crash landing.

It was getting gloomier all round us. If there was a sun anywhere, it must have set by now. A quarter to five. Cliffs, clouds, sea, snow, foam on the rocks, noise, turmoil, nausea, thickness in the head, pain in the ears, fatigue.

Suddenly the cliff ended again. Visibility improved a bit. *Here's a bay. A village in snow by the shore. Shingle, rocks. The village and bay we saw an hour or more ago. We must have flown all the way around an island and got back again.*

I got up and made my way forward to the compartment.

"Let me see your map," I said to our navigator, Flt. Lt. N. Anderson.

About forty miles off the mainland there was an island something like the shape of a hand pointing. Sado, it was called.

"That's it," I said. "And that village must be Takachi."

Anderson looked, nodded. Then he said, "The nearest airfield is Tokyo, the other side of the mainland. That's nearly two hundred miles over the mountains and clouds in the dark. Not too good."

"And no gas," I replied.

That rocky, desolate shingle shore beside the breakers down there was our only possible destination. Just as Dewing had said. In snow and storm, in the evening.

I turned to Campbell. He looked at me, smiling and determined as he said, "Bad show, sir, I'm afraid. If you agree, we must land on this little beach. No question of jumping for it—clouds too low and too much wind."

"Yes."

"Would you land wheels up or down?"

"I think you'd slide faster and farther," I said, "if you kept your wheels up and landed on your belly. But if you keep them down and don't crash the big rocks, we shall certainly turn over. What about keeping your wheels down ready to retract, and as we begin to slow up retract as quickly as you can?"

Campbell nodded. He was sweating.

I went aft to do what I could to protect the bodies of my crew and my companions. Everyone but the skipper should come into the cabin to keep the tail down. We'd be safer there and could get out of the plane faster. All must fix themselves so that they could not be thrown and be swathed in blankets, covered with mattresses.

And so I saw to their dressing up for this queer play with death. I, at any rate, was sure I was about to die.

When we were ready two crewmen staggered aft to open the door so we wouldn't be stuck inside. Off it came with a sudden roar as the full blast of snow-filled air burst in. There was a crash of china, cutlery and trays in the pantry.

The picture of what was going to happen in the next few minutes had been in my mind for the past twenty-four hours. Now I could hear, above the roar of air, the hiss-squeeze of the wheels going down. Then down went the flaps, and the *Sister Ann* banked close to the northern cliff, nose down for landing. The engine roar subsided.

I looked round at Ogden. He smiled in a pain-racked way. I looked at Dorita. Her eyes were closed. I couldn't see Berry's face.

Banked over as we were, I could see the curving beach with its jagged rocks and a steeple of rocks at the end. Down we went, straightening out and flattening out at the same moment. Then the engine noise died out. High black rocks sped by to port.

Now we are in for it.

A rippling, jingling sound began. Wheels ripping swiftly over shingle. It grew harsher. The deceleration began.

Let the wheels back, I prayed. And Campbell had. The *Sister Ann* was flopping down.

Bang . . . Bang! Cr-runch . . . *Stop.*

A huge shape hurtled by me, striking the back of my head. It was Ogden, seat and all.

Motion ceased. The *Sister Ann* had stopped dead.

There was a stillness. Then the splashing flop and hiss of breakers on the shingle . . . a quiet whistle of wind.

"My chair came off!" cried Ogden, almost apologetically.

Unstrapping, we began to laugh. I went forward to Campbell as he was coming aft. We met in the aisle and shook hands.

That night we sheltered in the little inn of Takachi. As I lay on the matted floor, I wondered whether Commander Dewing really had "seen" me, personally, in a state of total inanimation—dead. I must write to Dewing, I decided, before he forgets what he did dream.

Months later I got a reply:

I am horrified to hear about your crash. I remember our meeting and I vaguely remember that dream. No, I can't say that I actually saw you dead, but I certainly thought the crash was a killer. Glad it wasn't.

For my next crash I want no prior information. Quite spoils the enjoyment of flying.

A black night,
a lonely highway,
a patch of ice—
and suddenly the car
overturned and plunged
the young family into a
freezing stream

Terror at Shoshone Creek

BY JOSEPH P. BLANK

HER LUNGS SEEMED about to explode for want of air as she desperately squirmed through the foot-wide opening in the window of the overturned car. Then she was out and standing in neck-deep water. It was ten degrees below zero and a forty-mile-an-hour wind lashed at her face. Half of the car's wheels, and a few inches of its chassis, were visible. And that was all.

As she gulped air she heard the screams of her children still trapped in the car, but there was no sound from Ben, her husband. *I must go back down and show them how to get out through the window,* she thought.

She dived and groped for the driver's window through which she had escaped. It was closed! She dived again and again, frantically feeling for the open window. It didn't occur to her that the current had carried her a few feet downstream; that she was scratching around the rear window rather than the driver's window.

Suddenly she realized that the screaming had stopped. Numbed, bewildered, she stood in the bone-chilling water, listening to the silence and feeling her face stiffen from the cold. She was alone. *God, I don't want to be out here alone. I want to be with my family. But something has to be done. Someone has to know what happened.*

She waded around the car, crawled up a ten-foot bank and ran into a barbed-wire fence. She wriggled under it, then realized that she was on the wrong bank. Returning through the fence she started down the bank, then twisted her ankle and fell.

As she pulled herself to a sitting position, she noticed that the car's flasher signals were still blinking under the black water. *All gone. My four beautiful children. And Ben. Ben is dead, too. What point is there in going on living?*

It had been a lovely Thanksgiving for the Roberts family. Ben, 31, dark-haired, slim and intense, had been working hard as a salesman for the General Electric Supply Company, and his firm owed him vacation time. He had not had much opportunity to enjoy his children—Kristin, 8; Karol, 7; Jack, 5; Sally, 22 months—and he yearned to get away with his family.

Another thought was also on his mind when he walked into his home in Twin Falls, Idaho, on the evening of Tuesday, November 21, 1972. Several years earlier, when the couple lived in San Diego, they had lost an infant son. "I'd like to visit the grave," he told his wife, Phyllis, a pretty, twenty-nine-year-old blonde. "The children have a school holiday. Let's drive down."

The family visited the grave, then spent four satisfying days calling on friends, returning to old picnic spots and playing in the surf. On Sunday morning they began the long drive home. At 9:45 that night, Ben turned the wheel over to his wife, saying, "Wake me up when we reach Jackpot. I'll drive home from there." Jackpot, a small gambling-casino town that straddled Highway 93 on the Idaho-Nevada border, was an hour's drive from Twin Falls. Then Ben fell asleep with Sally snuggled against his side. The other three children slept on the rear seat.

Two miles south of Jackpot, Phyllis knew she was in trouble as the car crossed the tiny bridge over Shoshone Creek. The car had hit "black" ice, a glass-smooth, difficult-to-detect coating on the road, and it had swerved into an uncontrollable skid.

Ben awoke as the car slewed like a wet bar of soap from one side of the two-lane road to the other. He grabbed the wheel. The car shot off the road toward the creek that ran parallel to the road. Ben yelled, "We're going to crash!" He bent over to shield Sally. Phyllis thought, *Look what I'm getting the children into.*

The car rammed down the bank, struck a rock, flipped over and landed on its roof in the middle of the thirty-foot-wide creek. Phyllis suddenly found herself on her hands and knees. Water was pouring in and filling the interior, and the children were screaming. No sound came from Ben. She frantically jerked the door handle, but it wouldn't budge. "Ben," she called, "we've got to get out of here!"

The water was rising. The children continued to scream. Again she pulled at the door handle. *This is not the way it must end.* She took one last gulp of air and attacked the window handle. She opened the window far enough to squeeze through. Then she pushed herself upright in the water and gasped for the frigid air.

Knocked out briefly by the impact of the car hitting the rock, Ben dimly heard Phyllis yell. He was swallowing water and realized that he was drowning. *I am going to die. My family must be dying. It's over. Why?* He quit and accepted death.

Then he heard a child scream. His children needed help; he had to do something. Holding Sally under one arm, he scrambled to the backseat. Suddenly his mouth was out of water. He coughed and inhaled air. Hands grabbed at his face and pulled at his hair. It was pitch-black. Sally was screaming in his ear. For a moment he could only think, *I can breathe. We're alive.* Somehow, water had not reached this one corner. Then it hit him: *Phyllis isn't here.*

"Kristin," he said, "give me your hands. Now take Sally. Keep her head above the water. I'm going to see what I can do to get us out."

Jack moaned. "I can't stand up, Dad. I'm too cold. I want to sit down."

"You can't sit down, Jack. You'll drown. Karol, keep your hands on Jack. Don't let him sit down."

He lowered himself into the water and groped toward the front of the car. His hands felt something soft and inert between the steering column and the brake pedal. He pulled, but it wouldn't come free. *It's Phyllis. She's dead.* He felt his heart breaking. (What he thought was Phyllis' body was actually a large pillow.) *I've got to leave her. I've got to take care of the children.*

Back in the rear, Ben took several breaths, then dipped into the water, felt around and pulled out the lock bolt on the rear door. He turned the handle and pushed against the door with his shoulders. It yielded.

He grabbed the door frame and propelled himself to the surface. On the bank he saw Phyllis's figure. *It can't be. Her body is in the car.*

Phyllis saw him at the same moment. "Ben!" she screamed. "Ben! The kids! Where are the kids?"

"They're all right. Come and help me."

"I can't stand."

He dropped into the water, reached into the car, grabbed Sally, waded to the bank and handed the baby to his wife. He did the same with Kristin, Karol and Jack. Phyllis gathered the children behind a clump of sagebrush. They were crying in pain from the terrible cold, and their clothing was growing stiff. Phyllis knew that it would take only a short time before frostbite attacked their hands and feet.

"Keep moving," she directed. "Clap your hands. Stamp your feet. Jack, I don't hear you clapping. All of you, move!"

"I can't, Mommy!" Kristin yelled in anguish. "We're going to freeze to death!"

"No, we're not," her mother answered. "God got us out of that car. He's not going to let us die now."

As soon as the children were clustered around Phyllis, Ben half-swam, half-waded across the creek and climbed the bank to the road. He was shoeless, shivering uncontrollably and sick from swallowing water. He stared north and south for a sign of auto headlights. Nothing.

Pacing back and forth, his clothing frozen stiff, he tried to think. Should he wait for a car? How long? Should he jog to Jackpot for help? How long would it take? Could he make it?

Then, far to the south, he saw a car's headlights. "A car is coming!" he shouted to his family. Standing in the middle of the road, his heart pounding, shaking from the cold, Ben watched the headlights approach. When the car was about a hundred feet from the bridge he began jumping and screaming and waving his arms. The car swept past.

Dumbly, Ben watched the red taillights recede. He couldn't stop the tears of despair. Then the lights seemed to halt and vanish. In their place, headlights appeared, moving toward him. "They're coming back!" he shrieked.

The car, a Volkswagen station wagon, was driven by Leonard Braden, who was accompanied by his wife, Gail. They were both schoolteachers in Pocatello, Idaho, and were returning home after a family visit in California. Just as Braden felt his tires lose traction on the bridge, he had seen a strange figure, with his clothes gleaming wetly and hair hanging like icicles around his head.

Concerned with the slippery road, he let the car coast until the patch of ice ended. For a few moments he wondered whether he should ignore the figure on the road, or check to see if something was wrong. He awoke his wife. "I think we just passed a man in trouble," he told her. "We're going back."

He returned to the man, rolled down his window and looked out inquiringly. Icicles *were* hanging from the man's head. He was crying and he appeared to be drunk. His words were incoherent. Braden finally made out "wife" and "kids." Then he saw the overturned car in the water. "Is anybody in the car?" he asked.

Ben shook his head. Then he scrambled down the bank, rocks cutting his feet, followed by Braden. Ben forded the creek three times, carrying back a child on each trip. Braden, on the bank, handed the hysterical children to his wife, who put them in the rear of the station wagon and covered them with sleeping bags and coats. Jack's frozen trousers crackled as she carried him.

Ben now had to make the last crossing for his wife, who had the baby in her arms. He stepped into the creek, stumbled and sank into the water. *I can't make it.* In contrast to the arctic air, the water felt warm and comforting.

Phyllis saw what was happening. Ignoring her painful ankle, she waded across the creek with Sally. Braden stepped into the water to meet her and took the baby. Phyllis then went back, grabbed her husband's arms and yelled, "Ben!" He struggled to his feet and clawed up the bank behind her.

In the three-minute drive to Jackpot no sound came from anyone except Ben, who was violently sick to his stomach. *Thank God I stopped,* thought Braden.

He pulled into a motel adjoining a casino. Casino employees and customers scrambled to get the family into motel rooms, turned up the heat and ran baths of hot water for the children. Fresh, dry clothing suddenly appeared, and eventually a county ambulance took the family to a Twin Falls hospital where their own physician examined them. None required medical attention except Phyllis, whose ankle was taped.

By 4:30 a.m., the children were asleep at home. Ben and Phyllis sat sipping hot coffee. They looked at each other, trying to absorb what had happened—and what had not.

"I thought you were all gone," Phyllis said.

"I thought I had lost you," Ben answered. His shoulders shook as he sobbed in gratitude.

A few hours later the family was up and bustling around the house. Kristin and Karol insisted on going to school, and Jack begged to be taken to kindergarten. Although Ben was happily astonished by their recuperative powers, he wanted them to stay home so he could keep looking at them. But they had their way. As Phyllis hobbled around the house, she couldn't stop smiling. Sally trailed her, shouting, "Mommy, c'ap you' hands!"

Hours earlier the children had clapped their hands to forestall frostbite. Phyllis now clapped her hands for another reason. She had learned of the uncertainty of life. Her family had been taken from her, then returned. She knew that this day was a rare gift.

At a small Alabama church
one spring Sunday, the parishioners learned
an enduring lesson about themselves
and the grace of God

The Tornado
and the Sermon

BY ALLEN RANKIN

AT SUNDOWN ON A MAY evening in 1972, people in the little lumber town of Brent, Alabama (population 2,500), listened with only half an ear to the tornado warnings being broadcast for neighboring parts of the state. For although more than 900 tornadoes career across the United States every year, few Americans ever see one of these most sudden and terrible of storms, and even fewer suspect that they will ever be hit by one. Tornadoes happen to somebody else. And so, though the people of Brent kept an uneasy eye on the brooding, oppressively still dusk that day, they continued about their normal Sunday evening activities.

At the Brent Baptist Church, a red-brick complex in the heart of town, about 150 men, women and children were gathering. Tonight, Arthur Walker, acting pastor for the past two months, was to deliver his final sermon before returning to Birmingham's Samford University, where he was a professor of religion and a vice-president.

In honor of the seniors in the congregation graduating from high school, the scholarly, forty-seven-year-old Walker had chosen the topic "Be Thou an Example," based on the text from Paul's exhortation to the young Timothy: "Let no man despise thy youth; but be thou an example of the believers . . . in charity, in spirit, in faith, in purity."

At seven-thirty, ten minutes before the service was to begin, Walker stepped outside his study for a breath of air. There he found a group of Youth Choir members exclaiming over the extreme blackness of the sky to the southwest. He had no more than joined them when an ominous, growing rumble set it. It soon sounded, as someone later said, "like a hundred freight trains." It was the first hint of the tornado that, a minute or so later, would topple the church, demolish ninety-five percent of Brent's downtown sector, destroy 127 of its 700 houses, damage all the rest and, in sum, inflict what National Weather Service officials later were to describe as possibly the most concentrated property damage in the history of Alabama.

It was also the moment in which people who had always thought of themselves as quite ordinary began to respond with a quick and instinctive rightness of action—and, in most cases, with a selflessness and valor—that later, upon reflection, astonished them.

Rushing into the sanctuary, Walker calmly announced to the fifty older persons already seated, "There's an awful roaring approaching. Let's move immediately to the basement."

Outside, Jerry Pow, a twenty-three-year-old service-station manager who was also chief of Brent's volunteer fire department, began herding dozens of young people into the basement of the education building at the rear of the church. "Open the windows!" he shouted, remembering that the airless vacuum in the center of a tornado often causes closed buildings (containing heavier air) to explode. He then sprinted to the front of the church where, spotting three bewildered small children, he yelled to the two adults closest to them,

"Get them inside!" The grownups scooped up the little ones and carried them into the church.

As the tornado approached, Walker, with a strength he had not known he possessed, held the church's rear door open against the rising wind, enabling many people to enter who otherwise would have been shut out. Moreover, when the lights went out, the open door illuminated the way to the basement for the adults who had been in the sanctuary and for those who had been meeting on the second floor of the education building.

Then, with a blackness like night and a roar like a continuous thunderclap, the great storm struck, tearing the door from Walker's hands, banging it shut and plunging the church into total darkness. Not everyone had reached the basement. Elderly Andrew Mitchell, nearly blind, took a wrong turn when he became separated from his wife and got lost in the sanctuary. On the second floor of the education building, middle-aged Mary Krout and her good friend Fay Dowdle held back to keep from crowding those ahead of them and were caught at the head of the stairway. John Oden, a sixty-one-year-old retiree, had time only to throw himself down in the sanctuary between two pews when the church began to disintegrate.

Maness Cottingham, a fifty-one-year-old electrician, who had snatched up a small boy in the churchyard, had run only a few feet up the church aisle when he heard a booming like cannon shots. Looking up, he saw the rear and side walls of the church crumbling. Shoving the boy under a pew, he dropped protectively on top of him. John Meigs, Jr., 19, who had grabbed up two small girls, did the same for them. From under the pew, Meigs didn't see the roof fly off; nor, in the incredible din, did he hear the walls come crashing down.

Jerry Pow made it inside only as far as the front vestibule. There he felt a knifelike pain in his ears (from the decompression) and a mighty lifting that seemed about to haul him out of his shoes. He was still there, pressed against a wall, when the havoc subsided as suddenly as it had begun. It had lasted, Pow figured, about half a minute. As the air cleared, he saw with numb shock that only the front wall of the church and the steeple under which he had taken refuge were still standing. Behind him the once-handsome sanctuary lay in roofless, gutted rubble. In the surrounding area, trees, buildings and homes had either vanished entirely or been blasted into unrecognizable shapes. *About a minute,* Pow thought dazedly, *and the old town's gone!* Then: *My God! Hundreds of people must be hurt or dead!*

At the rear of the church, Meigs and Cottingham crawled from beneath the pews where they had leaped. They pulled forth, unscratched, the three children they had saved. Gratefully, Meigs looked up and saw the steel-reinforced balcony that had kept the falling roof from burying them all.

Nearby, John Oden staggered to his feet. When tons of brick and stone had thundered down toward him, the debris had struck the two pews he had thrown himself between, folded them together and formed a sheltering wooden tent above him. Although he had suffered smashed ribs and a broken collarbone, he was amazed just to be alive. Mary Krout, though buried to the waist in concrete blocks, was only slightly hurt. Fay Dowdle, however, was covered with blocks and bleeding from a critically mangled leg. And Andrew Mitchell lay by the organ, fatally crushed beneath a fallen wall.

All over Brent, which stretched for more than a mile along State Highway 25, others caught in the path of the grinding, funnel-shaped cloud were now beginning to stir from similar ruins. A cold torrential rain slashed down, bringing premature night. Children cried out for missing parents, and parents shouted for missing children. Except for a few glimmering flashlights, there was no light. All communications had been severed; downed telephone and power lines lay, with their snapped poles, in hopeless and potentially deadly snarls. Virtually all cars and trucks were battered out of commission or hemmed in by debris.

In the church basement, the more than one hundred people there began to get up—all except Pauline Hunt. A sweet-faced woman in her fifties, she had felt a slight *ping* in the back of one leg as windows exploded and glass flew. Now, in the semidarkness, she felt blood spreading around her, and discovered that the calf of her leg was dangling from the bone. She slipped off a stocking and twisted it into a tourniquet above her knee. The blood still spurted, and she realized that unless medical help came quickly she wouldn't live very long.

Soon she heard the voice of Linda Hammitt, the pretty R.N. who was director of nursing for the Bibb County Hospital. Linda hadn't been at evening church services for two months; she had been caring for her new baby. But here she was now, inspecting the tourniquet and saying gently, "That won't do. Let's try this." And she applied pressure on the artery above the wound. Realizing that several other people were in critical condition, she said to some of the men, "We've *got* to get these people to a hospital. Please find a way."

Several men who had run to the church after the storm struck decided that the quickest way to clear the roads to surrounding hospitals would be to commandeer some of the heavy equipment at the highway shop and the lumberyard. Twenty-two-year-old Phil Cottingham, an automobile salesman, spotted a forklift. He knew nothing about forklifts, and had never dreamed of trying to operate one—especially at night in a blinding rain. His uneasiness grew as he noted that the lift was wrapped in a tangle of downed power lines that might well be "hot." *This may kill me,* he thought, *but I've got to take the chance.*

He mounted the contraption. No shock—emergency circuit breakers had cut off the juice in the lines. After fumbling with some levers, he found he could make it go. In the meantime, district road commissioner Bob Elam had located a front-end loader, and a third man (unidentified) had found another machine. Together, the three vehicles soon cleared a path through the trees, power poles, demolished houses and piles of brick and debris that blocked a 600-yard stretch of highway near the church. Minutes later, Phil Cottingham and his brother Steve, whose cars had survived intact, were speeding the injured to the hospital at Marion, twenty-seven miles away. For Mrs. Hunt and Mrs. Dowdle their arrival was none too soon. They had hardly any pulses at all and were probably saved by the quickly administered blood transfusions.

Local power- and telephone-company men set to work almost immediately, and by midnight, National Guard units, the Salvation Army and civilian-rescue groups began to arrive from neighboring towns. Floodlights powered by portable generators lit up the ruins. Rescuers soon pulled from the wreckage in various parts of town five dead or dying persons and about fifty injured, some seriously. But before long it became clear that the hundreds of bodies the searchers had expected to find after such a disaster simply were not there! Instead, most of the people who emerged from the ruins were unhurt.

They had been spared, they told each other incredulously, by fantastic luck and the grace of God. What would have happened, those in the church wondered, if the storm had come five minutes later, when all 150 people would have been in the sanctuary listening to the sermon?

As more and more families were reunited, a mood of blessed thanksgiving enveloped the shattered town. People who had lost practically everything they owned stood in the wreckage and wept for joy. Many neighbors who had hardly spoken for years hugged each other on sight. Those still lucky enough to have houses with roofs threw open their doors to less fortunate relatives and friends. As the night wore on, others found their way to improvised dormitories being set up in adjoining Centreville.

About midnight, Arthur Walker went to the home of a church member to change into dry clothes. He was drenched and blood-spattered from his efforts to help the injured. In an inside pocket he carried an envelope given to him by Dot Mitchell, the church training director, minutes after the tornado had struck. In tears she had thrust it at him, saying, "I wish we could have given you a better sendoff. We intended to give you a surprise gift. Here it is!" The envelope contained a check.

In dry clothing, Walker walked back to the church through the devastated town, thinking of the concern shown for him by people who had now lost their homes and businesses. Struggling with his own emotions, he thought, *You people have given me the finest present, the greatest experience a minister could have—the strength, the courage, the faith, the concern for others that I saw enacted here tonight. My sermon, "Be Thou an Example"—I didn't need to preach it at all.*

Trapped
on a narrow ledge
deep within an Alpine crevasse,
husband and wife waited,
slowly freezing as the
desperate hours ticked away

Prisoners
of the Ice

BY FRANCIS SCHELL

THEY LIVED IN ROME and were on a holiday visit to the Italian ski resort of Cervinia on a group tour in February 1976: Claudio Turella, forty years old and darkly handsome; his wife, Maria Antonietta, six months younger, fair-skinned, brown-eyed and slender. Although neither was athletic, they spent the first week of their stay conscientiously attending beginners' ski classes.

On Sunday, February 29, to avoid the crowded slopes, they decided to take the cable car to the scenic upper ski areas to indulge Claudio's passion for photography. At breakfast, they asked for box lunches and briefly discussed their plans with the other members of their group. Should they go first to Fürggen, a rock wall at the foot of the Matterhorn on the Swiss border? Or to the 11,480-foot-high Plateau Rosà below the Breithorn, a vast snow-covered glacier field? It would depend on the crowds, they decided.

When they reached the cable-car station, the line for Fürggen was temporarily closed, so they headed for Plateau Rosà. Shortly after noon, they reached the top, and set out to find a quiet spot for a picnic. Higher up, in the distance, Claudio and Maria Antonietta could see six people walking, probably hikers. They headed in that direction. The sun beat down hot and intense. After a few steps, Claudio stopped and took some shots of the Matterhorn. Farther up the slope, he snapped more pictures; then his wife, who had wandered a few steps toward an inactive summer ski tow, called to him to come over and start their picnic.

Seconds later, as he was putting away his camera, he heard his wife scream "Claudio!" Looking up, he saw her literally being swallowed by the earth, her arms upraised, the plastic picnic bag still in her hand. In an instant the only trace of Maria Antonietta was a hole in the snow.

Claudio stopped dead. Then he gave in to a normal human reaction: He ran to the spot where his wife had vanished—and he, too, broke through the layer of snow and instantly disappeared.

Next to avalanches, crevasses are the greatest mountain danger, especially when warmer temperatures soften the snow covering. As sections of a huge glacial mass move down a mountain at different speeds, giant fissures form, from a few to several hundred yards long, and sometimes just as deep, in the brittle upper layer of ice. When they are V-shaped cracks, they are more or less visible (depending on the accumulation of fresh snow). When they are shaped like an inverted V, they are almost impossible to detect; Maria Antonietta and Claudio had tumbled into one of these.

Maria Antonietta had slid like a letter in a mail chute down an icy, slanting shaft hardly wider than herself, eventually slowing to a landing on a small ledge some sixty feet underground. Unhurt but stunned, she stood on a sloping ice shelf some two feet wide and about a yard long, with the opposite ice wall less than half an arm's length from her face. Beyond the shelf, the crevasse plunged downward. Looking up, she could see a small patch of sky, no bigger than a handkerchief. With all her force, she shouted, "Claudio! Claudio!"

Almost immediately she heard an answer—"I am here!"—from her left. About two yards away, she saw Claudio lying across some slabs of ice, his legs dangling down into the void. He seemed shocked and hurt. Nevertheless, he managed to ease himself out of his precarious position and onto Maria's platform. As he moved, he felt a sharp pain in his back and chest.

Their predicament seemed hopeless. Above, the icy walls extended sheer and smooth toward that tiny spot of sky, with no toehold, nothing for them to grab onto. Since climbing up was clearly impossible, their only salvation lay in rescue from above. So Claudio and Maria Antonietta began shouting, "Help! Help!" They did not know that snow and ice are poor sound conductors. Their cries, trapped by the slanting walls, would be barely audible on top.

By six o'clock no rescuers had come, and now it was dark. Hardly daring to move for fear of slipping off their perch, they kept each other awake by talking, shouting and praying. Occasionally their devotions were interrupted by an eerie, frightening sound: the intermittent loud cracking of the ice as it melted, froze and shifted.

When daylight returned, they tried to eat some of the sandwiches in their picnic bag, but these were half frozen and tasted like cold rubber. Instead, they scraped snow from the wall and swallowed that.

Their worst problem was the frigid air that kept sweeping through the crevasse. Maria Antonietta was wearing a silk body stocking, heavy ski pants, a woolen sweater and a fur-lined raincoat with hood. She also had gloves and sealskin boots. Claudio was more lightly dressed: thin woolen underwear, flannel shirt and slacks, knee-length corduroy coat and cotton socks under his boots. To keep as warm as possible, they began shaking their arms and shifting their weight from one leg to the other.

All that day, periods of hope alternated with times of near despair. "I am sure they will find us," Claudio kept saying. But when no one came, gloom would again settle over them. By the second night, Claudio felt feverish. His teeth were chattering, and he was hallucinating. "Look, there is an elevator there. People going up. Let's take it!"

"Yes, yes," Maria Antonietta murmured, holding on to him so he would make no rash move. Later, to keep him warm, she massaged his legs and tucked his cold, gloveless hands under her arms.

As darkness fell the next day, it became very cold. (That night and in the days to come, icy winds above would lower the temperature in the crevasse to 14° F.) To protect Claudio, Maria Antonietta dumped out the uneaten food and put the picnic bag on his head, then stuffed the paper napkins inside his shirt and boots.

In the night Maria Antonietta imagined that a cable-car attendant was flashing a light into their hole, telling her rescue would come in the morning. She told Claudio, and they waited excitedly until midmorning. When she realized it had all been a dream, she sobbed uncontrollably.

After the Turellas had been missing for a full day, a search was finally organized. But people at the hotel remembered conflicting stories about the couple's Sunday destination: some said Fürggen, others Plateau Rosà. So the *pisteurs* (ski-slope maintenance men), the customs police rescue squad, the carabinieri and local mountain guides began looking in both places.

At Plateau Rosà, the searchers checked every suspicious hole far up the glacier for traces of an open crevasse. On the Swiss side of Fürggen, a helicopter crew spotted something in the snow. A party sent to investigate made a grim discovery: the frozen bodies of a young Swiss couple missing for two months.

Alerted by phone, Mario Turella, Claudio's brother, arrived by plane from Rome on Tuesday. Twelve years older than Claudio, bullish and energetic, he dearly loved his brother and threw himself with all his heart into the search, which was soon extended as far as the next village about three miles down the valley from Cervinia. Mario himself checked every mountain shepherd's summer hut, every scenic spot where a photographer might have been tempted to linger, sometimes wading up to his calves in the mountain streams.

On Thursday, the searchers met at Mario's hotel. Four days had now elapsed, the weather had turned much colder and there was practically no chance of finding the missing couple alive. A sad understanding seemed to have been reached. Finally, one of the men broke the silence, "It's no use going on," he said.

Mario Turella thought of his daily calls to his old mother, who did not know precisely what had happened but had sensed disaster and spent the days praying for *something*. He thought of the elderly parents of Maria Antonietta, an only child. "Just one more day," he pleaded. "Please, just one more day. We will go back to where we started. We *must* find something."

His sincerity swayed them. The men looked at each other and nodded. They would search until noon on Friday.

On Thursday, Maria Antonietta realized they couldn't last much longer. Despite her efforts to warm them up, Claudio's hands and feet were becoming frostbitten, and his hallucinations were giving way to long periods of apathy. His pains were now so acute that he was constantly hunched over, and at any moment might slide off their narrow perch into the depths below, perhaps dragging her with him. And, after three days on their feet, they no longer had the strength to stand.

Craning her neck, Maria Antonietta saw that at the edge of the nearby ice slabs there was a cave-like indentation in the ice wall. Carefully, she let herself down onto the slabs, then coaxed Claudio to follow her. Slowly, painfully, she got him into the cavity. There was just room for her to stand at the entrance, from where she could still keep her eyes on the patch of sky. She felt an almost serene resignation: They were in God's hands now and He would help them to live, or to die.

Early Friday morning, two young customs agents, Gianfranco Ponzo and Gianpietro Chieia, joined a mountain guide, Germain Ottin, to search the Plateau Rosà. Ottin—a small and wiry man— had spent forty-two of his sixty-three years leading skiers and climbers over the local mountains. Retired two years before, he was still occasionally summoned in emergencies.

From the cable-car station the little group zigzagged upward beneath the summer ski tow, looking into every depression. After half an hour, Ottin stopped. He sensed that the unathletic Turellas would never have ventured even this far. They went back to the station and started anew. Ottin, walking in front of the two young men, suddenly stopped again. His experienced eye had spotted a slight variation of color in a patch of snow near the ski tow's second pylon.

He called to the others. "Hey, do you see anything from over there?"

Chieia backtracked and saw a hole. As he moved in to get a closer look, his shadow momentarily moved across the opening. Ottin thought he heard a faint cry. He motioned Chieia to stop. The sound came again.

On his hands and knees at the hole's edge, Chieia shouted into the cavity: "Is anyone down there?"

"Help! Help!" came the incredible reply.

With a rope knotted around his waist, Ottin was lowered into the hole. On the way down, he called out, "Don't worry, we have found you. You are safe now."

He heard a woman's voice say: "Who are you? An angel from heaven sent by the Madonna?"

As Ottin landed on the ice, a pathetic sight greeted him. The man was huddling inside an icy cavity, a plastic bag on his head, his five-day stubble making his skin look even whiter and sallower than it was. The woman was leaning against the ice wall, her eyes staring in wonderment, drained of all energy. Ottin checked for injuries, then uncapped a small flask he carried with him and gave each a swig of brandy.

With ropes, the two were quickly brought to the surface, and helicopters whisked them off to a hospital. It was 107 hours after Claudio and Maria Antonietta had taken their fateful steps, and less than two hours before the search was slated to end. Shortly after noon, fog rolled in, and it began to snow; the bad weather would continue for two days.

Many people called the survival of Claudio and Maria Antonietta a miracle. Both suffered from shock, exposure, exhaustion and bronchial pneumonia. In addition, Claudio had four broken ribs and a collapsed lung, frostbitten hands and feet, and bruises and lacerations on his hands. But after a month in the hospital they returned to Rome to convalesce, and by late spring they were both back at work.

Was it really a miracle? Doctors attribute the couple's survival to their robust health and to the fact that they were together: a person alone might more easily have lost the will to survive. Germain Ottin points to their incredible luck in having their plunges halted by ice formations, and to "Maria Antonietta's alertness to the very end in noticing us and calling."

But Claudio and Maria Antonietta feel in their hearts that there was a much more vital reason for their survival: their faith in prayer. It was to celebrate that faith that they created a lasting memorial on the mountain—a small bronze statue of the Virgin and Child erected on a stone high up on the Plateau Rosà. On a plaque next to the statue appears this inscription: *"O Heavenly Mother, our prayers and faith in you sustained us and you showed your infinite goodness by granting us salvation. In eternal gratitude and remembrance, Maria Antonietta and Claudio Turella."*

The statue is there today for all to see, and its lesson clearly has not been lost. For, on a nearby rock, someone has written this postscript: "Thank God for being alive."

When the U. S. plane crash-landed
in flames on a Vietcong-controlled airstrip,
there was no chance at all of rescuing the man inside—
yet Bernie Fisher decided
to go in and bring him out

"A Pilot
Is Down!"

BY RICHARD ARMSTRONG

THE WORKHORSE OF the air war in Vietnam was the Douglas Skyraider, officially designated the A-1E, an ancient holdover commissioned just after World War II. It had a cruising speed of 150 knots and could carry a huge load of what pilots call "ordnance": napalm, high-explosive bombs from 100 to 1,000 pounds, rockets, antipersonnel weapons.

Burdened with all this ordnance—up to 7,000 pounds of it—a Skyraider could still hang above an advancing ground force for two hours or more while the high-speed jets had to strike and get home before they ran out of fuel. Many infantrymen say that they are alive today because of a strike at the right time by an A-1E.

One of the men who flew the Skyraider in Vietnam was Air Force Maj. Bernard Francis Fisher, 39, of Kuna, Idaho; another was Maj. Dafford Wayne Myers, 46, of Newport, Washington. Fisher, a freckled, sandy-haired Mormon, was an elder in his church and did not drink, smoke or curse, although he was at ease, and much loved, in a squadron of men who did all three. "Jump" Myers was a chain-smoking nonconformist who once made his living running billiard parlors. Coincidentally, each of them was married to a woman who was a registered nurse, and each had five children.

Fisher and Myers had known each other casually since 1959, when they were both flying jets for the Air Defense Command in the U. S. Northwest. They met again in Vietnam. Myers commanded a detachment of the 602nd Fighter Squadron at Qui-nhon in the central highlands; Fisher was eighty miles away, in the First Air Commando Squadron at Pleiku. But during the battle of Ashau Valley, in that brisk and impersonal radio-code world of the fighter pilot, they were strangers.

Ashau was a desolate place, sere and brown, socked in by clouds most of the time. It lay seventy miles west northwest of Da Nang, at the eastern point of a mountain valley that broadened out until it crossed the Laotian border only three miles away. The U. S. Special Forces camp at Ashau was a triangular fort still under construction, with a 2,500-foot airstrip made of pierced-steel planks. It was a key spot for observing and harassing the infiltration of North Vietnamese regulars across the Laotian border into South Vietnam, and on March 9, 1966, the North Vietnamese decided to wipe it out with a major infantry assault.

That afternoon at 2:30 in the prefab operations shack at Pleiku, Fisher was being briefed for a mission when he was handed a "divert" to a new target of top priority: the Ashau Valley. Fisher flew there on top of the clouds by radio beam and found a thick cushion of clouds that began at 200 feet and extended all the way up to 8,000 feet, hiding the mountain peaks. A covey of planes milled around on top, looking for a hole.

Fisher found the hole. "It wasn't exactly a hole," he said later, "but a kind of light spot in the clouds." Once he got down to the valley floor, he began his strafing passes around the Special Forces fort. He had a copilot with him, Capt. Robert Blood, new to Vietnam, who was much impressed: "The ceiling was so low, and he made his strafing runs in such a tight bank between the ridges, that one wing was in the clouds and the other almost scraping the ground." Fisher went back up through the hole and down again three times that afternoon, to bring in other planes.

Next morning Fisher took off at 10:05 on a routine bombing-and-strafing mission with Capt. Francisco "Paco" Vazquez, 29, flying another A-1E just off the tip of his wing. They had been airborne only ten minutes when Control radioed a divert, once more to Ashau. Again Fisher reached the clouds above Ashau, to find four other Skyraiders—one of them flown by Jump Myers—looking for a hole. Once again it was Fisher who led the other planes down. Two of the Skyraiders took up a holding pattern, and the other three followed Fisher down the valley, six miles long, that led to the fort.

The pilots called this narrow valley "the tube." It was less than a mile across, and the ridge lines along it were studded with at least twenty enemy antiaircraft weapons positions. Every pilot who came into Ashau that day felt bullets thudding into his plane, but under the low cloud cover there was no room to maneuver.

The radio operator in the fort told them to hit the south wall of the fort, which had now been breached by the North Vietnamese. Myers had just pulled out of his second strafing pass when he got hit by a burst from an automatic weapon.

"The engine started sputtering and cutting out, and then it conked out for good," Myers said. "The cockpit filled up with smoke. I got on the radio and gave my call sign—Surf forty-one—and said, 'I've been hit and hit hard.' Hobo fifty-one—that was Bernie, though I didn't know it at the time—came right back, 'Roger, you're on fire and burning clear back to your tail.' I was way too low to bail out, and I said, 'Roger, I'll have to put her down on the strip.'

"I never saw the runway because of the smoke blowing back in my face, but I got a rough fix on it and Bernie talked me down. He was very cool about it, and that helped."

At the last minute he was too fast, so Fisher told him to retract his landing gear and belly it in. As Myers touched the runway his belly tank of high-octane fuel exploded with a roar. Surf 41 was a ball of flame that skidded a hundred yards, veered off to the right and slammed up into a dirt embankment.

Myers had seen pilots burned alive. "It is my only fear about flying. But the fear got the adrenaline pumping, and I just went through the motions I had thought out a thousand times." He stripped down to his flying suit, leaving survival gear behind, so he could get through the flames more quickly. It took at least a minute. Then he pushed the hydraulic lever. "The canopy popped right open. A strong breeze down the runway opened a path through the flames that seemed to me like the path through the Red Sea. I ran out along the wing, jumped off and squatted in a patch of weeds.

"I still thought I was a dead man because the strip was under enemy control. They don't take prisoners in the middle of a battle. I remember thinking, *How is Betty going to manage with all those kids?*"

When Myers headed into the strip, Fisher called Control and told them a pilot was down and to get a chopper in there fast. "When he hit the runway and exploded, I was sure he was dead. And then I saw him scrambling off with smoke pouring out of his flying suit."

The pilots overhead kept laying their ordnance in close on both sides of the runway, and they attacked the east ridge line from which heavy fire was coming. Fisher called Control again. "They told me the chopper was having trouble finding the hole, and could I go out and bring him in? Well, that was what cut it. I couldn't go off looking for a chopper. I told Control that I was going in to get the pilot. And I radioed the flight of A-1Es in the holding pattern just north of the fort to give me suppression fire."

This flight was led by Capt. Jon Lucas, 28, of Steubenville, Ohio, with Capt. Dennis Hague, 28, of Kellogg, Idaho, flying wing. "Roger, we'll cover you," said Lucas. Then, to Hague: "Set 'em up for strafe, we're going in." Paco, Fisher's wingman, fell in as third man in the string. "So we hit the east side of the runway and really hosed it down."

Evenly spaced, they flew in a tight-left pattern, so one or another was hitting the target every fifteen seconds. Meanwhile, Myers had crawled farther away from the plane. "I was hiding against an embankment ten feet high just west of the runway. There was at least a company of enemy on top of the bank, but they couldn't see me. Also, I think they thought I was dead.

"The last thought in my mind was rescue. I knew a chopper could never survive the ground fire, and it never occurred to me that somebody would be crazy enough to put an A-1E down on that strip. It was too short to begin with. The steel planking was all buckled up into spikes by mortar rounds, and it was littered with rocket pods, fifty-five gallon fuel drums and the debris from my plane. When I saw Bernie circle and then head into the north end of the runway, all I thought was *Well, now two of us are down.*

"I dropped my last string of bombs west of the runway to keep their heads down," Fisher said. "All I remember going through my mind was *Can we do it?* and *Yes, I think we can.* I was sure the poor guy was down there burned pretty badly."

"I was coming in on my final from the north end, just about right, when the wind blew a great big blob of smoke from the fort across the end of the runway. When I got out of the smoke, I saw I was too hot, so I put her down on the strip for just a couple of hundred feet. Then I gave it the power and took off again. I bent it around real tight in a teardrop turn and came in from the south, holding it right at ninety-five knots. That's the key speed for short-field landings. I touched down, put the flaps up and started hitting the brakes even before the tail came down. I steered around the mortar holes, but I just didn't worry about the rocket pods. I hit a bunch of them and knocked them aside.

"Then I saw the end of the runway coming up much too fast. That was the first time all day I was scared. I had to make a decision: Do I really slam on the brakes and probably tip her over, or do I take a chance on the overrun off the end of the strip? I decided to take a chance on the overrun. It was grass and soft dirt, and littered with these empty fuel drums, but it worked out real fine.

"After using up about twenty yards, I hit the left brake hard and swung the bird around in a big cloud of dust. I gave it a lot of power and taxied back down about two thirds of the runway. Jump waved to me from the weeds, and I stopped as quick as I could, about two hundred feet past him. I hit the parking brakes and unstrapped to go and get him." Bullets were thumping into the plane, one of them two feet from his head. (Crewmen later found nineteen bullet holes.)

At this point the other three A-1E pilots were flying strafing runs fifty feet off the ground. The lead pilot, Lucas, had just been hit hard, and his cockpit was full of smoke. Hague, his wingman, called him. "You're burning. Better get the hell out."

"Roger, can't leave Bernie yet. We'll make one more pass."

"Okay, but I'm out of ammunition," Hague reported. Lucas said, "Roger, me too, but they don't know that." So Hague and Lucas made the last pass dry. For this bit of gallantry and leadership, Captain Lucas was awarded the Silver Star.

Jump Myers still could not believe what was happening. "Even after I had seen Bernie make his teardrop and come in to land from the south, I was thinking, *Well, they got another one.* It wasn't until he had taxied back past me and waved that I knew. *Why, that crazy SOB has come in here to get me out!* I started running for the plane."

To Jump Myers, who set a record for the sprint at Williams Air Force Base, Arizona, back in 1943, the run seemed an eternity, although it took only ten to fifteen seconds. He was dashing down the middle of the runway in full view of every North Vietnamese who happened to look his way. "The gunfire was deafening, and bullets were whining all around. My shoulder blades were really puckering. I can tell you I made that run as fast as any old man of forty-six ever could."

Fisher was just about to jump out and go get Myers when he saw two big red eyes leaping up over the back edge of the wing. "They were so red from the smoke that they looked like neons," Fisher said later.

Myers scrambled across the wing on his hands and knees and dived into the cockpit head first. Fisher grabbed Myers and set him right side up again. Then he whipped the end of the plane around and shoved his throttle forward to its limit.

"The takeoff went real nice," said Fisher. "I had to give the bird full power, dodge the mortar holes and use up the last foot of runway, but I had hit flying speed by then, so I just lifted her off. I held her right down on the bottom of the valley until we got out of the tube. Then I just took her right up through the hole in the clouds and leveled off.

"Jump couldn't talk to me because he didn't have a radio headset. He gave me a couple of hugs and a thumbs up. He was a mess— mud all over, and the smoke from his flying suit stunk up the whole cabin. But we couldn't help turning to each other and laughing all the way home to Pleiku."

As soon as Lucas got above the clouds, just behind Fisher, he hit a lever that bypassed his hydraulic system, and the fire in his cockpit began to subside. "I thought that was where the trouble was, but I couldn't do it any sooner," Lucas recalled. "You want your hydraulics working in the middle of a fight."

Bernie Fisher and Jump Myers landed at Pleiku just after one p.m. on March 10. Myers was whisked off to the flight surgeon, who gave him some drops for his red eyes and told him that otherwise he was in splendid shape. Then they were both ushered in to see the deputy commander of the 7th Air Force, Major General Gilbert Meyers. By the next day Fisher's recommendation for the Medal of Honor was already being drafted. It was awarded to him on January 19, 1967.

Before going back to flying missions in their A-1Es, Fisher and Myers took a leave in Bangkok.

"What can you do with a guy like Bernie?" Jump Myers wondered after it was all over. "I would like to furnish him with a year's supply of whiskey. But he doesn't even drink coffee. So I bought him a Nikon camera—he's the biggest camera buff in the squadron— and had it engraved, ASHAU, MARCH 10, 1966. For the first few days I felt like a dead man walking. I couldn't believe it. Then I got over that, and it's great to be alive."

Could the seven desperate,
thirst-crazed men continue together for their own good?
Or would they strike out
one by one toward certain death?

Seven
in the Sea

BY MAURICE SHADBOLT

ON A DEEP-BLACK SEA, *under the stars of a tropic sky, seven men cling to a swamped and slowly sinking boat. Desperately they kick in unison, trying to propel their craft toward the shadow of land on the night horizon. Fierce currents fight them; again and again the tide tugs them away from shore. The seven share a certain knowledge: If they all stick together, they have an equal chance to survive—or drown. If they split up, however, each going it alone, one or two of the stronger swimmers might make it to safety, but the majority will certainly drown—or worse, for they are not alone in these reef-ridden Fijian*

waters. A gliding shadow hints of a shark lurking in the dim depths. The men try to pretend it isn't there, but it is. And maybe, soon, there will be more. With fear thick in their salt-swollen throats, the seven kick. And kick.

No one could have been better prepared for the ordeal that night than Graeme Coote, a short, muscular, twenty-seven-year-old New Zealander. A schoolboy swimming champion, he had also been a member of a surf lifesaving club in his native country and was skilled in the art of survival at sea. He knew the Pacific, too. For months he had roamed its coral-girded tropical islands as a crewman on a yacht. Now, settled into an insurance job in balmy Suva, he spent most of his spare time adventuring with a spear gun among the reefs and islands of Fiji.

With Graeme that night was his companion of many a fishing expedition, Fritz Bower, an athletic twenty-eight-year-old of mixed Fijian and European blood. Fanatical about the sea, the stocky, 212-pound Fritz was something of a legend in Suva for his daring and underwater prowess.

At first, that weekend in March 1974 was like many others Graeme and Fritz had spent together. They were joined by three schoolteachers—a New Zealander, an American and a Canadian— and two Fijian friends. Their plan was to fish a submerged coral outcrop called Horseshoe Reef, ten miles off Viti Levu, the main Fiji island. Fritz knew it well. "A paradise," he told Graeme, "full of fish and turtles."

Graeme had his first qualms when he saw the boat that was to take the seven men into the capricious Pacific. Only about thirteen feet long, it was little more than a crudely built dinghy with a makeshift cabin. But he stifled his dismay. The sea was calm, bright and inviting. He did not want to be a spoilsport.

They were quick into the water, and once they reached the reef the day became pure joy. The sunlit sea was flooded with the colors of coral; swarms of brilliant fish exploded everywhere they swam. The hours sped past; Graeme found it difficult to remember a day so spectacular.

Around four p.m., though, sharks, excited by the smell of fish and blood, started to make a nuisance of themselves. One charged Graeme, and he drove it off only by smashing it across the gills with his spear gun. It was time to call it quits.

Their catch stashed, they set out for home. All were cheerful, laughing, sated with sun and sea, and satisfied with the successful hunt.

Their little boat's outboard motor had taken the seven men perhaps half a mile clear of the reef when a huge wave slammed over the bow. The forward hatch had been carelessly left open, and the boat, already perilously low in the sea with its load of fish and men, suddenly started taking in water by the gallon. "Grab your gear," Fritz shouted, and they snatched up flippers, masks and snorkels. In a matter of moments it was all over. With a long, violent shudder, the little craft tipped on its side and flung the men into the sea.

They clung desperately to the rolling hull. There was no mistaking the danger in their situation. Viti Levu's safe green shores were still remote on the horizon, at least seven miles away. Graeme was conscious that he was the only single man in the group; the others were married with children. Fritz, for example, was the father of two, and his wife, Lily, was waiting to give birth to twins any day now.

"Let's swim back to the reef," someone shouted above the babble of voices.

"No," Fritz, Graeme and others argued. "The tide's too strong." And no one really needed reminding of the sharks on the reef.

Arguments exploded as each man tried to roar the others down. From his experience as a lifesaver, Graeme knew that panic could kill. "Shut up, all of you," he bellowed. "We'll each talk in turn."

But even one at a time, the men, in a state of shock, still talked unrealistically. "Let's all swim to the mainland," was one suggestion. Swim? They had just one life jacket for seven men. That was all the boat had carried, in casual Fijian style. The bickering began again.

Fritz intervened. "The first thing is to stay with the boat," he insisted. "And stay together. Together we've got a chance. Alone, we've only got our individual strength—with the sharks and tides ready to take us."

Why not, Fritz proposed, try to push the swamped boat back to shore? Even submerged, it was something to grip, to keep them together. Graeme supported this suggestion. It had to be all for one, one for all—or disaster.

Action subdued panic. They cleaned out the remainder of their catch from the hull, then laboriously wiped down every inch of it to rid the boat of all trace and taint of fish, anything that might be tempting to sharks. Next, they managed to right the boat by having some of the men stand on its keel while others pushed from beneath. When it was finally upright, they quickly jettisoned the heavy outboard motor and jammed empty gas tanks and drink coolers into the cockpit area for buoyancy. Only the top of the cabin showed above water at the moment—but this wallowing hulk was still their best hope of survival.

The men took places in the water—two on each side of the boat and three at the rear. Fritz instructed that no one was to break the surface with his feet or flippers; this would bring the sharks in. Also, the seven men must keep their legs working in unison. With any luck, a shark would be scared by a large object with fourteen legs moving together.

Within an hour Viti Levu seemed perceptibly closer, and they were all still moving strongly in the water. What the men did not realize, though, was that the current was carrying them parallel to Viti Levu's shore. Parts of the coast were closer; but it was a passing coast.

The quick tropical dusk came, then it was dark. "Let's all get back into the boat," someone said. "We'll be safe there."

Fritz would not hear of it. "We'll get home tonight," he promised.

The truth was that Fritz feared they might drift too far from land in the dark, out of range of search parties. He also knew it was important to keep his companions moving as a team, believing in survival.

With darkness came a fresh hazard—human exhaustion. A cramp seized one of the schoolteachers; paralysis even invaded his throat muscles and made him speechless. The others helped him into the hull of the boat. Wearing the only life jacket, he sat there with his head just above water. Now they were six against the sea.

"Come on," Fritz urged. "Keep moving."

There was no release, no respite. Again and again they seemed only a few hundred yards offshore; at times they could see fires and even people. But the tide, with a confusion of currents, pulled them tantalizingly in and out.

"Just another hour," said Fritz.

But that hour went by, and then another. Onshore, the lights went out and the fires faded. In the dark, Fritz began to think again of sharks slashing suddenly out of the deep. He began checking regularly to see that no one was lost.

There was more desperate talk of swimming for shore, of each man's taking his chances alone.

Fritz and Graeme argued, "We're in this together. One of us is certain to drown on his own." They were referring to the huddled figure of the schoolteacher in the hull.

As the others flagged, Fritz redoubled his efforts. His secret was simple: Whenever he weakened, he thought of his family, of Lily waiting. Fiji's communal society was a part of his upbringing; he could not consider striking off alone and leaving his companions. Life was a team business; it had to be to make any sense.

"There's a shark down there," one man shouted.

The others looked down—was that a pale underbelly glimmering in the sea below? Fear made their weakened bodies again work steadily. But soon two of them were near collapse, their legs weakly fluttering. Fritz was afraid that they might lose all will, drift away and drown quietly in the dark.

So, near three a.m., after ten hours of unbroken effort, they all slid one by one into the nearly submerged hull of the boat. There they collapsed, half sitting, half floating, heads just above water.

But with the collective effort temporarily ended, their confidence ebbed quickly. They were all suffering from exposure now. One man began shouting vehemently that the boat had to be abandoned, that they must swim for it. Graeme and Fritz, who were the ones most likely to survive alone, continued to argue strongly for team effort.

Somewhere in the early hours, before sunrise, with Viti Levu still barely visible on the horizon, they went into the sea again. Fritz had an inspiration, a use for the boat's two oars. Improvising oarlocks with rope, they lashed the oars to the gunwales. Two men sat in the boat, neck-high in the sea, and rowed—underwater.

Before long, however, cramps hit two of the men, and they had to rest in the hull. Now there were only three to swim and push from the rear. And their boat had started to founder. By eight a.m. there could be no doubt; it was gradually sinking. They were also fast passing by the coast of Viti Levu. Before long only one extremity of land was left. Beyond that was the open Pacific.

By now, search parties were out looking for them. But, imagining a motor breakdown, they were searching around Horseshoe Reef.

The tropical sun began to rise in the sky. The men felt their lips cracking open, their tongues swelling. Another man crawled helpless into the hull. Only Graeme and Fritz were left pushing.

They had been struggling in the water for fifteen hours. The collective effort, which had seemed the wisest thing at the time, might now mean they were collectively doomed. Graeme began to doubt as he kept forcing himself to go on; the more effort he exerted, the less chance he would have to save himself at the end. Should he not try to conserve his energy?

But Fritz, as committed to the group as ever, was a constant inspiration. Graeme was awed by his friend's strength of will; he could not let such a man down. Often Fritz seemed to be pushing the craft singlehandedly through the sea. Graeme found himself trying to keep pace.

Endurance suddenly had its reward. Nothing substantial: A thin rod, a reef marker—a tenuous last hope—rose slowly from the sea between them and the last of Viti Levu. Sight of that marker, indicating a reef ahead, brought wild shouting. If they could gain the reef and lash the boat to the marker, they might be able to bail it out, and get it afloat again. They might survive together after all.

"Let's put everything into it for an hour," Fritz said. "We're going to make it for sure, so let's keep at it." And the boat, even though sinking, surged through the sea with their great gust of new energy.

Suddenly, wonderfully, they were there, against the reef, leaping on rocks in shallow water, tying up the boat. Fritz found some clams, split them open and passed the tough raw flesh around as sustenance. For a while they relaxed in ecstatic exhaustion.

But another two or three miles of water still had to be crossed and the bailed-out boat was clearly falling to pieces; its stern was about to break away.

When they resumed their effort at nine a.m. only three men were in fit condition to propel the boat—Fritz, Graeme and one faltering Fijian. The other four were helpless, drifting betwen sleep and delirium.

Once again, Fritz urged the others on. "We must try harder," he said. "Keep on and don't stop."

Before long the third man collapsed. Now Fritz and Graeme, the two who had argued for collective survival in the first place, had to accomplish it alone.

Working an oar, Fritz set the pace. His renewed effort fired Graeme, too. An hour passed; and another. Soon, both knew, the tide would change, ebbing away from land. If they did not reach shore before that, their eighteen-hour struggle across at least twelve miles of sea would all be for nothing. The Pacific would surely finish them off. Both men bent to their oars, heads down. Graeme was beyond pain, almost beyond the world. Yet still he worked mechanically.

Suddenly, Graeme heard Fritz shouting: "Look! Look!"

Graeme looked up and saw tall coconut trees . . . a village . . . Fijian children returning from church in their Sunday best . . . and a dignified old man waiting to welcome them, in the formal Fijian way, on a beach of pale coral sand.

No nightmare ever had gentler end. Their boat, creaking and cracking, nudged the beach. And Graeme, nearly ten pounds lighter than when he last walked land, staggered ashore with the others.

"We heard about you on our radio," said the old man. "But we didn't think you would ever arrive here."

"Nor did we," one of the seven responded.

For more than a week,
thousands of volunteers had searched in vain
for Kevin Dye, a nine year old who had vanished
in the wilds of Wyoming.
Now time was running out

Lost Boy
on Casper Mountain

BY E. D. FALES, JR.

TOWARD FOUR P.M. ON SUNDAY, July 18, 1971, the annual plan-ning conference of the Casper, Wyoming, Christ United Methodist Church was breaking up. The fifty or so members who had pic-nicked and conferred high up on wild, 8,200-foot Casper Mountain were preparing to leave the camp where they had gathered when thirty-five-year-old Phillip Dye, the church's popular treasurer, asked, "Has anybody seen my boy Kevin?"

An hour earlier, blond, nine-year-old Kevin had squabbled with a friend over a swing. Kevin, who could not speak like other boys, had cried out shrilly and flung his arms about, and his dad had taken him to sit by himself in the family car. After fifteen minutes, Phillip Dye let Kevin return to play. Thirty-five minutes later, Kevin was gone. Other children said that he was either playing Ping-Pong or hiding in a nearby tree house. "You go on home," Dye told his wife, Carolyn. "I'll bring the children down after I help clean up here."

For accountant Phillip Dye, Carolyn Dye and their three other children, the episode was nothing new. Kevin was a child tormented by brain damage, possibly due to an injury suffered at birth. To his physician, Dr. Robert Fowler, he was an "expressive aphasic." "He's like a little radio set with a damaged speaker," Dr. Fowler had told Kevin's parents. "The input is perfect, but the speaker connection doesn't work." Yet Kevin was bright, not dull or "retarded," and this made his torture great. It was no wonder, his parents reflected, that he often flailed his arms and babbled, groping in despair for words that he could not say.

Yet, when all the inquiries and a search of the tree house failed to locate Kevin, Phillip Dye became worried. With the help of the Reverend Paul Hood and a few remaining men, he began to search the dense woods. After two hours, he drove to a resort restaurant called the Circle A to phone Casper Sheriff Bill Estes for help. Estes was out, but a deputy promised to send up a posse.

It was about sunset when Carolyn Dye received a telephoned message that Kevin was lost. She felt her throat tighten as she looked out her big picture window toward the mountain, a gloomy lump of granite towering over Casper like a great wave about to break. Moments later, she was rushing to gather warm sweaters and coats for herself, her husband—and Kevin. Because she was too upset to drive, she let a neighbor speed her back up the switchback mountain road.

The Dyes and Pastor Hood, who had established that the Ping-Pong paddle Kevin had been playing with was missing, searched with the posse until three a.m., stumbling through acres of heavy forest—to no avail.

At breakfast, the people of Casper read in the *Star-Tribune* that Kevin was missing on Casper Mountain.

Not long before Kevin Dye's disappearance, the nation's press had pointed a disapproving finger at Casper. This city of 40,000 had been found to have among the highest murder and divorce rates in America. Its morals were said to be lax. In such a town, then, how many people could be expected to turn out to help look for one troubled boy?

At nine a.m. Monday, when Sheriff Estes looked down from the mountain, cars were coming from as far as the eye could see. Mothers, National Guardsmen, cowboys, businessmen and Boy Scouts began reporting in to a search base set up at the Circle A. By Thursday, Sheriff Estes estimated that 3,000 people had checked in.

Not for many hours was it known that on the day Kevin vanished, two cottagers on the mountain had glimpsed a small boy in checkered shorts and a blue pullover short-sleeved sweater wandering happily toward the Crimson Dawn trail. "He was singing and whistling and talking to the birds," they told Sheriff Estes. "And he was slapping a Ping-Pong paddle against trees the way kids do." At dusk, a camper had seen Kevin approaching one of the radio and TV towers on a summit near the Crimson Dawn trail.

On Wednesday, a team of Boy Scouts tracked Kevin's loafers toward frightening Elkhorn Canyon, a place of giant cliffs and deep chasms, of lodgepole pines, brown bears and rattlesnakes. "Normally, no one would ever go in that canyon," said Boy Scout leader Marvin Miller. Still, Carolyn Dye went down into Elkhorn with an escort of Boy Scouts.

The next day, Kevin's parents drove their car up the Crimson Dawn trail and parked it on the highest cliff. Then for hours Carolyn Dye called. Sometimes she used a police loud-hailer, which caused her voice to echo weirdly against the cliff.

All night two men stayed at the cliff, broadcasting Kevin's favorite songs from *Sesame Street*. When Kevin still did not appear, his mother hung a toy clock from his schoolroom on the family car. She set the time at 3:20, the hour that Kevin's school bus usually came to pick him up. And because Kevin had learned to read, she left a sign that said: "Kevin, the clockwatcher says it's time to go home. Wait here for Mama."

Meanwhile, helicopters beat the woods, sending down showers of pine needles and actually blowing one searcher off his feet. And all around the mountain hundreds of watchers, armed with field glasses, lodged themselves on crags, looking for the flash of blue that would be Kevin.

But there was no Kevin. And now there had come a strange summer snow, freezing nights, fog—and despair.

Not that there weren't "sightings." Over and over came reports that people had seen Kevin running. They'd call out, they told Sheriff Estes, but he always ran on. Sometimes on craggy ridges he'd appear for an instant against the sky. He'd snatch food left for birds. At night, he'd break into cabins and steal peanut butter or raid garbage cans.

The greatest fear that the psychologists and Kevin's parents had was that he would forget all that he'd learned in the special school he was attending, even lose all ability to think. After five days of anguish, his mother expressed her dread: "He's become a small animal pursued by big animals, and he's frightened."

When she was on the mountain, Carolyn Dye kept her composure. "I'll never let them see me cry," she told Paul Hood. But at home she sobbed out her anguish.

On Friday, the fifth full day of the search, everyone was called off the mountain to "let the boy rest." By now, Carolyn Dye was beginning to despair, and the search teams were wearing out. On Sunday evening, the veteran Colorado Search and Rescue Board sent two fifteen-man teams of volunteers—the Rocky Mountain Rescue Group and the Alpine Rescue Team—to join the search.

The next day, a curious thing happened: Twice during the morning, a lanky nineteen year old appeared at the search camp to report, "I've seen Kevin." When it was learned that sometimes the youth attended a work-training class at Kevin's special school, no one put much stock in his report. "Then, at noon," recalls Sheriff Estes, "he came in again, this time carrying a bloodstained Ping-Pong paddle. We were stunned." The boy claimed he'd found the paddle in Middle Fork Canyon—part of the grim Elkhorn region—but he kept changing his confused, rambling story.

The Colorado teams had now taken full charge of the search. One skill that has greatly helped the Rocky Mountain Rescue Group in its twenty-four-year history has been its members' ability to evaluate clues. "The teenager's story was so horribly contradictory that we finally felt that this was in its favor," says Chuck Demarest, the group's field commander. "We decided to send our best men down into Middle Fork in the morning."

With engineer Bill May in command, a group of five shoved off soon after dawn in sweep formation, thirty feet apart. The men searched a summit meadow, negotiated a ridge, then began their descent toward a little stream, where it was thought that Kevin, if he was alive, would have to go for water. They'd gone only a few yards when the right anchor man, strapping forestry student Mike Murphy, came to a halt. Off to his right, leaves were moving, and he saw a lovely little doe take off in long, smooth leaps. Murphy now had an idea what some of those "sightings" of a running boy might have been.

In the dimness of deep forest, they found the stream, and Murphy felt the icy water in his boots. They began to follow the stream, heading north down the canyon. The canyon now became so steep that the team had to close ranks, moving in to twenty feet apart. The stream kept disappearing, then reappearing in foaming waterfalls. Murphy slipped on rocks, pushed through cool, shady grass that could conceal rattlers. Above, he could hear May's radio chattering. Then, from a bushy area below, he heard a splash and saw something dragging itself up from the stream: a large, bristly porcupine, spines erect. He thought he knew now what had been stealing food from cabins.

"In the next hour," Murphy says, "we circled a million trees, scrambled over a thousand logs." Finally, he saw a little glade ahead. The sun shot a long, probing shaft into the natural clearing where the stream shone bright blue.

What a great day for a hike! Murphy thought. And when he glanced toward the water again, there was something he hadn't seen at first. Near the stream was another patch of color, bright as the Wyoming sky. It was a small blue pullover sweater. And in it, like a crumpled fawn, lay a small child, on a patch of sun-dappled grass.

Murphy took a deep breath and held it. Says Chuck Demarest: "There is a mystical moment when you rescue someone whom you've been seeking for a long, long time. It's reverence. You don't want to approach him—for suddenly you have discovered how wonderful a human life is."

"Hi, Kevin," Murphy called gently, at last. As he advanced cautiously to kneel by Kevin, a pair of hungry eyes searched his face. There was no smile in them. "But there was a child's gratefulness and relief," says Murphy. He touched the terribly thin face, glad to find no feeling of fever. The small arms and legs were scratched and thin as matchsticks. "Kevin wouldn't have lasted another night," Dr. Fowler said later. Then Bill May was on the radio, calling calmly for a stretcher.

"Kevin, do you want to go home?" asked Murphy.

A small voice quavered, "Ye-e-e-s."

And suddenly Murphy knew. This was no cunning animal-boy who had been robbing cabins, scuttling madly over crags and outwitting 3,000 people. "We'd just found a scared and tired little boy," he says. "Like any kid, he got in a little trouble, ran away, rambled happily up a trail—and then got lost. He'd probably never been out of this canyon. And now, too weak to crawl to water, he'd lain down to die."

Carrying Kevin in the stretcher, the team started the tough, two-hour walk out. "But, suddenly," says Mike Murphy, "the going became easy." The birds sang, the sun was warm, and the shade was cool. It really had become "a great day for a hike!"

Kevin recovered from his ordeal, and in a curious and wonderful way it wrought a change for the better in him.

"*Something* surely happened," says a puzzled Dr. Fowler. "His whole troubled attitude has changed. He seems at peace now with himself—and his family. He still has a long way to go, but he no longer flings his arms and throws tantrums in school.

"Someday," Dr. Fowler adds, "we may have a pretty useful citizen named Kevin Dye. That's what I hope."

Terror
on Train 734

BY EDWARD HUGHES

The hijacked train sat motionless
for thirteen long days in the Dutch countryside,
while the strange captors
meted out death sentences

THE SEVEN SWARTHY youths on the station platform in Assen, northern Holland, struggled to get their bulky packages aboard the 9:53 a.m. train for Amsterdam. To the curious conductor, they explained that they had been buying presents for friends. But, minutes later, as the two-car train sped south, the men suddenly donned hoods and ripped the wrappings off an ugly assortment of pistols and submachine guns. One of the terrorists pulled the emergency brake, bringing the train to a screeching halt. "You're captives!" he shouted to the thirty-seven stunned passengers. Thus, on December 2, 1975, began the bizarre siege of Train 734.

The terrorists were South Moluccans, demanding independence for their distant Pacific Ocean archipelago, an obscure group of islands that had been absorbed by Indonesia in 1949 after the former Netherlands colonies won their independence. When the fighting ended, thousands of the islanders had been allowed to come to Holland; now, twenty-six years later, many of them, especially the young, still blamed the Dutch for their expatriate plight.

The gunmen's first victim died only seconds after the hijacking began. Engineer Hans Braam rushed from his cab to see why the emergency brake had been pulled. Glimpsing the terrorists, he ducked inside the cab, but the South Moluccans tore open the door and cut him down with a volley of bullets.

As the passengers watched helplessly, the terrorists thrust stacks of newspapers and masking tape into the hands of some of the men on board, with orders to use the paper to black out the windows. As the men complied, some of them complaining, an eerie twilight fell over the train, bringing with it a growing sense of isolation. Although they couldn't know it then, most of the occupants of Train 734 would be prisoners in their cold steel-and-glass island on wheels for thirteen days.

Shortly after 10:30 a.m., Mrs. Zwaantje Etten looked up from the chores outside her farmhouse and noticed the stopped train. Curious, she walked across the meadow toward it, but passengers peeping out signaled frantically to her to leave. She was almost home when the gunmen caught sight of her; five shots zipped past her head as she ran inside.

By then, the Assen police station had already received a "missing train" alert from the Dutch railways. As a radio car set out to investigate, a train from the nearest station rolled up to within ten yards of No. 734. Greeted with a burst of automatic gunfire, the engineer reversed his engine and went back down the track at top speed.

The Dutch government was no stranger to spectacular hijackings. In September 1974, Japanese terrorists in The Hague held the French embassy staff hostage for five days. Soon after, in the chapel of the Scheveningen penitentiary, the chaplain and a score of guards and visitors were held by convicts for 105 hours.

In the light of these experiences, the Dutch Ministry of Justice had worked out detailed plans for dealing with future hostage crises. By 11:15 a.m. on December 2, key officials and specially trained troops were speeding toward Beilen, a little town seven miles from the hijacked train.

When they arrived, Beilen's town-hall offices were quickly turned into an improvised siege headquarters. There, for most of the next thirteen days, would sit the five officials charged with management of the emergency. They would work closely with the Ministry of Justice, and at their elbows would be explosives experts, medical specialists, psychiatrists and psychologists. Their basic strategy had four elements: make no deals whatsoever; offer nothing to the terrorists, make them ask; stall for time to induce fatigue and give officials a chance to develop a plan; try to instill friendship between gunmen and hostages.

But while these broad guidelines were clear, precise tactics were difficult to formulate. At this point, the authorities at Beilen were not sure of the terrorists' ultimate intentions. The hijackers had demanded a bus and an airliner, but then threatened to kill a brave police sergeant who approached the train in an effort to make the initial contact.

That first afternoon, to prove that they meant business, the gunmen began choosing a victim. "There is a time to live and a time to die," intoned one terrorist, quoting the Bible. "This is a time to die." They all then pulled their hoods back over their faces and moved down the aisle, stopping finally by the seat of Robert de Groot, a thirty-four-year-old real-estate agent who had argued earlier over helping to paper the windows. Led out to the baggage car, de Groot was told to stand at an open doorway. "May I pray?" he asked. His captors turned away briefly, then wheeled around and fired a volley of shots at him. Incredibly, they all missed, probably because the gunmen were nervous. De Groot let himself fall out of the door and rolled into a drainage ditch where he lay still, feigning death. The gunmen fired two more shots, both of them wild, and returned to the other passengers. Ten minutes later, de Groot jumped out of the ditch and ran to safety.

The next victim chosen by the terrorists, twenty-two-year-old Leo Bulter, wasn't so lucky. Ordered to stand by the forward car's rear door, the young soldier was mercilessly gunned down. He died instantly, and pitched forward onto the gravel beside the track.

The remaining hostages, some of them weeping and moaning, wondered who would be led away next. They were also beginning to be bothered by the cold. Few were dressed warmly enough to withstand the bitter winter weather, and some of the elderly were already suffering. Every passenger's hero was a radiobiologist, Hans Prins, 40. The South Moluccans permitted him to move about, offering advice, giving encouragement. Soon he was "Doctor" Prins to everyone.

Prins's main worry was the Reverend Pietje Barger and his wife, both in their eighties, who seemed to be in shock. Hallucinating, the retired minister once rose from his seat and began looking for his suitcase. "Sit down, Grandpa," a terrorist snapped, raising his gun. "No," replied Barger. "We change trains here." Hurrying to his side, Prins calmed the old man.

Meanwhile, throughout Holland, the Dutch people watched in horror as the grotesque drama unfolded on their television screens. A ring of steel had been drawn around the train. One heavily armed cordon of police and marines formed a circle about 900 yards away; another surrounded the entire area for two miles around. Marksmen with infrared sights on their rifles lay behind trees and in frozen ditches, waiting for that moment-in-a-million when they might pick off all seven terrorists at once. It never came.

At the command post in Beilen, frustration was mounting. Thirty hours had passed, and two people had been killed. But satisfactory communications had not yet been established with the terrorists. Then, toward the end of the second day, they allowed a military field telephone to be brought to the train. Now the authorities could begin, slowly and patiently, to gain control.

The terrorists, as they would do most mornings over the coming days, presented a long list of the train occupants' needs. But command-post officials pared the list to necessities—food, blankets, medicines requested by "Doctor" Prins, toilet paper and water. One effect of the authorities' stinginess was to make the hijackers repeat their demands, forcing them into the role of supplicants; another was to infuriate the hostages, to make them feel abandoned. Pained as they were to add to the distress of the passengers, the command-post psychologists knew from experience that even the most hostile groups trapped together can become friendly if their mutual anger can be transferred to an external force—the authorities. Once this companionship is rooted, the hostage group is often safe from harm.

On the train, Prins was concerned about seventy-two-year-old Mrs. Johanna Jansen—known to passengers as Auntie Jo—who was suffering an acute attack of asthmatic bronchitis. While the terrorists watched impassively, Prins applied artificial respiration.

Meanwhile, another passenger, Walter Timmer, received permission to comfort the hostages with Bible readings. Although the passengers took strength from the eternal message of I Corinthians 13:13—"And now abideth faith, hope, charity, these three; but the greatest of these is charity"—the reading did not cool the South Moluccans' rising anger. The authorities had not yet answered the hijackers' new political stipulations: that they be allowed to state their case on television; that the Netherlands bring pressure on Indonesia to grant some autonomy to the Moluccans; that the case be taken to the United Nations.

Impatiently, the South Moluccans decided to kill still another victim. Once again, the ugly black hoods went over their faces. "Is Auntie Jo ready to die?" one asked. As they led the frail old lady toward the front of the train, Prins called out, "You cannot do that. Don't do it!" His words apparently carried weight, for ten minutes later, Auntie Jo walked shakily back to her seat.

But one victim's reprieve meant the selection of another. Paul Saimima, 31, who seemed to be the terrorists' leader, pointed to "the one with glasses," thirty-one-year-old Bert Bierling, who had also complained to the hijackers on the first day.

Police watching through field glasses gasped as Bierling's body toppled from the train. Then, suddenly, the authorities' attention was riveted by news of a second terrorist attack. Seven South Moluccans had burst into the Indonesian consulate in Amsterdam, and were holding forty-five hostages at gunpoint.

With two sieges going on at once, the tension mounted throughout Holland. On the train, however, the tension was receding. Bierling's murder seemed to have triggered an emotional release among the South Moluccans, who were now talking to the hostages in a relaxed, even friendly manner. Saimima himself had begun to feel pangs of remorse; at one point he sobbed uncontrollably on Prins's shoulder.

The new mood soon made itself felt at the command post. The terrorists began asking for things, instead of harshly demanding them. And they allowed Red Cross stretcher bearers to collect the bodies lying beside the tracks.

Toward evening on December 5, the hijackers needed the Red Cross themselves. For amusement, they had been firing and reloading their weapons. There was an accident: A bullet fired into the ceiling sprayed fragments of metal, one of which struck Saimima directly in the eye. Blood pouring over his face, he was carried from the train to meet Red Cross stretcher bearers.

Meanwhile, Prins was ministering endlessly to a growing number of sick passengers. Frequent shipments of medicine arrived in reply to his requests, including tranquilizers for Mr. and Mrs. Barger, who thought they were elsewhere. When the Bargers were allowed to leave the train on the sixth day, followed by another elderly couple on the tenth, hope arose that the ordeal might soon be over.

But the siege continued. On the eleventh day, the outside temperature fell sharply to 26° F. More than 150 blankets had been sent to the train, but anxious doctors agreed that another day or two of severe cold could be fatal to the elderly on board. Should the marines abandon caution and mount an all-out assault? Not quite yet, officials ruled.

In fact, the passengers were doing surprisingly well in the frigid temperatures. But the cold was sapping the will of the South Moluccans. On the evening of the twelfth day, a mediator brought back word to the command post that the hijackers were wavering. The next morning, although the hijackers sent in their usual request for food and medicines, the passengers sensed that the end was near. Gathered in another part of the train, the South Moluccans had reached a crucial decision.

Suddenly, a train door opened and the six terrorists stepped down. As they were surrounded by police, they shouted what had become their battle cry: *"Mena! Muria!"* ("Freedom! Our Cause!"). Then they were led away.

The siege was over. But so deep was the habit of obedience that the hostages remained in their seats until the police and marines actually entered the train. "Please, may we move?" asked a bewildered passenger. "Of course," replied a marine. "You're free." Then they all embraced, weeping and laughing.

Five days after the ordeal on Train 734 ended, the Amsterdam siege (in which one man died trying to escape) also collapsed in surrender. Three months later, following a three-day trial, each of the Beilen terrorists was sentenced to fourteen years in prison.

The veteran smoke jumper knew he had
only one desperate chance to survive as the
towering forest fire surrounded him

Trapped in a
Sea of Flame!

BY GERALD MOORE

UP FRONT IN THE FORWARD AREA of the DC-3 where the heat was
most intense, some of the younger smoke jumpers were getting sick.
In the hour since they had left their base in Missoula, Montana, that
July day in 1973, they had been battered by extreme air turbulence
and roasted by the sun. Now first one of them and then another
dropped his head low between his knees and began to vomit.

Squad leader Rod McIver, 33, a taut, rangy jumper with six sea-
sons experience, watched them from near the open rear door of the
plane. If Lowell Hanson, the plane's spotter, didn't get them out
soon, McIver figured, they would all be too sick to jump.

Hanson, lying on his belly at the door, his head thrust out into the
prop blast, knew that time was running out. But everything seemed

to be working against him. He had thrown out three drift streamers and watched the fifteen-mile-per-hour wind carry them toward the rugged upper slopes of Bald Mountain, just above the fire that had already burned for three hours, scorching over 600 acres. The only clearings he could see that were within hiking distance of the fire were too small for a safe jump in such strong wind.

Hanson looked down the line of vomiting men. Most of them were in their mid or late twenties and were physically tough, he knew. Yet he had no stomach for shoving them out where they might hang up in tall trees, or break a leg in front of the fire.

McIver felt his own stomach begin to roll as he watched Hanson. He was glad it was Hanson who was making the decision. He himself had made enough decisions for other men as a Marine platoon leader in Vietnam. The missing finger on his right hand and the silver plate in his head reminded him how easy it was to make a mistake.

Suddenly Hanson saw, halfway up the mountain, very near the fire, a small, grassy clearing—perhaps ten or fifteen acres. Just opening enough among the trees for a drop, if every man kept his head. He radioed the pilot.

McIver felt the plane bank. He watched the first two men go out. Now he was at the door. Hanson pointed out the jump spot and then slapped McIver's leg. Curling forward, McIver leaped out into the clear Montana sky.

The opening shock of the big orange chute jerked him straight up. He threw his head back to check the rigging. It was perfect. He pulled on the toggle held in his left hand, allowing a jet of air to escape from an opening in the back of the chute. This maneuver compensated for the strong wind, and he drifted steadily toward the landing site.

The clearing came up fast. McIver clamped his feet together and rolled forward as he hit. But his chute caught the wind and began to drag him. Rocks banged into his back and shoulders. McIver clawed at his harness release but could not get a grip on it. The chute picked up speed and dragged him toward the fire. McIver grabbed the fastener with both hands, but his speed was so great now that his hands were knocked loose by the rocks. Suddenly the chute hit the fire and melted. McIver jerked the fastener loose and scrambled away.

It was a bad beginning, but he had no time to reflect on what might lie ahead. He saw his crew chief about twenty yards away. Together, they watched the rest of the men come in, followed by fire packs dropped on quick-opening chutes from treetop level: Each pack included a shovel, chain saw, first-aid gear, and a Pulaski, a combination ax and hoe that is the basic tool of all forest fire fighters. When Hanson finally ordered the DC-3 back to Missoula, twelve well-equipped men were in position.

The fire on Bald Mountain had started along the highway that follows the Clark Fork River through the Lolo National Forest. Within an hour it had spread along the road and moved up the mountains, burning a huge triangle-shaped chunk of forest. It was near the apex of that triangle that the crew had jumped, hoping to build a line along its western flank to contain the fire. (Building a line involves the primitive, backbreaking process of scraping and digging a swath through the forest about six feet wide, removing anything on the path that might burn.)

"We were making good progress," McIver recalls, "building over half a mile of line an hour. We had worked about three hours when I looked up and saw smoke half a mile off to the west, nearly behind us. The fire seemed to be 'toeing out,' like a big spearhead. It looked as though we might get trapped. I volunteered to hike over to where I could see the toe, and if it looked like it was moving, I'd hustle back and let them all know."

McIver set a quick pace for himself, moving easily over the rocks and fallen trees. He found a narrow ridge and followed it for about a mile. It broke into a grassy clearing about a quarter of a mile above the fire, at the top of a long meadow. He was relieved to see that the fire was moving slowly. He sat down and dug out a candy bar.

Suddenly the wind picked up and changed direction. Within seconds it was directly behind the fire, coming hard.

Off to his left, the fire broke through the woods and came toward him in a wall of flame a hundred feet high. To his right, gray smoke billowed up so high that he lost sight of the sky. The fire seemed to gallop toward him, gobbling great chunks of forest as it came. The roar of exploding trees grew deafening. There was no hope now of getting back to warn the others. He was trapped.

McIver knew what happened to smoke jumpers who gave in to

panic and tried to outrun a fire. He was determined to keep his head, even while every instinct screamed out for flight. He watched the angry flames hit the bottom of the meadow, turning it into a sea of fire, and committed himself to a plan. If it failed, then his photograph would join those on the memorial wall back at the barracks.

McIver tied his bandanna over his face. Then, with the fire at his back, he struck a match and held it to the grass in front of him. Then he moved a few feet to one side and repeated the operation. Soon he had a line of small fires burning away from him up the mountain. By comparison with the inferno racing up behind him, they seemed to creep. But they were his only hope.

As the heat grew more intense, too intense for him to stand up, McIver fell to his hands and knees behind his line of fire. The big fire would overtake him soon. If he could endure its heat, and hold his breath in the little patch of burned-out grass behind his fires until the main fire passed over, he would make it.

Crawling now, pushing his face as close to the flames as he could, trying to lengthen the patch of burned grass behind him, McIver worked on getting his timing right. As the main fire closed in, he began breathing deeply. Then, lungs filled to bursting, he closed his eyes and held his breath.

Flames swirled around him. The heat was even more terrible than he had imagined. He moved closer to his own fire and felt his face begin to burn. He stopped. His legs and buttocks began to sear. He moved forward again.

His mind seemed to float away from his suffering body in an odd, detached way. "Will this dude make it?" one part of his mind asked. "Don't know," another part seemed to reply.

He inched forward again until the pain was too intense to bear, then stopped. The heat ate at his legs. His mind returned to its strange conversation. "When the pain gets bad enough, this dude will lose his head," one voice said. "He'll just jump up and start screaming." And again that other voice replied: "No, no, he will not. . . . He will *not* scream."

Then the sensation of smothering came upon him. He was running out of oxygen. If he didn't breathe soon he would lose control, and breathe involuntarily. And the rush of superheated air into his lungs would kill him. He had only one option now: to run back through the fire and hope that it had moved high enough so that he could reach an area of the meadow already burned over.

McIver jumped up and wheeled around, running blind, his legs pumping with all their strength. As he did so, his oxygen-starved lungs overrode his conscious command, and he sucked in a deep breath of air. He expected the awful pain of lung tissue searing. But it did not come.

Breathing now, he ran faster, praying he would not stumble. And suddenly the horrible flames were gone. He fell to his knees, panting, blinded by tears, hardly able to believe he was alive. He felt his face. It was hot, but there were no blisters. His ears were burned. His hands were a bright pink. Some of his thick black hair was gone. But he was alive.

When he could see again, McIver retraced his steps to where his Pulaski lay in the smoldering ashes. Motivated now by what he later called "a deep sense of personal vengeance," he picked up the Pulaski and, walking hard, moved up the flank of fire until he found a quarter-mile stretch where he figured he could hold it. Then he went to work, backfiring along his line. He was determined to beat back the fire that had almost killed him.

It was close to midnight when he heard voices nearby. It was another crew of smoke jumpers, and they had a radio. McIver immediately radioed his own crew to report that he was well, and then joined the new crew in digging line. Around five a.m., the two crews met, and McIver was able to tell his buddies how he had made it through the fire storm.

The smoke jumpers succeeded in containing the fire by about eleven a.m.—some eighteen hours after they had climbed aboard the DC-3 in response to the original alarm. After lugging all their gear to an open spot where it would later be picked up by helicopter, they hiked slowly down Bald Mountain to meet a yellow school bus that was waiting to haul them back to Missoula.

By the time the bus stopped at a roadside grocery, where the thirsty men picked up a case of beer, McIver's hands were covered with ugly blisters, and he had trouble holding the cold can that was offered him. But he knew the blisters would heal. And he knew, too, as the bus whined through the night, that he had learned something important on Bald Mountain: The dude would not scream.

The blizzard struck with paralyzing swiftness,
high on the flanks of the great mountain,
trapping the father and his two young children

Whiteout
on Mount Rainier

BY PHILIP YANCEY

ALMOST AS SOON AS THE SKY lightened that Friday morning,
Sharon, 12, and David Reddick, 11, began pulling on their long underwear and boots. Their dad, James Reddick, a busy dentist in
Seattle, had picked the 1968 Memorial Day weekend to take them
on their first long hike. Besides, a five-mile climb up Mount Rainier's snowy slopes would earn David a Boy Scout skills award.

Trails on Rainier—Washington's highest peak, at 14,410 feet—
had just been opened, and the three Reddicks chose an ascent from
Paradise Inn, elevation 5,420 feet, to Camp Muir, at 10,000 feet.
Mrs. Reddick, hampered by a hip injury, would stay behind in the

camper with the two other Reddick children in the Cougar Rock campground.

At eight a.m., Sharon, David and their father checked out of Paradise, the day's first hiking party. The trail was still packed with about ten feet of snow (Rainier's snowfall is legendary: Paradise Inn holds the world's record for 93.5 feet in one season), and the Reddicks followed a boot-trampled furrow marked with flags on sticks. Rivulets of water trenched across the trail, a sign of spring thaw. The temperature was 38° F. and rising. Reddick had insisted that his children wear extra clothing in case of a storm, but soon Sharon and David had shed their heavy outer coats, tying them around their waists.

Mount Rainier's weather, however, is notoriously fickle. Just an hour after the Reddicks set off, rangers at Paradise observed a thin cloud cap high on the mountain and warned a five-man party about to depart that a cloud cap often presages a storm.

The Reddicks could not see the summit cloud as they climbed along Nisqually Glacier. At Panorama Point, they stopped for a breathtaking view of the snowcapped Cascade peaks, curled out like a string of giant pearls as far as their eyes could see. Sharon gathered clean snow to melt on their tiny camp stove to make soup, and the others dug out candy bars, sandwiches and graham crackers from their packs. David and Sharon were amazed at how quickly they recovered their strength after a meal and a brief rest. They returned soon to the gradually steepening trail.

At noon, the five-man party caught up with the Reddicks and passed on the rangers' weather warning. But since Camp Muir was closer than Paradise, Reddick decided to continue climbing. The other party veered off on a different route.

Two hours later, David spotted a thick cloud around the volcanic peak of neighboring Mount Adams. Within minutes, clouds began to obscure the sun, and Reddick quickened their pace. Sharon sensed her father's nervousness. Wind gusts were soon stirring up snow around them, and Sharon and David put their coats back on. There was an urgency to the hike now as Reddick strained to keep the trail markers in sight. Here, on the snowfield above the timberline, there were only a few rocks to guide them.

Up at Camp Muir, meanwhile, the storm had hit with fury and

the temperature plunged to 22° F. Ranger John Dalle-Molle emerged from the guide building into sixty-mile-an-hour winds. As he headed for the hikers' building a hundred feet away, the wind lifted him off his feet and slammed him into a snowbank. Amazed at the wind's force, he scrambled to his feet and returned to the guide building.

Soon snowclouds swallowed the camp, bringing a dreaded "whiteout." In a whiteout, moisture—be it from fog or snow—is so dense that all perspective is lost. A hiker has no sense of direction and cannot tell the ground from the air. Dalle-Molle thought of the hikers who had started out from Paradise that morning. "God help them!" he muttered.

At 3:30 p.m., the storm engulfed the three Reddicks with paralyzing quickness, battering them with winds of hurricane force. Snow fell in thick, wet sheets, swirling everywhere and buffeting their faces. It was almost impossible to move or see in the whiteout. On the steep terrain, to take even a few steps might be suicide.

Reddick said quietly, "Well, let's dig in." While Sharon and her father tramped around in a six-foot circle, kicking snow outward, David took an aluminum mess kit and began scooping up great hunks of wet snow. Panting and sweating, they managed to clear an oblong trench big enough for three people.

Reddick worked furiously, widening the depression, building wind blocks and unfolding a canvas tarp he had packed for such an emergency. He did not realize it, but hypothermia—a debilitating condition in which the body begins to lose heat faster than it is produced—was overtaking him. His reasoning powers and coordination were being sucked away.

He struggled to cover the snow trench with his tarp and weight it down with their three backpacks. Every time he raised the tarp to spread it out, the wind would grab a corner and jerk it from his hands. When at last he got the tarp closed and collapsed into the trench, he helped David and Sharon into one sleeping bag so they would be warmer. He himself couldn't summon the energy to climb into his, and so slumped on top of it. All three promptly fell asleep in their wet clothes.

Reddick had positioned himself within reach of the opening in case the wind blew the tarp off, and in such a way that his body protected David and Sharon from the howling wind. "Don't leave this cave until the storm is over," he said just before drifting off to sleep. "The rangers will come. Lou Whittaker is one of the best rescue guides in the country."

Some time later, the Reddicks awakened. For morale, they sang songs. Sometimes they prayed. They felt very alone and helpless— buried under a tight wedge of snow, almost surely invisible to a rescue team—but they believed in prayer. "No matter what happens, God will send help," Reddick kept telling them.

Sharon noticed that her father seemed to lose energy as the hours passed. He lay still, his back against the drafty tarp. Frequently a corner would blow loose, and he would slowly reach up and secure it. Ironically, the temperature was not cold enough. If it had been colder, the snow cave would have worked as an igloo and stayed hard, allowing their body heat to warm them. But at 22° F., their body heat simply melted the snow. The three became steadily wetter and more miserable.

After many hours of waiting. Reddick raised his head and said, "I don't think I can go for help. I don't think I can make it down the mountain."

Until then, Sharon had believed completely that everything would be all right. Now she felt concern for the first time: *Will we all survive?* She volunteered, "Daddy, let me try to follow the trail of flags down to Paradise Inn."

Reluctantly, her father agreed. He wrapped her clothing tightly and hoisted her out of the trench. She scrambled upright, and fell back immediately, unable to stand. The wind on the steep slope was too much. David tried, too, and was blown back. Discouraged, they closed the tarp and climbed into their sleeping bags.

"Whatever happens, don't leave the cave now," their father said weakly. "Help will come."

On Saturday morning, Mrs. Reddick awoke to the monotonous sounds of a downpour beating on the camper. The rain made her wonder if her husband and two children would delay their return, planned for that afternoon. She drove to Paradise Inn and, a little before noon, asked rangers if anyone had seen the Reddicks. No one had.

At 2:15 p.m., rangers at Camp Muir checked in by radio and were asked if they had seen the three Reddick hikers. "Nobody here named Reddick," came the reply. "They must still be out there!" They reported temperatures at Muir of 18° F., with heavy snow and wind. No search party could operate in those conditions.

Mrs. Reddick spent a sleepless, anxious night listening to the rain. Somewhere above her, all that moisture was snow, piling on top of her husband and children. Would they ever be found?

At 5:50 a.m. on Sunday, despite dense fog and heavy rain, volunteers from Tacoma's Mountain Rescue Council, led by chief guide Lou Whittaker, left Paradise. By ten, the storm had abated somewhat at Camp Muir. Another party of six, including Dalle-Molle, started down from there. The searchers had few clues. The Reddicks could have turned back and holed up anywhere, or they could be lying in a cave inches from where a searcher was walking. The snow cover was deadly camouflage.

Dalle-Molle, district ranger Jim Valder and three other men were hiking toward a formation called Moon Rocks when they spotted something black barely protruding from the snow. It was a corner of one of the backpacks holding down the Reddicks' tarp. And beside it was a small hole. Dalle-Molle stuck his head in.

Almost directly in front of his face was a young boy, very much alive. David Reddick stated matter-of-factly, "We've been waiting two days for you to come." Sharon sat up beside David. The body of James Reddick lay against one wall of the snow cave.

Dalle-Molle gently helped the two children out of the trench and hugged them. Valder radioed the other searchers, and he and the men erected a tent, stripped the children of their wet clothes and nestled them into a dry sleeping bag.

Hours later, down from the mountain, rested and warm, the children began to tell their tale to their mother. Lou Whittaker had already described how Reddick had "taken the cold spot," using his own back as the outer wall of the snow trench. Sharon described their attempt to leave the cave for help—until they were blown back by the wind.

"It's hard to remember anything after that but sleeping and the sound of dripping water," David told his mother. Finally, they had realized that their father was not joining in the conversation. David reached over and shook him. When he got no response, he felt for his father's pulse. None. He looked up and said, "Sharon, I think Dad's dead."

Sharon was quick to comfort her mother. "Mom, Daddy died doing something he loved," she said. "And we kept praying and waiting, just like he'd told us. He promised that help would come for us, and he was right."

Years after the tragedy, those involved in the rescue still remember it well. The rangers cite it as a classic warning to nature lovers—of the need to respect, always and forever, the power and ferocity of nature's elements.

"Dad gave his life for us," says Sharon. "Now, when I see Rainier gleaming off there in the distance, I think of it as a special memorial to him."

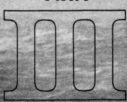
Man
is not made
for defeat

Ernest Hemingway
THE OLD MAN AND THE SEA

He met danger in the same way
he had always met life—head-on

Granpa and the Atlantic Ocean

BY DAVID O. WOODBURY

MY MOTHER USED TO SAY that the summer we spent in Maine when I was seven was the most terrible she ever lived through. That was the time Granpa taught me to handle a boat and insisted I "make friends with the Atlantic Ocean." As a girl, Mother had nearly been drowned in this same ocean, and she wouldn't have allowed us to live anywhere near it if Father hadn't made her. He was a marine painter, and the sea was his life. To her, it was malevolent and murderous.

But through Granpa's eyes the ocean was a vast new world of adventure and excitement. "The sea is your friend, Davy, if you don't abuse her confidence," he said.

This philosophy appalled my mother. But then she and Granpa were in a perpetual battle over my education. A retired cabinet-maker, gentle and considerate, he could fix anything around the house, and I was his devoted helper. Mother, on the other hand, wanted me to play music, paint pictures and read. Granpa said that first you must learn to be practical. You wouldn't live to grow up if you didn't.

Granpa had been a drummer boy in the Civil War and grown mature in courage and wisdom while still a youth. To him, danger was an essential part of growing up. It brought you alive, kept you keen, taught you to take risks and win. What really alarmed Mother was that he not only took chances but *enjoyed* them—and made me enjoy them, too. He called this habit his "capacity for surprise."

When the wind piled the sea into monstrous waves and the ledges in front of the house were buried in foam, Granpa and I would put on oilskins and clamber down over the rocks, bracing ourselves against the gale. Sometimes we went too close, and a wave would slam us down and wet us to the skin. When Mother protested, Granpa would cry, "Marcia, he has to learn to handle himself on those rocks. We're in luck to have so many storms!"

There were plenty of times when the sea was calm and I could get on with learning to manage a boat. Granpa turned for help to the little band of fishermen who inhabited the inlet we called the cove, though the small indentation in the rugged ledges was wide open to the waves, except at the upper end. Here there was a huddle of graying old fishhouses and a few square feet of pebbles on which to drag out the boats.

Granpa, with his tall, gaunt frame and bristling halo of beard, intrigued the stolid old-timers, and his delight in personal danger fascinated them. "Them waves knows him," they would say. His courage quickly made him one of them, a distinction that few summer folk attained.

One old lobsterman was called "Deef Al." No one could make

him hear, but everybody liked him and he liked everybody. The only way to communicate with him was by pointing and acting things out.

At first Granpa tried to shout into Al's dead ears, but a fisherman set him straight. "You can't make him hear, Mr. Woo'b'ry," he said. "He won't even hear Gabriel's trumpet when his time comes. They'll have to set it in writin' or Al won't go. Them ears is just ornaments."

In sign language we made a deal with Al to borrow his dory whenever he didn't need it himself. She was as old as he was, but rugged—a fine deep-bellied eighteen-footer, lapstrake, like a woman with many petticoats. She was just the boat for me, safe and unruffled in any sea.

Al was dirt poor. His traps were homemade from bits of wood he found, and in a storm he would lose every one he had. He never tried to beat the weather and get them in, as some of the other men did. He would just stand on the beach, gazing off into the turmoil, then go back to his hut and start lashing up more scraps of wood to replace them.

Granpa quickly improved on that. Buying some good hardwood withes, he skillfully fashioned a set of traps that were the envy of the cove. I helped by weaving the little nets that closed their ends, imprisoning the lobsters once they were in. Al hadn't wanted any pay for lending us the dory, but he was grateful when we offered him the new traps.

So the summer went by, one of the happiest in my childhood. Then one morning in September we woke to a blow that was the grandest of all. The sea was white to the horizon, and the cove itself was in turmoil.

"We'll have to make Al some new traps, Davy," Granpa said. "He's going to lose all he's got this time for sure."

We went down to the beach. The fishermen were standing in a silent little knot, staring out into the misty savagery beyond the point. Al wasn't among them. "Didn't he come down today?" Granpa asked.

One of them jerked his head seaward. "He's out there now, tryin' to get his traps in. We couldn't stop him. He sets more store by them traps you made than anything he ever had."

"He can't stay out there in this sea!" Granpa cried. "We must signal to him to come in."

They were silent for a moment. "Can't *git* in," one grunted finally. "He's snapped off one of his oars."

Granpa went into action like a lighted rocket. "We'll go out and get him," he said grimly.

"Who'll go with me?"

Not a man moved. Granpa looked from one to another. One man shrugged. "Go if you want to. You won't come back."

Granpa hesitated only a moment, then strode down the beach to the boats. The next minute I was running after him, screaming, "No, Granpa! Don't go! Don't go!"

He had lost his hat in the wind, and, as he turned, his thin, silvery hair made a halo around his head. His white beard stood straight out, and he looked like God, the way I had imagined Him in Sunday school. "I'll be all right, Davy," he called. "I'll just tow him in." Then he leaped into one of the dories. I was right behind him.

"No, Davy! Get out!" He took me roughly by the shoulder. "Do as I say."

"I won't. I'm going with you."

He looked at me a moment. Then he picked up the heavy oars and slipped them through the tholepins. I was in the bow of the dory and Granpa stood above me, pushing on the oars instead of pulling, as he had taught me to do when the ocean was rough. He did not look like God anymore, but like one of those great knights that Mother had read to me about in King Arthur. I loved him for taking me with him. I wasn't even scared.

As we got out of the protection of the cove, there was too much noise even to think. The bow of the boat would soar into the air and then plunge down until it seemed as if we were going to the bottom. Granpa kept pushing: slow, long strokes, keeping time like a pendulum. He seemed to me to be the strongest man in the world.

Outside the point, the waves were so big we went down out of sight between them. But when we were on top of a roller and Al was, too, we could see him for a second. He was rowing hard with his one oar, first on one side, then on the other, but he wasn't getting anywhere. He had hauled up all his traps, and they were piled around him in his dory, sinking it so deep that some of the waves washed in.

The seas were edging him in toward the ledges, where green water was smashing and bursting fifty feet in the air. We hadn't much time.

Granpa made straight for him. When we were alongside, Granpa leaned over and shook him by the shoulder. I will never forget the look on Deef Al's face. It was like the sun coming out suddenly, when the clouds break up. Granpa pointed at the killick in Al's bow. Al understood and passed it over to us. It took us a while to get it over the thwarts into the stern. It was heavy.

When we looked up, our boats were within a hundred yards of the rocks. We could feel the suck of the waves as they drew back and then crashed on the point. Granpa put his whole strength into rowing again, heading straight out to sea. At first we didn't move. Finally, we began to, till we had taken the slack out of Al's bow line—then it was even harder.

I ached to help, but there wasn't a thing I could do. All I could think of was to shout, "You'll do it, Granpa! You'll do it!"

Al was helping with his one oar, but every time Granpa finished a stroke, we would slip back toward the rocks. It seemed to take hours before the waves got longer and rounder and we knew we were in deep water again.

Then Granpa swung slowly around and headed us back toward the cove. Anybody who knows about boats knows that it is dangerous to have the waves behind you. They come slamming up like sixty and seem to pick you up and throw you ahead. If you can steer, it's all right. But you can't steer a dory pulling another one behind it in a big sea.

Somehow Granpa kept us from broaching to, but then a big wave got us, and Al's boat came slamming down on us from behind. Another wave got us, and I thought we were gone. I could see the water pour into Al's boat. He was bailing for all he was worth.

A minute later, there was a sudden calm. That happens in any storm. Right after the biggest waves there will be none at all. Granpa looked out to sea, and then he did a thing I couldn't understand. Putting both hands on one oar, he slued our dory around with all his might till it was pointing out to sea again. I was too little then to know what Granpa's maneuver was for, but I marvel at it now, after fifty years. It was the only thing to do to save our lives.

Granpa had never been caught in a storm like this before, but some instinct told him what to do. If we were to go in at all, we must go in backward, with our light boat holding Al's heavy one in line.

"I guess we can do it after all, eh, Davy?" Granpa shouted, smiling. I realized that for once he had not been sure he could win.

In another fifteen minutes we were paddling up to the beach. The fishermen helped us climb out. One of them had an old quilt that he threw around Granpa. The rest stared at him and shook their heads. It was the biggest tribute they knew how to give. Al waded ashore. He stood a little to one side, and reached into his pants pocket for a plug of tobacco. When he had stuffed it into his mouth, he stuck out his arm and shook Granpa's hand. That was all. But he and everybody understood what Granpa had done.

Father came running across the beach and threw his arms around Granpa and hugged me. "Papa, that was well done! But we won't tell Marcia a word."

He was shaking all over.

Unless help arrived quickly,
his critically injured wife would probably die.
Then the first in a succession of Samaritans
appeared from out of the night

"I Think I'll Try the White House!"

BY TREVOR ARMBRISTER

THE RAIN HAD STOPPED before midnight that Friday in June 1970, but the winding highway was still wet as David Urey, 34, guided his '68 Oldsmobile convertible through the West Virginia mountains. It was now almost one a.m.; he saw few other cars or trucks in this sparsely inhabited area. His wife, Donna, 27, who was almost five months pregnant, dozed next to him. On a pillow in the back slept their two-year-old son, Brian. How lucky he was, Urey thought, as he glanced quickly at them.

He made the four-and-a-half-hour trip from his home in the Washington suburb of McLean, Virginia, to his parents' home in Elkins, West Virginia, several times a year. Normally, he set out earlier but as the host of an evening reception for fellow patent lawyers, he hadn't been able to break away until nearly nine p.m. Even so, he thought, they would all be safely in bed in an hour.

Outside Petersburg, West Virginia, the road curved slowly to the right. Urey turned—too sharply—and the right front tire slipped onto the soft shoulder. He yanked the wheel to the left. Suddenly the car was sliding sideways out of control. It shot across the road, plunged through a fence, tumbled down a thirty-foot embankment and came to rest with a sickening crunch.

Urey was bleeding from minor cuts. He saw that the jagged chrome frame of the splintered windshield had sliced into his wife's scalp like a can opener. He tried her door, but it was jammed. "Honey, can you get out on my side? Please try!" he pleaded. Donna moaned and said she couldn't move.

In the darkness, Urey heard a faint cry—Brian had been thrown clear. Urey ran and scooped up his son, whose face was smeared with blood. Cradling the terrified child in his arms, he clawed his way up the embankment. Gasping for breath, he shouted and waved frantically as first a truck, then a car, roared past and vanished into the night.

Urey knew that unless help arrived soon Donna might die from loss of blood. He removed a bloody handkerchief from his pocket and vowed to stand in the middle of the road until the next car stopped—or knocked him down. He waited for what seemed an eternity.

At one-thirty a.m., Gary Arbaugh, 23, was driving his new Ford pickup home after an evening of running the Ferris wheel at a carnival in Petersburg. Attendance had been good; with a few more nights like this he'd be able to pay for the engagement ring he'd promised his girl.

Suddenly, just ahead, he saw a man in the middle of the road waving something. His face was bloody and swollen. Gary hit the brakes.

"Please help us! We've had a bad accident," Urey shouted. "Stop at the first house and call an ambulance. Then take Brian here to the hospital. My wife is down there in the car. She's hurt pretty bad. . . ." Gary laid the sobbing child on the seat and raced toward Petersburg.

Urey was beside himself with remorse as he climbed back and

forth between the car and the road. What if Donna or Brian died? Could the unborn child possibly survive? He thought of the young man who'd taken Brian away—he hadn't even asked his name! What if no help came?

Then he saw the flashing lights of an approaching police cruiser—and an ambulance! Driver Renee Schaeffer, 22, had been parking the ambulance at her father's funeral home when Gary's call came. Now she and her seventeen-year-old brother, Tommy, were climbing down the embankment. They pulled open Donna's door and lifted her onto a stretcher. In the dim light, Tommy could see that her scalp had fallen off backward. It was lying between her shoulder blades, attached to her skull by a sliver of flesh. "Please hurry," Urey said. "Please don't let her die."

At two-fifteen a.m., Dr. Robert E. Roberts, 42, was awakened by a telephone call. "We have a wreck," the night supervisor of Petersburg's Grant Memorial Hospital informed him.

"Bad?" he asked, rubbing his eyes.

"Yes. You'd better hurry."

When Dr. Roberts entered the emergency room ten minutes later, Brian Urey was semiconscious. He had suffered a severe concussion, a fractured skull and a broken neck. The first thing to do was to treat him for shock. While attendants gave Brian oxygen, Dr. Roberts started a "cut-down"—inserting a tube in a vein in Brian's ankle to carry blood and intravenous fluids. He was closing the boy's wounds when Donna Urey was carried in.

Looks like she was scalped, he thought as he examined her. *Shock. No blood pressure. No pulse. Condition critical.* He noticed that she was pregnant. She'd undoubtedly have a miscarriage—but that would be the least of her problems.

Dr. Roberts began a second cut-down. Donna received oxygen and nine pints of blood. A nurse cut her long brown hair, cleaned her wounds and wheeled her into the operating room. It took sixty stitches to sew her scalp back into place.

At eight a.m., Donna regained consciousness. "Try to move your legs," the doctor said. She shook her head. She could feel nothing below her neck. X rays showed that her back was broken and that she had a severe dislocation of the spinal cord. "There's hope," Roberts told Urey. "We get a faint knee reflex. She's not paralyzed yet."

But time was important. She needed an operation to relieve pressure on her spinal cord.

Dr. Roberts was not trained in neurosurgery, and he didn't have the necessary instruments. The nearest neurosurgeon was in Winchester, Virginia, eighty-two miles away, over mountain roads. The ambulance's slightest lurch could snap Donna's spinal cord. Still, *something* had to be done.

At ten a.m., Dr. Roberts telephoned Winchester. The neurosurgeon was on vacation. The only hope now was Washington, some 160 miles away. Roberts called several neurosurgeons there, but none was available. Then he had an idea. Years before, when he was practicing on Maryland's eastern shore, the Navy had flown patients from the islands by helicopter. Why not get a helicopter now?

David Urey's cousin was an Air Force colonel assigned to the Pentagon. David telephoned, but Colonel Urey was on a trip to Iran. The colonel's wife suggested he try Andrews Air Force Base. The duty officer there tried to locate the generals who might authorize a flight—with no immediate success. Every minute that went by seemed to Urey to lessen the chances of his wife's recovery. There had to be a way to make the Air Force respond *now*.

For the next two hours Urey called everyone he could think of who might conceivably help—from the governor of West Virginia, Arch Moore, Jr., to Senator Barry Goldwater. But this was Saturday afternoon, and not one of them could be reached.

At two-fifteen, Urey received a call from Andrews Air Force Base. The flight was approved, but severe thunderstorms were forecast over the Alleghenies. The small choppers available couldn't make it without refueling, and there was no place to refuel en route to Petersburg.

Urey paced back and forth in frustration. "There must be a chopper somewhere," he said. "I think I'll try the White House!" He got the number from information, and placed the call "to the man in charge of helicopters."

The President's military assistant, Air Force Brig. Gen. James D. Hughes, was at his desk when his telephone rang at two forty-five. Urey explained his predicament. "Stay where you are," Hughes replied. "I'll be in touch." A call to Andrews confirmed Urey's story.

Hughes knew of at least one helicopter that would fill the bill—

the President's. But Hughes had never authorized its use for a civilian evacuation and didn't want to establish a precedent. He telephoned the duty officer at the Andrews base hospital. "Do you *really* think that we can do any good if we bring that woman back?" The reply: an unequivocal "Yes, sir!"

Hughes decided to go ahead. His assistant telephoned Petersburg: "We are dispatching the President's helicopter with an Air Force doctor and a medical corpsman. They should arrive at five-thirty."

At first, Urey didn't believe him. Then, realizing that help was actually on the way at last, he broke down and cried.

The rotors on the President's chopper were already turning as Lt. Col. John Wanamaker, 36, a cardiologist and trauma specialist, ran down the Andrews flight line, followed by a medical corpsman, Tech. Sgt. Howard Stoller. No sooner had they lifted off than Stoller realized that there was no way to bring a stretcher through the chopper's narrow doorway. "Why not stop at Quantico," Wanamaker suggested, "and borrow a Marine Corps bird? With the White House behind us, we can get anything we need."

Changing at Quantico to a large helicopter with its doors removed, they set out through sheets of rain for Petersburg. Minutes after landing, they were headed back for Washington with Donna—sandbags next to her head and neck and along her sides to keep her immobile—and Brian, on a stretcher at her side.

At nine p.m., David Urey's neighbor in McLean, Dr. Robert P. Nirschl, was standing on the football field adjacent to Washington's Georgetown University Hospital. In response to a frantic phone call from Urey, orthopedic surgeon Nirschl had called a neurosurgeon, Dr. Alfred J. Luessenhop, alerted the police, secured an ambulance and even had flares placed on the field. Suddenly he heard the chopper overhead.

Donna's condition was still critical. Yet, as they examined her, Nirschl and Luessenhop marveled at the "fantastic" job Dr. Roberts had done. "Her spine's so badly fractured," Luessenhop commented, "that normally she would be completely paralyzed." For several reasons—because she was very weak, because she still had a few reflexes, because she was now under expert supervision—the doctors decided to postpone surgery until she had gained strength. Even then, they agreed, her chances of ever walking normally were less than fifty-fifty; her chances of keeping the unborn baby were even slimmer.

The operation took four hours. First, Luessenhop performed a spinal laminectomy to relieve the pressure on the spinal cord and to straighten her vertebrae. Then Nirschl grafted bone from her hip around her spinal cord, and inserted a stainless-steel "stabilizing" wire. Nurses wheeled her back to her room. Suddenly her condition began to deteriorate. Luessenhop reopened the wound. A blood clot was pushing against her spinal cord. He operated again—this time successfully.

Despite his injuries, Brian did not require surgery; three weeks after the accident, he was discharged. On July 22, Donna walked, with the help of a brace, down the hospital corridor. One week later, she went home. She was limping, but she hadn't lost the baby. That night, David and Donna Urey sipped champagne.

The baby was due the last week of October. When the date passed, Urey feared complications. Finally, on November 6, Donna began feeling labor pains. At eleven-thirty p.m., Urey drove her back to Georgetown University Hospital.

Waiting, he relived the agonizing hours he'd spent in Petersburg five months before. He thought about Gary Arbaugh, who had returned the check he'd sent him, explaining that he had a "moral obligation to help." He thought about General Hughes and all the others who had made this day possible.

Urey had not planned to be with his wife in the delivery room. But now, suddenly, he knew that he *had* to be there. Wearing a mask and gown, he held Donna's hand as the baby was delivered.

"It's a boy," Dr. George E. Stevens, the obstetrician, announced. "And he looks perfectly healthy."

As the doctor cut the umbilical cord, the baby started crying. But David Urey hardly noticed, for he was crying, too.

Amid the terror
and confusion of the crash,
the dazed girl
remembered a lesson
her parents had taught her
—always follow
running water downstream

Nightmare in the Jungle

BY JULIANE KOEPCKE

SHORTLY BEFORE NOON on December 24, 1971, LANSA Airlines Flight 508, a turboprop Electra, took off on a regularly scheduled flight from Lima, Peru, to Pucallpa, a jungle town 475 miles northeast across the high Andes. It carried ninety-two passengers, one of whom was seventeen-year-old Juliane Koepcke, who was traveling with her mother. Half an hour after takeoff, the plane's captain radioed that he expected to land in thirty-eight minutes. Then the plane vanished. Search planes found no wreckage. Eleven days later, Juliane Koepcke came out of the jungle—alone, tattered, barefoot, bleeding, pocked with worm lesions but alive. Here, she tells her own extraordinary story.

I have always enjoyed flying, and that sunny December day Mother and I had a good reason for taking a trip: I had just graduated from high school in Lima, and we wanted to spend Christmas with my father in our jungle hut. Daddy, an ecologist, and Mother, an ornithologist, had come to Peru from Germany twenty-five years before. Although they held professorships at San Marcos University in Lima, we spent a lot of time in the jungle where they carried on research.

I was sitting in the third row of seats from the rear, next to the window. Mother sat beside me, and a man we didn't know was on the aisle. Everything seemed quite normal—the takeoff, the climb over the snow-covered Andes, breakfast, the smiling stewardesses, then the green jungle stretching east to the horizon. People were reading or chatting; everyone was in a holiday mood.

In clear weather, the one-hour flight from Lima to Pucallpa can be one of the most beautiful in the world. But thirty minutes after takeoff, when we were over the jungle, visibility diminished. Rain began to beat against the windows, and the air grew turbulent. Suddenly there was a flash of lightning, terrifyingly near. The plane was shaking terribly. Hand baggage fell from the overhead rack. Someone screamed. Outside, I saw a bright yellow flame shooting from the right wing. I looked at my mother, and she said, "This is the end of everything."

An instant later, there was a hefty concussion and I found myself outside the plane, flying apart from it, still strapped in my seat. I can remember turning over and over in the air. I remember thinking that the jungle trees below looked just like cauliflowers. Then I lost consciousness.

The rain woke me up. It was still light. I was lying under a section of three seats turned upside down. There was no sign of my mother, or of any other passenger, or of the plane. All I could hear were frogs croaking—and the rain.

One shoe, one ring and my glasses were gone. One eye was so swollen I could hardly see. I had a bump on my head and a gash in one foot. I felt no pain, but I couldn't muster the energy to move and look around. Thus, I spent the whole night lying under the seat, half-asleep and in shock.

The next morning I crawled out slowly while everything swam

dizzily before me. I saw a small package and opened it. It contained some hard candies and a Christmas cake. I tasted the cake, then dropped it. It was soaking wet and revolting. I took the candies and picked up a long stick with which to probe the ground to avoid snakes, poisonous spiders and ants. My parents had taught me about the perils of the jungle during the years we had lived in it. One lesson I learned was that it's not the big animals —the ocelots, jaguars and tapir—that are most dangerous, but rather the snakes and the tiny ones, the insects.

Feeling ahead with the stick, I started looking for my mother. I was so dizzy that every time I took a few steps I had to rest. After hours of poking around I heard gentle splashing nearby—a tiny brook. My parents had impressed on me that when lost in the jungle one should always look for streams and follow them to larger streams. Rivers are the roads here, and the Indian tribes and the white plantation people live on their banks.

But rivers in the tropical forest of Peru meander and circle. You can walk for miles along a bank and advance only a hundred yards toward your destination. Moreover, rivers are alive with mosquitoes—billions of them, all bloodthirsty—and caimans. But the most frightening creatures are the piranhas, and they would be attracted by the blood from the gash in my foot; if they attacked, they would strip off the flesh with their sharp teeth.

But I *had* to stay near or in the stream. Its banks were overgrown with tangled vines, making every step arduous. Sometimes I had to wade through the water because huge, rotted tree trunks barred my way. It was slow going. At one point I heard the buzzing of flies and followed the sound—to a row of seats from the aircraft. Three girls were strapped in them, dead. Flies covered them. I moved on.

Nights in the jungle are scary. There was always a rustling somewhere: snakes? There was something crawling over my legs: a tarantula? Even the air seemed poisoned by decaying trees. I slept fitfully.

On the third day I heard vultures. Where there are vultures, there are usually bodies. I came upon a piece of airplane fuselage. But I could find no survivors.

During the afternoon of the third day, I heard the noise of aircraft. I shouted. I knew it was senseless, but I yelled, "Hello! Help!" over and over again. They must have been quite near, though I never saw them and, of course, they didn't spot me. Then the noise of the planes faded and I was once again alone. But not disheartened. I could walk, I wasn't hungry and I could drink from the clear stream.

On my fourth day I finished the candy, the only nourishment I had. I was swollen from the stings of mosquitoes and horseflies. Here and there armies of ants on the march blocked my path. And struggling through the tangled undergrowth to avoid them, I covered only a few hundred yards an hour. However, my stream did run into a larger river.

As I pressed on downstream along its bank, huge, dark toads jumped awkwardly and fell back to earth with a frightening slap. I considered eating parts of these toads, but didn't. Amazingly, I wasn't hungry. I resisted delicious-looking fruit because here many things that look tempting are poisonous.

The open wound on my foot was now getting worse, because it was infested with maggots. Every time the flies stung me, they laid eggs in my wounds and now the eggs were hatching. Helplessly I watched the maggots emerge, wagging heads that looked like tips of canned asparagus. I still had a ring—a spiral that could be stretched—so I started using it to gouge them out of the wounds on my legs and arms. They were eating me alive. One sore was now large enough to hold a finger. *God help me,* I thought. *They will amputate—if I ever survive.*

The river was widening. Whenever I could get a good view ahead, I risked swimming. It was faster because the current carried me along. On land I picked my way, careful to watch where I put my feet because the rotting foliage could conceal a snake or a poisonous thornback crab.

Walking had become progressively harder. The lack of food and the humid, 110-degree heat had made me weaker. The river was now so swift that I couldn't swim in it. Late one afternoon—the tenth day, as I later reconstructed it—I was looking for a spot to lie down for the night when I saw a boat moored on the riverbank. And there was a path leading to a small hut. I entered and saw on the floor an outboard motor, carefully wrapped in plastic, and a can of gasoline. Clearly someone would be back. But when?

I lay down on the floor. I slept badly. I kept listening for human voices. But I heard only the screaming of monkeys and the screeching of parakeets.

The next morning I wanted to push on. It might be days, even weeks, before the people came for their boat. But I didn't want to take the boat—it was somebody else's. However, because the rain was pouring down, I stayed in the hut. With a sliver of palm wood, I gouged out more maggots. Then I heard voices, and three men plunged in from the downpour. "Well!" one of them exclaimed in Spanish. "What have we here?"

The men were hunters. They told me they kept several huts in the jungle for their expeditions. They knew about the crash. One man had been in a search plane that flew over the jungle after the accident. "We could see nothing," he said. "No people, no wreckage."

They poured gasoline on my maggot sores and extracted the worms from the wounds on my legs and arms. They washed me with salt water and put salve on my wounds. They made fruit mash for me, but I was unable to eat.

Early next morning they took me downriver in their boat. My river—it was the Shebonya—became wider, swifter and more dangerous. I looked at the shore where I would have had to walk and saw that it became more and more impassable. At the junction with another large river, the Pachitea, there were nasty rapids and whirlpools.

It took us hours to get to the settlement of Tournavista. People came running and shouting to stare at me. One of my rescuers explained why. My eyes were so bloodshot that they looked entirely red. My face was disfigured and swollen out of shape from the insect bites. My arms and legs were pocked with worm lesions. I was a living nightmare.

Tournavista had a small dispensary where I was washed and my wounds were treated. Eleven and a half days after our crash, I again boarded an airplane, a small twin-engine machine that took me to the U. S. mission base of the Summer Institute of Linguistics near Pucallpa, where an American physician looked after me. With the help of my directions, search planes found the wreckage. Daddy arrived to stay by my side. He told me what I had suspected: my mother was dead.

Searchers found the Electra scattered over ten miles of jungle. The cause of the crash, and how Juliane survived, are unknown. One theory is that the plane exploded at 10,000 feet and that the fall of some pieces was cushioned by an enormous updraft of air in the storm.

Though Juliane alone came out of the jungle alive, she was not the only passenger to survive the crash. The first searcher to reach the scene reported: "At least twelve people, perhaps fourteen survived, some of them for ten days. The proof is simple: When we found them, their bodies had decomposed very little or not at all. Those who died outright in the crash had been eaten, right down to the bones, by the vultures and flies."

Juliane Koepcke recovered from the ordeal. Her fears about amputation were unfounded. She was lucky on several counts. The hunters who found her in the hut said that they went there only about once every three weeks. Fortunately, this trip had come at the right time. Had Juliane not waited because of the rain but started downstream again, she would never have walked out. There were no settlements that she could have reached.

An almost incredible saga
of endurance—nearly seventy hours alone
in the icy, storm-racked North Atlantic

Only One
Came Back

BY ØYSTEIN MOLSTAD-ANDRESEN

IT WAS A GLOWERING EVENING—March 21, 1973—when the 20,787-ton Norwegian freighter *Norse Variant* eased out of the harbor at Norfolk, Virginia, bound for Glasgow, Scotland, with a cargo of coal. From the bridge, Capt. Jens-Otto Harsem could barely tell where the wind-streaked sea ended and the sullen sky began. Yet both the captain and the crew had a good feeling about their ship, despite the weather. Storms had been routine that winter, but the freighter had always shrugged off the North Atlantic's worst moods.

Below decks, as the *Norse Variant* plowed ahead, Stein Gabrielsen, twenty-three-year-old ship's mechanic, began stowing away the food and drink that he had purchased for a birthday celebration. A ship-mate would be twenty-five the next day, and Stein planned to surprise him with a party.

Thursday, March 22, dawned cold and raw. The wind shrieked out of the north, and huge seas bore down on the freighter, exploding heavily against her bows. Inside, the twenty-nine-man crew had to brace themselves against bulkheads to keep from being tossed about like dice in a cup. Stein realized that the celebration must wait; the going was simply too rough.

Around ten a.m., the *Norse Variant* ran headlong into an enormous wave that thundered down on her bow and smashed the forward hatch. The No. 1 hold began to take on water as waves kept sweeping across the deck. Although the pumps were handling the problem, Captain Harsem decided to return to Norfolk for repairs.

About an hour later another great wave struck with such devastating force that the welds holding the forward crane to the deck zippered open, and the sea poured into hold No. 2. Now, under an almost continuous battering of wind and water, the *Norse Variant* started to come apart. With leaks erupting, the ship grew increasingly nose-heavy.

The radio officer began signaling the U. S. Coast Guard for assistance, giving the *Norse Variant's* course and position.

The lifeboat alarm sounded at 1:45 p.m. Grabbing his life jacket, Stein rushed to the afterdeck where the crew was gathering. The *Norse Variant* was now wallowing like a harpooned whale. Captain Harsem ordered: "The life rafts! Throw them overboard and jump after them! The Coast Guard will pick you up." Almost as he spoke, two monstrous breakers crashed amidships, plunging the freighter down under the water. In a matter of seconds, the *Norse Variant* was gone.

Stein found himself fighting the suction of the sinking vessel as it dragged him downward toward the Atlantic floor. After what seemed an eternity, the pull weakened. Lungs near bursting, Stein struggled to the surface, boosted by the buoyancy of his life jacket. *Keep calm,* he told himself, amazed at being alive. *Save your strength. The men on the rafts will pick you up.*

He hung limply in his life jacket, trying to catch his breath in the almost unbearably cold water as waves lifted, then dropped him. Each time he was swept up to a fifty-foot crest, he scanned the sea around him for his shipmates. *There must be others,* he thought. Then he spotted a raft. *There they are!* He struggled toward it and heaved himself aboard. It was empty.

As Stein tried to pull his thoughts together, waves swept over the pitching, tossing raft, threatening to wash him back into the sea. Hurricane-force winds drove needles of sleet and spray into his face. Stein was determined to cling to hope. *The Coast Guard is out looking. It will be only a few hours.*

The Coast Guard *was* looking. The *Norse Variant's* distress signals had been picked up at 12:28 p.m., and the search was underway even before she sank. All through the rest of the day, rescue planes crisscrossed the storm while Coast Guard cutters plowed the heavy seas. But no clue to the *Norse Variant's* fate could be spotted. The Atlantic, it seemed, had swallowed the ship whole.

Clinging to the ropes inside the reeling raft, Stein was grateful that he had put on his windbreaker under his life jacket. Like a diver's wet suit, it gave some protection from the cold. He had just learned to parry the tossing effect of each wave by shifting his weight when, suddenly, a churning breaker drove him deep beneath the surface, chewed up the raft and spat it out in little pieces. Again Stein fought to the surface, and there bobbed helplessly in the mountains and valleys of the seething sea.

Once more now, he began scanning the horizon at each opportunity. *Incredible!* Over there, a few hundred yards away, another empty raft was bucking! He fought his way into its path, hauled himself aboard, tied its lifeline securely to his left arm and settled back to wait. *Hang on,* he kept telling himself. *It won't be long now.*

Shortly before nightfall, Stein heard a welcome sound above the roaring of the wind. *A plane!* He grabbed a rocket flare from his raft's emergency compartment, and—with numbed fingers working in maddeningly slow motion—managed to release the safety and fire it off. As the drone of the plane grew steadily weaker, in desperation Stein fired a second rocket—his last one. But the plane was gone. The young seaman was alone once more with the pitching raft and the roar of wind and sea.

Several hours later, a ship's searchlights appeared, sweeping wide arcs through the murk. Stein waved his arms, shouting vainly into the howling wind, "I'm over here! Can't you see me?" But the searchlights blinked off, and the ship churned past only a quarter of a mile away.

At least they're looking, he consoled himself. *There will be another chance.* He settled down to parrying the seas and keeping himself awake.

The next morning—Friday, March 23—Stein was exhausted. His feet were blue and numb, and he knew he had to get the circulation going in his legs. Sliding into the water and holding tight to the side of the raft, he began slowly kicking until he felt a measure of warmth returning. Still worried about the condition of his legs, however, he tried to wrap them with the tattered remains of a canvas shelter. It was a mistake. A mighty wave capsized his craft again and hurled Stein beneath it, his feet imprisoned in the canvas.

Kicking and clawing frantically, he managed to free himself, only to find that his life jacket was so buoyant that it had trapped him against the raft's floor. Fighting for air, he pushed up with all his strength and barely managed to squeeze out from beneath.

Late that afternoon, the storm dealt its cruelest blow. An immense breaker—a great, gray monster the size of a five-story building— thundered down on Stein. The turmoil of raging water tore away his life jacket, snapped his lifeline and sent the raft swirling out of reach. Once more he made a desperate swim—and barely got back aboard.

By dawn Saturday, Stein was almost ready to give in. It had been nearly two full days since he had last closed his eyes. *How pleasant it would be to stretch out and drift off to sleep,* he thought. *No, Stein. If you doze, you are finished. Hang on just one more day.*

As the day went on, the storm began to taper off. But the sky remained empty. Stein began to wonder: *Could the search have been called off?* His muscles ached; his eyes were swollen and nearly blinded by the driving spray. And now his throat was too raw to swallow any of the raft's emergency rations. He felt giddy from lack of sleep. His strength was ebbing fast.

That morning, the search was continuing full-scale. At Coast Guard headquarters in New York, a computer had calculated wind and current and mapped out the area most likely to contain survivors. Coast Guard and Air Force planes had been sent to search a grid of 12,600 square miles, but engine trouble had forced one of the planes back early. When the last aircraft returned to base, 2,200 square miles out of the 12,600 had not been covered—and that was where Stein Gabrielsen was fighting his battle against the sea.

As daylight faded that Saturday, the temptation to sleep was overwhelming Stein: *Even if you freeze to death, there are worse ways to die.* The word brought him to his senses. *Don't be a fool,* he kept repeating. *You are not going to die.* Somehow, he managed to stay awake another night.

On Sunday morning, the seas were calmer. The exhausted seaman decided that it was finally safe to allow himself the luxury he had not dared yield to for almost three days. He closed his eyes and dozed off.

Minutes later, at nine a.m., the roar of a jet plane jolted him awake. It streaked by, several thousand feet above, and disappeared. *How could they miss again?* he asked as he gazed with frustration at the empty horizon.

The men aboard the HC-130 search-and-rescue plane had been out for nearly three hours when—at 9:06 a.m., Sunday, March 25— copilot Lt. Ronald Balleu spotted something off to starboard. It passed out of sight behind them before he could tell what it was. On the return pass, it was clearer: an orange bubble shining like a tiny beacon on the empty sea. It was unmistakably a life raft.

"My God, there's someone in there!" screamed Balleu. The entire crew jammed into the cockpit as the pilot, Lt. Cmdr. Edward L. Weilbacher, brought the plane down for a closer look. They could not believe their eyes. Not only was there someone there, but he was very much alive, jumping up and down. Balleu dropped flares to assure him that he had been seen, then radioed his base. Within minutes, the nearest vessel, an oil tanker about half an hour away, had set course for the little raft.

At the same time, two frogmen aboard Weilbacher's plane got suited up and bailed out, carrying plastic-wrapped medical equipment, blankets and a radio transmitter. They splashed down a few dozen yards from the raft. Then, as they pulled themselves aboard it, Stein, who a minute before had been dancing for joy, went limp as a rag. "He's okay," they radioed to the plane circling overhead. "It's unbelievable."

There was something Stein had to know. "Have you found any

others?" His voice was so hoarse it was barely audible. "I'm sorry," one of the frogmen answered gently. Stein lay back and closed his eyes.

For nearly seventy hours Stein Gabrielsen—alone in a stormy sea without sleep and unable to eat or drink—had survived conditions that no man should have been able to survive. In an incredible feat of human endurance, he had struggled against screaming seventy-five-mile-an-hour winds and fifty-foot killer waves. He had endured snow, sleet, hail and freezing temperatures. Amazingly, he was not frostbitten. He was dehydrated, cut and bruised, but that was all. After a few days of rest, he would be on his way home to his native Norway. For Stein Gabrielsen, the long ordeal was over.

The extraordinary story of what
a 66,000-volt charge did to a man's life

Shock!

BY JOSEPH P. BLANK

LEE FOLKINS WAS FEELING good as he sat on a rock and watched some new construction equipment being tried out in the town of Fort Towson, Oklahoma. He was thirty-three years old and, at six-foot-five and 230 pounds, the picture of finely conditioned physical power. He had an attractive wife, three bright children and a comfortable home in Norman, Oklahoma. Retired from professional football after playing offensive end for the Green Bay Packers, the Dallas Cowboys and the Pittsburgh Steelers, he now was a partner in an Oklahoma construction company. He was earning $50,000 a year as company president and was zeroing in on his target of success: to be worth a million dollars by the time he was forty. In all, the future looked as sunny as the weather.

On this hot mid-July afternoon in 1972, Lee was watching as his superintendent, Herman Wood, raised and lowered the long boom of a new backhoe, a machine that dug ditches for sewer pipe. Supported by metal towers above the boom were 66,000-volt electrical transmission wires. Lee ambled over to check an oil leak—and touched the machine.

At that moment, the current in the wires overhead jumped to the raised boom and shot through Lee. He was flung to the ground. An unseen force seemed to be crushing him, he said later, and he was forced to gasp wrenchingly for air. Then a tingling sensation ran through his body.

The charge passed through the backhoe without hurting Wood, since, like a bird perching unharmed on a high-tension wire, he was not grounded. Wood leaped off the machine to assist Folkins as he struggled dazedly to his feet, his eyes large and round.

"I got shocked," Lee said to his frightened companion. "I'm all right, but I think I'll go back to the motel." He slurred his words and moved as if he were very drunk. Wood thought, *Thank God he's alive.*

At the motel, Lee was excited and tense. His thumb and two fingers on his left hand were burned. When he removed his boots and socks, he saw burns on his left big toe and on the heel of his right foot. The charge had entered through his hand and left through his feet.

He spent a restless night. His muscles and joints hurt. He felt strange, unfamiliar to himself.

The next morning, he drove home and told his wife, Carolyn, about his experience. She telephoned the family doctor; it was the doctor's day off. "Don't bother to call him tomorrow," Lee said. "I'm really okay. Just a little sore and tired."

But he wasn't okay. Over the weekend, he stumbled without cause several times. He felt remote from his wife and children. His good memory suddenly disappeared. He remembered that an important change had to be made on the Fort Towson job, but he couldn't remember what it was. Five minutes after he asked his wife a question, he had to ask the same question again. Carolyn wondered whether she should leave as planned with the children the following Tuesday to drive to Seattle to visit her mother and Lee's parents.

When Lee awoke Monday, he awoke to a different world. He knew that he had changed. Throughout his football and business careers he had been aggressive, confident. Now he felt weak and fearful. *What the hell is going on?* he asked himself.

At the office, he couldn't concentrate. By the time he read the second paragraph of a letter, he had sometimes forgotten the contents of the first. He was unbearably uncomfortable. A loud, persistent ringing sounded in his ears. His skull felt too small for his brains. Desperation gripped him. *I can't stand it,* he thought. *Maybe I'm having a nervous breakdown. I have to get away.*

He drove to a bank and cashed two checks totaling $4,000. He "came to" as he was standing in the bank lobby and staring at the pack of hundred-dollar bills in his hand. *How peculiar,* he thought. *What's this money for?*

Again he slipped into mental nothingness. Suddenly he was aware that he was in Dallas, 200 miles away, driving around the old neighborhood where he had lived while playing for the Cowboys. Something was happening to him over which he had no control. He had no memory of parking his car and leaving his suitcase and keys in it. He walked the hot streets.

At a bus station, he noticed a sign: "Take a Trip to Denver." *I'll get on that bus. No one will know me. I'll sleep. But I must appear natural. They mustn't know that I'm going crazy.* His hands were wet with sweat as he took the ticket from the agent.

Three hours later, Lee was awakened by the driver's announcement of a supper stop in Wichita Falls, Texas. He stepped off the bus feeling utterly wretched and exhausted. *What I've done doesn't make sense.* He phoned Carolyn. "I'm in a bus station in Wichita Falls," he told her. "I've tried to get control of myself, but I can't. I've got four thousand dollars, and I'm going to Denver."

"Lee, stay there, please," she pleaded. "I'll drive right over and get you."

"No, I'm going to Denver. You leave for Santa Fe tomorrow. I'll meet you at your motel. I'm tired, just tired." He hung up.

Frightened and confused, Carolyn called a psychologist friend. She described the electric-shock episode and repeated his telephone conversation. Her friend offered to check with experts familiar with the effects of shock. The friend called her back and reported: "Lee apparently is suffering a classic reaction to deep shock. He can hurt himself. Call the police and have him picked up for his own protection."

"No," Carolyn said, crying. "He sounded very determined and very upset. If someone tries to stop him, he may do something violent. I'll call the police if he doesn't show up in Santa Fe."

At three a.m., she loaded the children into the car and set out to drive the 550 miles to Santa Fe. After checking into the motel, she drove to the bus station to await the next bus from Denver. When Lee didn't show up all afternoon, Carolyn became desperately afraid. *Where is he?*

Lee had slept for eleven hours when the bus pulled into Denver at seven a.m. He stepped off the bus feeling terrific. His senses, it seemed to him, were keener than they had ever been. Every color in the drab little café where he went for breakfast was vividly lovely. The aromas of coffee, sweet rolls and frying bacon were fantastic, and he ate with a zest he had never before experienced. *Oh, I feel great. I'll show Carolyn that I'm fine. I'll just buy a motorcycle and tool on down to Santa Fe.*

Lee had never been on a motorcycle, but he found a dealer and for $1,700 bought the biggest, most powerful cycle in the shop. A mechanic showed him how to operate it, and Lee took off for Santa Fe. He felt free and unburdened. The throbbing, powerful machine beneath him seemed like a living extension of himself.

When Carolyn saw him outside the motel at seven that evening, she wept in relief. She quickly told him that he was suffering "classic electric-shock reaction," and that his symptoms would gradually disappear. Lee was relieved, but he refused to return to Carolyn and his family. "I have to be alone for a while," he said. They argued, but Lee convinced Carolyn that she and the children should go on and visit their parents in Seattle as planned; he would return home.

For a while, Lee exulted in the drive to Norman. Then, suddenly, a police car flashed him to the side of the road. Pleasure turned to panic. He had no driver's license or identification. He carried a wad of hundred-dollar bills. He had no reasonable explanation for being where he was. *If he orders me to the police station, I'll take away his gun and make a run for it.*

But the officer only inquired about the absence of a license plate and was satisfied when Lee showed him the bill of sale and the remains of the temporary cardboard license tag, most of which had been demolished by rain. As Lee pulled away, the tension of the incident brought back the ringing in his ears and the hot pains shooting through his head. In time, his head began to clear. *How could I have thought of taking that cop's gun? That's irrational. What is going on with me?*

Back in Norman, things were not right. Lee decided not to return to work. The prospect of dealing with even routine business matters appalled him. On one occasion, he tried playing golf with three friends, but the need to make decisions overwhelmed him. Which club to use? How hard to hit the ball? It was too much. His head pounded. He felt sick. He flung a club fifty feet, then sat down on the grass and cried.

One of Lee's companions located Carolyn in Los Angeles, on her way to Seattle, and advised her to get home quickly. She left the children with friends and was on a plane within three hours. Lee wasn't glad to see her; she represented responsibility, and he didn't want it. But he did agree to see a neurologist.

After examining him, the doctor told Lee: "Your behavior follows a definite pattern experienced by shock victims. You should recover your stability, but it may take months. Take it easy for a while. Relax. Avoid stressful situations."

Lee couldn't relax. Any effort to read, think or make a decision gave him a banging headache. He didn't want Carolyn with him and insisted that she continue her planned vacation with the children. He slept sixteen hours a day but usually awoke feeling miserable and depressed. He tried to do some work at the office, but it was impossible. His secretary's voice alternately faded and grew loud, as if someone were playing with the volume control. Sometimes he couldn't complete a sentence because he forgot what he wanted to say.

He tried to distract himself by repairing the children's bicycles, but he couldn't thread a nut on a bolt. Any challenge at all overwhelmed him. He took the phone off the hook, disconnected the doorbell and refused to answer a knock.

When Carolyn and the children returned from Seattle, Lee was at first delighted, then dismayed. The door kept slamming as the children and their friends ran in and out of the house, and he was afraid of his impulse to slap them. The dog barked. The phone rang. He was drowning in confusion and torment, and he had to escape. Telling Carolyn that he had to go to the office, he stalked out of the house and climbed on his motorcycle.

That night, Lee called Carolyn from Garden City, Kansas. "I don't know what I'm going to do. I'll call you soon."

Lee now motorcycled to Seattle—to his parents' home and the scenes of his childhood. There was his kindergarten, the playground where he played ball, the window he had broken with an apple. Tears rolled down his cheeks.

Carolyn called Lee's parents and pleaded with Lee. "We need you. The doctor says you have to get into a hospital for a checkup. I can fly up tomorrow, and we can return together." She expected resistance, but this time Lee meekly said, "Okay."

When four days of tests confirmed that Lee had "acute brain syndrome," a reversible condition, the psychiatrist recommended that he return to work. But Lee had left his company; he felt incapable of holding any job. He couldn't stand any pressure. At a restaurant, his head throbbed when he was confronted with a menu. He threw it down and said to his wife, "You order for me."

During frequent, long spells of black depression, Lee would not communicate with anyone. Then, ever so slowly, he improved. A turning point came in February 1973 when Lee and Carolyn sold their house in Norman to conserve money and moved to a forty-acre farm they owned in Little Axe, about fifteen miles away. It was a new life-style for them. In their isolation, members of the family became dependent on one another. Before the shock, Lee had been so preoccupied with his career that he had never really got to know his children. Now he had the time to get to know them better.

At first, he cared for the pigs, built fences and cleared land only when he felt like it. When overcome by the "bad" feeling, he would sleep it off. Gradually, without really being aware of it, Lee found that routine jobs had become simply routine again. He spent less time thinking about himself. Farm work offered him satisfaction in ways he had never dreamed possible. He found delight in watching a litter of pigs grow, in building a good, strong fence, in the silhouette of his favorite tree against the sunset.

The test came in September 1973, when Carolyn and Lee realized that their savings were almost exhausted. Carolyn said, "If you get a job, the children and I can manage the farm." Six months earlier, Lee would not have been able to accept this pressure and would have flipped back into a state of depression. Now he went out and got a job.

But he was afraid. Could he handle the give-and-take of the business world? The job was selling sewer pipe, but at first he could work only part-time before the headaches drove him back to the farm. Even that haven reminded him, however, that his family needed money. Soon he was working full-time. In a few months he was promoted to a decision-making position in the company. He led a double work-life for several months: the job during the day, farming with his family evenings and weekends. But now the farm was producing enough so that he could make a choice between farming and industry. He chose the farm.

Lee will probably never know just how his body and mind recovered. He still thinks frequently about the shock and the hellish ordeal it imposed on him and his family. "That shock also changed me," he concludes. "Before the accident, I was primarily concerned with a big future goal. I measured success in terms of business status and money. Now I live each day for its own sake, what I give to it and what I get from it. I feel good with these values, and I sometimes wonder if I'm not coming out of this horrible experience with more than I had before it."

The hijacking of Southern Flight 49
spanned thirty hours, three countries and 4,000 miles.
When it was finally over, the twenty-seven passengers
shared a common conviction: They owed their lives
to the cool courage of Capt. William Haas

"We're Taking Over This Plane! And Let's Not Have Any Heroes"

BY JOSEPH P. BLANK

ABOARD SOUTHERN AIRWAYS Flight 49, stewardess Donna Holman was pouring a cup of coffee for Capt. William R. Haas in the small galley near the cockpit door. Suddenly, a passenger, Henry Jackson, a burly, round-faced man with a mustache and an Afro haircut, rose from his seat and strode forward. Entering the galley, he spoke a few quick sentences to the stewardess, encircled her neck with his left arm, then turned her to confront the passengers. Her face was pale and frozen, her eyes were glassy with terror. Jackson's right hand gripped a chromium-plated Smith & Wesson .38.

"Nobody move!" he shouted. "We're taking over this plane! And let's not have any heroes, because they'll be dead heroes."

Mid-cabin, Louis Moore stood on a seat, waved a Luger and repeated the threats in a tense, high-pitched voice. And at the rear of the plane, Melvin Cale pointed a .22-caliber "Saturday Night Special" at the neck of stewardess Karen Chambers.

The twenty-seven passengers were variously shocked, terrified, incredulous or calm. Business consultant Frank Morkill looked at Jackson's eyes and felt a sharp fear cutting inside him. Margie Brennan reached out, clutched the hand of her fifteen-year-old son, Patrick, and whispered, "Everything'll be all right." Alvin Fortson, an eighty-three-year-old farmer with a lung problem, began wheezing and coughing. This was his first airplane trip. Gale Buchanan, an agronomist, thought of his wife and children and figured that he wouldn't be home in time for the dinner party he and his wife were giving that night.

Five minutes earlier, at six p.m. on Friday, November 10, 1972, Haas, 43, and his copilot, Billy Halroyd Johnson, 37, had lifted the twin-jet DC-9 off the runway at Birmingham, Alabama, for a short hop to Montgomery. The flight had originated an hour previously at Memphis, Tennessee, and was scheduled to terminate in Miami. It wasn't Haas's turn to fly; he had taken over Flight 49 as a favor to another pilot.

Haas now heard a key turn in the cockpit door and swiveled around to take his coffee. Instead, he found himself staring into the muzzle of a gun. Stewardess Holman, with Jackson's arm around her neck, breathlessly announced, "This is a hijacking—he's not kidding."

Haas's face never changed expression. He saw that Mrs. Holman was virtually paralyzed with fear. In a soft, even voice, he told the hijacker, "Keep calm. We don't want anyone hurt. We'll obey your instructions."

As the stewardess returned to the cabin, where the other two hijackers were flourishing guns and hand grenades, Jackson remained in the cockpit, shouting commands. "Get this plane to Detroit! We want ten million dollars from the city of Detroit, or we're gonna start killing people on this plane."

Haas quietly explained that the plane would have to be refueled for the trip to Detroit. "Then get gas at Jackson," the hijacker ordered. "And nobody and nothing near this plane except the gas truck and driver in undershorts."

At Mississippi's Jackson airport, the hijacker pulled the safety pin on a grenade and held it at Haas's ear, manually depressing the safety lever to prevent it from exploding. As the fuel truck began pulling away, Jackson snapped, "Take off!" They did, and he slipped the safety pin back into the head of the grenade.

Shortly after Haas began circling over Detroit, the FBI reported the ransom demand to Mayor Roman Gribbs. "Are you kidding?" he exclaimed. "That much money! Why would they want it from the city?"

Mayor Gribbs soon got his answer. Jackson, 25, and Moore, 27, both faced charges in Detroit for rape and were free on $500 bonds. Prior to these charges, they had filed a four-million-dollar claim against the city for police brutality related to another arrest. When the city offered to settle for twenty-five dollars, they were outraged. "I think their minds kind of blew," their attorney said later.

Cale, 21, from Oak Ridge, Tennessee, was Moore's half brother. In 1971, he had been sentenced to a five-year term for larceny. He had escaped from a minimum-security rehabilitation program about two weeks before the hijacking.

After two hours of circling, during which the Detroit tower kept assuring the hijackers that the money was being rounded up, Southern Flight 49 began to run critically low on fuel. The hijackers ordered Haas to land at nearby Cleveland for refueling.

As they headed for Cleveland, Buchanan wrote a brief letter of love to his wife, in case he never saw her again. He then volunteered to help Fortson, who was coughing violently and complaining of pains in his legs. Buchanan removed the elderly man's boots and socks and rubbed his legs to increase circulation. Hijacker Cale occasionally grasped Fortson's wrist, stared at his watch and nodded approvingly. He appeared to enjoy playing doctor, even though he didn't actually have his fingers on the ailing man's pulse.

After refueling in Cleveland, Jackson directed Haas to Toronto. "And tell 'em," he growled, "that they goddamn better have the money there." Each stop had made the hijackers more furious and increased the pressure on the crew. Anything could happen. En route to Toronto, Haas got permission to use the lavatory. He casually strolled down the aisle, pausing to reassure the five women passengers and pat a few men on the shoulder. He gave not the slightest hint of the grinding tension he had been under in piloting the aircraft with a gun or grenade at his ear. He was using his own calmness to keep the hijackers as calm as possible.

At four a.m.—ten hours after the takeover—Flight 49 cruised in big circles through rain and snow over Toronto. Some passengers dozed fitfully. Others stared numbly into space. Mrs. Brennan was now caring for Fortson. Wan, weak, struggling for breath, Fortson was sprawled across three seats. After taking his pulse, Mrs. Brennan told Cale, "We have to get an oxygen mask down for this man, sir. He's dying." Cale consented. The pure oxygen eased Fortson's breathing difficulties.

Southern Airways flew $500,000, borrowed from the city of Detroit, to Toronto. The hijackers refused it as insufficient. Again the plane had to land for fuel. Back in the air, Jackson told the Toronto control tower, "We're tired of all this bull. No more foolin' around. We're taking this [obscenity] to Oak Ridge and dive it into a nuclear reactor."

At eight a.m. on Saturday, Haas began circling the Oak Ridge–Knoxville, Tennessee, area. Two hours later, he was forced to land at Lexington, Kentucky, for fuel. He then resumed circling over Oak Ridge. Officials of the Atomic Energy Commission at Oak Ridge shut down three nuclear-research reactors and evacuated all but the most essential emergency personnel. The hijackers set a twelve noon deadline. "I was born to die," Moore told a few passengers. "And if I have to take all of you with me, that's all right with me."

Exactly at twelve, since the money had not been collected, Jackson leveled his gun at Haas and said, "Dive it into a reactor."

"I can't," Haas replied. "There's an overcast beneath us, and there's no way to tell where the reactors are." He asked for another hour of time, explaining that there was probably confusion on the ground because of the difference between Eastern and Central time. Although Haas spoke matter-of-factly, he was bargaining hard for an extra hour of life for every person on the plane.

Jackson agreed, then dictated the hijackers' demand to copilot Johnson for radio transmission to the ground: "The one o'clock

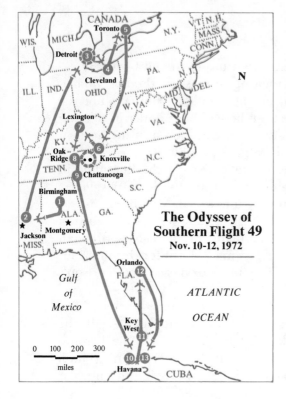

The Odyssey of
Southern Flight 49
Nov. 10-12, 1972

deadline isn't far off. We must have the money, seven bullet-proof vests, helmets and a document from President Nixon granting us the ten million dollars. We must have stimulants for the crew, food, a six-pack of Pabst Blue Ribbon beer, coffee, water and cigarettes for the passengers. If the conditions are not met, we take this thing into an atomic-energy plant."

Shortly before the deadline, Southern radioed that the hijackers' demands would be met at the Chattanooga, Tennessee, airport. The airline had assembled two million dollars in cash. On the assumption that the captured plane would head next for Havana, authorities figured that the hijackers would not have time to verify the amount of money.

As Haas began the descent toward Chattanooga, he suggested to Jackson that the passengers, having served their purpose as hostages, ought to be released after the ransom was obtained. But it wasn't to be. The hijackers were shaken and infuriated by the crowds staring up at the plane from the hilltops and shopping-center parking lots around the airport. "Pull down the shades!" Moore shrieked at the passengers as the plane leveled off to land. "Get your heads between your legs! No talking!" The hijackers saw an FBI agent in every man, woman and youngster. They desperately wanted to get away from the airport; unloading the passengers would only delay them.

A fuel truck, and a smaller truck bearing the ransom, crawled toward the isolated plane. As the items demanded by the hijackers were being unloaded from the small truck, the man handling the fuel hose stumbled over the containers of coffee and kicked over sandwiches. Concluding that he was an FBI agent deliberately prolonging the loading period, Jackson cocked his .38 and aimed. "I'm gonna kill him," he said to Haas.

"He's just nervous in this situation," Haas explained. He called through the open cockpit window to the fuel man: "Take it easy! You won't be hurt. Just get the gas in."

The instant the fuel nozzle was removed from the wing, Jackson said, "Let's go. Take her to Havana. And tell them we want Fidel Castro waiting at the airport." Copilot Johnson duly transmitted the latest demands over the radio.

In the air, the hijackers paraded about in flak vests and riot helmets with plastic visors. They each swallowed a few amphetamines, washing them down with miniature bottles of liquor. Moore waved the Presidential "grant," a piece of paper bearing official-looking seals, and repeated, "Ain't this great? We're millionaires! The money's ours!"

The bulging sacks and bags with their enormous wealth seemed to intoxicate Moore. He grandly announced, "Folks, we got nothin' against you. Some of you businessmen have missed a day's work. You all have things you want to buy, and you got payments on your houses. We're gonna share the wealth." He grabbed a handful of bills and started down the aisle, giving the passengers $150, $250, $300—depending on whim. No passenger dared offend the hijackers by refusing the money. In the cockpit, Moore began piling money around Haas and Johnson. After he had counted out more than $200,000, Haas asked him to stop because the clutter of bills was interfering with the operation of some controls.

When Haas began making his approach turn into Havana's José Martí Airport, Moore yelled, "Shades down! Heads between legs!"

As soon as the plane came to a stop after landing, Jackson and Moore, armed with pistols and grenades, climbed out the cockpit window and down an escape rope. A group of Cuban soldiers and officials surrounded them. The hijackers kept demanding to see Castro, apparently to arrange a financial deal; but the Cubans refused to negotiate and edged closer to the hijackers. The two men threatened them with grenades, then climbed back into the plane. "Get me Fee-del!" Jackson kept raving. "And get me a fuel truck, or we're going to start throwing dead people out of this airplane."

After the plane had been on the ground for an hour, it occurred to

Frank Morkill that his ability to speak Spanish might help to conclude the hijacking. He tapped the man in front of him and said, "Pass the word that a passenger can speak Spanish, if needed." Within a few minutes, Moore yelled. "Where's the guy that talks Spanish?" Morkill moved to the cockpit jump seat and pleaded with the tower: "This situation has been going on for more than twenty-two hours. The hijackers are desperate. For the love of God, comply with their demands."

Meanwhile, in the forward cabin, Moore was indignant. "Those people wanted to arrest us," he told the passengers. "Can you believe that? Why, they're nothing but a bunch of Spanish-speaking George Wallaces!"

Finally, a fuel truck reached the plane, but the driver only partially filled the tanks before hastily pulling away. Jackson ordered Haas to get the plane off the ground immediately. Haas then flew to the U. S. Naval air station at Key West, Florida, for a complete refueling. There, Jackson told the pilot, "Take it to Switzerland."

Haas explained that this wasn't possible. The DC-9 engines needed a type of oil not available at that air station; the aircraft didn't have the range for a direct transatlantic flight; charts were needed for a northern crossing to Europe. "We should change aircraft," Haas suggested. "This is now the worst aircraft Southern has, and we're the worst crew in the airline."

"Just get what you need at Orlando," he was told.

As the airplane took to the air again, Gale Buchanan felt the sickening effects of perpetual anxiety. He accepted the flight as a crazy nightmare that had to end in tragedy. How much longer could the engines keep going without proper maintenance? How much longer could the sleepless pilots control the aircraft with sound judgment? *My God,* he realized, *we're going into our second night.*

As the plane approached Orlando, a decision of vital importance to the occupants of Flight 49 was being made over long-distance phone lines. Acting FBI Director L. Patrick Gray III, calling from his home in Connecticut, told his special agent in charge at McCoy Air Force Base in Orlando, "This aircraft will not take off." The FBI planned to shoot out the tires. Once the aircraft was immobilized, agents expected to board it, according to a method rehearsed earlier in the day, and rescue the passengers and crew.

Director Gray decided not to consult Captain Haas, although the late J. Edgar Hoover had had an understanding with the Air Line Pilots Association that the FBI would take no action against a hijacked plane without the agreement of the aircraft commander. Independent action was justified in this case, Gray concluded, because the pilot and copilot were "not free to exercise their best judgment . . . nor was the pilot free to command his aircraft." Unknown to Director Gray, Haas thought he had just about persuaded the hijackers to release the passengers.

While the plane was being refueled, fifteen agents crept through the darkness to the rear of the plane and crouched beneath the fuselage. As the fuel truck drew away, they opened fire on the tires.

The shots sounded like dull pops inside the cabin. The plane sagged to the left as the twin tires on that side went flat. The twin tires on the right and at the nose remained inflated.

At first, bewilderment and consternation crossed the faces of Jackson and Moore, standing at the cockpit door. Then they became screaming maniacs. Moore fired twice at the departing fuel truck. Jackson fired twice past Haas's head through another window, twice through the galley floor at the gunners under the plane. He shrieked, "We're gonna start shootin' people and throw 'em out the window! You're first, Harold!" (He meant copilot Billy *Halroyd* Johnson, who had been handling radio communication between the plane and the tower.) "You did it! You told them to do it! We're gonna kill you."

The two hijackers dragged Johnson out of his seat, across the jump seat and into the cabin. The stewardesses screamed. "No! Please! Don't shoot him!"

Johnson flung himself to the floor between the second and third rows of seats. Jackson fired. The copilot screamed in pain as the bullet tore through a seat and into his upper right arm, shattering the bone. Jackson pulled the trigger again, but the gun misfired. Moore said to Jackson, "That's enough, man. Don't kill him. We may need him. Let's get out of here."

Johnson, ashen-faced, rose slowly, clutching his right arm. The sleeve of his white shirt was red with blood. Jackson shoved him into the cockpit, then turned to Haas. "Take off!" he screamed.

"They've blown our tires. We can't go anyplace."

"Get into the air, or we'll start killing people."

Haas didn't think he could make the plane fly, but he poured full power to the engines. The sudden blast from the twin jets sent the FBI agents under the plane rolling like oranges. One agent was blown some 150 feet and had his clothes torn off.

The plane bounced, creaked and vibrated wildly as it roared down the runway. Rubber peeled from the two flattened tires and flew into the left engine. The two left rims cut grooves into the paved runway and gave off long streams of sparks.

The two stewardesses gripped each other by the hand and prayed aloud, tears running down their cheeks. Morkill, his head on a pillow across his lap, thought, *It'll never take off. There'll be a skidding, then a crash, then an explosion.* Buchanan didn't want the plane to leave the ground. *Let it come to an end. Let it crash. Let it burn. At least some of us will have a chance of getting out.*

Haas watched the air-speed indicator. The lift-off speed of this DC-9 was normally between 140 and 150 miles an hour. At a speed of about 120 miles per hour, Haas gauged the remaining runway ahead of him and decided he had to fly or abort. Almost imperceptibly, he pulled back on the controls. The vibrations ceased. For several hundred yards the plane rode the cushion of compressed air that builds up between a rushing plane and the ground. Then Flight 49 climbed into the night. "Someone above pulled us up," Haas later told a passenger.

As the plane left the lights of Orlando behind, Haas turned to the hijackers. His plane had only one more landing, probably a crash landing, left in it, he told them. Another takeoff was impossible. Jackson believed him. "Take it to Havana," he said. Despite his pain and useless right arm, copilot Johnson helped Haas with the cockpit chores.

Haas flew southward slowly to avoid stress on the engines. He turned off the air conditioning and depressurized the cabin when a red light indicated a malfunction. Everyone in the aircraft was drenched with sweat. Many suffered sharp ear pains from the reduced cabin pressure.

At eleven-thirty p.m., Haas called Morkill to the cockpit to act as an interpreter with the José Martí Airport tower. After being briefed on the condition of the aircraft, Morkill talked with the tower and requested a foamed runway for an emergency landing.

"We do not have enough foam for an entire runway," the chief operator replied. "But a foam truck will meet you after you land. How much fuel are you carrying?"

"One and a quarter hours. The pilot will hold at two thousand feet and burn it off."

"Very well. But keep away from the downtown area."

The stewardesses prepared the passengers for an emergency landing: "At the final approach, put a pillow on your knees and your head on the pillow. Grasp your ankles. Stay in position until the aircraft has stopped. Then hurry out, either by the emergency chutes at the front doors or the emergency exits that we'll open over the wings." And Karen Chambers added, "Stay calm—and pray."

Donna Holman stepped into the cockpit to speak with the pilot. "We've done all we know to do," she said. "Is there anything else?" He took her chin between his thumb and forefinger and shook it reassuringly. "Go back to your seat," he told her gently. "You'll live to be old and gray and have lots of kids."

She looked at him through wet eyes. She knew that he was the kind of man who had to say that, but she didn't believe him.

As his fuel tanks neared empty, Haas wheeled the plane slowly for a landing approach. The three hijackers, each with a plastic flight bag crammed with money, sat near the exits to be the first out of the plane. Some passengers prayed. Others shook hands in farewell.

Mrs. Brennan, crying, held Fortson's hand with her right hand; with her left she reached across the aisle toward her son.

"I love you," she said. "I'll see you in heaven, Patty."

"I love you, Mother."

Now the ground rushed up toward the stricken aircraft. Lightly, delicately, like an aerialist stepping out on a high wire, Haas brought the plane down. As the two left wheels hit the runway, twin streams of sparks shot out. The craft bounced and jarred. Windows rattled. Cabin walls creaked. The plane came to a halt, its undercarriage smoking.

It was 12:32 a.m. on Sunday, November 12. After more than thirty hours, nine landings in three countries, and more than 4,000 miles of hopscotching, Southern Flight 49 had finally terminated.

The hijackers fled, dashing for the tall grass near the airport. They were rounded up within three minutes. Jackson, with two machine pistols at his back, held the bag of money on top of his head and pleaded, "Don't shoot me, baby. Don't shoot me."

After the passengers had safely reached the ground, a Cuban officer asked for the interpreter. " 'The Man,' " he said to Morkill, "would like to talk to the pilot." Castro appeared in his pressed fatigues, shook Haas's hand and said, *Magnifico! Magnifico!* That was a fantastically skillful landing. We are very relieved that a potential disaster was averted."

Castro asked if they could have done more to help. Haas said, "You did all we could ask for. *Gracias. Muchas gracias.*"

While Haas and Castro talked, the passengers and stewardesses were assembled in a terminal lounge and offered coffee or frozen daiquiris, the preliminary to a dinner of celebration. Many faces were streaked with tears. Some passengers were numb and still shaking. Others were exhilarated. Many believed that God had taken a direct part in their deliverance.

All of them, however, were tightly bound by a common conviction about their survival. They expressed it when Captain Haas walked into the lounge. In a spontaneous reaction, they rose from their seats and gave him a long, heartfelt ovation.

Later that day, Southern Airways sent another DC-9 to Havana to bring back the passengers and crew to the United States. In 1980, the hijackers were returned to the United States. Tried and convicted in February 1981, Jackson was sentenced to twenty-five years in prison, and Cale and Moore each received twenty-year sentences. Southern Airways' two million dollars was returned by Cuba in 1976.

The hijacking of Southern Flight 49 prompted the United States and Cuba, through the offices of the Swiss embassy in Havana, to enter discussions about a mutually agreeable method for dealing with air and sea piracy. These discussions resulted in the signing of an agreement on February 15, 1973, which provided for the punishment or extradition of hijackers using violence or extortion. This agreement expired in 1978 and was not renewed.

As they studied the forbidding rocks
and the sullen seas, the islanders were certain of just one thing:
The children would be found alive
—or not at all

Emergency Whistle
on Block Island

BY FLOYD MILLER

THE SINGLE LONG BLAST of the whistle could be heard from one end
of Block Island to the other—seven miles north to south, three and
one-half miles at its widest. The summer people—swimming, surf
casting, pleasure boating—were hardly aware of the sound. But the
year-round island people knew the whistle was a cry for help, a
summons to the Block Island Volunteer Rescue Squad.

It was the afternoon of August 4, 1969, and the sun was shining
for the first time in a week. After the long days of fog and wind and
rain, the drenched but refreshed island began to sparkle—a small
green jewel set in the sea off the shore of Rhode Island at the eastern
entrance to Long Island Sound. Several hundred visitors had poured
out of Victorian hotels, cottages and rooming houses, eager to enjoy
at last the sand and the sea.

The Kramek family, of Parsippany, New Jersey, had left their
rented cottage at about two-fifteen and, at the urging of their eighteen-year-old daughter, Diane, headed north to Cow Cove. The cove
is a rocky inlet at the storm-scarred northern tip of the island, a
place of somber beauty inhabited by gulls and the ghosts of
drowned mariners. On this forbidding shore stands a concrete-and-
stone lighthouse, which looks not unlike a small, stern church with
an automated light in its belfry. Just north of the light, the island
narrows to a fifty-foot-wide spit of sand called Sandy Point, which

runs beneath the water to become the treacherous Block Island North Reef. It was here that Diane wanted to be.

Her diary entry for August 3 reads, "Tomorrow I'll go and spend all day at Sandy Point. I've fallen in love with the view. Plan to build a house there; it is such a perfect place to go on a honeymoon."

Near the lighthouse, Stanley Kramek, a retired Marine Corps major, began to surf cast. His wife, Gudrun, a handsome woman then recovering from a recent hip operation, set up an easel and began to sketch. Their thirteen-year-old son, Stephen, and his friend and houseguest, Matthew Hikel, 12, went exploring to the west. Diane walked north and settled herself on top of a dune next to the lighthouse, there to lie in the sun and daydream. The time was 2:30.

After an hour and a quarter, as Stanley was throwing back his first catch, a sand shark, his wife called to him in alarm: "I hear Stephen shouting!"

He listened and heard only the surf, but Gudrun's ears heard something more. "It's Stephen, and something is terribly wrong!" she cried.

Then Stanley saw his son. Stephen had run through the sand

dunes all the way from the lighthouse; he was staggering from exhaustion and hysteria.

Gudrun saw her husband reach Stephen just as he dropped to his knees, tears streaming down his face. Then Stanley came racing back, his face set and white. A man and a woman were parked in a car nearby, enjoying the view. Stanley shouted to them, "Two children have been swept into the sea out there at the point! Send for help!"

The car sped away, and Kramek himself set off for the point. He floundered and scrambled his way along the "road" through the dunes, where the deep, dry sand sucked at his feet. He made it past the lighthouse and finally came onto the wet hard sand of the point. The roar of wind and sea was pierced by the shrill cries of the gulls that wheeled above his head. The surf broke to his right and left; straight ahead was the reef. There was nothing else.

Ironically, the very emptiness of the place gave him a moment of hope, for there was no evidence that Diane and Matthew had ever been here. Then he saw a small bundle of blue cotton fabric on the sand, the work shirt Diane had been wearing over her bathing suit. Beyond the shirt were prints of her bare feet leading directly into the sea.

When the emergency whistle blew, the twenty volunteer members of the rescue squad went into action. They were merchants, carpenters, fishermen, power linemen, highway maintenance men—all bound together by shortwave radios in their homes and cars. Weathered, fifty-five-year-old Charles "Ed" Conley, captain of the squad, was just arriving home from work when the dispatcher's voice crackled on his radio: "Possible drowning at Sandy Point." Conley's wife was standing in the back doorway, and he yelled to her, "Call the Coast Guard." Then he turned his car and headed north.

Twelve minutes after the alarm, Conley and several other island men had joined the lonely figure of Stanley Kramek at Sandy Point. To a casual observer, the scene might not have seemed threatening. The sea appeared calm; the sky was clear. But Conley knew the place intimately, and at this moment he was scared. A strong ebb tide sweeps the vast waters of Long Island Sound over Sandy Point eastward into the Atlantic; no swimmer had ever made headway against it. As he began to search with his binoculars, he was certain of just one thing: They would find the children alive or not at all. The sea never returns bodies from the east.

Slowly, disjointedly, young Stephen Kramek told his story to his mother. "Matt and I were exploring," he said, "and we saw Diane sitting on a sand dune and asked her if she wanted to look for driftwood, and she said okay. She wanted funny-looking pieces to arrange with flowers."

Eventually the three of them arrived on the point, where the sand was hard packed and led into the water with a most gradual descent. "We decided to go wading," Stephen said. "Dad had told us not to go swimming, and we didn't plan to; we only wanted to wade. We got out to where the water was up to our knees, and it gave us a funny feeling. The waves came together from both sides, and they would lift us straight up a few inches off the bottom, then drop us back down real gentle. It was real cool, kind of like walking on the moon. We went out a little farther, up to our waists, and we were lifted up and down quite high, and Diane said we'd better go back to shore."

The next wave lifted them higher, and when it dropped them down there was nothing beneath their feet and they were swimming. Matthew Hikel was small, and the Kramek brother and sister put him between them and tried for the shore in single file, Stephen leading. Shouting encouragement, Diane shepherded the boys forward a yard, two yards, three. Suddenly Stephen felt rocks beneath his feet. He scrambled forward and pulled himself up on the sand, then turned to give the others a hand. In that brief moment the tide caught Diane and Matthew and pulled them out to sea.

Stephen screamed, "Diane! You can make it! Matt! Swim!"

He started to wade back into the water, but Diane yelled sharply, "Go back! Go tell Daddy. Hurry, Steve . . . get help!" He turned and ran.

A small crowd had gathered, perhaps fifty people, islanders who had known what the whistle meant. There was no carnival atmosphere such as is often generated at disasters on the mainland. These plain-faced men and women born of sailors and fishermen had stood here before, as had their ancestors.

Then there came a collective sigh as the crowd saw the low, gray silhouette of a Coast Guard utility boat appear beyond the swirling waters off the reef. She began a slow run down the west side of Sandy Point and disappeared from view. Ten minutes later she reappeared, her search obviously fruitless. Ed Conley waved her to the east, and she came through a cut in the reef and began to search off the mile-long shoreline of Cow Cove.

The children had now been in the water for nearly an hour and a half, and after a brief surge of hope upon seeing the Coast Guard boat, Gudrun felt the grip on her emotions slipping. She began to whisper her daughter's name, "Diane ... Diane ... oh, my golden girl." To Gudrun it seemed that Diane, at the threshold of so many wonders, had earned a chance at life. To be cheated of it now was an unbelievable injustice.

Stanley Kramek also began to feel despair. Diane was a strong swimmer, and he knew that if she had only herself to care for she might survive the tide and eventually get back to shore. But how could she save both herself and Matthew? He knew she would not abandon the boy.

Fog began to crowd northward over the island, heavy and fast-moving. Cow Cove was taking on a pale, pearly opacity. Conley exchanged significant glances with his men. If the Coast Guard did not find the children in the next ten minutes, the boat might just as well head back to its base.

Running southeast at half speed, the vessel, under the command of boatswain's mate Robert Widerman, came slowly about. From the shore, the utility boat seemed to pause for a minute, rocking slowly on the swells. Then she abruptly headed northwest to a point about 600 yards offshore. There her engines were cut and her bow turned into the wind.

Sure that something had been found in the water, the crowd on shore pressed around the rescue squad ambulance to hear the radio. A voice came through with a metallic boom that was interrupted by static. "Coast Guard ... retrieved ... person ... headed Old Harbor."

As the voice ended, the boat could be seen heading south at full speed. The ambulance started off for Old Harbor, four miles away. Gudrun and Stanley Kramek followed, saying little, searching the dispatcher's words for a meaning. Does one "rescue" a living person but "retrieve" a dead one? And had the dispatcher said "person" or "persons"?

When they arrived at the harbor the sleek gray Coast Guard boat was already there. Stanley ran to the dock, battling his way through the crowd. "Please," he called out, "please let me through!" On the boat's stern deck he found two small figures wrapped in blankets. They were sitting up; they were alive! They smiled at him and laughed and wept all at once. And so did he.

The rescue squad nurse checked Matthew's and Diane's blood pressure and pulse, gave them some oxygen and pronounced them fit to leave the boat. When the family stepped ashore, a burst of applause came from the crowd. There were tears in many eyes, and hands reached out to touch them as they passed. "We prayed for you," a few said.

Safely back at their cottage, the Krameks laughed, talked and touched each other, intoxicated with the knowledge that the family was intact. Diane—with her mother's candid gray eyes and self-possession, with her father's determination to face up to a job, with her own sweet gentleness—was looked upon with a new awareness by her parents.

"I knew Stephen had got help," Diane told them, "because I could see all the men at Sandy Point and I told Matt that pretty soon a boat would come for us. I kept Matt on my back while I swam the breaststroke most of the time, but when he'd get cold I had him swim by himself awhile to get his circulation going. He was very good and did exactly what I told him to do and never once complained."

Matthew, his face flushed by the excitement of an adventure safely concluded, said, "We talked and Diane told me jokes and asked me if I knew the song 'True Grit,' but I didn't. She called me 'Matt, Matt, the water rat,' and I pretended to get angry. Sometimes she'd turn over and swim on her back while I rested on her stomach and held her around the waist. I'd kick my own feet real hard to help keep us afloat."

"The fog worried me," Diane admitted. "Each time a swell lifted us up I prayed I'd be able to see the lighthouse. I always could, but it got dimmer and dimmer. When we saw the Coast Guard boat, Matt and I waved our arms and screamed, but they went on by without seeing us. That was the worst moment of all. But then they saw us."

At dusk that evening Stanley Kramek left the cottage, announcing he was going to take a walk. A quarter of a mile away he came to the Town Hall, a small frame building where the Town Council was holding its regular meeting. Kramek entered the crowded room and took a seat at the back. He felt like an intruder, but he had come to make a short speech, and so he asked for the floor. When it was given him, he could only express his thoughts in the bluntest words.

"My name is Stanley Kramek, and I've been bringing my family to your island for vacations for a couple of years. This afternoon my daughter and a young friend of my son's were caught in the tide and taken out to sea. If it had not been for the prompt action of your rescue squad and the Coast Guard, I would have lost my daughter and the boy. What I want to say is . . . from the bottom of my heart—" His voice broke, and his face flushed with the effort he made to continue. He cleared his throat and said, "From the bottom of my heart I thank you." Then he quickly walked out of the building.

The people of the island often talk of Diane Kramek. Coast guardsman Robert Widerman says, "When my boat got to her, she had supported that boy on her back for an hour and a half, but there was no panic. She had a big smile for us. I've rescued a number of people at sea but none quite like her." Rescue squad captain Conley adds, "She is the gutsiest girl I've ever seen."

It will be a long time before Block Island forgets Diane Kramek. And a long time before the Kramek family forgets the people of Block Island.

One wrong turn, one misjudgment,
a few short miles—
the difference between life and death.
A gripping account of two days
of burning horror

Trapped
in the Desert

BY GARY BEEMAN

IT BEGAN INNOCENTLY enough, when I turned off U.S. 91 in the middle of California's Mojave Desert and headed the old black coupe down a gravel road. I was only eighteen that hot June night in 1959, and I didn't understand how in the desert in midsummer a moment of thoughtlessness can lead you, step by step, to disaster.

An aged prospector had told us—my sixteen-year-old school friend Jim Twomey and me—that the road led to derelict Rasor Ranch, on the edge of an area called the Devil's Playground. Desert "ghost settlements" fascinated me, and so did the prospector's report of rattlesnakes there. As a budding zoology major, I collected animal specimens to help pay for such wandering vacations as this.

We had food for a couple of days in the car, and there was supposed to be a good well at Rasor. Still, I'd never have turned off the highway with only two pints of water in our canteens if I hadn't been so tired. It was almost midnight. We'd driven more than 400 miles from San Francisco.

Turning off the highway at a half-buried tire the prospector had told us about, I drove down the moonlit gravel road. After a long way—I didn't notice just *how* long—we hit a little finger of sand that had drifted across the road. I gunned the car, and we plowed over it, then over three more drifts. After the fourth, our headlights showed only pale, undulating sand ahead. For a few feet the car gained

momentum. Then its spinning wheels began to dig down. We shuddered to a halt.

Obviously I'd taken a wrong turn. We got out and paced the distance back to the road: 200 feet. Jim wanted to go to sleep and dig out in the morning. "No," I said. "Let's get out now. It'll only take a few minutes."

An hour later, we hadn't moved an inch. The rear wheels had just dug in deeper. Then, searching for rocks in the moonlight, we stumbled onto the remains of an old railroad track. The steel had been salvaged, but we found nine ties in various degrees of preservation. Using one of them as a firm base, we jacked up the car and laid down a double strip of ties, starting at the front wheels and extending out behind. Then I eased the car backward. It moved slowly but steadily: two feet—six feet—ten feet. Then one wheel slipped off a tie and the car stopped.

All through that long, frustrating night we jacked up the car, rearranged the ties, reversed a few feet until the inevitable slip. I figured we'd come at least twelve miles from the highway, perhaps twenty. But what really mattered was that 200 feet of sand between the car and the gravel road. By five o'clock in the morning we'd covered perhaps fifty feet—still 150 to go. Exhausted, we drank all but two cupfuls of our water, then slept on the bare sand.

Almost at once, it seemed, the sun was beating down fiercely. Now, in stark daylight, things looked more serious. We could see why this sandbowl was called the Devil's Playground. Only scraggly bushes broke the barren, stony slopes.

Stripped to the waist, we went to work on the car. Within half an hour the sun was burning our skin. The sand soon grew too hot to touch. "Let's rest till evening," I suggested. "We'll get her out once it cools down." Jim didn't need much persuading. We decided we'd shelter in one of the rock faces of a hill that thrust up a quarter mile away across the sand. I still wasn't really worried. In fact, before we left the car I shot a few feet of movie film.

We found two shady hideaways, thirty feet apart. Sprawled under a shallow overhang, I dozed fitfully. The sunlight moved steadily closer, beating savagely up from the pale sand. Soon a bare foot of shade remained. My lips began to crack.

About noon we shared the last two cupfuls of water. Afterward, I lay and watched the line of sunlight, waiting for it to retreat. I kept wondering how hot it really was. (Official June temperatures near the Devil's Playground have been as high as 121° F.)

At last a wedge of shade moved up unexpectedly from one side. The sun set; a wonderful coolness fell. Somewhere out in the desert, a whippoorwill began its plaintive song. Jim and I went down to the car and ate our first food in twenty-four hours—the first we'd wanted. We each finished a can of chicken noodle soup—heated by the inferno inside the black coupe—then shared the juice from a small can of pineapple.

The food revived us, and we discussed whether to try walking out. Jim felt too weak for such a long trek, and I rated my own chances a bare fifty-fifty. We decided to keep working on the car. I didn't really grasp, even then, that we were in desperate danger. I knew that unwary motorists had died of thirst in the desert; not long before, in Death Valley just thirty miles to the north, the dried-out corpses of two young men had been found close beside their stalled car. But somehow I felt it couldn't happen to us.

My memories of that second night are blurred. It was all we could do to jack up the car and run it back a few feet until it slipped off the disintegrating ties. We kept resting, I remember, and half-dozing. About four o'clock we fell asleep.

When I awoke, the half-risen sun was already burning my skin like an infrared lamp. Every movement demanded effort. And now for the first time I understood our peril: During the night we had moved the car barely fifteen feet; more than 130 feet remained! Jim, weak and listless, seemed to have lost hope. With rocks and twigs I laid out a four-foot SOS; then we started toward our rock shelters.

Right from the start, that second day was terrible. Even under the shady overhang, I could feel the heat sucking moisture out of my body. And it wasn't only the heat. The silence was almost as bad. I found myself straining for sounds, but all I could hear was my heartbeat. The drumbeat inside me swamped everything.

Occasionally I'd hear Jim's heavy breathing. Then he began to babble. He might have been dreaming—or delirious. "What about my grape drink?" he kept saying. "I've paid for it, and I want my grape drink." At last he fell silent.

Soon the noonday sun was compressing my strip of shade tight up against the overhang. Once, I heard the lisp of sifting sand. Four feet away, a rattlesnake was moving past, from shade to shade.

I lay in a daze now, never quite dozing, never fully awake. I had given up hope that the day would ever pass its peak. Once, when I squinted out at the car, shimmering in the haze a quarter of a mile away, there was another car parked beside our coupe—and a stream of vehicles rushing up and down the black highway on which they stood. Had I, after all, walked out to the highway? I twisted my head, then squinted out again: The old black coupe stood on pale sand, alone.

Panic swept me. I knew that dehydration eventually unbalanced your mind. If I could already see a nonexistent highway, had I been *acting* irrationally?

At last, in midafternoon, I could stand the terrible dryness no longer. Struggling to my feet, I went out into the sun. When I looked down toward the car, I saw for the first time that the flat sand near it had once been a lake. *If I dig*, I thought, *perhaps I'll find water*. I staggered down the hill.

There were green-leaved creosote bushes growing on a small sand dune, and I remembered that when digging for lizards in such places I had found moisture. I began digging into the side of the dune, in among the roots. There was no water; but suddenly I realized that my hands felt almost cool. Perhaps I could dig a cave and crawl into that wonderful coolness!

I don't know how long it took me to scoop out a hole. But at last it was big enough. I stripped off all my sweat-stained and grimy clothes and crawled in. The cool sand soothed me like a balm. I fell asleep.

I woke to see the sun sinking below a line of hills. The plaintive whistle of the whippoorwill came at last. I felt cool and rested. Then, without warning, Jim staggered past. His head lolled; his arms hung loose at his sides. Suddenly he sank to one knee, then pitched forward and lay still. I shook him. He moaned faintly.

Alarmed, I hurried to the car and searched feverishly through the inferno inside it. Under the seat I found a bottle of after-shave lotion. I wrenched off the top and put it to my lips. The shock of what tasted like hot rubbing alcohol brought me up short. Again I had that horrible, fleeting comprehension of my unhinged state of mind.

I began rubbing lotion on my face and neck. It felt good, so I went back to Jim, rubbed lotion on his face and poured it over his T-shirt. He was deathly pale, his mouth hung open, and dried mucus flecked his scaly white lips. *We need a drink,* I kept thinking. *We both need a drink.*

Desperately, I ran my eyes over the car. And suddenly I was thinking, *The radiator!* I'd always known that in the desert your radiator water could save you; yet for two days I'd ignored it! I grabbed a saucepan, squirmed under the front bumper and unscrewed the radiator drainage tap. A stream of rusty brown water poured down over the greasy sway bar and splashed into my saucepan. It was the most wonderful sight I had ever seen.

Still lying under the car, I took several huge gulps. The water was thick with oil and rust. Almost at once, though, I began to feel better. When I had drained the radiator and filled a canteen, I went back to Jim and poured water into his open mouth. He stirred.

Then I returned to the car, got a can of chow mein and ate half of it. Soon Jim was sitting up and eating his half of the chow mein.

My mind felt clearer, and I realized that if we were going to get out I'd have to try something new. After a while I saw what would have been obvious if I had been thinking clearly: that I would have to run the car back off the ties at high speed and just hope I could keep it going.

We were still pitifully weak. When Jim tried to help he collapsed over the jack, and the rest of that third night he lay prostrate. I must have spent five or six hours over a job that would normally take twenty minutes: aligning the car perfectly on the ties for our final attempt. I knew that if we failed the first time I wouldn't have the strength to try again. At last, utterly exhausted, I fell asleep.

I awoke in the hot sunlight. Hurriedly, we drank the last of the water. I helped Jim into the car, started the motor, and let it idle for a few moments. Then I looked at Jim, sprawled across the seat. "This is it," I said. He didn't seem to hear.

I revved the motor, slammed the automatic transmission into reverse and stamped on the accelerator. The car leaped backward. It gained speed, slipped off the ties . . . kept going. All at once, a tie banged hard, somewhere up front. The car faltered, almost stopped. Then the tie snapped, and we were moving again.

But soon we were slowing down. The rear wheels started to dig in with a horribly familiar sinking motion. They would spin, grip for a moment, then spin again. And, all the time, the motor was slowing down, the car sinking into the sand. We'd almost stopped when I felt the tires grab something solid. They spun again . . . grabbed and spun . . . grabbed. For interminable moments we hung poised between life and death. Then the tires took a firm grip and we were moving smoothly. At last we were out on the gravel road, and I was whooping like an idiot. Beside me, Jim was smiling weakly.

Four hours later, after many sweltering halts for the now-dry motor to cool, we turned onto the highway: We'd been stuck only six miles off U. S. 91. And within another mile—less than seven miles from the desolate sandbowl where we'd faced a terrible death—we came to a modern roadside café.

We parked the old coupe and went inside.

"Kinda warm today, boys," the man behind the counter said. Then he took another look at us and saw that we were drained dry, caked with grime and dead tired.

He put two glasses of water on the counter.

"Just sip it a little, boys," he said, "until you get used to it."

We sat on the clean stools, sipping the cool water gratefully, each sip confirming what we were beginning to dare to believe: We were going to be permitted to stay in the land of the living.

When a case of smallpox erupted in Germany,
disease control experts faced a showdown with a deadly killer.
The only question was: Could they win?

A Town's
Race Against Death

BY CLAUS GAEDEMANN

I N THE TWILIGHT HOURS OF MARCH 27, 1972, a Mercedes sped
through the streets of Hanover, West Germany, and braked to a stop
before the Institute of Virology. The vehicle's occupants were Dr.
Bernd Liess, the institute's director, and his associate, Dr. Karl-Peter
Olberding, on whose lap rested a small aluminum box. Getting out
of the car, the men hurried into the institute's laboratory and began
examining the contents of the box under a powerful electron micro-
scope.

An hour and a half later, at 8:30 p.m., the scientists looked up at
each other in mute horror. There could be no doubt: The lymph
specimens they had just examined contained smallpox virus. They
had come from the arm of a Yugoslav admitted two days previously
to one of the clinics in the city. Doctors Liess and Olberding realized
immediately that Hanover and its 520,000 people were facing a race
against a dangerous epidemic, for smallpox is an acute, highly con-
tagious disease. There is no specific treatment, and every third victim is likely to die a horrible death. In the nineteenth century one
smallpox epidemic caused 130,000 deaths in Prussia alone. The
question was: Could Hanover be saved from a similar fate?

Liess and Olberding acted quickly. It was now 8:40 p.m., Liess
noted as he put through a telephone call to Dr. Kurt Wickenhäuser,
deputy head of Hanover's health department. The race against

death was on. Dr. Wickenhäuser, following a detailed and previously well-thought-out plan for such an emergency, alerted city, state and military authorities, the fire department, the police, the Red Cross, doctors, hospitals and the news media. Most of these in turn activated their own contingency plans. The state government passed the alert on to all German health departments and also to the World Health Organization.

Meanwhile, the smallpox victim, Ejup Hodzaj, a twenty-four-year-old construction worker from the Serbian village of Trnja, lay prostrate with fever at the Linden Dermatology Clinic on the city's west side. Dr. Jo Hartung, the clinic's chief surgeon, ordered all the outside doors locked and the posting of signs that read: DANGER OF SMALLPOX! ENTRANCE STRICTLY PROHIBITED! The patients and all clinic personnel were vaccinated on the spot, and preparations were made to transfer Hodzaj to an isolation ward at Stolzenau Hospital.

The transfer was accomplished on the morning of March 28. Two firemen, wearing face masks and plastic suits, carried the desperately ill patient from the clinic and placed him in a specially disinfected ambulance for the thirty-five-mile trip. At the hospital, Hodzaj was placed behind a shield of elaborate safeguards, and everyone coming near him, including the cleaning woman, was required to wear a respirator. Afterward, they all had to change their clothes, pass through a disinfection chamber and wash their hands and face in a strong alcohol solution.

But the real fight against killer smallpox had only just started. Scores of people—even hundreds perhaps—had come in contact with Hodzaj. City officials were faced with the difficult task of identifying them, and with the seemingly even more impossible job of tracking them down. Could it be done before an epidemic erupted?

Precious time was lost when an interpreter called upon to question the smallpox victim refused to go near him; another couldn't understand his Serbian dialect. Finally, one was found who had been born near Hodzaj's home village.

The victim himself cooperated as best he could. He had arrived in Hanover from Yugoslavia on March 13, and spent his first few nights in the city in a crowded flophouse. During the day he had boarded streetcars looking for work. At one period, he had mingled with countless fellow job-hunters at the city's labor office. A construction firm had finally hired him as a carpenter's laborer and had assigned him to quarters with two other Serbs and a German.

When the smallpox erupted and his face and hands began to be covered with blisters, his foreman sent Hodzaj to a doctor. He wasted an hour in the crowded waiting room of a specialist in ear, nose and throat ailments, where he came in contact with no fewer than sixty-eight persons. Unable to help him, that doctor sent him to the nearest dermatologist, where he might have exposed another 125 patients to the disease. He was given a prescription for a salve, which he bought at a nearby pharmacy. The next day, he visited the dermatologist again.

On Saturday, March 25, Hodzaj recalled, he was running a high fever and his roommates called a doctor, who diagnosed chickenpox and had the Yugoslav admitted to the clinic.

Walter Teuber, an official from the city's Office of Records, was assigned the staggering task of finding and quarantining every single person with whom Hodzaj might have had contact. He and his fellow workers found themselves repeating an order that was soon to become second nature to them: "You may be infected with smallpox. You must enter quarantine for eighteen days. Please pack the most necessary things and be ready for the quarantine bus that will come to pick you up."

There were endless frustrations. For example, a child exposed to Hodzaj in one of the doctors' offices was finally located, but her parents couldn't recall which of them had accompanied her on the day in question. Normally, the parents took turns taking their daughter. However, it was grandpa, the mother finally remembered, who had volunteered on this occasion. For the "smallpox detectives," it meant another address, another trip across town, mounting more stairs—until grandfather and grandchild were safely on the quarantine bus.

Shortly before midnight of the first day, 200 newly discovered persons with whom Hodzaj had had contact had been identified—but only forty-nine of them had been located and isolated. Hundreds of contacts were as yet unidentified.

Then Hanover's smallpox fighters received additional bad news: Yugoslavia reported seventy-five smallpox cases, with seven dead. The disease was also rampant in Bangladesh, Ethiopia, India and

Pakistan. It appeared impossible that Hanover could escape an epidemic. However, there was hope, for the city and its citizens were demonstrating amazing valor. "It's simply unbelievable how everybody helps in this hour of need," said one city spokesman.

Werner Eichlseder of the City Hospital Administration, in search of suitable quarantine centers, utilized summer camps and youth hostels. They were cleared out, cordoned off by the police and then equipped to become self-contained units, complete with food supplies and facilities for decontamination. Nurses and other personnel from all over town volunteered and soon the centers were operating efficiently.

Upon first learning of Hodzaj's illness, Dr. Gunther Terbeck, the epidemiological expert of the state Ministry for Social Affairs, had rushed a request for 300,000 units of vaccine to Düsseldorf's Vaccination Center. It was delivered within hours by refrigerated van. And by now seven of the eleven planned vaccination centers had been opened. Six thousand Hanoverians were immunized on the first day.

Later, health-department physicians had to be reinforced by eight military doctors to cope with the seemingly endless lines of people waiting to be vaccinated. Members of the police force, welfare organizations, the fire department and other agencies put in thousands of overtime hours. Many worked around the clock, taking only naps at their stations.

On the Wednesday before Good Friday, officials finally located the flophouse where Hodzaj had spent his first nights in Hanover. It was occupied by sixty-two foreign nationals—Turks, Malaysians, Indonesians and others. The number of persons known to have had contact with Hodzaj was soon to reach 679. Most of them—but not all—had been rounded up and quarantined. Two waiting room contacts had been found in East Germany and were isolated there; another was picked up by military helicopter at a Spiekeroog Island hotel and taken straight to one of Hanover's isolation centers; a small boy was found visiting his relatives in the Black Forest region.

It was a derelict, however, who was causing officials their biggest headache. He had been treated for minor burns on his hand in the dermatologist's office—and had vanished. No one knew him, and the address he had given proved to be fictitious. If he had become

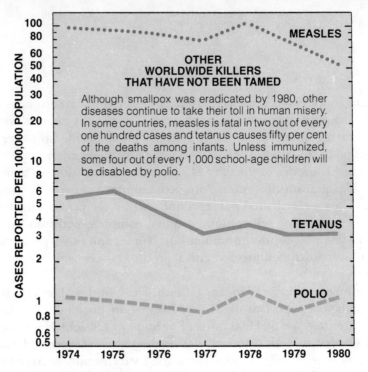

contaminated, his disease would now be in the infectious stage and might infect hundreds of others.

City authorities and police set up a huge dragnet for the one missing man. Newspapers and radio stations started disseminating this message: "Wanted, Heinz Kowitz, born February 16, 1936. Acute suspicion of smallpox!" Thus, a vagrant had begun to play the most ominous role in the city's battle against the threatened plague—and everybody seemed to be convinced that all danger would pass if only Kowitz were found.

Hanover's Easter holidays were somber. Clergymen prayed for the threatened city. Because of the danger of infection, those taking Holy Communion were not offered the usual chalice. And as the faithful left services, they avoided the customary handshaking.

However, the holiday mood had not entirely disappeared. It could be found even in the city's quarantine centers. For days, nurses and aides had been secretly painting Easter eggs. For each isolated person the municipal authorities donated a chocolate-filled Easter egg, a bottle of wine and fifty cigarettes. The center's sixty children gleefully gathered the colorful eggs that had been hidden for them. At the Riepenburg center, trombone players of the Hamelin regional church community entertained the inmates with catchy tunes from outside the fence.

But somewhere a man was still at large who might yet infect any number of people—the vagrant Heinz Kowitz. It took four more anxiety-filled days before a student spotted the derelict in front of Hanover's main post office. "Kowitz!" he yelled. For a moment, the man remained frozen, then scurried away. The student quickly alerted the police, who cornered Kowitz a few minutes later. The last of those who had come in contact with Hodzaj was finally safely isolated, and the remainder of those quarantined were released on Sunday, April 16. Ejup Hodzaj recovered and was released from the hospital on April 19.

Thanks to the selfless dedication and calm discipline of everyone involved, the miracle had come to pass: No one else contracted smallpox. Hanover had won its race against death.

By 1980, "the total eradication of smallpox from the globe" was proclaimed by the World Health Organization, the culmination of years of work devoted to vaccinating people around the world in high-risk areas. The last case of smallpox was recorded in October 1977, in Merka, Somalia.

The old boat
didn't look very seaworthy,
but none of the excursionists
recognized her
for the death trap she was

The Sinking
of the *Comet*

BY MICHAEL REILLY

THE BOAT WAS FORTY-FIVE minutes late, but the guys were taking it well—considering the fact that many of us had been on night runs and had driven directly to the Point Judith harbor without sleep. We were mostly truck drivers from Rhode Island, and we had chartered the *Comet* for six o'clock this morning of May 19, 1973, for a day of deep-sea fishing.

Joe Faria was taking a lot of kidding because the whole thing had been his idea. About a month earlier he'd told me, "Mike, I ran into this old friend, Bill Jackson, and he's bought himself a boat that he'll charter for ten dollars a head if we guarantee twenty-five men. He'll supply crew, tackle and bait."

I was a supervisor-dispatcher at the St. Johnsbury Trucking Company in Pawtucket, Rhode Island, and I began talking it up to the drivers: "You guys are always complaining that we don't do anything together. Well, Joe's got something great."

Soon the required twenty-five men had signed up, and the trip was on. But when the *Comet* hadn't appeared by 6:45 that morning, we began to kid Joe. "How much did Joe lift off of us so far—a hundred and twenty-five dollars?" a voice demanded. "Not bad for a

boat that don't exist." The four teenage boys in the group with us—eighteen-year-old Steven Gercey, his brother William, 16, and their cousins, Andrew Girczyc, 14, and Stanley, 13—began to worry that their first ocean trip might not take place.

At five minutes before seven, however, we saw the *Comet* coming in. We were disappointed—her hull planking was battered, her deck seams needed caulking—but a cheer went up and we all rushed aboard. There was some delay in letting go. The deckhand was a young boy named Ralph Nickerson, and it was clear that this was his first trip to sea. Also, Jackson's orders shouted from the wheelhouse were sometimes confusing. We finally got under way at about five after seven.

I noticed then that *Comet's* stern had very little freeboard. There couldn't have been over eighteen inches between the sea and the afterdeck. Comparing it with other boats I had been on, I knew that the distance should have been greater. I saw my friend Al Charron staring at the afterdeck with a worried look, too. If only we had spoken to each other about it!

The day was clear, but a flood tide was bringing three- to five-foot waves while a southwesterly wind was whipping them in the opposite direction, creating a bad chop. As the *Comet* moved into the open sea, the first wave heeled her sharply to starboard, lifted her as it ran beneath her, rolled her back to portside and then sent her plunging into the following trough.

Everybody on deck staggered and clutched at the handrails. After about fifteen minutes of this, Joe told me he was going to talk to Jackson about turning back. In a few minutes he reported, "Jackson says it's up to the guys."

We talked to them, but they laughed and joked about getting their money's worth. They didn't seem to understand the danger. And so the *Comet* continued on, shuddering as each wave hit her.

"She doesn't seem very seaworthy," my buddy Brian Beaudette said.

"No boat can take on passengers without a Coast Guard inspection certificate," I assured him. "They check everything—engine, hull, wiring."

At that moment I heard a shout from Al Charron. He was pointing to the lunch pails we'd placed on the deck along the starboard railing. Each time the *Comet* dived into the trough between waves, water flooded part of the afterdeck and, as I watched, the water rushed up and set someone's lunch pail awash. The water was rising higher and higher as the boat settled. That was the reason she had been so low in the water when we first boarded her—the bilge was slowly flooding!

Al ran to the wheelhouse to tell the skipper, but the door wouldn't open. He pounded on the window, shouting, "She's taking on water! She's gonna swamp!" Jackson seemed not to hear.

Brian and I were beginning to toss life jackets to the men when the engine died. The *Comet* began to roll badly. Jackson came bursting out of the wheelhouse, shouting, "Stay with the boat!"

"Radio the Coast Guard," I heard Charron shout at him, but again he appeared not to hear. Eerie creaks and groans came from the rolling ship's timbers as we scrambled from side to side, trying to keep her level. Then Nickerson appeared at the wheelhouse door clutching the radio microphone.

"How does this work?" he called out to us.

"Try turning on all the switches and talk into it," Al shouted.

At this moment, the *Comet* began her final plunge. There was a muffled report—the cabin was breaking off.

Everyone was thrown free. Wreckage began to bob to the surface, and we survivors grabbed for it.

"Mike! Mike! Over here," I heard a voice calling. It was Walter Girczyc, who had shepherded his sons and nephews to a fairly large raft I had seen tied to the roof of the cabin.

Soon fourteen of us were clinging to the lifelines along the sides of the raft. Our situation didn't seem too bad. Suddenly everyone felt optimistic and began talking at once: "I can see Block Island . . . the tides will take us there . . . we're in the transatlantic shipping lane and freighters go through here all the time . . . the Coast Guard must have heard our SOS."

Al Charron and I looked at each other. We were both pretty sure no radio call got out. But our immediate problem was the raft, which was covered with a sheet of slippery fiberglass. In these seas no man could stay on top of it. We all had to remain in the water, holding on to the lifelines. I clamped my jaws on my chattering teeth and fought the leg cramps that jerked my heels up under me. As the cold penetrated, a sort of stupor came over us.

Suddenly one of the men was crying shrilly, "A ship! A ship!"

Jolted awake, we saw a tanker headed in our direction. When she was about two miles off, Al and I held Brian on top of the raft while he waved his orange life jacket wildly. The rest of us yelled, cheered and laughed. She came within 150 yards of us, but her rust-streaked hull kept on sliding through the water. We could hear the continuing throb of her powerful engine. She wasn't going to stop!

We thrashed our arms and legs in frantic efforts to raise ourselves out of the water. But, as the ship grew smaller with each turn of her screw, our screams turned to curses. Finally she was a smudge on the horizon, then nothing.

Now the cold resumed its deadly work. It stunned us and sapped us of our will to survive.

Al Charron suddenly began to strike the water and yell. "No, by God, no! I'm not gonna die out here without doing something. I'll swim for help."

Thinking he was delirious, I grabbed his arm. He jerked it free and pointed to a wood bench that we'd salvaged and lashed to the raft. "I can keep afloat with that bench. We gotta do something or we'll all die anyway."

"I'm a better swimmer than you are, Al," I said. "And you've got a wife and kids. I'm not married. I'll go."

The bench was about eight feet long and two feet wide. When we got it free, I positioned my left arm over it—leaving my right arm and my legs free for swimming. Brian's head appeared suddenly opposite me. "I'll go along," he said. "If I have to drown, it might as well be with you."

I gave him a grin and said, "Well, let's go."

We swam as hard as we could, but we were just two antlike figures on a chip of wood. The sea would take us where it wanted to.

For a time we joked to keep up our spirits. "Hey, I've still got my wallet," I said. "Let me know if we come to a toll booth."

"Don't be a big spender," Brian warned. "Remember you already blew ten bucks to go fishing."

When we could no longer joke, we talked quietly about the things in life we'd miss. Brian said, "It's hard to believe that we'll never have another brew together at Murphy's Lounge."

I felt tears in my eyes and looked away. Then I saw a triangle of white cloth nearby. We stared at it dumbly, finally realizing it was a sail. We screamed and waved—or thought we did. We were drugged by the cold and couldn't lift our arms out of the water. The sail moved past. We were invisible men. We gave up.

Yachtsman Richard Lemmerman was sailing his forty-foot sloop, the *Decibel,* to her home port of Manchester, Massachusetts. She was about in the middle of Block Island Sound when crewman Mark Standley called out, "There's something out there in the water. Looks like a couple of damn-fool kids in a kayak. I wonder if they need help."

Lemmerman said, "Let's not take any chances. Bring her around, Mark."

When the sailboat came alongside, strong hands wrestled me onto the deck where I lay gasping. "Others out there," I whispered. "The *Comet* sank. . . ."

The next thing I knew I was below deck in a bunk, wrapped in a blanket and being fed coffee. In the bunk across from me I saw Brian. Over the next forty-five minutes we heard the creak of rigging and the growl of the engine as the boat maneuvered, stopped and started. As each survivor was brought below, I said a silent prayer of thanks.

I began to hope all had been saved, but when the *Decibel* finally headed back toward Point Judith I knew they had not. Joe Faria and Al Charron told us that after Brian and I had gone for help, Steve Gercey had lost consciousness and slipped away from the raft. His uncle, Walter Girczyc, had drowned, as had the young deckhand, Ralph Nickerson, and the *Comet's* owner, Bill Jackson. In all, sixteen men had died.

On May 22, 1973, the U. S. Coast Guard convened a Marine Board of Investigation. When the hearings ended, two stark facts were revealed: The *Comet* had no inspection certificate because Jackson had never submitted his boat to a safety inspection. Nor did he have a personal license to skipper a boat for hire.

Now I wonder. Had I thought to go into the wheelhouse before we sailed and found no Coast Guard certificate, would I have tried to talk the men into walking off the boat? I'm not sure. I know I will next time!

The story of a night
when the Congressional Medal of Honor
seemed to be a modest award

Sergeant Erwin
and the Blazing Bomb

BY COREY FORD

SOMETIMES I'M ASKED which I like best of all the pieces I've written. I guess the answer is something I wrote one night back in 1945,
on the island of Guam. It was never published; I didn't even sign it;
but it was more rewarding than anything else I've ever done.

Guam was our base in the Marianas from which the B-29's took
off for their nightly incendiary raids on Japan. As an Air Force colonel, I had flown with them, and I knew what those missions were
like. The seven endless hours over the Pacific to the hostile coastline.
The wink of ack-ack guns and the flak bursts all around us, the
ground searchlights that lighted up our cabin as though a car had
parked beside us in the sky, and, after our bomb run, the red ruins of
an enemy city burning. We would throttle down to cruising speed;
there were 1,500 miles of empty ocean between us and home.

This particular night I was not flying. I sat in the group headquarters tent with Col. Carl Storrie, waiting for the mission's strike
report. Storrie, a lean, tough Texan, was the group commander, and
he paced up and down the tent, restless as a caged animal, as the

first news filtered in. The lead plane, commanded by Capt. Tony Simeral, had been forced to turn away from the target and had made an emergency landing at Iwo Jima. It was on its way back to Guam now.

We could make out the drone of its engines, see the red flares that signaled distress, and hear the fire trucks rumbling out to meet it as it touched down. A few moments later Captain Simeral entered the tent. His face was white; he seemed to be in a state of shock. He fumbled for a cigarette with his left hand, and I saw that the back of his right hand was pockmarked with deep ugly holes that had burned clear to the bone. He took several drags before he could trust himself to talk.

It had happened as they approached the enemy coast, he said. They were flying the pathfinder plane—the one that drops a phosphorus smoke bomb to assemble the formation before proceeding to the target. On a B-29 this task is performed by the radio operator, back in the waist of the plane. At a signal from the pilot he releases the bomb through a narrow tube.

The radio operator on Simeral's plane was a chunky, red-haired youngster from Alabama, S. Sgt. Henry Erwin. His crewmates liked to mimic his soft southern drawl, and he was always ready with a grin, always quiet and courteous. He received the routine order from Simeral, triggered the bomb and dropped it down the tube.

There was a malfunction. The bomb exploded in the tube and bounced back into Erwin's face, blinding both his eyes and searing off an ear.

Phosphorus burns with a furious intensity that melts metal like butter. Now the bomb at Erwin's feet was eating its way rapidly through the deck of the plane, toward the full load of incendiaries in their racks below. He was alone; the navigator had gone up to the astrodome to get a star shot. There was no time to think. He picked up the white-hot bomb in his bare hands and started forward to the cockpit, groping his way with elbows and feet.

The navigator's folding table was down and latched, blocking the narrow passageway. Erwin hugged the blazing bomb under his arm, feeling it devour the flesh on his ribs, unfastened the spring latch and lifted the table. (We inspected the plane later; the skin of his entire hand was seared onto the table.)

He stumbled on, a walking torch. His clothes, hair and flesh were ablaze.

The dense smoke had filled the airplane, and Simeral had opened the window beside him to clear the air. "I couldn't see Erwin," he told us, "but I heard his voice right at my elbow. He said—" Simeral paused a moment to steady his own voice. "He said, *'Pardon me, sir,'* and reached across to the window and tossed out the bomb. Then he collapsed on the flight deck." A fire extinguisher was turned on him, but the phosphorus still burned.

Simeral's instrument panel was obliterated by the smoke, and the plane went out of control. It was less than 300 feet off the water when he righted it. He called to the formation that he was aborting, jettisoned his bombs and headed back to the field hospital at Iwo Jima, three hours away. The crew applied first aid to Erwin, gave him plasma and smeared grease on his smoldering flesh. "He never lost consciousness, but he spoke only once the whole way back. He asked me—" Simeral took another drag on his cigarette. " 'Is everybody else all right, sir?' "

At Iwo, he was still exhaling phosphorus smoke from his lungs, and his body had become so rigid that he had to be eased out through the window like a log. They carried him to the hospital. When they removed the unguent pads there and exposed his flesh to the air, it began to smolder again. The airplane flew on to Guam— with eleven men who would not be alive except for the one they left behind.

Simeral finished talking. A young lieutenant looked at the holes in his right hand, where the phosphorus had spattered, and said tactlessly, "You ought to put in for a Purple Heart, Captain." Simeral, his control snapping, took a wild swing at him. Then the flight surgeon arrived, gave him a sedative and led him away to have his burns treated.

We spent the rest of the night writing up a recommendation for the Congressional Medal of Honor. It was simply worded. There was no need to speak of heroism and sacrifice; the facts were enough. It ended with the conventional military phrase: "Above and beyond the call of duty," but that expressed it pretty well. At five in the morning Colonel Storrie carried the single typewritten page to Air Force headquarters. Gen. Curtis LeMay was awakened. He read and signed it, and the recommendation was flashed to Washington. The reply arrived in record time: Approved.

Iwo Jima reported that Sergeant Erwin was still alive, but no one could say how much longer he would survive. There was no Congressional Medal of Honor on Guam; the nearest was in Honolulu, and a special B-29 was dispatched to fly the Pacific to Hawaii.

The medal was in a locked display case in Gen. Robert C. Richardson's headquarters, and the key was missing. They smashed the glass, took the medal from the case and sped back to Guam. General LeMay flew to Iwo and personally presented it to Sergeant Erwin, in a ceremony at his bedside. He repeated the final line about the call of duty, and Erwin said, "Thank you, sir."

Several years after the war I heard that Erwin was back in Alabama, happily married; he had regained the use of his hands and partial vision in one eye. I hope he can read over his citation now and then. I hope it gives him as much satisfaction as it gave me to write it.

When the raging storm
finally trapped them, Hazel Miner knew just what to do
to save her brother and sister

Girl
Against a Blizzard

BY HELEN REZATTO

THE MORNING OF MARCH 15, 1920, was pleasant and sunny as William Miner, finished his chores on his farm near Center, North Dakota. A thaw had set in, and the snow in the fields was patchy.

"Snow should be gone by night," he reported optimistically to his wife when he came in at noon. After the couple had eaten a leisurely meal, Miner glanced out the kitchen window. "Good Lord!" he exclaimed.

In the northwest a black, billowy cloud loomed over the horizon. It moved stealthily, inexorably across the sky, its dark blue edges spreading toward the sun.

Blanche Miner spoke with the sure instinct of a homesteader. "A spring norther!"

They watched the advance of the formless, faceless monster. Abruptly, Miner said, "You get the stock in. I'm going to school to get the kids. I don't like the looks of it."

Miner piled on his storm clothes, saddled his best horse, Kit, and started down the slushy road to the school two and a half miles away. By now the writhing apparition had swelled and blotted out the sun. All nature was poised, breathless, apprehensive. Then an avalanche of blinding snow and wind slammed into the horse and rider. Miner fought through it to the school barn, tied Kit among the other stomping, nervous horses and hurried into the schoolhouse.

The teacher and pupils had observed the approach of the blizzard, but were still pretending to concentrate on lessons. Although many children had their own horses and sleighs in the school barn, the rule was that no child could leave during a blizzard unless called for by a parent.

"Hi, Dad!" fifteen-year-old Hazel Miner exclaimed. She turned to her brother, Emmet, 11, and her sister, Myrdith, 8. "I guess *somebody* doesn't trust us to drive old Maude home!"

Her father smiled briefly. "Hurry! Get your wraps—here are extra scarves."

Hazel bent down to fasten her sister's overshoes and said to Emmet, "Don't forget your history book." Hazel was wonderfully dependable, Miner thought. She always far surpassed expectations.

He carried Myrdith outside to their homemade sleigh with its rounded canvas cover, settled the two children in the straw lining the bottom and covered them with two blankets and an old fur robe. Then Hazel perched on the driver's seat while her father hitched Maude to the sleigh. Above the roar of the wind he shouted to Hazel, "Stay right here! I'll get Kit and lead the way."

Maude was facing the north gate that led toward home. She had always been a placid and easily managed horse, but just then a thunderclap startled her, and she bolted and swerved through the south gate, pulling the sleigh behind her. Hazel, knocked off balance and hardly able to see through the swirling snow, did not realize at first that Maude was headed in the wrong direction. She shouted to the wide-eyed younger children, "Don't worry, we'll beat Dad and Kit home! Maude knows the way."

Hazel could do nothing to control the horse, for the reins trailed out of reach beneath the sleigh. Finally, Maude slowed to a walk and then stopped, her sides heaving.

Emmet called, "Are we home? Did we beat Dad?"

Hazel stepped down into the snow. Through the dizzying gloom she could not tell whether they were on a road or in a field. The whole world had become a white, foaming, lashing sea, threatening to swallow them all. Panting for breath, she crawled back into the driver's seat with the reins. "No, we're not home yet, but I think we're close. Now that Maude's calmed down, she'll know the way."

Maude, under control now, obediently plowed along through the deepening drifts. Once she plunged into a low place filled with water from the spring thaws and choked now with ice and new snow. A tug came unhitched, and Hazel stepped down into the chilling slush, reached her bare hands into the icy water, fumbled for the tug and fastened it. By the time she led Maude out of the water, she was soaked to the waist and her clothes were turning into heavy armor.

Then, close by, she saw the top of a fence post sticking above the snow. She dug into the snow until she located the barbed wire. The fence would lead them to a farm and safety.

Emmet got out to see what she was doing. Together, they broke off the crystal mask that had formed over Maude's face. They held Maude's bridle to keep her on the fenceline, but a huge drift blocked their way and they had to turn off the course. Frantically trying to get back to the fence, Emmet and Hazel pawed for the wire or another post to guide them. They could find neither. (The gate, buried in a big drift, opened to a farm only 200 feet away.)

Almost suffocating from the onslaught of wind and snow, Hazel and Emmet climbed back into the sleigh. Stubbornly, Maude kept on going until the sleigh lurched over a concealed obstacle and tipped over on its side. The children were thrown against the canvas top.

Again Hazel and Emmet got out. Blindly, they pushed, they

heaved, they pulled. The sleigh, jammed into the snow, was too heavy for them to right.

In the howling darkness, Hazel realized that it was up to her, the oldest. She fumbled inside the canvas. "See," she said, "we're in a little cave. We'll fix it nice and cozy."

Since the sleigh was on its side, the narrow wooden floor formed a low wall to the east and the canvas top, uncurtained at the ends, made a tent. In the dark, Hazel found the blankets and robe. Despite her frost-crippled hands, she placed the two blankets on the canvas floor. Following her instructions, Emmet and Myrdith lay down, curled together tightly. The wind snarled through the north opening, and Hazel tried to improvise a curtain with the fur robe. It blew down again and again. Finally she tucked the robe around her brother and sister.

The hellish wind ripped the canvas top. Hazel tore away the flapping scraps and piled over the robe all those she could salvage. There was only one way to keep them in place—to fling herself on top of them. Now there was nothing between the three children and the blizzard except some dangling strips blowing from the bare wooden framework.

The snow fell incessantly. Three human specks lay motionless, their minds and bodies stupefied, benumbed by the terrifying force of the wind. Hazel roused herself. "Emmet! Myrdith!" she shouted. "You mustn't close your eyes. Punch each other! I'll count to a hundred. Make your legs go up and down as though you're running. Begin—one, two, three—" She could feel the small limbs moving underneath her. She tried to move her own; her brain instructed her legs, but she wasn't sure that they did move.

"I'm tired. Can't we stop?" begged Myrdith's muffled voice.

"No!" came the stern answer. "We're only at seventy-one."

Next Hazel ordered, "Open and close your fingers one hundred times inside your mittens."

Emmet stuck his head out from under the robe. "Come on, Hazel, get under here. We'll make room."

"No, I can't." Little warmth her ice-mantled clothes would provide the others. "Everything blows away. I've got to hold it down. Besides, I'm not very cold. Let's sing 'America, the Beautiful' like in opening exercises this morning."

From underneath the robe came the thin, childish voices and the words they had sung only that morning—but a hundred years away. *For purple mountain majesties above the fruited plain.* They sang all four verses.

"Let's pray to God to help us," suggested Myrdith. " 'Now I lay me down to sleep—' " she began.

Hazel interrupted. "No, not that one. Let's say 'Our Father' instead." Solemnly they chanted the prayer.

On into the timeless night Hazel directed them—in exercises, stories, songs, prayers. Several times she sat up in the never-ending snow and forced her nearly paralyzed fingers to break the crusts of ice that formed around Myrdith's and Emmet's legs; then she brushed and scraped away the creeping menace.

She said to the two children over and over, "Remember, you mustn't go to sleep—even if I do. Promise me you won't, no matter how sleepy you get. *Keep each other awake!* Promise?"

They promised.

More than once Myrdith voiced the question: "Why doesn't Daddy find us?"

When William Miner discovered that his children had disappeared from the schoolyard, he urged Kit mercilessly through the fast-forming drifts, sure that Maude had gone home. His wife met him at the door. They gazed, stricken, into each other's eyes.

Immediately, he gave the alarm over the rural party lines. Nearly forty men, risking their lives, were soon moving slowly, persistently, over the fields and roads between Miner's farm and the school. They stopped at neighboring farms to change teams, to treat their frostbite, to gulp coffee, to devise new plans. All the other children were safe in their homes. But the men found no trace of the Miner children.

The wind became a sixty-mile-an-hour gale; the temperature dropped to zero; the gray became utter blackness. And the maddening snow kept falling. The searchers had to give up until daylight.

The next morning one group of searchers reported tracks made by a small sleigh and a horse that went out the south gate of the schoolyard—then were obliterated by the falling snow. The search was quickly reorganized. Men with teams and sleighs, men on horseback and men on foot fanned out for half a mile. Back and forth they forced their way across the shrouded land.

At two o'clock on Tuesday afternoon, twenty-five hours from the time the Miner children had disappeared, a search party spotted something in a pasture two miles south of the school. It was the overturned sleigh. Next to it, like a sentry, a ghostlike horse stood motionless but still alive. They saw a bulky snow-covered mound under the arch of the naked, skeletonlike staves.

The rigid body of a girl lay face down with her unbuttoned coat flung wide open. Her arms were stretched over her brother and sister, sheltering and embracing them in death as she had in life.

Tenderly, the men lifted her, then slowly removed the matted robe and torn canvas pieces that she had been holding down with her body. Underneath were Myrdith and Emmet, dazed and partially frozen but alive. They had promised never to fall into the dread sleep from which Hazel knew they would never awaken.

Today, on the courthouse grounds in the town of Center, these words are engraved on a granite monument rising, like a challenge, above the plains:

In
Memory
of
HAZEL MINER
April 11, 1904
March 16, 1920
To the dead a tribute
To the living a memory
To posterity an inspiration
THE STORY OF HER LIFE AND OF HER
TRAGIC DEATH IS RECORDED IN THE
ARCHIVES OF OLIVER COUNTY.
STRANGER, READ IT

A jet pilot's harrowing account
of what has been called
"the most prolonged and fantastic
parachute descent in history"

I Fell
Into a Thunderstorm

BY LIEUTENANT COLONEL
WILLIAM H. RANKIN, USMC

IT WAS JUST BEFORE six p.m. on July 26, 1959, when I heard a thump and a rumbling sound behind and beneath the cockpit I was sitting in. Another Marine pilot, Lt. Herbert Nolan, and I were making a routine high-altitude flight in two F8U Crusader jet fighters. We were en route from South Weymouth, Massachusetts, to our home base at Beaufort, South Carolina, and I had just climbed up past 47,000 feet to get over an unusually high thunderstorm in the vicinity of Norfolk, Virginia.

Quickly I scanned my instruments. I was at Mach .82 (82/100 of the speed of sound), and nothing appeared to be wrong. Still, the thump and rumble were abnormal sounds. I was about to call Herb to let him know I was expecting trouble when I heard the sounds again. Then, suddenly, the red fire-warning light flashed on!

I knew I had only seconds to analyze my situation and decide what to do, for the red warning light meant, in effect: DON'T WASTE TIME. EJECT!

Instinctively, I cut back on power and called Herb: "Tiger Two, this is Tiger One. I'm having engine trouble. I might have to eject."

Herb replied instantly: "Roger, Tiger One. If you have to go, let me know." That was my last communication with him.

The fire-warning light went out now, but my rpm indicator started unwinding frighteningly. In five or six seconds my indicated engine speed went from about ninety percent to zero. I was having a one-in-a-million kind of emergency—"engine seizure." Some awful friction, perhaps due to loss of oil, had caused the engine to "freeze."

Without an engine, I lacked both electrical and hydraulic power to control the plane. Even at subsonic speeds, the aerodynamic forces on the airfoils of the F8U are so great that no one can exert sufficient pressure on the control stick to move the control surfaces.

I reached to my left and pulled the handle to actuate the emergency power turbine. Nothing happened. I pulled again. The handle came completely out of the cockpit wall.

There was nothing more I could do. Without power, I could not dive to a lower, safer level for ejection. Nor could I stay with the plane much longer, for it might stall and fall into a wild spin. But no one, so far as I knew, had *ever* ejected at this altitude, at any speed, supersonic or subsonic, with or without a pressure suit or some protective clothing. The temperature outside was seventy degrees below zero, and I was wearing only a summer-weight flying suit, gloves, helmet and Marine field shoes.

Perhaps I could survive frostbite without permanent injury, but what about decompression? I was almost ten miles up, where the air is so thin that the blood in a man's body, lacking the shield of a pressure suit, could literally come to a boil.

And how about those dark, massive, rolling thunderclouds below? If there was one thing I'd learned in flight training, it was to avoid thunderstorms. I vividly recalled flying through one several years before in an F4U Corsair. The turbulence was so violent that it flipped the plane over on its back and I'd barely managed to regain control. If thunderstorms were so hazardous for an airplane in flight, what would one do to a mere man?

Still, there was no alternative. I gripped the ejection-curtain handles and pulled—hard.

The nylon curtain that protects the pilot's face from windblast during ejection came down before my eyes. Then I heard and felt the ejection-seat fire—a tremendous kick in the rear.

As I shot up and out of the plane, a wall-like blast of air hit me. The coldness of the air, as I hurtled through it at 500 miles an hour, was shocking. My face, neck, wrists, hands and ankles felt as if they were on fire. Then, seconds later, the burning sensation turned to a blessed numbness.

At the same time I felt the almost unbearable pain of decompression. I could feel my abdomen distending, stretching, until I thought it would give way. My eyes felt as though they were being ripped from their sockets; my ears seemed to be bursting; my entire body was racked by cramps. Once I caught a horrified glimpse of my abdomen, swollen as if I were in a well-advanced pregnancy. I had never known such savage pain.

Strangely, there was no immediate sensation of falling, only of zooming through the air and spinning like a pinwheel, my limbs trying to go in every possible direction at once. Brilliant colors rotated against a purplish void; the sun swept past in streaks of blurred reddish orange.

After a while I felt a surge of elation. In spite of everything, I was conscious! *Hang on,* I thought. *You might make it yet.*

I was in a free fall, which I knew must continue until my parachute opened automatically at 10,000 feet. Now, what was that beating against my face? My oxygen mask! I had just left an airplane where I had been breathing one-hundred-percent oxygen. I would soon need more to avoid unconsciousness and possible serious brain damage. But my body was spread-eagled, and the g forces were so great that I could not move my arms to get at the mask.

Suddenly, as I entered a dense overcast of gray and white clouds, I was able to pull in my hands. I grabbed the oxygen mask and held it to my face. Connected with an emergency oxygen bottle in my chute pack, it would give me a three- to five-minute supply.

In denser atmosphere now, I was feeling a little better. By remaining conscious, I said to myself, I would be able to report in detail what had happened. It would be good news to high-altitude aviators: *We can survive decompression at extreme altitudes.*

Something was streaming down my face and freezing. Taking my right hand away from the mask, I saw that it was covered with blood. As I was to learn later, I had bled from the eyes, ears, nose and mouth as a result of ruptures caused by the decompression.

The clouds were darker now. I looked at my watch—and all my confidence in survival vanished. The luminous dial was barely visible, but it seemed to indicate four or five minutes after six. I knew I'd left the airplane at exactly 6:00 p.m. at approximately 47,000 feet. Undoubtedly I had slowed to terminal velocity in a few seconds and was now falling about 10,000 feet per minute. Why hadn't my chute opened? Had I fallen past the 10,000-foot mark? In this blind overcast, I might be only a few hundred feet from crashing into the ground.

I felt a tremendous desire to open my chute. Just then, however, my confidence was somewhat restored by the realization that my body was being pelted by hailstones. The freezing level for rain? Must be 10,000 feet or more. Good. Keep on free-falling.

Suddenly my body lurched violently. My chute had opened by itself. I made a rough calculation: *I'm at the 10,000-foot level. Descending from here at the rate of about 1,000 feet per minute, I should be down in about ten minutes.*

Utterly elated, I took off the oxygen mask. It was all over now, I thought; the ordeal had ended.

But it hadn't. I was about to enter the center of the thunderstorm. With incredible suddenness and fury, a massive blast of air jarred me from head to toe, sent me soaring up and up and up. Falling again, I saw that I was in an angry ocean of boiling clouds spilling over one another, into one another, digesting one another. I was buffeted in all directions—up, down, sideways, clockwise, counter-clockwise, over and over. I was stretched, slammed, pounded. I vomited repeatedly.

At times my chute seemed to lose its precious billow, and I thought it a miracle that I did not go streaming toward earth with a long, narrow white tail—my collapsed chute.

The wind had savage allies. The first clap of thunder came as a deafening explosion that literally shook my teeth. I didn't *hear* the thunder, I actually *felt* it—an almost unbearable physical experience. If it had not been for my closely fitted helmet, the explosions might have shattered my eardrums.

I saw lightning all around me in every shape imaginable. When very close, it appeared mainly as a huge, bluish sheet several feet thick. It was raining so torrentially that I thought I would drown in midair. Several times I held my breath, fearing that otherwise I might inhale quarts of water.

The storm seemed endless, and there were times when I felt I must die of sheer exhaustion. One thing, however, sustained me: the ability to continue to *think*. Once, when a violent blast of air sent me careening up into the chute and I could feel the cold, wet nylon collapsing about me, I was sure the chute would never fill and blossom again. But, by some miracle, I fell back, and the chute *did* recover its billow. *Well*, I thought, *if this damn thing can survive, so can I!*

Finally, I sensed the turbulence lessening. Coming out of the overcast at last, I caught my first joyous glimpse of green earth. *Now*, I thought, *gather your wits. Don't get killed, after all this, in a bad landing.*

I was over the tall, sharp treetops of a dense evergreen forest—sweeping past them, I estimated, at thirty-five to fifty miles per hour. At the rate I was zooming toward them, I was likely to be impaled. Instinctively, I gritted my teeth, closed my eyes, crossed my legs and cupped my groin.

I felt a tremendous jerk. Luckily, my parachute had caught in the treetops, and like a large pendulum I swung out wide and then crashed back against a tree trunk. I slid the rest of the way to the ground and lay there stunned.

Every part of my body ached, and my entire face felt raw and sensitive. *Don't lie here doing nothing*, I thought. *You need medical help—and soon. Get going!*

I looked at my watch. It read 6:40. A descent that should have taken a little more than ten minutes had taken forty! Shaky and shivering, I struggled free of the chute.

Now, jungle knife in hand, I stumbled through a tangle of underbrush to a cornfield. Over the tops of the cornstalks I could see the headlights of moving automobiles. A road! I half-ran, half-stumbled toward it. Several cars passed me, ignoring my shouts and frantic gestures. I must have been a terrifying sight standing there in the purplish twilight in my tattered flight suit and Buck Rogers helmet, with a large knife in my hand, blood caked on my face and oozing from my mouth, nose and ears.

Finally, as a car went by, I sank to my knees. About fifty yards down the road I saw its red brake lights go on. It turned and came back. The driver motioned me into the front seat. He was Judson Dunning, a farmer, and with him were his wife, three young sons and a teenage cousin. I asked where we were. Near Rich Square, North Carolina, he said. That was some seventy-five miles from Norfolk.

For two weeks I was kept under constant observation at the naval hospital at my base in Beaufort by a small army of flight surgeons, cardiologists, general surgeons, eye-ear-nose-and-throat specialists and orthopedists. They were astounded that I had suffered no serious damage, apart from severe bruises, lacerations, a badly cut finger, a slight hemorrhage in one eye, generalized swelling (especially of the eyelids), some early difficulty in focusing on small print, widespread discoloration of skin (mainly due to frostbite), and sprains and strains of ligaments, joints and muscles. My sense of equilibrium was impaired, and there were signs of personality changes and forgetfulness. But gradually my equilibrium and memory returned to normal.

Around mid-August I was discharged from the hospital. After a program of physical rehabilitation, a long session with the psychiatrist and a pressure-chamber test, I was cleared to fly again.

Two days later I went up in an F8U. As soon as I was airborne, I knew I was back where I belonged.

The tourists watched in horror
as the little boat passed the point
where nothing could keep it
from going over the Falls

The Boy Who
Plunged Over Niagara

BY LAWRENCE ELLIOTT

JUST AFTER EIGHT A.M. on Saturday, July 9, 1960, James Honeycutt came off the night shift at a Niagara Falls hydroelectric project. Sleep, though, was not on his mind—not on a fine summer morning with a trim new outboard motorboat tied to the dock at Lynch's Trailer Court, where he lived.

Honeycutt was forty, an affable man who had had to leave his family in Raleigh, North Carolina, when he came north to work. He found the weekends long and lonely. So, after breakfast, he drove to the home of Frank Woodward, a carpenter on his crew. Over coffee Honeycutt sprang his surprise: How would the Woodward youngsters, seventeen-year-old Deanne and her seven-year-old brother, Roger, like to go for a boat ride?

Deanne, awed by the tumultuous river, which she had seen only once, was reluctant. But with little Roger jumping with glee, and her mother urging her to go along—"You'll have a chance for a swim at Lynch's later"—Deanne changed into a bathing suit, and the three set out.

Soon Honeycutt was easing his green aluminum runabout away from the Lynch dock, his pride and inexperience both obvious in the cautious way he maneuvered clear of other boats. At midstream he turned the sleek fourteen-foot craft downriver and offered the tiller to Roger. His face grinning above his brilliant orange life jacket, the boy took hold.

Deanne, in the bow, relaxed. If Mr. Honeycutt was confident enough to let Roger steer, what was *she* worried about? When they passed under the Grand Island Bridge, gateway to the American side of the falls, she waved gaily at the cars passing far overhead.

John R. Hayes, a trucker and special police officer from Union, New Jersey, had crossed the bridge an hour earlier. He and his wife had come to Niagara Falls for the weekend, and now, like the thousands of other tourists, they were snapping pictures and marveling at the incredible power of the famous cataracts.

Just past noon, they crossed the footbridge to Goat Island, which splits the Niagara into two sets of leaping rapids, its sheer northern end overlooking the awesome cleft into which both the American and the Horseshoe falls plunge. Downriver from the falls, so far below him that it looked like a toy in a bathtub, Hayes could see a vessel docked under the Canadian cliffs.

It was one of the two *Maid of the Mist* ships that take turns cruising up into the "Shoe." There, within 150 feet of the wet black rocks at the very foot of Horseshoe Falls, surrounded by wild flying spray and deafened by the roar of the torrent, tourists come face to face with one of nature's great extravagances.

The Niagara River is, in effect, an ever-narrowing trough, draining the North American midcontinent. Plunging north with the overflow from Lake Erie and the three Great Lakes to the west, it drops a precipitous 326 feet in its thirty-six-mile length, flings 823,650 gallons of water a second over the 161-foot falls and swirls through the world's most treacherous rapids before spending its fury in the vastness of Lake Ontario.

Its violence has always attracted daredevils. In steel drums or padded barrels, at least seven stunters have gone over the Horseshoe. Only four survived. Suicides find in the falls the savage end they elect. Scarcely a month passed in 1960 that one wasn't washed over the brink. Dashed to the rocks below, thrust into wild eddies and currents, their broken bodies were almost invariably cast to the surface at the *Maid of the Mist* landing dock exactly four days later.

Jim Honeycutt, back at the tiller again, seemed unconcerned as the little outboard, now four miles downstream from Lynch's and only a mile or so above the falls, came bouncing past the long breakwater that evens the river's flow. Deanne, though, was getting nervous. This was not the broad, friendly river they'd started out on. It was roiled, leaping turbulently along the pronounced downhill pitch, breaking white against glistening rocks. The thunder of pounding water grew louder in her ears.

About this time, a Goat Island sightseeing guide was telling a group of tourists that the control structure out on the river was the point beyond which nothing could keep from going over the Falls. One tourist gestured at the little green boat and said, "What about that?" The guide ran for a telephone. But it was already too late.

With the runabout almost abreast of Goat Island, Honeycutt finally brought the bow around. For one tenuous moment, the seven-and-a-half-horsepower motor beat against the relentless force of the current, barely making headway. Then, with a piercing whine, it began to race futilely; the propeller pin had sheared.

As the boat was swept downstream stern first, Honeycutt lunged for the oars. Though he pulled frantically, he hardly slowed the boat's backward rush. He yelled to Deanne, "Put on the life jacket!"

The girl's fingers were stiff as she laced up the boat's only other life jacket. In the stern, face suddenly turned white, Roger called, "Dee-dee, I'm scared." He began stumbling toward her.

"No!" she screamed, terrified that he would tip them over. "Stay there, Roger! We'll be swimming at Lynch's soon."

"No, we're going to drown!" he cried. But he sat down and, cling-ing to the thwart, began to sob quietly. They were in full rapids now, the water solid white and tearing them toward the falls. Smashing off a rock, then caught by a vicious rip, the stern flew straight up.

"Hang on!" Honeycutt cried out, but there was nothing to hang on to. He and Roger were thrown over Deanne's head. Then the water snatched at her. She grabbed for the overturned hull, but it slid from beneath her fingers.

Honeycutt grabbed Roger's arm, fighting to hold the boy's head out of the water. But the furious currents tore them apart. The rap-ids wrenched Roger down and spun him around. Then all at once he was free, thrust out over the edge of the Falls, dropping through space.

John Hayes saw the boat turn over. He and his wife had been walking toward Terrapin Point, the railed tip of Goat Island that looks out over the lip of the Horseshoe. "Look!" he shouted, racing for the river.

As he ran, he spied Deanne Woodward's vivid life jacket. He dashed upriver, past dozens of stunned tourists, trying to get closer to her. Above the roar of the cataract he heard her crying out for help. He leaned over the guardrail so she could see him.

"Here!" he called out. "Hey, girl! Swim over here!"

Deanne saw him but shook her head hopelessly. She was unable to make any real progress.

"Try!" Hayes called. He ran downriver to get ahead of her, and leaned farther over the rail. "Try!"

The current was sweeping her inexorably closer to the jagged rim of the Falls. Hayes stretched his arm out, though the girl was still far beyond reach. Deanne was at the very edge of exhaustion. Her legs ached from being pounded against the rocks. "Help me!" she pleaded with Hayes, the thunder of death a bare twenty feet away. Quickly he climbed over the guardrail. He was only a foot above the rushing water, clinging to the rail with one hand. He cried out, "You got to try, hear? *Try!*"

The sharpness of his voice stirred a last, hidden resource in Deanne. Doggedly she buried her face in the water and pulled once more against its clutch. When she looked up again, Hayes was almost directly above her. Desperately she flung out her hand as she went sweeping by—and caught his thumb. Hayes's hand closed around hers.

His foot wedged behind the rail, the weight of the girl and the awful force of the rapids tearing at his fingers, Hayes thought they would both go over. He called for help. A man broke out of the cluster of spellbound sightseers. Vaulting the rail, John A. Quattrochi, another tourist from New Jersey, leaned down and grabbed Deanne's wrist. For a long moment the three hung on, straining. Then the two men pulled the girl from the rushing water and lifted her over the guardrail.

Deanne Woodward had been just ten feet from the falls, closer than anyone had ever come before being plucked to safety. As she lay on the ground, she gasped, "My brother! My brother's still in there. Please save him!"

But Quattrochi had seen Roger go over the falls. Softly he said, "Say a prayer for your brother."

Maid of the Mist II, its decks heaving, drenched by spray and surrounded by thunder, was almost to its turning point just below Horseshoe Falls. At the wheel, Capt. Clifford Keech peered into the chaos of white water. When, at 12:52, he spotted a bobbing orange object dead ahead, he craned forward in amazement. He barked into his ship-to-shore phone: "This is Keech. There's a kid in a life jacket floating around up here and—maybe I'm crazy, but I think he's alive!"

Though Roger Woodward was indeed alive—the first human being to survive a drop over Niagara Falls without elaborate protection—his peril was not yet past. He was drifting close to the huge intake port of an Ontario hydroelectric plant and might yet be sucked into it.

The *Maid* came about and bore down on the boy from upstream, using the full reverse power of both engines to hold a position against the driving current. From the starboard bow, Mate Murray Hartling and deckhand Jack Hopkins threw a life preserver toward the tiny figure in the water. It fell short. They hauled it in and threw again.

On the third try the life preserver bobbed to within an arm's length of the thrashing boy. He crawled up onto it. A moment later,

Roger Woodward lay on the deck of the *Maid,* shivering under the blankets piled on him. "Please find my sister," he said. "She and Mr. Honeycutt fell in the water, too."

An emergency launch, responding to Keech's call, searched the swirling caldron for half an hour but found only the auxiliary gas tank, all that was ever recovered of the boat.

Meanwhile, high up on Goat Island, hundreds had seen the boy in the orange life jacket pulled aboard the *Maid of the Mist.* "They've got your brother," Hayes told Deanne just before she was whisked off to the hospital. "I think he's okay."

"Thank you, God," said the girl, and closed her eyes.

Roger was taken to a Canadian hospital, where an hour later his mother and father came to tell him that Deanne, too, had been rescued. In a few days both youngsters, incredibly uninjured except for superficial bruises, were released.

How did Roger Woodward survive? River men reason that one possibility is that Roger's lightness held him atop the water's surge; that, as he was thrust over the brink, he flew along and down the crest as though going over a slide, thus avoiding the deadly rocks and turbulence at the base of the Falls. Though he had dropped 161 feet at an estimated seventy-five miles an hour, his life preserver had forced him back to the surface before he lost consciousness.

But the mighty Falls did not go completely unappeased. On Wednesday, July 13, the body of Jim Honeycutt turned up at the *Maid of the Mist* landing. It was four days, almost to the hour, from the moment he was swept to his death.

For eight days
and seven nights,
the crippled climber
lay helpless—
as scores of brave men
struggled to save him
in one of the most spectacular
rescue attempts
in mountaineering annals

Ordeal
on Mount Kenya

BY LAWRENCE ELLIOTT

THE AFTERNOON OF Saturday, September 5, 1970, suddenly cleared. The two young Austrians who had just climbed to the top of Mount Kenya, higher than the highest of the Alps, looked out over the green land three miles below and exulted at the magnificence of the moment.

They were both doctors—Gerd Judmaier, 29, was studying to be an internist at the Innsbruck University Hospital, and Oswald Oelz, 27, was engaged in medical research in Zürich. They had been climbing together for four years, but never had they won out over a mountain of such immensity, such solitary splendor. So sharply does Mount Kenya rise up from the East African jungle that each year only a handful of climbers attain the 17,058-foot summit of Batian, the taller of its twin peaks. Just the day before, a party of four Zambians and two Americans had been turned back from the top by a blizzard; they were still resting in a shelter about 2,500 feet below.

Atop Batian, the two Austrians took some photographs and then, around two p.m., started down the sheer face of the mountain. Roped together, they descended about one hundred feet to a patch of flat ground at Shipton's Notch. Here Oelz searched for a solid rock around which to secure the rope tied to his waist. Judmaier, also bound to the rope, leaned out over a massive boulder to study the route down.

Suddenly there was a sharp cry. Oelz spun around—he was alone—the boulder had given way beneath Judmaier. Oelz dived for the rope as it whizzed over the edge. It went ripping through his palms, and he felt first the shock of knowing that his flesh was burning, then the pain. Desperate, he dug in his heels and managed to wind the rope on his arm and check Judmaier's fall down the steeply pitched mountainside.

Heart pumping fiercely, Oelz found a place to tie the rope and scrambled down to his friend's side. Judmaier lay on a sliver of rock shelf that tilted out toward the void. His head was bloodied, but Oelz saw at once where the real trouble was: His right leg had been so badly shattered by the tumbling boulder that a jagged end of bone had torn through his trousers. Another piece of bone, perhaps two inches long, lay on the ground beside him. The wound was spurting blood.

Working swiftly, Oelz used an elastic bandage for a tourniquet and tightened it around Judmaier's right thigh. "I'm done for," Judmaier said.

Oelz didn't answer. He went on working, cleaning the abrasions on Judmaier's head and tying him to a rock so he wouldn't slip off the ledge. He could not disagree with his friend's bleak assessment.

If this were Switzerland or Austria, where there were many skilled climbers trained in rescue techniques, he might have a fighting chance.

But this was Kenya, where no professional mountain-rescue teams existed. Even if there had been any, it seemed clear that his friend would be dead of shock, blood loss or exposure long before Oelz could round them up.

Having considered the realities, Oelz put them out of his mind. There had to be something a man could do. "I'm going to get medicine and some people to carry you down," he said. "There is a chance."

Judmaier nodded weakly. "Maybe if they are quick," he said, "and if you are lucky. . . ."

It had begun to snow. Although Mount Kenya stands only ten miles from the equator, the disappearance of the sun at that great altitude can, in minutes, bring on below-zero temperatures. Oelz put both their down jackets and a blanket on Judmaier and zipped him into a bivouac sack. He left him their only food—a can of preserved fruit. Then he fixed a rope, touched his friend's shoulder in farewell, and slid over the ledge.

The descent was harrowing. Oelz's burned palms kept shredding on the rope, and often he had to stop because the pain was so frightful. The rocks were slick with ice, and the snow fell so thickly that he could not see more than a step or two ahead. But he kept thinking of Judmaier, alone up there in the cold, and he pushed on. Around six p.m., he stumbled into Kami Hut, where he found the Zambian and American climbers and told them what had happened.

One of the Zambians, a transplanted Briton named Bev Burrage, volunteered to set off for the 15,700-foot-high shelter at Top Hut, where there were emergency medical supplies and a solar-powered radio. After two and a half hours of hazardous night climbing, he reached it and alerted the police at Naro Moru, a village at the foot of the mountain.

Burrage's SOS set in motion a rescue plan evolved by officials of Mountain National Parks, the Kenya police and the Mountain Club of Kenya, an association of climbing enthusiasts (mainly Europeans), residing in and around Nairobi. In a short time, Mountain Club president Robert Chambers was speeding to the mountain with rescue gear. Police and park officials were setting up backup services, and all the available climbers were being marshaled. Unfortunately, only a few of these men had done any serious climbing in months, and most were neither fit nor acclimatized for the task. But they decided to try nevertheless. They couldn't just leave him there.

Meanwhile, Burrage was on his way back to Kami Hut with the emergency medicine; he arrived at about four a.m. Oelz, who had slept a little, now asked if anyone would climb back up to Shipton's Notch with him. Richard Sykes, an American, volunteered. He stood up and said, "Let's go."

They started up at first light. It snowed steadily all that morning; they were heavily loaded, and Sykes's courage exceeded his experience. Within 300 feet of Judmaier, they had to turn back. By the time they struggled into Kami, eighteen climbers were on the way there, as well as twenty Kenyan porters. In the evening, Chambers and four other climbers reached the shelter. They brought radios and a cacolet (a backpack litter for carrying injured climbers). A helicopter was also en route to Kami.

Monday, September 7, dawned clear and warm. Oelz and Silvano Borruso, an Italian, started climbing toward Shipton's Notch with a radio. One of the other two teams following had the cacolet.

At 4:30 that afternoon, with snow falling hard, Oelz and Borruso reached a height above Shipton's Notch and called down to the still, dark form on the ledge. No answering stir; no sound. For Gerd Judmaier—alone there for fifty hours—the two nights had been bitterly cold. He had been haunted by the sensation that he was slipping off the ledge. By day the equatorial sun sapped precious body fluids and left him unable to fight off the agony spreading up from his shattered leg.

Oelz and Borruso clambered down. To Oelz, Judmaier mumbled weakly, "At least *you're* alive. I thought you'd fallen, too." While Oelz gave Judmaier an injection of a pain suppressant, Borruso tried to radio Kami to tell them that Judmaier was alive and to urge all speed. But the set would not transmit! They settled down to wait for help.

Early the following morning, a helicopter piloted by Jim Hastings, a thirty-eight-year-old American who had volunteered for the

Stretcher Traverse, September 11
Bation
Shipton's Notch
Top Bivouac
Direction Top Hut
Direction Kami Hut

flight, landed at Kami with plasma, glucose and other vital medical supplies. A climbing team started up with these while Hastings took off again to get some badly needed rope.

A little past noon, the cacolet was finally hauled up onto the ledge by a climber named John Temple. He took one look at Judmaier's ghastly pallor and said, "We'd best start down right now. I'll carry him." Oelz gave Judmaier another injection and immobilized the broken leg, using a camera tripod for a splint. Then he and Borruso strapped Judmaier into the cacolet and hefted it up on Temple's back. But spasms of unbearable pain tore at the injured man, and Oelz cried, "Put him down—he's dying!" Only the arrival of the team carrying the plasma and glucose saved Judmaier that afternoon.

The next morning, Wednesday, the urgent beat of the helicopter's rotors again reverberated up toward Kami, and a surge of hope ran through every man on the mountain. They knew that the helicopter hadn't the power to lift Judmaier off a ledge at 17,000 feet, but if it had brought rope and other equipment, there was a chance. They could move Judmaier to Kami. From there the helicopter could fly him out.

But even as they listened, they heard a terrible crash. One moment, Hastings was maneuvering for a landing; the next—perhaps caught by an updraft—he was flung against the mountainside and he was killed. Spent and heartsick, Judmaier turned his face into the bivouac sack.

Meanwhile, the injured man's father, Professor Fritz Judmaier, was en route from Austria, having alerted a crack mountain-rescue team in Innsbruck to stand by in case of need. The elder Judmaier learned how the international band in Kenya had tried valiantly to save his son, but now seemed thwarted by exhaustion and inexperience. After landing in Nairobi on Thursday, Fritz Judmaier telephoned Innsbruck, 4,000 miles away. "Please come at once," he said to a member of the Austrian rescue team. Within two hours, six expert Austrian climbers had gathered their gear and were airborne. They were led by Dr. Raimund Magreiter, a medical colleague of Oelz and Judmaier's.

Wednesday night was the worst of all for the critically hurt man on the ledge. Sleeping fitfully, feverish, all ten toes frostbitten, he cried out for water, but when Oelz put some to his lips he threw it up. In the morning, however, Judmaier was still alive. He muttered, "If I die now, that American's life is wasted."

That day and the next, defying all odds, there were thirty-four climbers on the mountain working to bring Judmaier down. Sapped by exertion in the rarefied air, lashed intermittently by blizzards and biting cold, they worked in relays. They managed to move Judmaier about 400 feet to a small natural resting place at the junction of the two ridges, which they called Top Bivouac. They got no farther that night.

On Friday morning, the Austrians arrived in Nairobi. They climbed into a police Cessna and flew to Nanyuki, where they began the thirty-mile trip up to Kami Hut, the last ten miles of which they had to cover on foot. They arrived around midnight and spent the rest of the night preparing for the final ascent.

At daybreak Saturday, the Austrians started up. By this time the men at Top Bivouac sat in a kind of despondent stupor. Oelz, despite his ordeal, steadfastly refused to leave his friend's side. Judmaier drifted in and out of a coma. He barely stirred when, with a herculean last effort, Chambers, Temple and the others brought him down another 400 feet. But that was absolutely the last of their strength, and they fell back, unable to go on. It started to rain; one of them covered Judmaier's face with a sheet of plastic.

After a time, Judmaier felt it drawn back. He heard Oelz say, "He's very bad." Then there was another voice: "Hey, we didn't come all this way for nothing!" Judmaier opened his eyes and saw a Tyrolean climbing helmet. "Do you hear me?" an Austrian, Horst Bergmann, said to him, grinning. "Don't make this a wasted trip."

They moved with astonishing speed, thanks in large measure to the preparations by the local climbers. The Austrians had the training and equipment to rig lines for the steepest descent in a few minutes, and were fresh enough to bundle Judmaier down rapidly. At treacherous Firmin's Tower, they ran 650-foot lengths of strong nylon rope through special pulleys that held the stretcher on an even keel. In sixty heart-stopping minutes they had lowered Judmaier some 130 feet down the sheerest part of the north face.

Then came the back-breaking job of carrying him over steeply sloping shale and ice-encrusted rock. By ten p.m., they had reached level ground. At midnight, they saw the lights of Kami. "By God, we've done it!" someone said.

Their mission was completed. In one of mountaineering's most astounding exploits, the Austrians had traveled 4,000 miles, climbed to the top of Africa's most dangerous peak and snatched from death a man who had lain there crippled and helpless for eight days and seven nights—all in fifty-four incredible hours.

Gerd Judmaier faced days of surgery and weeks of recuperation. But he felt undying gratitude for the men who fought to save his life. Perhaps the most meaningful tribute came from his father, who after thanking all the volunteers, spoke warmly of Jim Hastings, the American helicopter pilot who had been killed on the mountain. "I bow my head in deepest respect to this young man who sacrificed his life for the sake of someone he had never seen. His name will never be forgotten in our household."

To save a life,
brave men sometimes dare the impossible

Miracle
in Midair

BY VIRGINIA KELLY

IT BEGAN LIKE ANY OTHER May morning in California. The sky was blue, the sun hot. A slight breeze riffled the glistening waters of San Diego Bay. At the naval airbase on North Island, all was calm.

At 9:45 a.m., Walter Osipoff, a sandy-haired, twenty-three-year-old Marine second lieutenant from Akron, Ohio, boarded a DC-2 transport for a routine parachute jump. Lt. Bill Lowrey, a thirty-four-year-old Navy test pilot from New Orleans, was already putting his observation plane through its paces. And John McCants, a husky, forty-one-year-old aviation chief machinist's mate from Jordan, Montana, was checking out the aircraft that he was scheduled to fly later. Before the sun was high in the noonday sky, these three men would be linked forever in one of history's most spectacular midair rescues.

Osipoff was a seasoned parachutist, a former collegiate wrestling and gymnastics star. He had joined the National Guard and then the Marines in 1938. He had already made more than twenty jumps.

That morning, May 15, 1941, they were headed for Kearney Mesa, where Osipoff would supervise practice jumps by twelve of his men. Three separate canvas cylinders, containing ammunition and rifles, were also to be dropped by parachute from the DC-2 as part of the exercise.

Nine of the men had already jumped when Osipoff, standing a few inches from the plane's door, started to toss out the last of the canvas cargo cylinders. Somehow the automatic-release cord of his backpack parachute became looped over the cylinder, and his chute was suddenly ripped open. He tried to grab hold of the quickly billowing silk, but the next thing he knew he had been jerked from the plane—sucked out the open door with such force that the impact of his body ripped a two-and-a-half-foot gash in the DC-2's aluminum fuselage.

Instead of flowing free, Osipoff's open parachute now wrapped itself around the plane's tail wheel. The chute's chest strap and one leg strap had broken; only the second leg strap was still holding, and it had slipped down to Osipoff's ankle. One by one, twenty-four of the twenty-eight lines snapped between the parachute and his precariously attached harness. He was now hanging some twelve feet below—and fifteen feet behind—the tail of the plane. The four parachute lines twisted around his left leg were all that kept him from falling to the ground.

Dangling there upside down, Osipoff had enough presence of mind not to try to release his emergency parachute. Since the plane was pulling him one way and the emergency chute would pull him another, he realized that he would be torn in half. He was conscious all this time. He knew that he was hanging by one leg, spinning and bouncing—and that his ribs hurt. He did not know then that two of his ribs and three vertebrae had been fractured.

Inside the plane, the DC-2 crew struggled to pull Osipoff to safety, but they could not reach him. The DC-2 was starting to run low on fuel, but an emergency landing with Osipoff dragging behind would certainly have smashed him to death. And the pilot, Harold Johnson, had no radio contact with the ground.

To attract attention below, Johnson eased the transport down to 300 feet and started circling North Island. A few people at the base noticed the plane coming by every few minutes, but they assumed that it was towing some sort of target.

Meanwhile, Bill Lowrey had landed his plane after his test flight, and was walking toward his office when he happened to glance upward. He and John McCants, who was working nearby, saw the figure dangling from the plane at the same time. As the DC-2 circled once again, Lowrey yelled to McCants, "There's a man hanging on that line. Do you suppose we can get him?" McCants answered grimly, "We can try."

Lowrey shouted to his mechanics to get his plane ready for takeoff again. It was an SOC-1, a small two-seat observation plane with an open cockpit. Recalls Lowrey, "I didn't even know how much fuel it had." Turning to McCants, he said, "Let's go!"

Lowrey and McCants had never flown together before, but the two men seemed to take it for granted that they were going to attempt the impossible. "There was only one decision to be made," Lowrey said quietly afterward, "and that was to go get him. How, we didn't know. We had no time to plan."

Nor was there time to get through to their commanding officer and request permission for the flight. Lowrey simply told the tower: "Give me a green light. I'm taking off." At the last moment, a marine ran out to the plane with a hunting knife—for cutting Osipoff loose—and gave it to McCants.

As the SOC-1 roared aloft, all activity around San Diego seemed to come to a standstill. People crowded the rooftops; children stopped playing at recess; at North Island every head turned toward the sky. With murmured prayers and pounding hearts, the watchers agonized through every move in the impossible mission.

Within minutes, Lowrey and McCants were under the transport, flying at 300 feet. They made five approaches, but the air proved too bumpy to try for a rescue. Since radio communication between the two planes was impossible, Lowrey used hand signals to direct

Johnson to head out over the Pacific, where the air would be smoother, and they climbed to 3,000 feet. Johnson held his plane on a straight course and reduced his speed to that of the smaller plane—one hundred miles an hour.

Lowrey flew back and away from Osipoff, but on a level with him. McCants, who was in the open seat in back of Lowrey, saw that Osipoff was hanging by one foot and that blood was dripping from his helmet. Lowrey edged the plane closer, and with such precision that his maneuvers jibed with the swings of Osipoff's inert body. His timing had to be exact so that Osipoff would not swing into the SOC-1's propeller.

Finally, Lowrey slipped his upper left wing under Osipoff's shroud lines, and McCants, standing upright in the rear cockpit—with the plane still going one hundred miles per hour at 3,000 feet above the sea—lunged for Osipoff. He grabbed him at the waist, and Osipoff flung his arms around McCants's shoulders in a death grip.

McCants pulled Osipoff into the plane, but since it had only two seats, the next problem was where to put him. As Lowrey eased the SOC-1 forward to get some slack in the chute lines, McCants managed to stretch Osipoff's body across the top of the fuselage, with Osipoff's head in his lap.

Since McCants was using both hands to hold on to Osipoff, there was no way for him to cut the cords that still attached Osipoff to the DC-2. Lowrey then nosed his plane inch by inch closer to the transport and, flying with incredible precision, used his propeller to cut the shroud lines. After hanging for thirty-three minutes between life and death, Osipoff was finally free.

Lowrey had flown so close to the transport that he'd nicked a twelve-inch gash in its tail. But now the parachute, abruptly detached along with the shroud lines, drifted downward and wrapped itself around Lowrey's rudder. That meant that Lowrey had to fly the SOC-1 without being able to control it properly and with most of Osipoff's body still on the outside. Yet, five minutes later, Lowrey somehow managed to touch down at North Island, and the little plane rolled to a stop. Osipoff finally lost consciousness—but not before he heard sailors applauding the landing.

Later on, after lunch, Lowrey and McCants went back to their usual duties. Three weeks later, both men were flown to Washington, where each received a Distinguished Flying Cross.

Osipoff spent the next six months in the hospital. The following January, completely recovered, he went back to parachute jumping. The morning he was to make his first jump after the accident, he was cool and laconic, as usual. His friends, though, were nervous. One after another, they went up to reassure him. Each volunteered to jump first, so he could follow.

Osipoff grinned and shook his head. "The hell with that!" he said as he fastened his parachute. "I know damn well I'm going to make it."

And he did.

*Battered but alive,
two-year-old Stacy Craine
is comforted by her mother
amid the ruins of their home*

In two and a
half terrible minutes,
half the city of Xenia, Ohio,
virtually disappeared
in a tornado

The Town
That Wouldn't Die

BY GERALD MOORE

ON APRIL 3, 1974, Bob Stewart, city manager of Xenia, Ohio, sat in his office at City Hall and watched a heavy bank of dark clouds hanging low on the southwestern horizon. Stewart felt uneasy about the weather, but he had other things on his mind. To celebrate their twentieth wedding anniversary, he was taking his wife, Yvonne, to dinner that evening. He shifted slightly so he could see his house a block away down Market Street. Then he phoned Yvonne to confirm their date. "The weather looks bad," she said. "Maybe we should stay home."

Bob felt a pang of disappointment. "Why don't you walk up here a little before five and I'll buy you a drink. Then we can decide about dinner."

As he finished up his day's work, Stewart did not imagine that the storm bearing down on Xenia, a town of 27,000 people just east of Dayton, would threaten everything he loved and hand him the greatest challenge of his life.

Shortly after four p.m., at Wright–Patterson Air Force Base, eleven miles to the north, Brig. Gen. Irby Jarvis, Jr., stopped by the Operations Center. "We have tornado activity headed this way, sir," the chief technician said. "It's moving very fast." With several B-52s out on a training mission, Jarvis did not hesitate. "Sound a base alert," he said. Nearly 6,000 men and women scrambled to their duty posts.

At about the same moment, Bob Stewart saw a giant, angry cloud approach his office. He called Yvonne. "I've got the kids in the cellar," she said. With the tornado only yards away, Stewart and several other city employees ran into the street to warn people who were still outside. With seconds to spare, they made it back to City Hall and took cover. Lying flat, trying to protect their heads, they felt their ears begin to pop violently as the atmospheric pressure dropped sharply. The storm was there.

Broken glass, plaster, books and papers rained down on Stewart's group. All over Xenia, buildings were exploding, collapsing, caving in under the weight of uprooted trees. Just out of town, live power lines sent great arcs of lightning through the sky as they tore in two and fell to the ground.

Sheila Fife was with her two sons and three neighboring children when the tornado struck. She pushed the five children into a back bedroom, made them lie on the floor and cover their heads. The storm grew deafening. Bricks, boards and chunks of asphalt torn out of roads began sailing into the yard. Nails suddenly tearing from rafters sounded like human screams. The roof ripped away, and as Sheila held the hysterical children, something heavy hit her head.

Then the carpet beneath the children was jerked up and out of the house. A wall suddenly disappeared into splinters and two-year-old Stacy Craine was wrenched from under Sheila. She looked around for the child. She could see nothing.

As the monstrous storm moved through the town, it cut a swath that was freakish as well as destructive. It ripped open the house above but left its furniture and pictures in place.

Xenia was in the grip of one of the most violent groups of tornadoes ever to pass over North America. In one eighteen-hour period on that April 3 and 4, 148 tornadoes wrecked parts of thirteen states and one Canadian province, killed more than 300 people, injured 6,000 and caused more than half a billion dollars' worth of property damage. Xenia was hit the hardest of all: Three tightly bunched tornadoes, generating winds of over 200 miles an hour within their howling centers, cut a swath of total destruction 1,100 yards wide and sixteen miles long through the town.

Two and a half minutes after they arrived, the storms were gone. An eerie calm followed the awful noise of the wind. The only sounds then were cries for help as people staggered, shocked and bleeding, into the littered streets.

Sheila Fife raised her head and saw that she and the children, but for Stacy, were left on a bare slab where her house had stood. Then she saw Stacy's hand, motionless, protruding from a pile of rubble. Wild with grief and fear, Sheila dug into the rubble with her bare hands. Stacy, against all odds, was alive. Sheila gathered the crying, bleeding children and herded them to the street to seek help. Hours later, after the children were treated, Sheila allowed herself to be examined. X rays showed that her neck was broken.

Bob Stewart ran to the west window of his office and looked down Market Street. His house was severely damaged. So was most of the downtown area. Horrified, he hurried to the street just in time to see Yvonne and three of their six children walking toward him—ironi-

Acres of rubble were all that remained in some areas after the storm. Yet, within hours, a remarkable rehabilitation was under way, with assistance coming from as far away as Britain.

cally, it was a little before five. It would be another ten hours before the Stewarts learned that their other three children were safe.

Bob and Yvonne embraced. Then the chief executive officer of Xenia turned to see what was left of his town. Although it would be days before anyone knew the figures, in the wreckage were thirty-three dead and fifteen hundred injured. Twelve churches and six schools were destroyed or extensively damaged, and many landmark buildings were gone. Wide streets were clogged with the twisted remains of once-magnificent maple trees. Damage was more than one hundred million dollars. It was apparent that nearly half of Xenia was a total loss.

What was not apparent that terrible afternoon was a spirit already working in the people. "What the *hell* are we going to do?" a city employee asked as he looked out over the wrecked town. The answer was prophetic. "We're going to clean the place up," Stewart calmly replied.

From the first, the people in Xenia and surrounding communities whose homes were spared threw open their doors to the storm's refugees. When a call went out for blood donors, so many people showed up that some had to be registered and turned away. The response to requests for food, water and bedding was so tremendous that offers had to be refused. Gov. John J. Gilligan and units of the National Guard were on the scene before midnight. Gilligan recalls that his two strongest impressions in Xenia that night were "the devastation—and the response of the people."

399

By this time, too, General Jarvis had sent huge trucks carrying bulldozers into Xenia, and now the bulldozers from the base were crawling through town, pushing out narrow passages before them. Fire trucks and ambulances followed, and soon the Wright–Patterson base hospital was receiving the overflow from Greene County Memorial Hospital. Citizens armed with chain saws and axes attacked the trees blocking their streets.

The Xenia *Daily Gazette,* even though its plant was hit hard and many of its workers were themselves victims of the tornadoes, did not miss a beat. Working by candlelight while rain poured through the torn roof, the staff put together the tragic story of what had befallen their town. (The paper and its staff would ultimately win a Pulitzer Prize for local reporting.)

The morning after the storm there were railroad cars in the streets and trucks perched on top of buildings. Distraught parents were searching for their missing children. One of the first out-of-town rescue workers to arrive on the scene summed up the city's physical condition: "This is the first time I've been to Xenia—and it's not here." One man, still dressed in the business suit he had on when the tornado hit and carrying a cardboard box through the streets, was challenged by a guardsman: "What have you got in that box?"

"My house," came the reply.

Everyone pitched in on the reconstruction. Local 82 of the International Brotherhood of Electrical Workers sent 150 men from Dayton to clear downed power lines. A caravan of twenty men in eight vans from Sayre, Pennsylvania, 600 miles away, brought food, clothing and $1,000 in cash. Only five days after the storm, private cash contributions reached $50,000. An Englishman who had served with a Xenia resident during World War II sent two pound notes; an Arizona woman who had once been given a traffic ticket by a courteous Xenia patrolman sent fifty dollars.

For a month, trucks loaded with wreckage moved bumper to bumper, until the debris was buried beneath a carpet of sod where a worked-out quarry had been. "The most depressing period was after the cleanup," Stewart said later.

"As long as there was wreckage there was at least something. After the cleanup it seemed like there was nothing. One of the first things county officials did was to start repairing the old stone courthouse downtown. We thought that seeing it restored would give people hope."

Psychological considerations aside, Xenia needed money, and, working together, Stewart and City Commission president Hewlett Mullins set out to get financial aid. The federal government responded quickly. The Small Business Administration set up an office to make low-interest loans to businesses and homeowners who were underinsured. The Department of Housing and Urban Development helped people find temporary housing and approved a forty-two-acre urban-renewal project for the downtown area.

Things moved quickly at the state level, too. The Ohio Legislature approved in only eleven days a $2.5-million aid bill for Xenia. Insurance companies paid $70 million in claims in two months.

The people of Xenia now realized they had a unique opportunity—a chance to rebuild a city. Jack Jordan, editor and general manger of the *Gazette,* helped organize the Spirit of '74 Committee, which met each week to discuss various points of view in the community. Businessmen, educators, doctors, librarians—all who had energy and ideas—were recruited. Out of those discussions and research, plans for a new Xenia began to emerge. On April 14, only eleven days after the disaster, school began again, on split shifts, using buildings in neighboring towns.

As the town was rebuilt, the pride of its people grew stronger. Stores came back with bigger and nicer buildings; businesses donated their first day's receipts to community projects; men with building skills offered their services to neighbors free of charge.

On April 3, one year later, the people of Xenia celebrated the determination that pulled them through the disaster, and they paused to reflect on what they had learned about themselves and the world. "Selfishness disappeared for a time in Xenia," one woman said. "That and a feeling that this storm just wasn't big enough to ruin us are what make it all possible."

Stewart commented that things seemed nearly back to normal because people were starting to call in about potholes and loose dogs—complaints he never before thought he would welcome. And no one who visited the town then could doubt the bumper stickers on local cars that said: XENIA LIVES!

Two things he was sure of:
that he was lost in the vast wilderness of British Columbia
and that civilization lay somewhere to the south.
So he began to walk . . .

Ron Woodcock's Long Walk Home

BY JOSEPH P. BLANK

RONALD WOODCOCK SAT on the trunk of a fallen tree, stared at the ground and tried to think. He was lost in the trackless, unspoiled wilderness of northwestern British Columbia. He marked the date on the calendar that he kept in his backpack: "June 5, 1971."

Woodcock wasn't worried about himself. He felt comfortable in the wilderness and figured he had plenty of time to find the cabin that he had been using. But he was concerned about his family; he had been out of touch with them now for forty days. His wife and six children were living in a rented house in Endako, more than 200 air miles to the south. The February before, their home and their pos-

sessions—all uninsured—had been destroyed by fire. Financially, he had been wiped out.

That, really, was why he had made this trip to the wilderness. He needed more money than he was earning at his railroad job, so he had taken a leave of absence to trap beaver. A good pelt brought twenty dollars. In late April he flew to Damdochax Lake, after arranging for a bush pilot, Bill Jenkins, to pick him up eight weeks later.

Woodcock, 48, was brown-haired, blue-eyed and stocky at 170 pounds. This venture was his third trip to the bush in ten years, and he loved it. He had often said, "If there was a way to have my family with me, I'd spend my life here. You're at peace. You're your own boss. Fish and game are plentiful. You're in a world you're making for yourself, and no other world exists."

The trapping went smoothly, and Woodcock garnered more than fifty pelts in the first three weeks. On May 31 he left his cabin to retrieve skins that he had cached twenty miles north. He wore rubber boots, a wool shirt and a light jacket. His thirty-pound backpack included a sleeping bag, an ax, food, a rifle and fifteen rounds of ammunition.

He worked his way up Slowmaldo Creek and into Groundhog Pass, where he located the skins and spent several days cleaning them. Then he packed half the skins—a sixty-pound load—and his remaining three-day supply of food. Because of the weight of his pack, he decided to seek a shorter route back to Slowmaldo Creek.

After trudging south for six hours through high underbrush, he broke out onto a creek that was backed up by several unfamiliar beaver dams—and from which he had a stunning view of mountains he had never seen before. For a long minute he was hypnotized by the beauty of the panorama. Then, sitting down, he faced the fact that what had so often happened to other woodsmen had now happened to him: He was lost. He had no means of knowing whether Slowmaldo Creek was east or west. In this land of untapped mineral deposits, he did not trust the accuracy of his compass. He couldn't backtrack because there was nothing to follow. His best course, he reasoned, was to stick with this unfamiliar creek downstream to the south. It might bring him to recognizable land or a river. And south was the general direction of the closest town, Hazelton, 125 air miles away.

Woodcock pushed along the creek, still carrying the heavy beaver pelts. Every step was work. The banks of the creek were so overgrown that there was no simple path to follow. He was continually climbing and descending hills and fighting through underbrush; worse, he met an endless obstacle course of windfalls—dead trees that had accumulated over the years and combined sometimes to form impasses twenty-five feet high.

On the evening of the second day, Woodcock reluctantly abandoned his furs. He cooked a handful of rice and zipped himself into his sleeping bag. As he lay awake, he realized that he was in trouble; other men in his predicament, he knew, had panicked, exhausted themselves and not survived. This would not happen to him. He resolved to pace himself and be careful. He *would* make it out, however long it took.

Although he plodded on for about thirteen hours a day, he always stopped when he was tired, rather than spent. He doled out his food sparingly, always on the lookout for game. He shot a woodchuck and a grouse, and on the tenth day he shot a moose. He spent the following day dressing a hindquarter and cooking it down to some twenty pounds of meat to take with him.

About six o'clock that evening, as he prepared his campsite, he looked up to see a giant grizzly approaching the moose carcass. Although he was a hundred feet downwind from the carcass, he knew he had to kill the bear. "The grizzly must have stood nine feet tall and weighed more than a thousand pounds," he remembers. "Those bears are touchy in the spring and inclined to attack. I couldn't have him around my camp while I was sleeping."

Woodcock's first shot slammed through the bear's neck and down into his spinal column, paralyzing him. Reluctant to use another bullet, he waited for the wounded animal to die. Finally, as light grew dim, he had to finish off the bear with a second shot.

On the fourteenth day Woodcock's path toward home was blocked by an icy river too broad and too deep to ford. He shoved his way westward for a day until he encountered another creek. He felled two forty-foot trees across the water, but the current swept each away. Now he was blocked to the south and the west, so he moved north along the creek, hoping that it would narrow enough to enable him to cross.

On the evening of the fifteenth day a storm struck. The wind howled, trees crashed and rain slashed down. He fixed a shelter and a high "mattress" out of spruce limbs. For two days, while the storm raged, he lay in his sleeping bag, hardly moving. He thought about his family and about what the bush pilot, Bill Jenkins, would think and do when he returned for their rendezvous at the Damdochax Lake cabin and found no one.

In fact, the pilot did return. Alarmed at Woodcock's absence, he searched the area for two days, went home and then came back again with Woodcock's brother and brother-in-law. They found an overturned raft at the place where the lake empties into a creek. They concluded that Woodcock must have been on the raft when it capsized and that he had drowned.

After the storm subsided, Woodcock, still totally lost, continued northward, looking for a place to cross the creek. "Take it easy," he told himself aloud. "You'll get out." He eventually found a narrowing of the stream, managed to cross and turned back southward. On about the twenty-fifth day he ate the last of his food.

One morning, as he worked through the underbrush, he suddenly caught a glimpse of a rotting pole—a telegraph pole! He had, he knew, chanced on the old telegraph trail, put through the wilderness by government packhorse expeditions in the late 1800s, now abandoned for many decades. If he could follow signs of the trail—a pole here and there, a piece of telegraph wire still nailed to a tree—the clues would lead him to Hazelton.

Although the trail was overgrown now, it had been trampled for many years by men and animals. Woodcock cut himself a walking stick. By poking it gently into the ground, he could differentiate between the packed earth of the old trail and the soft virgin soil on either side of it.

Now, his odyssey became a step-by-step ordeal as he kept prodding the earth and looking for old poles and pieces of wire. Frequently, he lost the trail in foot-high moss, dense brush and trees. He had to detour for swamps and stands of impenetrable willows. When he lost the trail, he patiently zigged to the east, zagged to the west, sometimes repeating the pattern for days until he picked up the trail again. All movement was a struggle. During one two-week period he estimated that he had progressed no more than twenty miles.

By about the forty-third day his stamina was ebbing, and he couldn't remain on his feet more than six or seven hours a day. Since the twenty-fifth day he had eaten only wild berries and leaves. His belt could no longer hold up his tattered trousers, so he removed the sling from his rifle and fashioned a single suspender out of it. In climbing, he had to pause after three or four steps, and he relied increasingly on his rifle and a walking stick for support. The sole flapped off one boot, and he tied it to the upper with a piece of string from his pack. His clothing was progressively shredded by the sharp brush. Mosquitoes were turning his forehead into raw, bleeding meat. He found nothing to eat except heavily seeded high-bush cranberries. The seeds lodged immovably in his intestines, doubled him up with cramps that shot through his middle like electric shocks.

On what he figured was about the fiftieth day, he lay on the ground, writhing and panting in pain. *Maybe it's time to give up,* he thought. But that's not what he wanted to do; he wanted to see his family. *Rest awhile,* he told himself. *You don't have much farther to go.* Somewhere ahead, he knew, was the dirt road to Hazelton.

So he got up and stumbled on. His rubbery legs felt boneless. He had to squint to focus his eyes. Saliva thickened in his mouth and throat, and he choked when he tried to scrape it out with his fingers. He knew he did not have the strength to climb each new incline, but somehow he did. He had to make it in two more days. He could not last a third day. Yet, even in his condition, he did not let himself indulge in hopeless thoughts.

Suddenly, around noon on the fifty-seventh day, he found himself in the open, on a road—the dirt road to Hazelton! The scene around kept wavering and swimming. He tried to lock his knees so they wouldn't buckle.

A car approached him. The two men in it, bent on an afternoon of fishing, stared at the mangy scarecrow of a human being and continued past him. One hundred and fifty feet down the road the car stopped, then backed. Woodcock staggered toward it. He opened his mouth to talk, but he couldn't utter a sound. He weakly motioned for a pencil and paper.

"I need water," he laboriously scrawled. One man opened a bottle of beer and handed it to him. He slowly got it through the saliva that clotted his mouth. Then he wrote, "If it's not too much trouble, please take me to my mother in Hazelton." Her house was closest.

The two men helped him into the rear seat. His head swam. He felt a mild sense of satisfaction and relief. He had made it. The fishermen helped him to the door of his mother's house. She couldn't believe the apparition before her. Woodcock's face was gaunt behind a three-inch beard. His eyes were glazed. He had lost seventy of his 170 pounds. The rips in his trousers revealed thighs that looked like white sticks.

He was hospitalized for two weeks and treated for malnutrition, exposure and intestinal disorders; and it took an additional two months for him to recover his health and strength. In the hospital, it was three days before he could talk even in a whisper. His wife sat by his bed and asked no questions. After four days, Woodcock's feelings surfaced. When friends asked him about his experience, he began whispering the details, then broke into tears, not even aware that he was going to cry. The visitors misunderstood his tears. He couldn't explain that he had passed through a great adventure. It had given him a conviction that all human beings seek: that he had the courage to face and deal with whatever test life brought.

A brush with the
terrible might of the sea
brings a new awareness
of all that's precious in life

"But
We're ALIVE!"

BY DORIS AGEE

As a child growing up by the edge of the sea, I used to wonder about the people who, on a mild summer's day, somehow managed to drown. I'd wonder how anyone could be frightened enough of the water to panic and sink instead of simply floating until help came. (This was a basic lesson I had learned early.) I'd wonder, too, why people—good and poor swimmers alike—would wander into heavy surf and allow themselves to be pounded into the sand or carried out to sea. Drowning seemed a ridiculous and unnecessary way to die.

On Tuesday, September 20, 1966, I learned that there is no special trick to drowning. Anyone can do it. Even a strong swimmer like myself, with years of ocean experience, can do it. On that afternoon, at 4:34, I came within a breath of it. Rust has fixed the hands of my watch at that time. My watch cannot be repaired, and I wouldn't want it to be. I want to remember that day.

There were three of us. Don Horan and Jess Paley were from a television-production firm in New York and had flown out to California that morning to scout locations for a film they were planning. Through a mutual friend, I had offered to show them some beaches near my home in San Mateo. Although we had only just met, we soon drifted into an easy, relaxed relationship. Our spirits were high

when, a little after four o'clock, we found the beach that seemed perfect for the film.

Sunlight blazed on the rolling surf. There were no swimmers, and only a few people sat along the wide expanse of pink-gold sand. Gulls swooped and settled along the ocean's edge. Just offshore stood an impressive mass of black rocks, and occasionally a wave would hit the base of these and send up a tower of foam. If I'd been thinking, and not simply enjoying the scene, I would have recognized the unmistakable signs of high tide. I missed them all.

We parked near the base of a large, flat-topped cliff whose appearance intrigued us: Its chocolate-brown sides soared straight up from the shore, and its wide, flat face was squared off to the sea. We decided to walk along the front of it and see what lay beyond.

Laughing at how ridiculous we looked on the beach in our street clothes, we moved in single file across the wet sand. Some thirty feet separated the base of the cliff from the edge of the sea; enough, we thought—or did we think?—for walking. Jess stopped suddenly ahead of us to remove his shoes, and I noticed with a rushing sense of danger that the rocks were wet to a point well above his head. I was just about to mention it when time ran out.

We all saw the big wave foaming toward us at the same time. There was no place to run, so we drew back against the rock. Instinctively, to cut resistance, I turned my body sideways.

The wave caught me with unbelievable force as it went under me, rode straight up the rock and fell back on itself. Suddenly I was being turned and twisted and thrown down again and again. Within moments I was far out in deep water. Other waves added to the rolling, boiling turmoil. I felt the stinging salt of the water as it entered my nose and throat. Something heavy—kelp?—wrapped around my legs and feet, pulling me down. I tried to kick away the dragging weight, but it stayed with me, tormenting me.

Occasionally my head would break through to the surface and, for a brief moment, I could breathe. Once I came up facing the cliff, and saw that it was a long way off. In the ever-changing turbulence I couldn't swim; the best I could manage was an attempt to tread water, to conserve my strength and keep my head above the waves. I concentrated on relaxing, hoping that new waves would push me toward shore.

Then I looked up and saw a huge wave rising, and felt the outward dragging and lowering of the water that always precedes such waves. In the next instant I was being shoved ahead of the wave as it sped toward shore. Surely I would be dashed to pieces against the cliff!

Mercifully, the wave took me to a point just short of the beach. Don was standing in the surf close by. His hand reached toward me. I wanted to shout, "Don't! You'll be pulled out, too!" But there was no need, for I felt myself moving, with incredible swiftness, back into deep water. The wave that had carried me almost to safety was now removing me from it with its backwash. I lost sight of Don.

Again there was the helpless turning and twisting, the gasping for air, the weight at my legs. Once more I was delivered nearly to the beach, and snatched away. It came to me, with shocking clarity, that I was hopelessly trapped. I couldn't get out of the breakers—either onto the beach or into the relative calm beyond the surf. I was going to die.

I saw my handbag floating over a wave and thought, "If I could only catch it when it comes this way." Then I realized that I had no further need of it. I thought of my husband, Bill, and of how much I loved him. When had I last told him so? Who would meet his six-o'clock train? When would he know what had become of me?

All thought was halted by an enormous wave that broke directly over my head. I recall little else. Once I heard someone shout, "Hold on! I've got you!" But it sounded faraway and strange, and I felt no hand on mine. (The wave had brought me directly to Don, he told me afterward. He clutched my hand, but it was completely lifeless and slipped from his as the surf tore me back into deep water. He thought I was dead.)

Suddenly, incredibly, I found myself face down on the beach, half in and half out of the water. Someone called, "Run! There's time!" Don crawled to me, grabbed my hand and fell to the sand at my side. I tried to get up, but couldn't even raise my head. I heard waves crashing behind me, and knew that within moments I would be swept into the sea for the final time. All my will, all my hope, went into the effort to rise from the sand. But I could not move.

Then Jess was there, a shadowy figure over us. Somehow he got Don to his feet and the two of them managed to pull me up. Stumbling, falling, crawling, we fought to get beyond the rocks. It was a nightmare in slow motion, an eternity before we fell in a sodden heap onto the safe, dry sand. We stayed that way for a long time, holding silently to one another, unwilling and unable to let go.

Suddenly we were all talking at once, with breath we couldn't spare, saying foolish, obvious things. We counted our losses—my handbag, Don's wallet. It was too soon to state the truth: We'd been careless, had suffered for it, and only a miracle had put the three of us back on the beach. Yes, we counted what we'd lost—and each account invariably ended with, "But we're *alive!*"

People, many of them now, were standing over us. We were told that we had been carried far out. One man said, "Only a fool would go in front of that cliff at high tide." High tide! I, raised at the edge of the ocean, had not even noticed. Another man said, "I live over in that cottage. I've seen a lot of people caught where you were. Most of 'em don't make it back, even after they're dead."

Finally we were able to stand, and compare experiences. Don had been thrown against the rock by the first wave, hitting his head. He had been carried into the breakers twice. Jess, luckily, had been pulled in only once, and so it was his greater strength that eventually had drawn us to safety. My sturdy wool suit testified to the might of the ocean and the action of the sand: It was riddled with holes, the hem torn and hanging nearly to my ankles.

For several days afterward, I slept very little. My body was bruised and aching, my mind restless. I thought, again and again, of how it had begun: the foolish way we walked in there, leaving ourselves no avenue of escape. I thought of the many times in my life when, with no fear of the ocean's power, I had put myself in equal jeopardy and not been caught. Those days are over. In the future I will swim—and live—with new respect for the forces of nature.

Since that Tuesday, many wonderful things have come to me. I have seen, with my eyes and my spirit, sunsets such as I've never seen before. I have heard a Chopin étude played by a fifteen-year-old genius. I have burned my tongue with steaming black coffee. I have heard people talking and laughing. I have watched the long grasses bend in the wind, a hummingbird hover, a tear on a baby's cheek. I have looked into my husband's eyes and told him of my love for him, and his eyes have returned that love.

And always I realize that in one careless moment I nearly gave up all these things. Because I came so close to losing them, I can never again take them for granted.

Seventy people owe their lives
to the heroic labors of one lone fisherman
who was almost forgotten
in the days that followed their rescue

John Napoli,
Rescuer Extraordinary

BY J. CAMPBELL BRUCE

ONE DAY IN THE FALL of 1950, John Napoli, a fisherman in San Francisco, made a deal to sell his crab traps. He had paid $3,200 for them; he let them go for $1,000. His reason: "I gotta eat."

When word of the transaction got out, the people of San Francisco were furious. For John Napoli was a hero. What he had done was incredible: single-handed, he saved seventy lives and in so doing, made himself a cripple.

The USS *Benevolence,* a Navy hospital ship, was returning from a trial run in a blinding fog in August 1950, when, two miles off the Golden Gate, she collided with an outbound freighter, the *Mary Luckenbach.* Because it was a trial run, the *Benevolence* was carrying two full crews—Navy and civilian—making a total of 526 persons aboard. The *Benevolence* sank within half an hour.

At two o'clock on the same morning, John Napoli had eased his thirty-four-foot *Flora* out of her mooring at Fisherman's Wharf. He still had seven weeks to go for salmon, then a month of the rich albacore run. After that, if he had the highest catch again in the crab season, he could pay off the $400 he still owed on a recent overhaul job on the *Flora,* and maybe he could even whittle down the mortgage on his new home.

At the fishing grounds thirty miles out the fog hung on all day. Napoli worked hard hauling in the salmon, some of them sixty

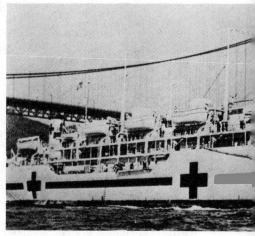

pounds of fighting fish. By late afternoon he had caught some 550 pounds, and he headed home.

About two miles off the Gate he saw what he thought was a turtle. And then, a minute or so later:

"All of a sudden I saw a big black spot. Was I scared! I thought I was on the wrong side of the channel."

It was the towering steel wall of the *Mary Luckenbach*. Abruptly, a Coast Guard boat slid out of the mist and a megaphoned voice boomed: "We need your assistance."

He thought they said something about a body overboard. He remembered the turtle and shouted, "Follow me." He went directly to the spot and hauled his first survivor aboard the *Flora*.

"I noticed he was wearing a Navy suit. I thought there must be a shipwreck. But I can't get nothing out of that man. His mouth was all cut and bleeding from chattering, he was so cold.

"What happened then was like a miracle, like God pressed a button and lifted the fog. You could see a three-block area with heads bobbing all around like seagulls sitting on the water. My hair stood up, my eyes got full of tears. And then the fog came down, like God said, 'Now you seen 'em, go to work.'"

It was slack water—the period between tides—and there were

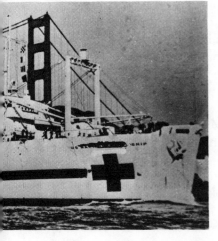

The Mary Luckenbach, *above, remained afloat and made it to safety after colliding with the* Benevolence, *shown at left as she appeared on an earlier run, with the Golden Gate Bridge in the background*

perhaps three hours before the swift ebb tide might sweep the victims to sea. Napoli set the *Flora* at a trolling crawl and began scouting for survivors. When he spotted a figure in a life jacket he would throw out a line, then put the *Flora* in neutral.

Now came the real job—incredibly difficult for one man. The survivors had been in the numbing water an hour and a half; they were sea-soaked, helpless. And the stretch from the *Flora's* rail to the water was better than three feet.

"I put my knees against the rail, then stooped down and grabbed them over the shoulders and under the arms. Wait for a wave, pull up, then grab them some more by the seat of the pants. Two hands ain't enough sometimes, so I used my teeth like a horse, bite his shirt or pants, then pull more, till his belly's over the rail. Soon as a body gets there, boy, he's safe. I grabbed a good hold on his leg and heaved. I have to make plenty of room so they don't hurt the other guys when they flop down. So I threw three of my four big boxes of fish overboard and pushed the other one back out of the way.

"Pretty soon I got a full boat. I figured these people needed first aid quick. They were all in shock from floating around in the cold water."

He came alongside the *Mary Luckenbach* and shouted for assistance.

Two men slid down the *Flora's* mast, and one of them shoved the last box of fish over the stern. "Don't worry," he assured Napoli, "*Luckenbach* will pay for it."

They transferred the eighteen survivors in wire-basket stretchers—a slow, dangerous business. The *Flora* bobbed and lurched and banged against the steel plates of the freighter. Her rail was chewed up and the turnbuckles securing her rigging were broken.

After that Napoli went trolling for more survivors. He was worried. This was taking too long; the ebb tide would catch up with them.

"All my life I never worked so hard. My arms ached like I got a charley horse. And all the time I kept saying in Italian, 'God give me strength to pull these people in.'"

A priest, Chaplain John J. Reardon of the *Benevolence*, was now on board the *Flora*. He understood and spoke up, "Don't you worry, signor. God will give you the strength."

The scene was like a painting of doom by an old master. The dark gray shapes of the rescue craft prowled in the gloomy mists. The shifting fog at times lifted to reveal the sinking *Benevolence*, the great red cross freshly painted on her white hull shimmering in the calm, glassy wash of the waves. The green combers were strewn with litter and upstretched arms. And over all dinned an unearthly tumult— the watery throb of the motors, the shouting of the crewmen, the piercing cries of those in the water.

"The noise was something terrible. When I get to thinking about it in my sleep, I'm done for the night. You hear five hundred people hollering and you never get it out of your system."

Napoli's muscles were beginning to ache with fatigue. His throat was parched, but he kept on.

Napoli grabbed one survivor under the arms, pulled up, then reached farther for a chest hold. "And I think, that's funny. He's all soft there. When I get him up I say to myself, 'Sonofagun, this is a woman!' She was barefoot and walked by herself up to the bow and sat down. She's purple like everybody so I give her my coat and say, 'You want my underwear, too?' She told me, 'No, thanks, I'm okay now.' And she smiled at me, she's that happy to be saved."

This was Ensign Helen Wallis, a Navy nurse. Napoli beamed as he recalled her pluckiness. "There's a brave one! She didn't complain one bit, not even a word. She told me, 'I'm gonna give these fellas respiration.' And all soakin' wet herself. She's got guts, that woman."

It was growing dark when he transferred his last batch of survivors. In all he had pulled fifty-four of them out of the water. As he finished unloading he heard with relief that "everything was under control," for the tide was beginning to ebb fast.

The *Flora*, battered and wobbly, had crawled about a city block when she plowed into a cluster of plasma boxes. Above the crunching noise came a solitary cry.

"I stopped and ran forward to get away from the *purp-purp* of the exhaust and I yelled, 'Holler again, fella, holler again!' "

He heard nothing more and started back to the pilothouse. And then he saw them, about twelve feet off midships.

"There they were on a big lazy swell, sixteen Navy men, all hugging each other in a ring. Another stroke of the propeller and I would have run by and maybe they'd have gone out to sea. I got them to the boat but I just didn't have the strength left to pull 'em up. I told them, 'Take it easy. I'll get you saved somehow.' "

He made them fast to the rail and carefully towed them until he found another rescue craft.

The complete tally next day showed that a total of 503 lives were saved; thirty boats in all had taken part in the rescue.

It was well past midnight when Napoli climbed the stairs to his home. His wife, Flora, after whom the boat was christened, took one look at him and almost fainted.

"I was so cold she gave me two hot baths but I didn't even feel it. Next day I had a time getting out of bed. I couldn't straighten out. Arms, legs, neck, everything was stiff. When I coughed I hurt all over, specially my chest and back. I tried to tie my shoes but I couldn't. When I stooped over it clicked here"—indicating the small of the back—"and I couldn't get up."

Despite his aches, Napoli went down to the Luckenbach Steamship Line to ask about that last box of fish pushed overboard. The claims agent suggested he see their attorneys.

"Why do I have to see attorneys?" Napoli demanded. "I ain't committed no crime."

The sinking of the *Benevolence* was of course a big story for the San

Francisco papers, but somehow Napoli's exploit received only a brief mention and was quickly forgotten.

As a reporter for the *Chronicle* I telephoned him on a slow, quiet Sunday afternoon about two months later, to ask how things were going.

"Oh, fine," he said. "Everything is coming along fine."

No particular story there. I was about to hang up when I remembered the fish. Had he been paid?

"The Navy says it is going to pay me, but things like that take time. But everything is fine. Tomorrow a man is buying my crab traps."

With crab season coming on? But why?

The answer was simple: "I gotta eat. My wife got a job, first time she's worked since we got married, but that don't catch up with the bills."

What about his fishing?

"I can't stand standing up, my back hurts. So I got to lie down. And you can't make a living lying down."

Of all the hundreds of pictures taken at the scene of the disaster, none had included Napoli. So we went down to the wharf one day to take a belated shot. And there my throat tightened up. Nailed to the mast of the *Flora* was a board and on it, newly written with care, was an announcement: FOR SALE. LO 4-3582. CALL AT 6:00 PM.

Napoli, a native San Franciscan and son of an immigrant Sicilian fisherman, had gone out with the boats for thirty-five years. After his heroic rescue work he had spent twenty-two days in the hospital— and lost twenty-seven pounds. "I feel kinda bad," he said. "But I figure there's no use fooling anybody, specially myself. If I go out there alone I want to be a perfect specimen. If I'm pulling in a wild one and my back locks up maybe I'd stay out there."

The *Flora* bore ugly scars of her encounter with the steel-plated ships. It would cost $1,000 just to put her in shape to sell.

After Napoli's story was told, dollars poured in to the *Chronicle*, unsolicited; readers quickly contributed over $1,100. Many of the letters to the editor asked why the people Napoli saved had not kicked in. Napoli explained that they tried to.

"They all came out to see me in bunches. The nurse, she looked sixty years old when I pulled her out of the water; when she came to the hospital, boy, she was a real doll. And she brought me a bouquet of roses. But what really got me was seeing those kids; they came to see me all together. I got so choked up I couldn't say hello, boys. They were very grateful and wanted to pay me. One even offered $1,000."

Napoli shrugged his shoulders. "You save somebody's life you don't take money for it."

In the days after Napoli became an outpatient at the hospital he was like a fish out of water: "Every day I go get my therapy. Bake the back, shoot electricity through the system, massage the back. If it's a nice day then I go down and bail out the *Flora;* she's leaking a lot now."

On other days Napoli sat alone and counted his blessings and awards: a glittering model of a sloop given to him at a banquet by Italian Americans in Oakland; a resolution by the San Francisco Board of Supervisors; a scroll in a gilt frame which read: "The United States Navy recognizes with gratitude the meritorious service . . . worthy of the highest tribute of all. . . ."

The Navy's gratitude took a more material form a short time later: the Secretary of the Navy approved a $4,422 check for Napoli's jettisoned catch and damage to the *Flora.*

And there's the sheaf of letters. John Napoli sifted them through his stubby fingers. "I didn't think so many people would . . ." His voice thickened a little. "I feel very kind to these people. I feel so happy about things."

The sudden volcanic eruption
forced the evacuation of the tiny island of Heimaey
and jeopardized a vital national industry.
But it failed to crush the islanders' spirit

How Iceland Fought
the Fiery Mountain

BY PAUL HENISSART

SHORTLY BEFORE TWO A.M. on January 23, 1973, a volcano
erupted on the small, windswept island of Heimaey six miles off the
southern coast of Iceland. A potential national disaster loomed: Iceland's economy is dependent upon its fishing industry, and Heimaey
was its largest fishing community. Its fish-meal and cod-liver-oil fac-
tories and its fish-freezing plants, the country's biggest and most
modern, stood only a mile from the center of the eruption.

Most of Heimaey's 5,237 inhabitants were asleep in their homes when the disaster struck. Roused by his wife, Armann Eyjólfsson, principal of the Navigation College and a teacher at the local Marine Engineering School, looked out his window and saw ash and stones raining down on his neighbors' roofs and giant blue flares of burning gas spurting in a crooked line along a ridge less than 600 yards away from his house. As Eyjólfsson stepped outdoors, a deep-throated, supernatural growl from the mountain's innermost recesses jarred the stillness of the night. Then he saw fire trucks racing in the direction of the flaming fissure, from which more than a dozen lava fountains boiled.

Rapidly, Eyjólfsson and his wife bundled up their four sleepy children against the bitter cold, grabbed a few bare essentials and drove off to a relative's house on the other side of the island. Within an hour most of the island's population would abandon their homes the same way. "Nobody can understand how fearful a full eruption is without experiencing it," a Norwegian journalist reported. "You are completely helpless and expect the earth to swallow you up."

Volcanic eruptions were no novelty for the local population. Aptly known as the "Land of Ice and Fire," Iceland boasts no less than 200 volcanoes, thirty recurrently active, some dormant under the glittering crust of immense glaciers. But the last eruption on Heimaey itself had occurred more than 5,000 years before.

The previous afternoon there had been a series of odd, seemingly unrelated phenomena on the island. What seemed like lightning flashes forked the sky unaccompanied by thunder. In several places, ground heat uncharacteristically melted the falling snow. On the main island, two seismographs recorded minor tremors—but their epicenter remained in doubt.

Then that night, along the slope of Eldfell (Fire Mountain), the earth opened, in one witness's words, "like a mile-long knife cut," hissing weirdly. Now volcanic ash began to fall, settling like a shroud over the town's broad streets and its gaily painted houses.

Word of the calamity reached Iceland's civil defense deputy director, Gudjon Pedersen, in Reykjavík, at 2:05 a.m. Promptly, he and his hastily assembled staff set to work activating a nationwide contingency disaster plan. But Pedersen noted one highly alarming fact: This was the first time in Iceland's history that a volcano had erupted in an inhabited area. Evacuation orders were flashed immediately via a coastal radio station to Heimaey's police chief, and Red Cross volunteers hurriedly began converting three elementary schools in Reykjavík into reception centers. Meanwhile, by rare good fortune, the island's entire fleet of seventy-seven diesel-powered fishing boats lay at anchor in the harbor. In a pinch, the larger trawlers could carry up to 400 passengers at a time across the icy forty-mile strait to the nearest port on the main island.

Local officials realized they had little time to act. The first reports indicated that the principal lava stream running down the mountainside and into the sea might soon block the mouth of the harbor. With temperatures as high as 1,800 ° F., the white-hot liquid rock advanced inexorably, turning cars into puddles of steel. Windborne lava bombs, some more than a yard in diameter, could set a house afire in seconds. The entire island—only 2.5 miles wide by 4.5 miles long—might even explode and go under.

By the end of the first four-hour boat runs from Heimaey, 3,000 people—more than half the population—had been evacuated. At Thorlákshöfn, the nearest mainland port, disembarking islanders were whisked into buses, driven quickly to the capital, given a hot meal and assigned cots in Red Cross centers. But the problem remained of transporting those who could not easily leave by sea—seventeen inmates at a home for the aged and thirty-seven patients at the Heimaey hospital. The island's airstrip, only 400 yards from the volcano, was still open, though for how long no one knew. Civil defense headquarters needed aircraft immediately to complete the evacuation.

Iceland had no air force, but U. S. Navy and Air Force pilots were stationed at the NATO defense base in Keflavík, twenty miles west of the capital. Lt. Col. Matthew Thome, U. S. Army, got a request for help at 2:30 a.m. Two twelve-passenger HH3E helicopters took off at once for Heimaey. Although the night was clear, pilots found that the strong turbulence and static electricity created by the volcano interfered with radio communications. Moreover, a muddy mixture of cinders and snow had transformed the short main runway into a mud slick. But, within two hours, all the disabled islanders had been removed to Reykjavík, and by midmorning on January 23—only seven hours after the initial eruption—most of Heimaey's population was safely off the island.

Once the first shock was over, many of the islanders were eager to go back to save whatever they could. But when, four days later, a few of them were authorized to land briefly, they discovered a black, unrecognizable landscape of desolation. Hills of volcanic ash as high as a two-storied house smothered entire streets. Returning to his cottage, Armann Eyjólfsson saw a chimney sticking out from a field of cinders—all that was visible of his former home.

The government was no less concerned about the damage to Iceland's economy. In 1972, Heimaey had produced over eleven percent of Iceland's total fish exports and the island had been counted on to contribute twenty million dollars in prized foreign exchange to the economy in 1973. The harbor's storage and processing facilities represented a staggering investment, impossible to replace during the winter fishing season. A new race against time now began. Within forty-eight hours of the eruption, freighters, steering perilously close to the offshore lava buildup, managed to reach the port. Ashore, a 1,000-man rescue force hurriedly disassembled and loaded costly filleting machines, cranes, even a new steel slipway. Working in twelve-hour shifts, teams then packed and stowed one and a half million dollars' worth of frozen fish products.

While the lava from Eldfell flowed on, U. S. Air Force and Icelandic planes began airlifting still-undamaged furniture and household goods to Reykjavík. The main torrent could not be checked, but Sveinn Eiríksson, an Icelander employed as the Keflavík base fire chief, set out to protect homes and buildings from a threat that could be averted—lava bombs. Some twenty homes were already burning when Eiríksson took charge of fire-fighting operations, assigning volunteer workers to scour the island for available sheet metal. Soon more supplies began arriving from other parts of Iceland, along with a special task force of a hundred carpenters. Within a week they had shoveled ashes off rooftops, capped chimneys, reinforced doors and nailed protective sheet-metal plates over some 8,000 windows. No more homes were lost to lava bombs.

Then Heimaey was confronted with a new threat. Three main vents had formed in the crater; now semiliquid basalt rock was flowing from them toward the town. An ominous new menace developed as the northwestern flank of the horseshoe-shaped volcano cone broke off and slid downhill. Advancing at a rate of 450 feet a day, the 150-

foot-high landslide threatened to flatten everything in its path.

Iceland geologists had observed that when the smoking lava mass crashed into the sea, the water's cooling effect and pressure deflected it from its normal course. At their request, thirty-eight powerful pumps provided by the United States were installed to shoot 13,000 gallons of seawater a second at the main lava flow. In addition, rescue workers hosed the lava front with water while bulldozers nudged makeshift ash dams into place at the town limits. Cooled by the water, the molten mass solidified and formed a wall that now rerouted the hot liquid lava behind it.

Three months after the first eruption, the lava flow from Eldfell had slowed markedly, and the situation seemed to be under control. But the upheaval had demolished 400 homes—one third of Heimaey's total—and property damage alone was in the millions of dollars. To raise an initial forty million dollars in emergency funds, Iceland's parliament adopted, virtually without debate, a bill providing for an immediate increase in taxes to share the burden equally among all citizens.

Several weeks later, the lava flow had slowed down, but the airstrip was still in danger. Apart from an occasional rumble from the volcano and the roar of the high-pressure water pumps arrayed near the harbor, a deadly silence enfolded the island. The air was polluted by a cloying stench and everywhere the once gaily painted homes lay derelict in a black sea of ash. Some scientists gloomily doubted that the island would ever be habitable again.

But they were wrong. A year later, like some latter-day Phoenix, Heimaey literally arose from the ashes. The eruptions of lava finally ceased in mid-June and within a few days energetic crews were on hand to begin a giant reconstruction plan spearheaded by a special Heimaey relief committee set up by the government. Bulldozers and shovels went to work on the mountains of residue and construction gradually began to blot out the moonscape. By mid-July, a handful of families had reclaimed their homes and Heimaey's Mayor Magnus Magnusson moved his municipal government back to the island.

On weekends the thrice-daily plane service from the main island to Heimaey was crowded with former inhabitants coming to observe the reconstruction in progress, to work on refurbishing their own homes, to savor the clean, crisp air. Eyjólfsson was back on the island teaching the winter term and public utilities were getting back to normal. The harbor was being cleaned out of its accumulation of pumice and the fish processing plants were in part reinstalled.

With stable living conditions and their old livelihood assured, the Heimaeyers were beginning to reclaim their land. "By next summer," said Helgi Bergs, who headed the disaster relief committee, "life should be humming along at a good pace. Heimaey can—and will—flourish again."

When the hunters
become the hunted,
few survive to tell the tale.
Here is one who did

Attacked
by a Killer Shark!

BY RODNEY FOX

KAY LOOKED QUITE MISERABLE standing there as I said good-bye at 6:30 that Sunday morning in December 1963. She was expecting our first child, and the doctor had told her firmly: Don't go.

I wish now that the doctor's advice had applied to me as well. Two hours later, however, found me standing on the cliff at Aldinga Beach—thirty-four miles south of our home in Adelaide, South Australia. This was why I had set out so early. Now I had time to study carefully the dark patterns of bottom growth on the coral reef that shelves to seaward under the incoming blue-green swells.

Aldinga reef is a watery paradise, a teeming sea jungle and happy hunting ground for underwater spearfishermen like myself. Forty of us—each in a black rubber suit and flippers, glass-windowed face mask, snorkel, lead-weighted belt and spearfishing gun—were wait-

ing for the referee's nine-o'clock whistle to announce that the annual South Australian Skin-Diving and Spearfishing Championship competition had begun. Each of us would have five hours to bring in to the judges the biggest bag, reckoned both by total weight and by number of different species of fish.

My own chances looked good. I had taken the 1961–62 championship and had been runner-up the next season. I had promised Kay that this would be my last competition. I meant to clinch the title and then retire in glory, diving thenceforth only for fun, whenever Kay and I might want to. I was twenty-three and, after months of training, at the peak of form. We were "free divers," you understand, with no artificial breathing aids. I had trained myself to dive safely to a depth of a hundred feet and to hold my breath for more than a minute without discomfort. At the nine-o'clock whistle blast we waded into the surf.

Each man towed behind him, by a light line tied to his lead-weight belt, a buoyant, hollow float. We would load our fish into these floats immediately on spearing them. This would minimize the amount of fresh blood released in the water. Blood just might attract the big hunting fish from out beyond the reef—the always hungry and curious great predatory sharks that prowl the deeper waters off the South Australian coast. Lesser sharks—like the bronze whaler and gray nurse—are familiar to skin divers and have not proved aggressive. Fortunately, the dread white hunter, or "white death" sharks, caught by professional fishermen in the open ocean, are rarely seen by skin divers. But as a precaution two high-powered patrol boats crisscrossed our hunting area keeping a wary lookout.

The weather was bright and hot. An offshore breeze flattened the green wavetops, but it roiled the water on the reef. Visibility under the surface would be poor. This makes it difficult for spearfishermen. In murky water a diver often gets too close to a fish before he realizes it's there, scaring it away before he can get set for a shot.

By 12:30, when I towed to shore a heavy catch of parrot fish, snapper, snook, boarfish and magpie perch, I could see from the other piles that I must be well up in the competition. I had sixty pounds of fish on shore, comprising fourteen species. It was now 12:35, and the contest closed at 2:00. As fish naturally grew scarcer in the inshore areas I had ranged out to three quarters of a mile off shore for bigger and better game. On my last swim in from the drop-off section of the reef—where it plunges from a depth of twenty-five feet to sixty feet—I had spotted quite a few large fish near a big triangular rock that I felt sure that I could find again.

Two of the fish were dusky morwongs—or "strongfish," as we Australian skin divers usually call them. Either of these would be large enough to tip the scales in my favor; then one more fish of another variety would sew things up for me, I decided. I swam out to the spot I'd picked, then rested face down, breathing through my snorkel as I studied through my face glass the best approach to the two fish sheltering behind the rock. After several deep breaths I held one, swallowed to lock it in, upended and dived.

Swimming down and forward, so as not to spook the fish, I

rounded the large rock and thrilled to see my quarry. Not thirty feet away the larger dusky morwong, a beauty of at least twenty pounds, was browsing in a clump of brown weed.

I glided forward, hoping for a close-in shot. I stretched both hands out in front of me, my left for balance, my right holding the gun, which was loaded with the stainless-steel shaft and barb. I drifted easily over the short weeds and should have lined up for a perfect head-and-gill shot, but . . .

How can I describe the sudden silence? It was a perceptible *hush,* even in that quiet world, a motionlessness that was somehow communicable deep below the surface of the sea. Then something huge hit me with tremendous force on my left side and heaved me through the water. I was dumbfounded.

Now the "thing" was pushing me through the water with wild speed. I felt a bewildering sensation of nausea. The pressure on my back and chest was immense. A queer "cushiony" feeling ran down my right side—as if my insides on my left were being squeezed over to my right side. I had lost my face mask and I could not see in the blur. My spear gun was knocked violently out of my hand.

The pressure on my body seemed actually to be choking me. I did not understand what was happening. I tried to shake myself loose but found that my body was clamped as if in a vise. With awful revulsion my mind came into focus, and I realized my predicament: *A shark had me in his jaws.*

I could not see the creature, but it had to be a huge one. Its teeth had closed around my chest and back, with my left shoulder forced into its throat. I was being thrust face down ahead of it as we raced through the water.

Although dazed with the horror, I still felt no pain. In fact, there was no sharp feeling at all except for the crushing pressure on my back and chest. I stretched my arms out behind and groped for the monster's head, hoping to gouge its eyes.

Suddenly, miraculously, the pressure was gone from my chest. The creature had relaxed its jaws. I thrust backward to push myself away—but my right arm went straight into the shark's mouth.

Now I felt pain such as I had never imagined. Blinding bursts of agony made every part of my body scream in torment. As I wrenched my arm loose from the shark's jagged teeth, all-encompassing waves of pain swept through me. But I had succeeded in freeing myself.

I thrashed and kicked my way to the surface, thudding repeatedly into the shark's body. Finally my head pushed above water and I gulped great gasps of air.

I knew the shark would come up for me. A fin brushed my flippers and then my knees suddenly touched its rough side. I grabbed with both arms, wrapping my legs and arms around the monster, hoping wildly that this maneuver would keep me out of its jaws. Somehow I gulped a great breath.

We went down deep again—I scraped the rocks on the bottom. Now I was shaken violently from side to side. I pushed away with all my remaining strength. I had to get back to the surface.

Once again I could breathe. But all around, the water was crimson with blood—my blood. The shark breached the surface a few feet away and turned over on its side. Its hideous body was like a great rolling tree trunk but rust-colored, with huge pectoral fins. The great conical head belonged unmistakably to a white hunter. Here was the white death itself!

It began moving toward me. Indescribable terror surged through my body. One tiny fragment of the ultimate horror was the fact that this fearful monster, this scavenger of the sea, was my master. I was alone in its domain; here the shark made the rules. To the shark I was no longer an Adelaide insurance salesman. I was simply a squirming something-to-eat, to be forgotten even before it was digested.

I knew the shark was attacking again and that I would die in agony when it struck. I could only wait. I breathed a hurried little prayer for Kay and the baby.

Then, unbelievingly, I saw the creature veer away just before it reached me, the slanted dorsal fin curving off just above the surface. And suddenly my fish float began moving rapidly across the water.

The slack line tightened at my belt, and I was being pulled forward and under the water again. At the last instant the shark had snatched the float instead of me and had fouled itself somehow in the line. I tried to release my weight-belt to which the line was attached, but my arms would not obey. We were moving very fast now and had traveled underwater thirty or forty feet, my left hand still fumbling helplessly at the release catch. *Surely I'm not going to drown now* rushed through my mind. Then the final miracle occurred: The line parted suddenly and I was free once more. They tell me that all I could scream when my head reached the surface was: "Shark! . . . Shark!" It was enough.

Now there were voices, familiar noises, then the boat full of friends that I'd been praying would come. I gave up trying to move and relied on them to help me. In this new world of people, somebody kept saying, "Hang on, mate, it's over. Hang on." Over and over. I think without that voice out there I would have died.

The men in the patrol boat were horrified at the extent of my injuries. My right hand and arm were so badly slashed that the bones lay bare in several places. My chest, back, left shoulder and side were deeply gashed. Great pieces of flesh had been torn aside, exposing the rib cage, lungs and upper stomach.

Police manning the highway intersections for thirty-four miles got our ambulance through in record time. The surgeons at Royal Adelaide Hospital were scrubbed and ready, the operating table felt warm and cozy, the huge silver light overhead grew dimmer . . . until late that night or early next morning I opened my eyes and saw Kay alongside my bed.

I said, "It hurts," and she was crying. The doctor walked over and said, "He'll make it now."

After a year and a half of recuperation, my lungs worked well, although my chest was still stiff. My right hand wasn't a pretty sight, but I could use it. My chest, back, abdomen and shoulder were badly scarred.

God knows I didn't want to, but Kay realized right from the start that I had to go skin diving again. A man's only half a man if fear ties him up. Five months after I had recovered, I returned to the sea to leave my fears where I had found them.

But my skin diving is different nowadays. I've got my confidence back, but with it came prudence. You can't count on getting through a second round with a shark; anyhow, there are plenty of risks you have to take in this world without going out of your way to add needless ones.

So now I stay away from competition, and leave the murky water to the daredevils who've never felt a shark's jaws around their chest.

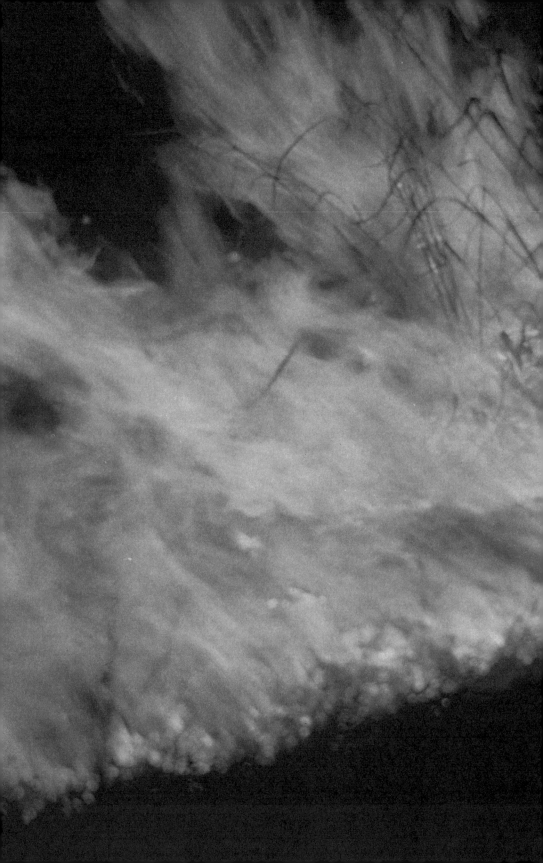

VI

I believe
that man will
not merely endure;
he will prevail

William Faulkner

The courage of two men
was all that stood between a sleeping town
and total disaster

Nightmare
in Laurel

BY JAMES H. WINCHESTER

TRAIN No. 154 was a potential bomb as it rolled north through the piny woods of southeastern Mississippi in the predawn darkness on Saturday, January 25, 1969. Midway in the mile-and-a-quarter-long freight were twenty-six special tank cars, each filled with 33,000 gallons of explosive, highly flammable propane gas. Ahead of them was a red and white tank car with an even more lethal cargo—hydrogen cyanide, a gas used for exterminating rats and insects in ships, so poisonous that it can bring rapid death to any person exposed to it for a few minutes.

Shortly after four a.m., the Southern Railway System train had passed downtown Laurel (population 23,500) and was rumbling at thirty miles an hour through a closely packed sector of homes, small businesses and light industry. Suddenly, without warning, the emergency air brakes slammed into place and the three huge locomotives pulling the 139 cars ground to a halt. Then a burst of white light from somewhere near the middle of the train turned night into day. In the head engine the fireman radioed the railroad's dispatcher in Hattiesburg, twenty-five miles away: "We're on fire, and it looks like Laurel's on fire, too!"

Laurel's greatest disaster had begun. So had the trial by fire of two veteran Southern Railway employees, forty-nine-year-old William Joel Chandler and forty-three-year-old Frank M. Wells.

The trouble had started when a wheel on one propane tank car broke as it passed over a crossing. When that car derailed, it pulled fourteen other propane-loaded cars off the track with it. The train had broken into three parts—the front and rear sections were *on* the rails, the center section was *off*—and the air hose connection to the brakes, running the length of the train, was severed. As the air in this line escaped, the iron shoes of the emergency braking system automatically descended on the wheels and brought the train to a screeching halt.

As they flipped over, some of the derailed cars had been torn open. The compressed gas inside was released, and as it mixed with the outside air, its explosive quality was increased 13,000-fold. Heavier than air, it crawled along the ground like flowing lava. Fiery sparks from the wreckage ignited it at once—and roaring white flames shot 500 feet into the sky.

From Hattiesburg, the railroad dispatcher radioed a curt safety order to No. 154's engine crew: "Cut away!" A brakeman clambered down and unhooked the three linked-together engines from the rest of the train. Quickly, they pulled ahead.

Now the crew had second thoughts: Perhaps some of the freight cars could also be saved. None of the cars still on the rails, however, could be moved until their emergency brakes were released. To do this, the valves in the train's air line would have to be closed off at the points where the line was severed from the derailed cars; then the engines would have to be hooked up again and air from them pumped back through the system until enough new pressure was built up to release the brakes. Someone had to go back to the broken lines and close the valves by hand.

Engine foreman Bill Chandler had been riding aboard the train as an observer of the crew's work. Now he left the separated engines, telling the engineer to stay with them.

The heat from the towering fire, already spreading to the houses and buildings on both sides of the track, was searing. Chandler, wrapped in an old army overcoat, lifted the heavy collar around his neck and face for protection. With a small walkie-talkie in his hand, he began to walk toward the flames.

"All I could think about was the hydrogen-cyanide gas," he recalls. "I knew that if it was afire or leaking, a lot of people were

going to die. If it was still on the rails undamaged, I had to get it out of the city."

Just then one of the blazing propane tanks in the middle of the fast-spreading fire exploded with an ear-splitting roar, almost knocking Chandler to his knees. This blast, five minutes after the derailment, shattered thousands of windows and awakened people for miles around; the huge fireball that followed and mushroomed high into the sky was seen from a hundred miles away. The one-hundred-ton tank car itself was hurled through the air like a blazing comet, dripping flaming liquid in its wake. Before it crashed into a street a quarter of a mile away, scores of homes were engulfed in fire.

As Chandler passed the first of the stalled freight cars, a second shattering explosion erupted a short distance ahead of him. Blazing cinders and debris rained for blocks. The thunderous roar of the flames was deafening. "I'm not ashamed to admit that I was horribly frightened," says Chandler. "I prayed out loud."

Then he saw that the red and white hydrogen-cyanide tank car was still intact on the rails ahead. *Thank God!* he thought. *I can get it out of here.*

"Couple up!" he radioed the engineer.

Chandler knew that it would take time for the engines to back up, link and build up pressure in the brake lines. So, compounding his personal danger, he decided to continue down the tracks and try to cut the brake-locked cars loose as close to the fire as possible, thereby saving the maximum number.

Now, directly ahead of Chandler, came a third explosion. A blazing tank car shot out of the flames. Hitting the rear of one house, it bounced across the street, tore down power lines and finally came to rest in a backyard. Within minutes a complete block of houses had been ignited. By this time, Laurel's entire fire-fighting force, with its equipment, was on the scene, but the men could get no closer than within two or three blocks of the core of the flames.

For Chandler, the heat from the fire was hardly bearable; already his exposed neck, face and hands were badly scorched. He pulled his overcoat over his head. For a few frightening moments the odor of the singed wool made him think he was inhaling gas escaping from the train.

Finally, he reached the far end of the sixty-one forward freight cars still on the tracks. Chandler turned his back on the incinerating heat and closed the air valve at the end of the car. As he did so, another great blast—the most powerful yet—erupted from inside the sheet of flames, knocking him to his knees. Two of the propane tank cars had exploded at once.

Half-stunned, Chandler still held on to his walkie-talkie. "I'm okay," he reassured the engineer. "I'm shutting off the line." Ordinarily it takes five minutes for the air to build up in a brake line. Chandler, his clothes smoking, called for the engineer to start pulling after only three. The wheels were still partially locked, but the cars moved. Thirty minutes had elapsed since the derailment.

South of the blaze and blasts, on the other side of the derailment, sixty-three cars, including eleven still-intact propane tanks, were also stalled on the rails. At the first blast, conductor Tom Scruggs and second brakeman P. E. Kidd, who had both been riding in Train 154's caboose, had headed for a small diesel-powered switch engine parked on a nearby siding. Though neither of them knew how to operate a diesel locomotive, they hoped to get the shuttle engine onto the main-line tracks, hook it up to the caboose, and pull the cars out of danger.

They were having trouble getting the engine started and had blown its electrical fuses when Chandler, walking away from his end of the flames, heard Scruggs appealing over his radio to the dispatcher for advice and help. "Get someone to pick me up," Chandler broke in on his own radio. "I'm on the tracks about a quarter of a mile north of the fire."

A Southern Railway agent, skirting around the fire on side streets in his car, found Chandler and drove him to the downtown depot. There Chandler came upon Frank "Sonny" Wells, a switchman in the Laurel railyards for twenty-five years. Off duty, the slightly built Wells had been awakened by the initial explosion, had bundled his family into his car, and had driven to the depot. "Can I help?" he asked.

Wells's wife drove the two men to the halted switch engine. Quickly, Chandler replaced the blown-out fuses from the emergency supply, then began moving the machine up the tracks toward the fire. Daylight was beginning to show as the tiny switch engine eased against No. 154's caboose. Kidd made the connection while Wells started toward the fire to close off the air line on the rear section of the train so that the emergency brakes could be released.

The smoke from burning gas was suffocating. Live electric lines, torn down by the blasts, littered the area like deadly snakes. In adjacent side streets, fuel tanks in burning automobiles exploded like strings of firecrackers. The last propane car on the rails was less than a dozen feet from the sheets of flame, and heat radiated from its badly scorched metal sides. It could explode at any second.

Unable, because of flames, to approach the end of the propane car nearest the fire, Wells disconnected the pin linking it to the rest of the train and closed off the air line. He was wearing heavy leather work gloves, but even so the metal burned his hands. "Let's get out of here!" he radioed to Chandler.

In the switch engine, Chandler released the emergency brakes and opened wide the throttles. The engine's wheels spun in a shower of sparks on the rails, but nothing moved.

"I can't move," Chandler called back to Wells. "You'd better get out of there."

"I'll cut farther back," came the response. Running back along the uneven roadbed for about half the length of the cars, Wells made a second cut. The engine finally began to move, and the cars were shifted to a siding two miles south. A second trip with the pony engine to rescue the remaining thirty-four cars followed. Only one propane car was now left on the rails, the one nearest the flames. Chandler said, "Let's try and get that one, too."

They moved the engine back into the inferno. Just one car length away from the last standing car, the derailed tanks spewed burning gas like flamethrowers. "I'll never know why that car didn't explode," says Chandler. The valve at the end of the car's air pipe was burned off and couldn't be closed to release the emergency brakes. Chandler and Wells pulled anyway. It was a little like hauling a one-hundred-ton sled, but the small engine did the job.

By midmorning, the fifteen derailed propane tank cars were still ablaze, as were blocks of houses and other buildings. Three persons had died, scores had been hospitalized and nearly a hundred homes and businesses had been destroyed or damaged. With property damage exceeding $7.5 million, Laurel was declared a disaster area. The greatest danger, though, was over: The eleven tank cars still filled with propane had been removed and, most important, the one containing hydrogen-cyanide gas was safe on a siding five miles away.

For their courage and exceptional presence of mind, Chandler and Wells both earned the 1970 Carnegie Hero Medal, the nation's foremost civilian award for bravery. Sums up Fern Bucklew, who was the mayor of Laurel at the time: "They saved the town."

Wells went back to switching cars in the Laurel railyard. Chandler, who maintains that "anyone would have done the same," resumed his job of riding freights across the South to check on engine crews.

"They said I was a hero," Chandler commented. "My wife said I was a damn fool."

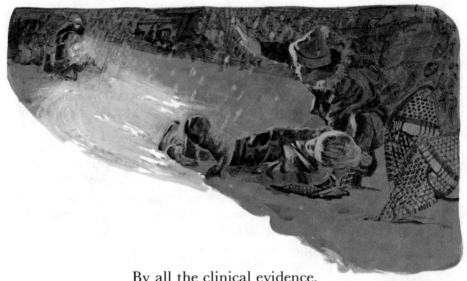

By all the clinical evidence,
Ted Milligan was Dead on Arrival—but,
for some reason,
the doctors refused to give up

The Boy Who
Came Back to Life

BY SIDNEY KATZ

SATURDAY, JANUARY 31, 1976, dawned clear, windless and sunny—seemingly just another day for the boys of St. John's Cathedral Boys' School near Selkirk, Manitoba. The temperature was a comfortable few degrees above freezing as sixteen-year-old Edward "Ted" Milligan checked his snowshoe fittings and headed down the frozen, snow-blanketed Red River at 1:45 p.m. His companions on the trek were teacher Bruce Handford and three fellow students. The plan: to cover a twenty-five-mile circular route as briskly as possible in training for the school's annual snowshoe race. They expected to be back in the dining room by seven-thirty.

THE BOY WHO CAME BACK TO LIFE

Until about four p.m., it was an uneventful trip. Exhilarated by the gleaming prairie landscape, Ted and his friends had covered about nine miles. But, by four-thirty, Ted began to feel cold. A sharp wind had come up and the temperature had plummeted seven degrees. Nevertheless, he forged briskly ahead. By five-thirty, he was feeling drowsy—and no longer cold. Then, six miles from home, Ted blacked out. "I was in serious trouble without even realizing it," he recalls. "My memory was a complete blank."

Bruce Handford had no way of knowing what was happening to Ted. He was aware that Ted had occasionally tripped and fallen, which was not unusual on a long trek. But, over the next two miles, it became obvious that something was wrong. Ted was stumbling every twenty yards or so and constantly asking, "Why am I falling?" Chilled by the icy gale now raging, two of the students ran ahead for home while Handford and seventeen-year-old Pat Williams remained behind to bring Ted back.

Handford now realized that Ted's endurance was almost at an end. The boy was drowsy, and finally, with two and a half miles to go, he collapsed. All efforts to arouse him failed.

What Handford didn't know was that Ted was suffering from a dangerous, deceptive condition known as hypothermia, a lowering of the body temperature to the point where the body begins to lose heat faster than it is produced. Unaware of this heat loss, the hypothermia victim becomes oblivious to his surroundings, loses coordination and suffers from slurred speech and thought disturbance.

Handford and Williams took turns carrying Ted's 138 pounds of deadweight before admitting defeat after a mile. Finally, Handford sent Williams back to the school to bring help while he stayed in the raging snowstorm sheltering the unconscious boy in his arms. "I wasn't worried," he recalls. "He was breathing deeply and regularly, as if enjoying the sound sleep of an exhausted man."

Twenty minutes later, the lights of a snowmobile pierced the gloom. At 9:45, the motionless body of Ted Milligan was placed on a cot in the infirmary. The headmaster's wife, Nancy Wiens, a nurse, was shocked by his appearance. "I knew we were in serious trouble," she says. "His skin was grayish green. He wasn't breathing and his eyes didn't respond to light. I thought I detected a faint pulse, but I couldn't be sure."

While an ambulance was called from Selkirk, Nancy cut away Ted's frozen outer clothing. The layers underneath were wet with sweat. She began mouth-to-mouth resuscitation while one staff member lay beside Ted to warm him and several hot-water bottles were placed on his body. After thirty minutes of strenuous effort, he showed no signs of life. "I was worried sick," recalls Mrs. Wiens. "Was he dead or alive?" Later, her anxiety increased. *If he were to survive,* she wondered, *would he be a retarded, crippled vegetable?*

The fear was a real one. If the heart stops beating, oxygen-bearing blood ceases to reach the brain and the cells begin to die. Three or four minutes of oxygen deprivation are enough to cause massive brain damage.

Doug Johnson, a driver for the Selkirk Ambulance Company, was cruising in his ambulance when the call came through. When he arrived at the school infirmary and saw Ted Milligan, his judgment, after a cursory examination, was that he was already beyond human help. Nonetheless, as Ted was being carried to the ambulance, Johnson walked beside the stretcher, alternately massaging his heart and administering mouth-to-mouth resuscitation. Inside the vehicle, Ted was given oxygen and Johnson radioed the emergency department of the Selkirk General Hospital that a "99"—a case of cardiac arrest—was on its way in.

Anne Ward, the nurse in charge of emergency, was waiting when the ambulance pulled in. She switched Ted onto the hospital oxygen supply, set up an intravenous feed line so that drugs could be administered and made sure that external massage was kept up. The only physician on duty, Andy Wozny, was delivering a baby, so Anne called the staff pediatrician, Robert Smith, who lived only a block away.

Ten minutes later Dr. Smith had completed examining the patient. A flat line on a monitor showed that the heart was lifeless and a reading on a rectal thermometer indicated that Ted's inner body temperature was 87° F., almost 12 degrees below normal. "Ted Milligan was Dead on Arrival," he recalls. "By all criteria known to medicine, we had a corpse on our hands."

The thirty-one-year-old doctor faced a crucial decision. As nearly as he could estimate, his patient's heart had stopped beating about forty-five minutes earlier. Should he still attempt to restore the boy's life? The answer flashed back. "My mind told me that he was dead. But my heart refused to accept the premature death of a healthy young man." Besides, he knew Ted had a slight chance for survival; when the inner body temperature dips far below normal, the rate of oxygen consumption slows down, and this in turn may impede the rate of brain damage.

The battle for Ted's life now began in earnest. A tube was put down his windpipe to force oxygen into his system while heart massage was continued. And Dr. Smith sent out an urgent call for anesthetist Gerald Bristow, a specialist in resuscitation. Arriving in the emergency room with street clothes over his pajamas, Dr. Bristow was mystified by his colleague's decision. "In my opinion, the patient was dead," Dr. Bristow remembers. "But I wasn't going to be the one to pull the plug. Like everyone else, I was caught up by Bob's dogged determination."

At first, the doctors concentrated on getting Ted's heart restarted. They injected stimulating drugs, including Adrenalin, into the right jugular vein, close to the heart. The line on the heart monitor remained motionless and flat. Clearly, traditional techniques were not going to work, so Bristow and Smith decided to provide as much heat to the body as they could and hope for the best.

Andy Wozny and another doctor had now joined the team. Anne Ward was joined by five other nurses. Even the ambulance crew had stayed on to help.

Ted was covered with hot, wet towels every three minutes while hot-water bottles were strategically placed on his body at points of maximum blood flow. The thermostat was pushed as high as it would go, raising the temperature in the crowded room to over 100° F. Dr. Bristow ordered a series of warm-water enemas and washed Ted's stomach with warm water through a nose tube. "I was grabbing for straws," he says. "After an hour and a half, Ted's body temperature had risen two or three degrees, but he was still totally unresponsive."

Usually, in cases of cardiac arrest, resuscitation efforts are abandoned after fifteen or twenty minutes. But, strangely, the weary, perspiring crew fought on. Dr. Bristow now decided on a last-ditch measure. He asked surgeon Ike Hussain to open Ted's chest and pour warm water directly onto his heart. As the instruments were being prepared, however, Bristow ordered everyone to stop. Acting on a hunch, he asked for Adrenalin again. The injection was given. All eyes turned to the heart monitor. Seconds later, the doctors were staring at each other in disbelief. The monitor revealed that Ted's heart was beating, though in a wild, uncontrolled fashion. Ted Milligan was alive!

In a concentrated effort to regulate the heart's erratic action, two circular metal paddles were placed, one on each side, and a 1,000-watt, low-current jolt shot through it. Almost immediately, Ted's heart began to beat in a normal rhythm. Finally, after almost two hours of backbreaking effort, Ted was breathing on his own. His blood pressure built up. His body temperature rose. "I watched his gray, cold skin turn warm and pink," Dr. Bristow remembers, "a lovely, lovely sight." Within twenty minutes, Ted's temperature was a normal 98.6°F.

The doctors could not yet relax their efforts. To improve Ted's circulation, they injected dopamine. When they detected fluid on his lungs, they administered a diuretic to help get it out. "We were delighted when Ted urinated a vast quantity," says Bristow. "It dispelled our fears that his kidneys might have been damaged."

At two that morning, the phone rang in John Milligan's home in Toronto. This was not unusual. He was an obstetrician and gynecologist. But he wasn't prepared for a call like this one.

Dr. Bristow gave Dr. Milligan a rundown on what had happened to his son. The father was well aware of the consequences of prolonged oxygen deprivation, and the fact that Ted was still unconscious was alarming. "Does the electroencephalogram show any brain damage?" Milligan asked. "I can't answer that question," Bristow replied. "Our hospital doesn't own a machine. But we'll find out soon because we're about to move Ted to Winnipeg for intensive care."

Like the boy's father, Smith and Bristow were haunted by the specter of brain damage. As far as they knew, no one had ever been "dead" as long as Ted—more than two hours—and survived intact. To expect that his brain had escaped the ravages of oxygen deprivation defied science and common sense.

At 11:30 a.m. on the longest Sunday of their lives, John and Lynn Milligan landed at the Winnipeg airport and rushed to their son's bedside in the Health Sciences Centre. Ted's life still hung in the balance. His heart was beating normally and he was breathing on his own, but he remained unconscious. The Milligans retired to a waiting room and began their vigil in two easy chairs near a telephone.

In the intensive-care unit, Dr. Joe Lee watched the motionless body on into the late afternoon. It happened in a fraction of a second, but the alert doctor noticed. Ted's face had twitched! Then, suddenly, the boy began to thrash about, muttering. Soon the words became intelligible. Evidently he was reliving his experience of the last few miles on the trail.

Now the boy's eyes were fluttering. A minute later they were wide open, and he was looking cautiously around the room. He stared at Lee, puzzled. "Where the heck am I?" he asked. "This looks like a hospital."

Lee pressed Ted's hand and replied, quietly, "It is a hospital, and you're okay." He motioned a nurse to the telephone.

Although worn out from sleeplessness and strain, John Milligan jumped up when the phone rang. "You can come in now," said the nurse.

Apprehensively the Milligans made their way to the intensive-care unit and found Ted sitting up, propped on pillows. He was amazed to see his father. "Dad! What are you doing here?" Then he caught sight of his mother. "Mom!" he cried. "What's going on anyway?" Dr. Milligan's worst fears vanished. "Those few words from Ted proved to me he was really back. It was like walking out of the clouds into the sunshine," he said later.

Ted Milligan's health improved rapidly during the next few days. As he listened to detailed accounts of what happened to him during his twenty-four-hour blackout, he shook his head in disbelief. "I remember heading for the trail. The sun was shining; I was feeling great. After that—nothing."

Within the next three weeks, the gap in his memory narrowed, to the point where he could recall certain details of the trip until about five-thirty p.m. But at no time was he even remotely aware that his life was threatened.

When he returned to school, after a three-week convalescence, his work was unaffected. "His academic record was excellent, as usual," says headmaster Frank Wiens. The only persistent physical symptom was some weakness in his hands, the result of frost damage to his flexor muscles. But after six months of physiotherapy, he regained complete control. The frostbite injuries on his hands and legs, as well as some burns caused by the hot-water bottles, have long since healed. Ted spent the next summer working in a youth camp in Algonquin Park in northern Ontario—reassuring proof that he was back in top physical condition.

With typical professional restraint, the doctors who doggedly coaxed Ted Milligan back to life describe the case as "highly unusual." Pediatrician Bob Smith is still puzzled by his decision to try to revive a boy who, by all clinical evidence, was dead. "I've often thought about it," he says, "but I don't have the answer. What I do know is that Ted is alive and well, and I feel humbled by the experience."

In an isolated Texas ravine,
the lives of three critically injured airmen
depended on the cool presence of one young rancher

Rescue
on the Pedernales

BY NILAH RODGERS

SITTING ON THE PORCH of his ranch home near Johnson City, Texas, Bobby Wilson removed his Stetson to mop his brow. It was a little after seven on the evening of June 28, 1976, and very hot. He spotted a dab of olive against the blue sky—a helicopter. It was skirting low along the Pedernales River Gorge, but the sound of it was obscured by the hum of the vacuum cleaner that his wife, Barbara, was using.

Bobby watched the aircraft as it dropped out of his view. Walking into the house, he thought, *Hope the pilot sees those telephone lines.* While fishing the day before, Bobby had noticed that the lines were almost invisible against the canyon walls and that the poles were totally hidden in live-oak trees.

Moments later, Bobby's mother, who lived only a hundred yards away, appeared at their door. Sensing her alarm, Barbara switched off the vacuum cleaner.

"Come quick!" her mother-in-law shouted. "Something awful's happened. I heard a terrible noise!"

As Bobby raced to his pickup truck with his wife, he feared the worst. He hit the accelerator and sped over the rocky trail until he reached the spot where the telephone lines crossed the river. Braking to a skidding stop, he leaped out and ran to the edge of the bluff.

The chopper had hit the lines. On a sandbar 200 feet below lay the wreckage. The waters of the Pedernales swept dangerously close to the helicopter. Later, Bobby surmised that everyone aboard surely would have been drowned or dashed to bits had the chopper not fallen just where it did.

The helicopter's jet engine had continued to run after the crash, and its high-pitched whine echoed deafeningly from below, assaulting the Wilsons' ears. They ran down the hillside. As Bobby neared the sandbar, he saw one man dragging himself toward the wreckage and two others motionless in the caved-in cockpit.

Pieces of metal and Plexiglas were strewn everywhere. The severed tail of the OH-58 Kiowa helicopter had been thrown a hundred yards. The doors had been ripped off, and the landing skids were twisted and partly buried in the sand. The pungent odor of jet fuel filled the air.

When he reached the crawling figure, Bobby saw that he wore an ID tag: Lt. Col. Charles F. Densford. "Got to cut off the fuel before this thing blows," Densford gasped, obviously in great pain, trying desperately to get to the cockpit. "Get them out!" he yelled, indicating the pilot and copilot, who were still strapped in their seats, either dead or unconscious.

Momentarily, Bobby froze, riveted by the thought of the chopper exploding. Then he remembered his wife. Whirling, he yelled, "Barbara, go back! Get help."

Bobby watched her start toward the pickup before he turned again to the injured men. (It was five miles of twisting, rocky roads to his nearest neighbor, twenty-seven miles to Johnson City, the closest town with a doctor and ambulance service.) *Good God!* Bobby thought. He was just a Texas hill country rancher—and suddenly he needed the knowledge and skills of a mobile hospital unit.

Desperately, he tried to remember what he knew about first-aid procedure. He could turn a breech calf before birth or doctor a lamb cut by shearers, but what was he supposd to do to help these downed airmen? The only rule he could remember was *Don't move an injured person.* But his common sense told him that these men had to be moved—and fast. He remembered one of his dad's sayings: *Son, believe in your own judgment.*

The copilot groaned as Bobby released his harness and eased him out of the cockpit. The name Bruce Palmer was stenciled above his shirt pocket, and he wore captain's insignia.

"Captain, how do you kill the engine?" Bobby shouted to make himself heard above the ear-splitting whine. He bent over, trying to catch the answer, but the copilot's face was ashen and his eyes stared without blinking. *Is he dead?* Bobby thought. *Did I kill him by moving him?*

Running back to pull the pilot out, Bobby found the stricken Densford still trying to find the chopper's fuel shut-off valve, beating on the instrument panel in his frustration. "Get out of here," Bobby ordered Densford. "Move, move before she blows!" He motioned to the sheltering ravine wall, then ran to the other side of the helicopter. He unfastened the pilot's harness, but before Bobby could stop him the pilot fell onto the sand. Bobby put his ear to the man's mouth and heard his deep, labored breathing. He was alive. His ID tag identified him as Capt. Thomas Nollner.

Hoping desperately that he was doing the right thing, Bobby started to drag Nollner to safety. After a few feet, the pilot screamed. Bobby stopped short—and noticed a fist-sized bulge under the captain's shirt in the middle of his back. A broken back! If he moved Nollner, it could kill or paralyze him. But if he left him and the chopper exploded . . .

A door, ripped from the plane, lay nearby. It would make a good stretcher. That moment, as Bobby weighed what to do, the engine whine reached a crescendo. He waited, rigid, expecting the inevitable explosion. But the high-pitched, nerve-shattering noise dropped to a whisper. Then the engine died, apparently out of fuel.

Limp with relief, Bobby looked about him. Everything was going to be all right now, he tried to assure himself. Surely, experienced help would arrive any minute. (But he didn't know that the phone lines to their house were cut in the crash and that Barbara would have to drive on to a neighbor's place to call for help.) He glanced at his watch: 7:55.

With the danger of an explosion past, Bobby set about doing what he could for the injured men. *Perhaps Densford knows first aid,* Bobby thought, *and can tell me what to do.* But the colonel lay staring blankly ahead in the twilight zone between consciousness and unconsciousness; his breathing was shallow and irregular.

"My back hurts," Densford half gasped, half sobbed. Only now did Bobby realize that the man couldn't walk, that he had been crawling and dragging himself all the while. The helicopter's sudden plunge to the ground—the equivalent of falling sixteen stories—must have compacted the colonel's back, and likely those of the other two, Bobby figured.

Gently, Bobby eased Densford into a more comfortable position. Then he ran to the chopper and tore out seat padding to pillow the colonel's back and head. "Lie still, you hear? I'll be right back."

Answering Palmer's piercing screams, Bobby found the copilot struggling to breathe. Carefully Bobby removed Palmer's headgear, hoping it would make it easier for him to get air. Palmer choked. Blood oozed from his mouth. With a thumb and two fingers, the captain reached up and pulled pieces of his teeth from his mouth. With trembling hands, Bobby flicked out remaining bits.

"Move me, please, somebody!" Palmer screamed. Bobby again ran to the helicopter and tore at the insulation. He removed some of the batting used for soundproofing, rolled it into a cushion and eased it under Palmer to support his spine. He tore off two more strips and folded them to cradle his sides.

Palmer vomited blood. Bobby hesitated. He suspected that Palmer's back or neck was broken—and that any movement would increase the chance of paralysis. But if he didn't do something, Palmer would choke to death on his own blood. Without lifting the copilot's head, Bobby turned it ever so gently to one side. Every few seconds, he kept assuring Palmer all was well.

8:25. An hour and ten minutes since the crash, and still no sign of help. The setting sun cast long shadows across the sand. Could rescuers find them in the dark?

For what seemed an interminable time, Bobby talked to the injured men, offering words of comfort and encouragement. Periodically, Palmer screamed. Bobby did what he could to ease the pain.

8:45. The lonely ravine was pitch-black. If help did not come soon, Bobby knew these men would die. With each tick of his watch, their lives were ebbing away.

9:00. High up on the bluff, a light appeared and moved slowly toward them. Then—*thank God*—Barbara was standing beside him with a flashlight and blankets. The ambulance from Johnson City and an Army MEDEVAC helicopter from Fort Sam Houston in San Antonio were on their way.

9:15. A dozen volunteer rescuers made their way down to the wreck. A doctor bent over the injured men, injecting painkillers. Again Palmer vomited blood; they gave him plasma. A volunteer bent to lift Palmer onto a stretcher. "Don't touch him!" Bobby shouted. "Wait for the medevac chopper!"

Minutes later, the helicopter, guided by the ambulance's flashing red light and the headlights of the parked cars, appeared overhead. With its own searchlights piercing the ravine's darkness, it set down behind a grove of oaks. That wouldn't do. The chopper *must* land on the sandbar. Bobby bounded toward the helicopter and yelled, "The wires are already down. There's no way you can get those men with broken backs over here without killing them. Land by the river!" The craft lifted off again, and landed by the crash. The voices of the army medics were music to Bobby's ears.

Three hours after the crash, the injured airmen were being flown to Brooke Army Medical Center. Only then did Bobby realize that he ached with fatigue—and worry over whether he had helped or hurt the injured men.

Six weeks later, Bobby received a letter signed by Lt. Gen. Robert M. Shoemaker, commanding officer of nearby Fort Hood, the helicopter crew's base, commending him for his lifesaving actions. All three officers had survived, but their recovery was going to be slow.

Densford had a crushed lumbar vertebra and several broken bones in both feet. Nollner had multiple back fractures and a severe concussion. In addition to three broken vertebrae and damage to his spinal column, Palmer had a crushed chest, eight broken ribs, lung punctures, a broken ankle, and nerve damage to his legs and lower body. Without Bobby's careful attention, Palmer's spine would probably have been so seriously damaged that he would have lost the use of his legs.

On February 14, 1977, while Bobby Wilson was napping and Barbara was washing the pickup, a car pulled into the yard. Two men got out slowly; they were encased from their necks to their hips in body casts. Still, when Bobby was called, he recognized them immediately: Palmer and Nollner.

They walked toward him haltingly, stiffly, their arms outstretched. Each clasped one of Bobby's hands in theirs. Bobby could barely swallow for the lump in his throat.

"If it hadn't been for you," Nollner said, "we'd have died. Thank you from the bottom of my heart."

"You made the right decisions under pressure," Palmer said. "We'll never forget you."

Bobby Wilson could lay his worries to rest. In all his thirty-two years, it was the nicest Valentine he had ever received.

Suddenly, in a Michigan city,
people began turning up with symptoms
of some strange and frightening disease.
Could its source be tracked down
in time to save lives?

Case of the
Deadly Hot Peppers

BY AL STARK

DIANE SPRENGER, a twenty-six-year-old nurse at St. Joseph Mercy Hospital in Pontiac, Michigan, was on duty the night of Tuesday, March 29, 1977. Toward the end of her shift she noticed that the lights in the hospital corridors bothered her. After work she went directly home and, before retiring, nibbled on a piece of cheese. She had trouble swallowing, but thought it was just because she was very tired. The next morning, she could hardly talk. She felt dizzy and couldn't focus her eyes.

Diane made a noon appointment with a doctor. He checked her over and thought she might be suffering from hysteria. (Recent bad news about her father's health had come as a terrible blow.) So the doctor gave Diane some medication and sent her home. She made herself a cup of hot chocolate but couldn't swallow it. Instead, she went into a choking fit. When it was over, she asked her mother to drive her to the emergency room at St. Joseph's.

When a neurosurgeon examined Diane, she was afflicted by facial paralysis and drooling, and she had double vision. He determined that she was suffering from a paralysis with neurological origins, which could be caused by a number of conditions, all of them strange and uncommon.

Diane was admitted to the hospital, where she would be under close observation, and another neurologist, Dr. Lionel Glass, was asked to take a look at her when he made his rounds the next day.

During the night Diane's condition deteriorated. In the morning, Dr. Glass found her "obviously quite sick. She had difficulty breathing. And she looked bad, real bad. When she tried to swallow, she felt as if there were a golf ball in her throat. It was acute bulbar paralysis."

Because of her precarious breathing, Dr. Glass had Diane moved to intensive care. There she was hooked up to a respirator, and two pulmonary specialists were called in to keep her alive while Dr. Glass tried to figure out what was wrong.

Tests were taken, including a spinal tap: no sign of anything infectious or inflammatory. Myasthenia gravis (a debilitating and often fatal weakening of the muscles) was eliminated. So was polio. In due course, almost every possible cause was eliminated—except botulism. This is an acute food poisoning produced by bacteria that breed in improperly preserved food. A vicious killer, botulism is fatal to about twenty percent of those who get it.

Says Dr. Glass, "I can't remember when I first said the word out loud. But when I walked across the room to the dictating machine, I had it in mind as my first guess. Another doctor there said, 'What do you think?' and I said, 'Botulism first.' "

As Dr. Glass finished dictating his notes on Diane Sprenger, something happened that made his guess look a great deal better. "At that moment," he recalls, "a resident stepped up and asked if I could come to the emergency room to look at a curious case. I asked what the symptoms were, and he told me difficulty swallowing, difficulty with vision, difficulty with speech, difficulty with breathing—everything Diane Sprenger had.

"We ran down to Emergency. And there lay John Slater." Slater, a twenty-six-year-old deacon at St. Hugo of the Hills Catholic Church in Bloomfield Hills, Michigan, had become mysteriously ill and had consulted his physician only hours before.

This was an enormous break in pinning down the diagnosis. It would be extremely rare for a hospital to admit two cases of myasthenia gravis or bulbar polio within hours of each other. But botulism almost always affects more than one person, since the poisoned food is usually eaten by several people.

As soon as Dr. Glass had examined Slater, he called the state

health department in Lansing to ask if botulism had appeared anywhere in the state recently. This was at three p.m. on Thursday,
March 31.

From Lansing, contact was made with sanitarians in Oakland
County, where Pontiac is located. They would have to determine
where the sick people had eaten the tainted food and try to prevent
anyone else from being poisoned. By four p.m., sanitarian Mel
Goldman and a public-health nurse were at St. Joseph's questioning
the patients' friends and relatives.

The Center for Disease Control in Atlanta is the nation's clearing-
house and command post in epidemics. Its man in Lansing was dispatched to Pontiac by car with the three vials of botulism antitoxin
on hand in Michigan. Meanwhile, health officials began lining up
more antitoxin across the nation. No one knew yet how large the
number of people involved might be, but already the doctors had
fearful suspicions that the outbreak could get very big and might be
difficult to control.

In the intensive-care unit, Mel Goldman was hunting for a lead.
Botulism, he knew, is most frequently caused by food that has been
improperly canned at home. Diane Sprenger and John Slater didn't
know each other. This suggested that they had been poisoned in a
public restaurant. But which one? And how many more people
might be poisoned if it weren't identified quickly and closed down?

The best Diane could do by now was nod or shake her head.
Questioning a member of the hospital staff, Goldman learned that
she and Diane had shared a pizza on Tuesday night. But since only
Diane was sick, he questioned her further. On Monday night after
work, he learned, Diane had eaten a mininacho (peppers and cheese
on corn chips) at Trini and Carmen's, a Mexican restaurant near
the hospital.

When the interview was over, Goldman went to the nursing station to phone his superiors. A nurse overheard him. She didn't feel
well herself, and her symptoms were similar to those Goldman was
describing. She told him so and, in response to his questions, said she
had eaten out only once that week—at Trini and Carmen's.

Slater, in a room nearby, overheard some of this. He was badly
paralyzed and couldn't speak but was able to ring for a nurse. "Were
you talking about nachos?" he wrote on a pad. "I had nachos, too."

Health officials rushed to Trini and Carmen's. They found a jar of home-canned peppers in a kitchen closet. It had been opened. On the busy night of March 28, the cook had used some of the peppers to make the hot sauce for the popular nachos.

At 8:30 p.m., Thursday, just five and a half hours after Dr. Glass had called Lansing, an order was issued halting food service in the restaurant. During the period when the suspect nachos were served, the restaurant had served some 400 customers.

By now botulism victims were beginning to stream into emergency rooms at hospitals throughout the area. When the vials of antitoxin arrived, one each was given to Diane Sprenger and John Slater, who were among the most seriously ill. As the crisis grew, the terrible implications remained: How many more were poisoned? How could they be warned so that they would go to a hospital?

The decision to make an announcement—there was excellent circumstantial evidence of botulism but no definite laboratory proof—wasn't reached until after eleven p.m. By then, with locally produced programs completed for the day, the radio and TV studios were largely deserted. When a doctor called the studios to ask that an alert be read over the air, the phones went unanswered. But someone got the stations' emergency numbers from the police, and the first announcement went out on television at about 11:45 p.m.

Soon, St. Joseph's was flooded with calls. So was nearby Crittenton Hospital. Crittenton's emergency room became so crowded that there weren't enough doctors to interview the people. All internists on the staff were called in to help determine who actually showed signs of botulism. At least ten persons were admitted to either St. Joseph's or Crittenton with botulism that night, and the phones kept ringing.

The number of cases continued to climb on Friday. Alerted by the media and by their friends, Trini and Carmen's customers showed up in hospitals for miles around.

Jars of peppers from the restaurant had been sent to the laboratories in Atlanta. On Saturday, April 2, the report came back: Some of the peppers definitely contained the botulism poison. So did the stool samples taken from the first patients.

That same day, word came from doctors at Little Traverse Hospital in Petoskey, Michigan, 260 miles to the northwest. Two hospital employees who had been to Pontiac and had eaten at Trini and Carmen's had been admitted there.

A National Guard airplane was dispatched from Selfridge Air Force Base to fly antitoxin from the Pontiac airport to Petoskey. But the military plane couldn't land at Pontiac because of fifty-mile-an-hour winds. Finally a private plane, piloted by Mike Bezzeg, took off in a storm with the serum. State police cars were waiting at airports along the way in case the plane was forced down short of Petoskey. It was a bumpy flight, but Bezzeg got the serum there in time to help save the two hospital employees.

The last new case was reported on Wednesday, April 7, and the next day public health officials announced that the crisis was over. Botulism may appear in a person up to eight days after eating the contaminated food; the eight days had now passed.

And—miraculously—no one died. Through fast action, excellent medical care, quick and effective detective work, and sheer luck, death was held off. It had been the biggest single outbreak of botulism in U. S. history: The number of victims totaled fifty-eight. Yet every one of them survived.

By April 14, John Slater was recuperating at his mother's home in Dearborn. Diane Sprenger remained hooked to the respirator at St. Joseph's until Easter weekend. But a few days later she was well enough to joke about the tracheotomy that had been performed to help her breathe. She wondered if smoke would come out of the hole in her throat when she lit up a cigarette. It did. Diane went home on April 15 and eventually returned to her job.

A couple of days later a doctor at St. Joseph's blurted out something that had been on his mind: "Has it occurred to you how lucky we were it was Mexican hot sauce that poisoned these people? Imagine if it had been applesauce, or something else that people eat by the spoonful."

An ordeal of endurance
that overshadows the classic trip of Captain Bligh
and his men of HMS *Bounty*

Two
Survived

BY GUY PEARCE JONES

On the night of Wednesday, August 21, 1940, the *Anglo-Saxon,* a British tramp steamer loaded with coal for South America, had left the Azores 500 miles behind and was making its way steadily in a southwesterly direction through a choppy swell. The night was pitch black, with low clouds scurrying across the sky.

Suddenly four explosions, so close together that they seemed to be one, shook the ship from stem to stern. A quarter of a mile away a dark shape raced toward her, guns flashing.

The first salvo from the raider killed everyone in the *Anglo-Saxon's* starboard fo'c'sle. Then a hail of lead and steel raked her fore and aft. The lifeboats were set afire and the radio antennas were shot away.

Two men crouching in the lee of the bridge saw the port lifeboat being lowered and scrambled into it. When it hit the water three men slid down the lifeline; a moment later two others dropped in from the boat deck.

The boat cleared the churning propeller blades by inches and drifted within a hundred feet of the raider. The men crouched like hunted animals and scarcely breathed. Near the *Anglo-Saxon,* lights suddenly appeared, bobbing up and down on the waves. The life rafts! The raider swung its guns and fired, and the lights went out. The rafts and the men clinging to them had been obliterated.

The white finger of a searchlight reached out and swept the

stricken *Anglo-Saxon*. Incendiary bullets played on the wreckage of the wireless room; no one was to live to send a message. Then the ship's bow rose up—almost perpendicular—as she went down stern first; the raider headed off into the night.

The seven survivors of the *Anglo-Saxon's* crew of forty huddled miserably through the night in the lifeboat. At dawn they could see nothing save empty miles of ocean and sky.

The chief mate, first officer C. B. Denny, took over command. His first concern was for the wounded. R. H. Pilcher was the most severely hurt. Shrapnel had torn through his left foot. With the aid of

the third engineer, Leslie Hawkes, the mate cleaned Pilcher's mangled foot in seawater as best he could. They moved him forward into the bow.

Gunner Richard Penny's right hip was badly torn by shrapnel. Cook Leslie Morgan had a jagged cut just above his right ankle. Seaman Robert Tapscott had a front tooth broken off, exposing the nerve, and Seaman Roy Widdicombe's hand had been severely bruised when it was jammed in the block while the boat was being lowered.

With the wounded men fixed as comfortably as possible, the mate set a course west-southwest for the Leeward Islands—2,800 miles in an eighteen-foot open boat! But they had to go that way; the wind and the current were against their going east. The able men bailed the boat, pulled in the sea anchor, stepped the stubby mast and set sail. Then they took stock of supplies. For food, they had three six-pound cans of boiled mutton, eleven cans of condensed milk and thirty-two pounds of sea biscuit. The water cask was a little over half full—about four gallons.

Only Pilcher had been able to bring anything away from the ship. He had a Rolls razor, a pound of tobacco, a pipe, his time sheets and radio-operator's log, and a book of Bible quotations, one for every day of the year. The men used the latter for cigarette paper and always read the verse before absorbing it in smoke. The mate made himself a logbook with the back of Pilcher's radio time sheets. For a calendar, he cut notches in the gunwale.

They had their first food that evening at six: a sea biscuit apiece. Their first drink came at sunup of the second day. The mate set half a dipper of water, a little of the condensed milk with it and half a biscuit as each man's daily ration every morning and evening.

They made fair progress until Sunday, when the wind dropped and the boat lost way. All that day they drifted aimlessly, the sun shining down intensely on them. Their bodies were already so dehydrated it was impossible to swallow the hard biscuit without wetting it first.

Pilcher and Morgan were both suffering from increasing pain. Their lacerated feet had swollen, and it was necessary to loosen their bandages. When this was done the horrible stench of gangrene permeated the boat.

At six o'clock, the mate doled out water. Then he said, "Sunday treat—mutton for dinner today."

The men watched fascinated while he opened the can and divided half its contents. They ate it carefully, making every morsel count. It was more cheering than drink.

But the next day—and the next—the men in the becalmed boat suffered fearfully. The burning sun was torture, and those who took shelter under the canvas boat cover found themselves in an oven. They were very thirsty now. Their pores, denied any liquid to evaporate, closed up; their skin became scorched; salivation ceased. The morning half-dipper of water, gulped with such eagerness, was like a drop on a blotter.

The able men bailed seawater over the wounded and then went over the side themselves, being careful to keep their faces out of water less they yield to the desire to drink. Their bodies took up moisture through the pores and the saliva returned to their mouths, but the relief did not last.

On the evening of the seventh day, to buck up morale, the mate held a lottery. Seven days—September 9 to 15—were listed as those upon which they would be picked up or make a landfall. The men's names were then written on slips of paper, scrambled in Pilcher's cap and drawn by the cook. The losers were to buy the winner all the drinks he could consume.

The lottery was a great success. The men argued in cracked and raucous voices over the dates they had drawn and settled down for the night still debating the matter. The mere act of holding a lottery based on their rescue seemed, somehow, to assure the fact.

Next day the wind was strong and the sea boisterous. They bowled along handily, making fine time and shipping buckets of water. No one cared about the water. They made ready for a wet night cheerfully. This, they told themselves in voices croaking with thirst, was the last lap. But they couldn't sleep. Pilcher was delirious, and his bursts of hysterical laughter and singing and invectives gave them no rest.

In the morning they decided that amputating his foot was the only hope they had of saving his life. But the sole available implement was an ax—dull and rusty—and they had no antiseptic or anesthetic.

Pilcher was lucid, though very weak. He agreed bravely to the operation, but at the last moment even the mate's resolute nerve failed him.

"Carry on, old boy," he said. "We're certain to be picked up soon and a proper doctor will make it right for you."

Pilcher smiled weakly and closed his eyes. When they took him his ration of water that night he told them to give it to someone who needed it more than he. At eight o'clock the next morning he died, silently and unobtrusively. The men looked at one another incredulously. So soon! It couldn't be possible. They stood by quietly, overwhelmed by the awful finality of death. In curt, low orders the mate arranged all that was left to do. Tapscott and the third engineer lifted the body over the gunwale and lowered it gently into the sea. They had nothing to wrap it in and nothing with which to weight it. It drifted away on the swell. They watched it until they could see it no more.

On the eleventh day the mate suffered some sort of internal collapse. Nausea and cramps seized him. His face was livid and lined with pain. His flesh, even where burned by the sun, had a lifeless, claylike appearance. In a hand that could just trace the letters he made his last log entry: *"Suggestion for life-boat stocks:* At the very least, two breakers of water, tins of fruit such as peaches, apricots, pears, etc."

On September 4, the mate was so weak he could scarcely move. He could no longer command. They drank their last meager ration of water at noon. A little later the boat suddenly yawed. There was no one at the helm. Penny, the gunner, who had just taken the tiller, was floating face downward some distance from the boat. It was useless to try reaching him.

Two days later there was still no sign of rain. And, as if to put the seal of finality on disaster, the rudder was carried away by a heavy swell. They shipped the steering oar in its stead.

After long hours, the mate raised himself on his elbow and said from swollen and discolored lips: "I'm going over. Who's coming with me?"

"I'll go," the third engineer said.

The mate turned his eyes to the others: One by one they shook their heads. But the dread of what they must see overwhelmed them. They stared at the self-condemned men.

"Just a minute," the third engineer said, almost gaily. "I'm going to have something to eat and drink." He dipped a can of water from the sea and gulped it down greedily. Then he softened a biscuit in seawater and ate it.

The mate drew off his signet ring and handed it to Widdicombe. "Give it—my mother—if you get through," he gasped. "And keep going west."

The mate and the third engineer struggled over to the port gunwale. There was a splash. . . .

The three men who now survived had nothing to maintain life—they had no water, and without water the biscuits were useless. Morgan was out of his head most of the time, and Tapscott and Widdicombe were too weak to steer for more than an hour at a stretch. But they clung to life tenaciously, conserving what little strength remained.

Then one morning Morgan got up from where he had been lying in the bow and announced in a clear, casual voice: "I think I'll go down the street for a drink." He walked aft rapidly and stepped over the side. When his body reappeared it was being carried away by the swell. He made no more movement, no outcry! Tapscott and Widdicombe stared at each other. Of the seven men who got away from the *Anglo-Saxon* they alone were left.

By noon their thirst was so terrible that Tapscott could stand the torture no longer. He drank a little seawater. Immediately, he was shaken with a paroxysm of vomiting, after which he lay quietly for a long time.

Cramping pains tore at Widdicombe's entrails, stretching him stiff in the bottom of the boat. He rolled about in agony, clutching at his belly and bursting into bellows of insane rage and hysterical imprecation.

The sun crossed the meridian and moved at a snail's pace down the sky. As the heat diminished they lay in a grateful stupor. When the sun rose the next morning they knew it was day—and little more. The boat had lost all way. It wallowed gently on an oily sea under a hot and humid sky. The tempo of the elements slowed down to the faint pulse of life in the boat.

Tapscott roused himself dully. "Oh, goddamn it all," he said. "I'm going over. Are you with me?"

Widdicombe nodded faintly. He lowered himself over the side and clung to the lifeline. Tapscott plunged into the water. Automatically, he floated. The cool water seemed to revive him; the shock stung his deadened nerves into action. When he looked up, he was five or six feet behind the boat. Widdicombe was still clinging to the lifeline.

"Come on," Tapscott called. Widdicombe gave no sign of hearing.

"Let go," Tapscott said. Widdicombe did not move.

Tapscott went into a laborious crawl. He was surprised to find that he could swim. When he came alongside the boat he said: "Why don't you let go?"

Widdicombe shook his head violently.

Tapscott felt a rush of rage. Widdicombe wasn't playing fair! He, too, took hold of the lifeline.

Hanging from the rope Tapscott and Widdicombe argued the matter. Having once made up his mind, Tapscott was determined to go. But he wasn't going without Widdicombe. And Widdicombe's pain had passed; immersion was making him feel much better.

"If you're strong enough to swim that far," he pointed out, "you're strong enough to go on some more."

Tapscott reflected that this was true. By this time he was quite willing to be convinced. With much effort, they got themselves back into the boat and crawled under the boat cover. They felt that they had been accorded a new lease on life.

Then Tapscott had an idea. Why not drink the alcohol in the compass? They decanted it into two condensed milk cans, about three quarters of a water glass each. As if standing each other a round in a pub they sat opposite each other on the thwarts and drank. The alcohol rasped their raw throats and burned their intestines. But it was liquid.

Several swallows and they grinned at each other. Peril and pain were forgotten. They laughed and ragged each other in strange, throaty croaks, their misshapen mouths grinning like gargoyles. They recalled famous binges in foreign ports. When the alcohol was gone they rolled over and went to sleep. It was the first relaxed sleep they had had since leaving their blazing ship.

Toward morning they were roused by a terrific peal of thunder. A moment later there was a splatter of drops on the boat cover. Rain!

The fresh water sluiced down in steady, heavy sheets, quickly making a puddle in the canvas cover they laid across the thwarts. They poured water down their throats by the canful, spilling it out of the corners of their mouths, down their chins and chests, with joyful, gluttonous, animal noises. Never had they known such pleasure in drink. Then they drained the water—about six gallons—off the canvas into a cask.

Their thirst quenched, they were aware of the first recognizable hunger they had felt in days. They soaked sea biscuit in water and ate it. Life flowed back into them. They were very weak, but the tide, definitely, had changed. Widdicombe was jubilant.

"I knew we'd make it," he declared. "I knew it the moment we got back into the boat. If we couldn't go then, it stands to reason we're going to be okay."

This was September 12, their twenty-third day in the boat.

For six days the breeze held, and for six days they had all the water they wanted. They were so profoundly pleased to have cheated death from thirst they laughed at their hunger. They scraped up the shreds of Pilcher's tobacco, filled the pipe and managed a few whiffs each.

But now the quality of the heat seemed more punishing, and the air heavier, more humid. The direct rays of noon burned and stung like heated needles. By the morning of September 18 they had reached the bottom of the water cask again. But their thirst did not seem as bad as it had been before. They had learned the technique of suffering. Rain came early on the morning of September 20. They rigged the cover and drank copiously. While the cask was filling they soaked six biscuits each in rainwater. Their supply was getting low, but they had been without food for two days.

They had no suspicion that miles and miles of the Atlantic lay between them and the nearest land. On September 24, they dribbled the last of the water into their cans. They fumbled in the biscuit box, but it yielded only broken bits and crumbs. They were now completely without food or water.

The five weeks that followed were like a long, bad dream. One day followed another in an unvarying pattern of hunger, sun and sea, an indistinguishable blur in the continuity of their suffering.

Rainfall became fairly frequent, but for many days they had nothing to eat. Then one day they heard a thud against the sail, and a desperate flapping in the boat. To their incredulous joy a flying fish had leaped aboard. Tapscott got out Pilcher's razor and cut it in two. He took the head half. Widdicombe had the other. They ate every scrap—including the eyes, bones and fins.

Later they encountered great patches of seaweed and were delighted to find a tiny variety of crab in its meshes. They winnowed out many of them, but it took hours of work to make a meal.

On October 9, a leaden, drizzly day, they sighted a large steamer, not more than half a mile away, bearing south. They stood up in the boat, waving their arms and shouting. They swung their oars, semaphore fashion, and blew the mate's whistle until they were breathless. The liner steamed steadily ahead.

Tapscott and Widdicombe collapsed on the seats, completely spent. Their hearts were beating as if to burst; their lungs heaved and they gulped down air in sobbing spasms.

Some time after midnight, four days later, they were awakened by the howl of wind and the violent tossing and pitching of the boat. The sea was running high and the boat was filled with water within a few inches of the thwarts. At that moment the crest of a huge wave poured in over the gunwales. Tapscott seized the bucket and Widdicombe a can, and they started bailing desperately. That night was an eternity of terror.

Dawn came as a lightening in a leaden sky. The gale blasted them with spindrift that stung like shot. It took both of them to manage the steering oar. Ahead was a howling, tumbling chaos of wind and water. All day and all the next night they fought the storm. There was no question of sleep. Drenched, cold and dog-tired they huddled in the stern.

The second day of the storm the wind blew more steadily. The boat raced with the forty-foot waves, driven at express speed.

"At any rate," Widdicombe said grimly, "we're making time."

The rising sun of the following day revealed a turbulent sea, but one in which they could safely lie to. They fell exhausted upon the seats. Then they looked at each other and grinned; another great danger successfully passed.

After the storm, pickings from the sea were poor. They became frantic with hunger. They stripped the peeling skin from their bodies and ate that. They tore the latex lining from Pilcher's tobacco pouch and chewed on that. They were very light-headed now, and their mounting hysteria found relief in bitter quarreling.

The next week was almost a blank. Then one night Tapscott thought he heard a fish flapping in the boat. With the first light of dawn he was in the bottom of the boat, looking for it.

"I've found it," he said finally. Widdicombe said nothing.

"I've found that fish," Tapscott repeated, looking up to see why

Widdicombe received this important news so apathetically. Widdicombe was staring straight ahead.

"Look," he said, pointing.

Tapscott, holding the fish firmly, raised himself on a thwart to see. Dead ahead lay a long line of lowland and beach.

"Land or no land," Tapscott said, "I'm going to eat this fish." He cut it in half with Pilcher's razor and they ate it, staring at the land.

That afternoon the radio flashed the news to the world that Robert George Tapscott, 19, and Wilbert Roy Widdicombe, 21, the only survivors of the torpedoed *Anglo-Saxon,* had crossed 3,000 miles of the Atlantic Ocean in an open boat, outliving seventy days of thirst, starvation and storm.

They were found on the beach at Eleuthera, one of the Bahama Islands, by a beachcomber. A rescue party took them to Governor's Harbor, where they were greeted as heroes by the commissioner and citizens.

In the Bahamas General Hospital it was found that in addition to the physical effects of exposure, starvation and prolonged thirst, their mental and nervous systems were badly deranged. They could not sleep; both were frequently hysterical or sunk in despondent apathy. However, weeks of skillful treatment and considerate care restored them to some measure of their former nervous and physical stamina.

The final irony of the epic fight for life was reserved for Widdicombe. In February he went to Canada to join a ship, the *Siamese Prince.* On February 18 the ship was torpedoed and sunk off Scotland.

The steamship line reported that "everyone on the *Siamese Prince* must be considered to have been lost."

In all respects, he was an outstanding naval officer. Why, then, did his mind so suddenly collapse, plunging him into a world of unspeakable horror?

The Lieutenant's Deadly Wardrobe

BY GERALD MOORE

SHORTLY AFTER FOUR in the afternoon of Friday, June 9, 1978, Navy Lt. Peter Chmelir, 27, stood crowded in with hundreds of other passengers at Florida's Pensacola airport, waiting to claim the two bags he had checked on a commercial flight from San Diego. When the first bag appeared, Chmelir (pronounced Kă mill′ er) lifted it off the conveyer belt and looked impatiently for the second. An old friend was waiting outside in the limited parking space.

The second bag arrived. As Chmelir grabbed it, he saw that the zipper and one side of the bag were coated with a liquid. He thought of lodging a complaint with the airline, but remembered his waiting friend.

Arranging the soiled bag so it would not stain the station wagon, Chmelir jumped in for the trip to the Pensacola Naval Air Station, where he would be spending a month at the prestigious Electronic Warfare School. They had driven only a few blocks when Chmelir noticed a strong chemical odor. Then his head began to ache.

In his room at the base, Chmelir opened the soiled bag carefully. He saw that whatever had stained the outside had also soaked through the bag, soiling all his civilian clothes and underwear. (His uniforms were in the other, clean bag.) Angry, Chmelir took the soiled clothes to the laundry. He had no soap, but he ran the clothes through a cycle with clear water and dried them. The smell was still strong.

Saturday morning the stench from the clothes woke Chmelir. He went to the base exchange, bought laundry soap, and washed the clothes again. They still smelled. He ran them through again. When they were dry, the odor was barely noticeable, and Chmelir thought he could wear them without offending anyone.

Late Sunday morning Chmelir put on a pair of the undershorts that had been wet by the mysterious liquid, dressed and went to lunch. Afterward he pulled bathing trunks on over the same underwear and went out to sunbathe. Sitting by the pool, he began to feel lightheaded, but dismissed it. As a man who had enjoyed nearly perfect health all his life, he was not one to fuss over minor symptoms.

Before dinner, Chmelir changed clothes and put on underwear from the same freshly washed supply. While he was watching TV after dinner he noticed a burning sensation in his groin. Gradually he began to feel drunk. He had had no alcohol at all, but a swirling disorientation came on him. Back in his room, he struggled into the shower. The burning subsided, but the disorientation grew worse. "I couldn't concentrate," he said later. "I was alert, but I couldn't focus on a single thought. Then I realized that my peripheral vision was gone. I had tunnel vision and it was out of focus."

Frightened now, Chmelir called the Officer of the Day and asked for transportation to the hospital. His nightmare had begun.

At nine-thirty p.m. Chmelir tried to explain to an emergency-room doctor what was happening to him. He had even managed to remember to bring a pair of the shorts with him in the hope that the hospital might identify the chemical which had spilled on his bag. He told the doctor about the odor. He insisted the doctor take the underwear and examine it, but Chmelir's condition made his story wandering and disconnected. The doctor dismissed the underwear as a factor.

When a blood test failed to show any reason for Chmelir's condition, he was told he might be having an allergic reaction. "Get some rest and go to the dispensary in the morning," the doctor said.

Terror welled up inside Chmelir at the thought of leaving the hospital. He knew he needed help. Back in his room, he called Cmdr. F. Lee Tillotson, the executive officer of his unit, Fighter Squadron 51, in San Diego. Chmelir recounted his story about the chemical and about getting sick, while Commander Tillotson tried to make sense of what was being said. Chmelir was one of Tillotson's best officers, a cool-headed young man who made good use of his 131 I.Q. and who had distinguished himself as an outstanding member of his squadron operating off the carrier *Franklin D. Roosevelt*.

The call worried Tillotson deeply. "Forget about the school," he said. "Just try to get well."

At three a.m. Chmelir woke up nearly hysterical with fear. He thought about his ginger-haired wife, Dorothy, and the two children, at that moment on a holiday with her family in Texas. Suddenly he was sure he was dying. He called the base fire department and when the corpsmen arrived he was barely in control of himself. His eyelids were like movie screens, with wild images and even wilder sequences playing before his eyes.

In the hospital emergency room, someone hit his arm with a hypodermic needle and his turbulent emotions began to quiet down. He rested without sleeping through the night. In the morning, however, things got worse.

He remembered nothing of most of that Monday. Chmelir would learn later that during those black holes in his recollection he lashed out, moaning and sobbing. He was tormented by unnamed fears and half-formed swirling horrors which his memory could not record.

Late Tuesday afternoon Dorothy arrived home in San Diego after driving from Texas. She lay down for a nap and was wakened almost immediately by a call from Cmdr. Lonny McClung, the skipper of Chmelir's squadron. "Peter has been sick," he said. "But he seems better now. They plan to discharge him from the hospital tomorrow."

Chmelir left the hospital on Wednesday. His native stamina had pulled him through the ordeal quickly. His head was still quite foggy, but his self-control was back and his emotions were quiet. On Thursday, he went to keep an appointment with his doctor. As Chmelir talked, the lightness of head suddenly returned. Then all emotional control went. Peter began to sob. He babbled something about his ruined career and then drifted off into madness.

Dorothy picked up the jangling phone. It was Commander McClung. "Peter is back in the hospital," he said. "I'm making arrangements for you to fly to Pensacola."

When Dorothy arrived at the hospital, she was not prepared for what she saw. "I was stunned," she recalled. "Peter couldn't walk. He didn't even recognize me." The diagnosis was "acute schizophrenic episode." Dorothy felt her world coming apart. None of this made any sense.

On Wednesday, June 21, Chmelir was moved by MEDEVAC to the Naval Regional Medical Center in Oakland, California. Dorothy was permitted to accompany her heavily sedated husband on the trip. Despite the drugs, Peter became aggressive and hostile during the flight. He seemed to Dorothy like a total stranger.

In Oakland, Peter became rational again. "I was scared," he remembered. "I felt sure I would never be free again. I expected to spend the rest of my life in a mental hospital."

The following day, Peter had his first interview with Dr. Gordon McCamley, a psychiatrist. McCamley wanted to know what had happened. "I don't know," was Peter's simple reply. The doctor then asked about the chemical; he said that the doctors in Pensacola had pretty well dismissed it as a cause. He added that he was inclined to agree.

Virtually no more weight was given to the contaminated-clothes theory in Oakland than it had received in Pensacola. Chmelir had, it appeared, simply cracked up.

Each day in Oakland, Chmelir felt better. His doctors began talking about release within a week. On Monday, June 26, Peter dressed in civilian clothes to go out to dinner with his brother John, a captain in the Army Corps of Engineers. Driving to the restaurant, Peter suddenly insisted they were lost and wouldn't be able to return to the hospital. Then his speech started to slur and they had to go back. He spent that night under his hospital bed screaming in terror.

At this point Dorothy's spirit crashed. She had allowed herself to feel some hope in the past week. Now it was gone. She was told that Peter had regressed to a catatonic state—he was physically frozen in a rigid position. Returning to Oakland, she wasn't permitted to visit him. Instead, she was taken aside and given some alarming and confusing news: A drug screen taken when Peter returned Monday night had shown PCP, the street drug commonly known as "angel dust," in Peter's urine.

The soiled clothes leaped to Dorothy's mind. Could that be the chemical that spilled on Peter's bag? The doctors said no. That exposure had occurred more than three weeks ago. The PCP in Peter's urine wouldn't have lasted three weeks. When Peter went out of the hospital, they said, he went crazy. When he was confined, he recovered. Clearly, he must be obtaining the drug on the outside. Dorothy was not convinced.

Peter was questioned about PCP. Where did he get it? How did it get in his system? He insisted that he had never taken the drug. His denials met with skepticism, and when PCP was still present in his urine ten days after his brother's visit, the entire ward was searched.

On July 14, Dorothy visited Peter and found him nearly normal. She told him she was doing intensive research into PCP. The drug had first been developed as an anesthetic, she said. It had been rejected for all human use after early tests showed that it had horrible psychological side effects. She found out that the San Diego police had established strict rules for handling PCP when it had to be stored as evidence because some officers had become ill after handling the powder.

That weekend Dorothy brought Peter some clothes from home. They went for a picnic and had a lovely day. Peter showed no signs of getting ill. "I felt the first real hope that day," Dorothy recalled. "When I dropped him off at the hospital and he was still all right I thought we might make it through."

Peter's doctors were also encouraged that he had left the hospital without a relapse. They were prepared to return him to limited duty for six months. Thus things were looking up when Peter went home on leave on Friday, July 21.

On Saturday he took Dorothy out to dinner and a movie. "While we were sitting in the movie," Dorothy said, "Peter gripped my hand very tightly. I looked at him and his eyes rolled back in his head. He said he had to go home."

Dorothy undressed him and locked him in the bedroom. In the morning, she and a relative took him to Balboa Naval Hospital.

When Dorothy was alone she went to the bedroom, fell across the bed and burst into tears.

As the tears rolled down Dorothy's cheeks, wetting her face, she became aware of an odd sensation. Her face felt warm. Then it began to burn. She wiped her face to see what was on it. Nothing. She looked down and saw that she had been lying across the pants Peter had worn to the movies. She pulled the curtains open and held the pants up to the light. There, along the waistband and down one leg, were yellow stains. She turned the pants inside out and saw countless tiny crystals. She called a doctor in Oakland (where Peter had been transferred) and told him about the stained clothing, her burning face and lightness of head. She was told that she was meddling in affairs where she had no training, and that the doctor would no longer receive her calls.

At the hospital, Peter's doctors were convinced now that they had a hopeless drug abuser on their hands. They confronted Peter with the results of a new drug screen. Where did he get the PCP? Proceedings were prepared for a medical discharge, with misconduct. This would not only end Peter's career with the Navy but also make any other career extremely difficult.

On August 16, the Chmelirs' wedding anniversary, Peter was released from the hospital and eventually transferred back to his squadron to await the discharge proceedings. A few days later Dorothy cut a four-inch strip of zipper out of Peter's suitcase and sent it, together with a sample of the clothes, to the Rocky Mountain Poisonlab in San Diego for analysis. The results were ready in two days and they were very interesting: The short piece of zipper yielded nearly two grams of PCP, enough to drive a small town mad. If the sample was an accurate indication of the total spilled on his clothes, Peter had been handling, sniffing and wearing enough PCP to dose half the Pacific Fleet.

Peter was ecstatic when he got the news. During the many interviews when he had insisted that he did not know the source of the PCP, unless it came from his clothes, the doctors assumed he was lying; their medical reports forwarded to Washington to support the discharge presented the case that way. Peter now filed a rebuttal that included a copy of the lab report. Then he waited confidently.

On October 1, Peter was found medically unfit for duty by virtue of misconduct (drug abuse). He was staggered.

Several things happened now in quick succession. Rear Adm. F. G. Fellowes, Commander of Fighter Airborne Early Warning Wing, Pacific Fleet, heard that one of his pilots was about to be kicked out of the service. He called Chmelir in. Peter told his story and reported the lab results. Admiral Fellowes made his own judgment about Chmelir's credibility. When the interview ended, Admiral Fellowes declared, "I don't think you have had a fair hearing up to now, Lieutenant, but I guarantee that you will be treated fairly from now on."

Shortly thereafter, the investigation was continued, using the resources of the Naval Investigative Service. Peter took and passed a lie-detector test. He was given a complete physical examination and underwent mental and personality tests. Medical experts from eight different fields were consulted. Drug Enforcement Administration experts tested the suspected suitcase and confirmed the earlier lab report.

A final hearing into the matter was held on January 4, 1979, at the Balboa Naval Facility. After nearly five hours of testimony from various experts who had examined Peter, it was time for Peter to take the stand. During his questioning he appeared healthy and alert. At 2:15 p.m. the board retired. Only twenty minutes later they returned and found Lt. Peter Chmelir fit for duty.

No one knows for sure just how the concentrated PCP was spilled on Chmelir's clothes, but the people who investigated the case guessed that the drug leaked from an illegal shipment concealed as baggage aboard the commercial flight which carried Chmelir to Pensacola. Much PCP is manufactured in makeshift labs in southern California, and some of it is sent by various means to the rest of the country. Chmelir, the investigators guessed, was a victim of one such shipment.

On a beautiful sun-warmed day in May 1979, as the carrier *Kitty Hawk* departed from San Diego on a seven-month cruise, Lt. Peter Chmelir rode a thundering F-14 over the sparkling water of the Pacific. "Fit for duty" had, for him, meant just that. Justice, painfully slow, had finally been served. The nightmare was over.

He lay pinned in a wreck
at the bottom of a deep
mountain ravine.
As time ticked by
he realized that no one
could tell he was there

The
Sixteen-Day Ordeal
of John Vihtelic

BY EMILY AND PER OLA D'AULAIRE

HE DIDN'T REALIZE what was happening until it was too late. One minute his car's headlights were probing the twilight along a winding mountain road; the next minute his world came apart. The station wagon strayed to the right, hit a depression in the narrow gravel road and bounced out of control. A few car lengths ahead, the shoulder of the road had washed away down the mountainside into a steep ravine. Now he felt his car tumbling, heard the crunch of buckling metal, sensed himself being tossed around like a rag doll.

When the crash ended, he found himself lying on his stomach on the inside roof of the overturned car near the base of the ravine. He ran his hands over his body. Everything seemed normal—just a few cuts and scratches. He glanced at his watch: It was 8:00 p.m.

He tried to pull himself free, but something was wrong. Twisting backward, he saw in the near darkness that a two-foot length of thick, six-inch root jutting from the base of a fallen tree had punched through the windshield, clamping the instep of his left foot against the dashboard as cruelly as if he'd been caught in a bear trap. He had the presence of mind to turn off the ignition, lessening the danger of explosion. But then, in growing panic, he began jerking and pulling at his leg. He kept this up most of the night, until the agony became unbearable and his strength ran out. Exhausted, he groped for his sleeping bag, pulled it over him and, dulled by pain, dozed fitfully. *Tomorrow,* he thought, *someone will find me.*

The accident happened on the evening of September 11, 1976. Just four days earlier, John Vihtelic had arrived in Portland, Oregon, from his home in Whitehall, Michigan, for a ten-day training course at Drake-Willock Systems, a manufacturer of kidney-dialysis machines. His new job would make use of the skills he had developed in the medical corps of the U. S. Army Green Berets and as a civilian working at St. Mary's Hospital in Grand Rapids. He planned to establish a service territory for the company in Philadelphia and also to marry Mary Fahner, a teacher from Whitehall whom he had known since childhood.

An energetic twenty-eight-year-old with black hair, a walrus mustache and lively blue eyes, John had borrowed the company station wagon the previous day and headed north from Portland to explore Mount Rainier National Park in southern Washington. He spent most of Saturday on the snow-covered slopes of Mount Rainier, hiking to an altitude of 9,000 feet before bad weather forced him back. It was late afternoon when he returned to the car, but there were still a few hours of daylight left, so he decided to drive to Mount Hood, about 150 miles south, that same evening.

Unknown to him, the route he chose through the mountainous Gifford Pinchot National Forest was one of the most treacherous in the Cascade Mountains region. As he headed south, he was forced to creep along a rough, single-lane gravel track cut precariously into the mountainside. After two hours of hard driving, he must have dozed off. A split second later, he hit the bump and plunged into darkness.

When John awoke that first Sunday morning, he realized he was lucky to be alive. The car was crumpled like a tin can, its roof crushed in places to below window level. He had at most a foot and a half of vertical space in which to move. His access to the outside world was a few inches of space still open through the buckled driver's window—space he could reach only by painfully twisting on his pinned leg. Beyond the window, a white-water stream thundered through the narrow ravine, and, on the other side, a steep embankment rose toward the road. Looking up through the trees, he could glimpse the grade he had come down before his luck ran out.

He saw a car go by early that morning and was sure he'd been spotted. He had no way of knowing that he was virtually invisible. His car had bounced 150 feet down the sixty-degree slide and now lay close against the base of the hill. Bottom side up, it blended with the dirt on the hill and the gray stones of the creekbed.

When John failed to report to work Monday morning, Steve Evarts, his boss at Drake-Willock, was worried. The Rainier region, he knew, has a savage reputation. He called the rangers there, described the car John was driving and asked for a search of the park. Within hours, 110 miles of park road had been covered, ravines and drop-offs checked. The head ranger informed Evarts: "That vehicle is not in this park."

As dozens of cars went by without stopping, John Vihtelic began to realize it could be days before anyone found him. An apple was all he'd found to eat in the car, but he was not worried about food. Over six feet tall and 190 pounds, he could exist for many days on his body's reserves of fat and muscle. What he did need was water. Thousands of gallons a minute were rushing by just twelve feet from the car.

Piece by piece, John began to dismantle the interior of the car. First he improvised a "fishing pole," yanking off the heavy metal headliner strips that held the inside lining to the roof. Then he assembled bits of electrical wires ripped from the door panels and roof, plus cord from his sleeping bag and nylon string from his tennis racket. He tied one end of this line to his pole, and the other around a T-shirt. Poking the whole contraption out the driver's window, he lofted the T-shirt into the creek, let it soak, pulled it back into the car and squeezed the moisture into his mouth. It took several successful casts to produce just one glass of water, and many casts weren't successful at all—the wires snagged on roots along the creek, or the tennis string snarled and broke. But he knew now that he would not die of thirst.

During his first days in the ravine, John worked steadily on the root that pinned his foot, jabbing at it with a lug wrench in an attempt to twist and break the wood fibers. But it was slow going and painful; as often as not, his desperate pokes struck his ankle instead of the root. He remembered what he'd been taught in the Army: *If taken prisoner of war, it is your duty to think always of a way to escape.* The words kept repeating themselves. He threw his body back and forth, hoping to rock the car free from the root. He tried to puncture his spare tire to get at the jack behind it, hoping to use that to lift the car from the root. But nothing he tried worked.

He kept to a strict daily routine. Each morning he would "fish" for water, then drink, sponge off his face and comb his hair. Between "work spells," he napped for two to three hours day and night. He kept track of his activities with paper and pencil, meticulously noting down the hour and day when he woke, when he drank, what he was thinking. He knew that keeping his mind occupied was important if he was to remain sane. The worst times came at night when it was too dark to work and he couldn't sleep. He would lie in the cold car and pray. *Please, dear God, get me out of here. I want to see my family.*

On Wednesday, September 15, John's older brother Frank, having flown to Portland from Detroit, set out on his missing brother's trail. In the town of Ashford, a few miles west of the park gates, a tavern owner said she thought she had seen a man answering John's description the previous Saturday morning and that he had asked directions to Portland. But this turned out to be a case of mistaken identity—John had never been in the tavern at all—and would result in a frustrating search west of Rainier instead of south.

By Friday, John's flagging spirits picked up. A weekend was coming; families would be out for a drive or a picnic. He attached the vanity mirror from the visor to his tennis racket with masking tape. The sun never hit the car directly, but for two and a half hours each clear afternoon it came close enough for him to reach with the outstretched racket. He would signal the cars as they drove by; he was confident he would be discovered.

Saturday dawned bright and clear, and traffic increased. At least sixty cars went by that weekend, and John flashed his mirror at dozens of them. One car stopped above him on the opposite side of the ravine. He was certain he had been seen and began to yell and bang on the side of the car with the lug wrench, but after a few minutes the car drove off. By Sunday evening he was angry and frustrated. Eight days had passed. *I can see the cars,* he thought. *Why can't they see me?*

By now Frank had been joined by two other brothers, Larry, 33, an airline pilot, and Joe, 25, an engineer. Three of John's friends from Whitehall, including Mary's brother Tom, had also flown out to join the Vihtelic search-and-rescue attempt. They rented three cars and split into teams, with one man driving, the other riding the fenders to get a good view into ravines and gullies. Whenever they saw a two-track road, they followed it to the end. They passed out flyers with John's description at gas stations, motels, taverns and restaurants. They cajoled local newspapers into publishing the story and running his picture. They visited local police departments. "We have more than one hundred missing persons reported," one detective told them bluntly. "If he is really out there, he'll have to help himself."

Inside the wreck that second week, John realized that the nights were growing colder. At 4,000 feet, it is not unusual for September temperatures to drop to freezing overnight. His sense of time running out became urgent. *One more weekend,* he thought. *If I'm not found by then, I never will be.*

From Wednesday to Friday, dump trucks went back and forth on the road above in an almost steady stream. John flashed his mirror until his arms ached and the sun slipped from his narrow ravine. When he counted a hundred trips on a single day, he knew that no one was ever going to see him. He'd have to get out himself.

On the second Saturday, with hope and money running out, Joe Vihtelic and Mary Fahner's brother Tom passed out flyers in the Mount Hood area, then headed back to Mount Rainier for a last try. To save time they cut through the mountains, taking the exact route, in reverse, that John had taken two weeks before. At about seven o'clock that evening, Tom slowed for a treacherous hairpin turn, then accelerated up the hill on the other side. One hundred and fifty feet below, John heard another car go by.

On the fifteenth day, John desperately turned his attention once more to the root; either it or his foot had to go. Stabbing with the lug wrench was obviously not going to work—the fibers were spongy and bounced back, and the misses were too painful. He needed another tool.

He opened his small leather suitcase and tossed it close to the creekbed. Then, bending a headliner rod in the shape of a shepherd's crook, he began scooping stones toward the suitcase, working them slowly up the side—only to have them fall away inches from going over the rim.

Finally, at dusk, he managed to nudge a rock the size of a cannon ball into the suitcase. Placing his hook through the handles of the suitcase, he pulled the treasure carefully back to the car and lifted it inside. Like a sculptor working with chisel and mallet, he placed an end of the lug wrench squarely against the root and hit it with the rock. For the first time he felt the iron bite across the grain and cut into the wood. He knew now that it was only a matter of hours before he could work himself free. But it was dark and he was exhausted. He forced himself to rest.

When the first gray light of dawn filtered into the ravine, he was ready. His foot had been pinned to the dashboard for sixteen days; now, as he chopped through the fibers and pulled out chunks of root, blood rushed back to the parts of the foot that were still alive. He groaned with pain, for it felt like hot pokers being driven through his flesh. But when the last bits of wood fell away, three hours after he began, he pushed himself through the window, threw his arms in the air and screamed, "I'm free! I'm free!"

He broke a limb from a tree to use as a crutch and began the difficult climb up the 150-foot embankment, dragging his injured foot behind him. Almost an hour later he pulled himself over the top, lay down by the side of the road and turned his pale, whiskered face toward the warmth and light. It was the first time in sixteen days that he had felt the sun.

John Vihtelic was found by a dump-truck driver and taken by ambulance to Portland, where doctors termed his condition "remarkable." He had lost twenty-five pounds but was otherwise in good health. However, because circulation to his foot had been cut off for so long, a great deal of tissue had died. The foot had to be amputated just above the ankle.

After three weeks in the hospital, John was discharged. Soon he was fitted with an artificial foot that functioned almost like the real thing, and he was hard at work as his company's service representative in Philadelphia. He and Mary Fahner were planning a summer wedding.

For John Vihtelic, the long ordeal was over.

The doctor had never even seen a brain operation,
but he knew he had to perform the delicate surgery
immediately—or watch a little boy die

Emergency at Waitangi

BY MAURICE SHADBOLT

ISLANDS DON'T COME much harsher or lonelier than the windswept
Chathams, almost 500 miles east of New Zealand. Eight of the ten
islands are but bleak pinnacles of rock, haunted by tern, albatross
and mollymawk. Two—Chatham and Pitt—are inhabited by a
scattering of farmers and fishermen and their families, many of
mixed Maori-European blood.

Amiable, reflective Neil Hutchison, 26, first began thinking about
the Chathams when he talked with another young doctor who had
served there. The Chathams, he said, made medicine—even daily
living—an adventure. Neil liked the sound of that and surprised everyone by applying to work as general practitioner to the Chatham
Islanders for the two years of government service he had agreed to
give in return for his Health Department scholarship.

In January 1975, when a Bristol air freighter dumped Hutchison, his wife, Lynne, and their two children on Chatham's grass landing strip, Neil wondered whether he'd done the right thing. The sky was overcast and the wind was cold. The welcoming party wore parkas and Wellington boots and drove four-wheel-drive vehicles. Neil and Lynne soon saw why, as they bumped forty miles over the island's untarred road to the settlement at Waitangi.

Until then, Neil had practiced medicine only as an intern, working under senior colleagues. Now, he was in sole charge of the health of 650 Chatham Islanders. Waitangi had a four-bed cottage hospital, a tiny operating room and three missionary nuns who served as nurses. Specialists, second opinions and experienced surgeons were a three-hour flight away; night landings were always impossible and bad weather often halted *all* air traffic. In a crisis Neil would have only the radio-telephone as support.

The minor ailments of the islanders set Neil working almost within hours of his arrival. Five times a week, he conducted office hours from ten a.m. to one p.m. For the first time since his marriage, he had free time to spend with his wife and children. In addition to beachcombing among seabirds, seals and sea lions—always a popular family activity—he hunted duck and swan in the swamps; dived for crayfish and perlemoen.

More and more, Neil came to relish the challenges of a doctor working alone. He stitched wounds, delivered babies, set broken limbs, dispensed medicine and at times was also dentist, physiotherapist and social worker. He was grateful he hadn't been obliged to confront the greater mysteries of surgery, not even a caesarian. Serious surgical cases were flown to the mainland; only three times—to remove appendixes—did Neil have to use the operating room for its true purpose. Twice, tragedy struck: A man was killed in an automobile accident and a baby died on tiny Pitt Island when high seas prevented Neil from getting there. So, for the most part, he and his family lived something of an idyll until nearly the end of his service.

October 22, 1976, was one of the loveliest days the Hutchisons had known. Finished with patients by one p.m., Neil was assembling his fishing gear when the telephone rang. It was Marie Prescott phoning from the remote century-old Waitangi West farm where she lived with her husband, Alby, and their lively young sons, Brent and Shane.

Seven-year-old Shane had been swinging on the arm of a tractor trailer when it tipped over and crushed his head. He was bleeding badly and losing consciousness. Alby was out fishing, and Marie had no transportation. The barely negotiable thirty-mile road between their farmhouse and Waitangi meant a rugged three-hour journey there and back.

"I'm coming," Neil said.

An hour out from Waitangi, Neil and Sister Falole, one of his nurses, met a Prescott neighbor driving over the primitive track like a man possessed. Marie had found him after speaking to Neil, and to save precious time they had set out for the hospital. Shane was unconscious and vomiting violently.

Neil and Marie transferred the boy to his Landcruiser and turned back toward the hospital. He drove carefully, but it was impossible to control the jolt and sway of the vehicle on the rough road.

The Waitangi hospital's X-ray machine was in New Zealand for repairs, but Neil didn't need it to see that Shane was in a bad way. There was obviously bleeding inside his fractured skull—and clotting could fatally compress his brain.

There were not enough daylight hours left to fly in a specialist from the mainland, so Neil radio-telephoned Wellington hospital and described Shane's condition to neurosurgeon Graham Martin. Martin was less than encouraging.

"Even if I could get there tonight," he said, "it would be too late. You'll have to operate. Get at that clot, ease the pressure on the brain, stop the bleeding—or watch that boy die. Ever done anything like this before?"

"No," said Neil. "I've never even seen a brain operation."

"Have you got the right instruments?" he asked.

"I don't know," Neil said. When he had first looked over the hospital's surgical tools, many had been unfamiliar.

First, Martin told him, he would need something with which to drill a hole in Shane's skull. Neil sorted through the instruments and found one shaped like a carpenter's drill with a sharp thistle on the end: a bone corer.

"That'll do," said Martin. Then, in a quiet and reassuring voice, the distant surgeon in New Zealand told Neil how to perform an operation he had never so much as glimpsed.

There was much to organize. Chatham constable Lorne Fell rounded up people with Shane's blood type and Neil extracted six units of blood from them. Neil would have to be his own anesthetist, with help from Fell and two of the nursing nuns. He had to set up the oxygen; the nurses sterilized the instruments and shaved Shane's head. The radio-telephone link with Wellington had to be kept clear, possibly all night.

Around 5:45 p.m., Neil observed that the pupil of Shane's left eye had enlarged perceptibly, a sign of increased brain compression. Neil gave the unconscious boy a sedative injection and a local anesthetic for his head. A breathing tube was slid down Shane's trachea; he rested on his right side, his head sterilized and draped with sterile cloths.

Scrubbed up and gowned, Neil realized that there were many simple questions he had not asked Graham Martin, such as precisely *where* to make the first incision without severing an artery or nerve. Now he was on his own—with only his instincts, prayers and now-vague anatomy lectures.

He did no damage making an incision a little over an inch wide into the back of Shane's head, but he didn't locate any bleeding or clotting between the skull and the fibrous layer that covers the brain. A small hole in the fibrous layer still did not disclose any bleeding. He would have to phone again. "Try a hole in the left front of the head," encouraged Martin. "That's where the bleeding and pressure on the brain must be."

Back in the operating room, Neil made a smaller incision into Shane's skull—and there, to his relief, was the clot that was crushing the little boy's brain. After it was suctioned away, a transfusion was necessary.

With the pressure on his brain released, Shane suddenly woke and began thrashing about violently. He tore the breathing tube from his trachea and kicked the sterile cloths to the floor. The nurses and the policeman had trouble holding him. His head, with two open wounds, banged against the operating table. Luckily, he did not lose his blood drip, and Neil used it to give more tranquilizing drugs to him. They soon calmed the boy, but he remained restless.

It was still necessary to locate the source of the bleeding. The shaken doctor began again, chipping into Shane's skull, enlarging the second hole to a width of about two and a half inches above and in front of the boy's ear. Finally, he reported to Martin: "I just can't find it."

Martin was consoling. "Never mind," he said. "Start packing cotton wool into the hole." It was a slow, delicate business, wedging small, damp balls of sterile cotton within Shane's skull. When it was accomplished, a small suction machine was applied to the cotton wool to draw the excess blood through. Then once again, the tired doctor tramped down the corridor to consult on the telephone.

"You've done all you can," said Martin. "Close the openings; leave the cotton wool with a small wick to the outside so the blood can find a way out."

This accomplished, forty slow stitches closed up the holes in the boy's head.

Neil had lost track of time. He thought he had been operating for two hours. In fact, it had been six; it was midnight. Shane was still unconscious when he was wheeled back to the ward. Neil could look up at last and thank Lorne Fell, Sister Falole and Sister Charlene; their eyes were as red and tired as his. After he had stripped off his bloodstained gown, he told the nurses to prepare the operating room for a possible second operation when Graham Martin arrived in the morning. Then he started the long night watch with Marie Prescott.

At 8:30 a.m., as they sat glassy-eyed beside the little boy's bed, Shane opened his eyes and sat up. They both looked at him with astonishment.

"Does your head hurt?" asked Neil.

"No," Shane replied—and went quietly back to sleep.

Soon after, Martin arrived to perform the second operation. He examined Shane, then said, "It seems you've stopped the bleeding. Another operation here won't be necessary. We can fly the boy to Wellington." While Shane was being prepared for the flight Martin said, "Oh, by the way, Neil, I have brought you a present—my book on head injuries in general surgery."

"Thanks," said Neil hazily. "I'll read it."

Shane Prescott recovered rapidly in Wellington Hospital, was sent home thirteen days after the accident and was soon leading a full and active life.

Trapped in the mud of the river bottom,
with a 500-ton barge above him
—and the tide moving out

Buried
Alive

BY JOSEPH S. KARNEKE
Master Diver, U.S. Navy, as told to Victor Boesen

IT STILL CHILLS ME to recall the nightmare events of that hour so
many years ago. Yet I felt no foreboding as I sat on the diving stool
on that gray autumn afternoon in 1940. I was preparing to dive
from a Navy barge tied up in the Anacostia River near the Navy's
underwater sound laboratories in Washington, D.C. It was a routine
operation.

Extending down through the 500-ton barge were three wells, each
three feet in diameter, in which the Navy tested its sonar equipment.
After each test it was necessary to empty the wells of water so that
the next underwater-listening devices could be installed. The usual
procedure was to seal the wells from the bottom, then pump them
dry. On this occasion the laboratories wanted the after well sealed.

Our crew from the Navy's Deep Sea Diving School began the job
with the self-assurance of old hands. We had all trained in these wa-

ters, and I had made some thirty dives in the area. We dived in rotation, and it was now my turn to go down.

The chief gave me his final instructions, then closed the faceplate in my helmet. The crew slid me feet first into the middle well, and in a moment I was on the uneven river bottom, scrunched down in the two-and-a-half-foot space between it and the underside of the barge. Using a seam in the barge's steel plates to guide me, I dug my feet into the mud and propelled myself backward, squidlike, to the well I was to close.

Crouched below it, I could feel the soft mud beneath me, studded with rock and pieces of scrap iron. Above me a dull halo of light showed through the murky water in the well. Out to the sides all was blackness. I felt out the cover plate at the side of the opening, unbolted it and swung it under the hole. This blacked out my last bond with the daylight world above. Working by touch, I began taking bolts one by one from my tool bag and putting them in place over my head.

The work went smoothly. The water buoyed up my arms, and as I leaned back a little each time I reached up I felt a support behind me that I thought was my combination lifeline and air hose. Loyd Skill, my telephone man, heckled me reassuringly from above.

The phone man is the most important member of the crew topside. He listens constantly to the sound of the air going into the diver's helmet and to his breathing. "How're you doing?" Skill would say every few moments to relieve that feeling of isolation a diver gets.

I told of my progress. "Ten more bolts to go," I said at one point.

"Well, speed it up," Skill answered, keeping the conversation going.

All at once I noticed that the barge was no longer at arm's length above my head but directly over my face. I ran my hand along the bottom. It was only inches away! I was flat on my back! Without realizing it I had kept leaning farther and farther back until I was now stretched out like a man working under a car.

"Hey, this barge is sinking!" I yelled.

Skill said, "Nah, everything's all right up here, Karneke."

"Get me out of here!" I yelled again. "The barge is sinking!"

There was a pause. Then Skill said tightly, "Be calm now. You're in a shallow spot. The barge isn't sinking—*but the tide's going out.*"

Now I remembered. We were such old hands at these routine jobs that we hadn't bothered to check the tide before I went down. The support that I had felt behind me as I worked was not my lifeline but the surge of the outgoing current.

"We're going to pull you up," Skill said. I felt the lifeline tug at my breastplate. "Can you feel us pulling?" he asked.

"Yes, but I'm not moving."

"You sure?" Sometimes when it's too dark to see and the movement is slow a diver can't tell.

But I could tell. By now the 500-ton barge was beginning to rest on my helmet and breastplate, pinning me against the river bottom. "Not an inch," I said.

"We can't pull any more," Skill said. "We're afraid we'll part the lifeline."

That shook me. The lifeline could take a pull of 2,600 pounds. I was in real trouble.

"What are you going to do?" I asked.

A minute or so passed. Evidently a plan was being discussed by the crew. Then Skill said, "The chief wants to know if you'll be all right if we move the barge."

I spread my arms—the only thing I could move now—and felt the bottom. "No, don't move the barge," I said. "Too many rocks. They'll grind me up." But maybe I had made a bad decision, for the 500 tons were pressing down harder by the moment.

"You'd better do something fast," I said. "This barge isn't getting any lighter."

"Take it easy," Skill called. "We're going to try to wash you out with the tunneling hose." (This is a tool that shoots a jet of water through a nozzle at very high pressure.) "The standby diver will come in with the nozzle from the side."

I started figuring. The barge was forty feet wide; a tunnel to where I lay under the middle would have to be twenty feet long. The job could hardly be done in less than an hour. Meanwhile, the tide would not be waiting.

I would have a lot of ways to die. If my helmet and breastplate collapsed, I would be crushed and drowned at a stroke. My air hose could be pinched against a rock, causing my suit to fill with carbon dioxide from my breath as the oxygen was used up. Even if neither of these things happened, the tunneler could easily miss me in this darkness.

Suddenly I had an idea. "Hey, Skill," I said, "how about tying the tunneling hose to my lifeline, dropping the nozzle down the middle well and letting me pull it toward me?" That way the nozzle could not go astray, and the distance to be dug would be shorter.

Skill passed along this suggestion topside. "The chief thinks that's a good idea," he said. "We'll let you know when to start pulling."

As I lay waiting in my world of darkness, sinking deeper into the mire under the weight of the barge, there was a strangling sound like a death rattle at my exhaust valve. The vent at the side of my helmet was being choked off by mud. To give the exhaust air another way to get out, I reached for the hand-operated spit cock at the lower left side of my helmet. It was jammed hard against the underside of the barge, its handle immovable.

The specter of death by asphyxiation came closer. So did death of another kind: My breastplate was beginning to sag against my chest. Surely, at any moment it must collapse like an eggshell. Icy sweat rolled into my eyes.

"Stand by," Skill called at last. "We're dropping the nozzle in the hole with full pressure. Start pulling."

This was the final bid for life. I pulled. Nothing moved. "I can't get any slack," I said.

"The line is probably pinched under the edge of the well," Skill answered. "We'll try to wash some of the mud away by swishing the nozzle around."

Suddenly the line gave. "It's moving!" I cried. Its progress was by inches, but after what seemed forever I heard pebbles bouncing off my helmet and felt them pelting my bare hands. Then I gave a final heave and the nozzle burst through at my feet, wrapping me in a storm of swirling water, mud and stones.

I groped through the boiling darkness and grabbed the nozzle. "I've got it," I yelled. "I'm going to try to blast myself loose."

"Easy now," Skill called back. "Untie the nozzle from the lifeline." This was necessary so that the crew could take up the now slack lifeline before it fouled on the rocks and debris.

I clawed at the rope that bound the nozzle to the lifeline. "It's too tight," I said.

"Can you cut it?" Skill asked.

"If I can reach my knife." By twisting my body and digging rocks out of the way with an elbow I managed to get my hand to the sheath on my belt. "I've got it," I said as I drew the blade out and began cutting.

"Be careful," Skill cautioned again. "Don't cut your lifeline!"

His warning came just in time. In my excitement I might easily have made the knife the means of my own execution. I forced myself to slow down.

"Okay," I called when I had finished. "Take up the lifeline."

As the line began snaking away, I directed the tornado spewing from the nozzle toward my underside. Deliciously, I sank away from the bottom of the barge. Then the lifeline went taut and I felt myself sliding through the mud.

"I'm *moving!*" I shouted. "Keep pulling."

I slid rapidly feet first along the trench blasted out by the nozzle, moving toward the center well and its promise of freedom. It was still only a promise, however, for the rocks in the trench banged against my helmet and raked at my suit as I passed. If they tore through my suit, I would drown.

Presently Skill said, "All right, Karneke, we can feel your feet. We're going to pull you up."

One of the crew had come down into the well to guide me home. He seized my feet and directed them upward. Other hands grabbed them from above, and soon I stood on the deck, helmet off, squinting in the light.

The chief eyed me up and down and bellowed with mock rage, "Dammit, Karneke, how many times I gotta tell you I don't want you coming up feet first?"

I grinned and looked around at the day, still as overcast as when I went down, and marveled at how bright it was.

For two terrible hours,
Jim Obenauf risked his life to save a crewmate
—one of the jet age's most heroic rescue feats

The Man in
the Burning Bomber

BY JOHN G. HUBBELL

IN THE FREEZING midnight skies above northern Texas and Oklahoma, 1st Lt. James E. Obenauf, a twenty-three-year-old Strategic Air Command copilot from Grayslake, Illinois, faced an agonizing decision. Should he save his own life or try—alone and against staggering odds—to wrestle with a flaming B-47 jet bomber for 400 miles to save the life of an injured crewmate?

Jim Obenauf took the job, and then for two hours and ten minutes on the night of April 28, 1957, he proceeded to carry out one of the most amazing rescue feats in Air Force history.

Jet bomber 2278, carrying four men, had left the Strategic Air Command's Dyess Air Force Base, Abilene, Texas, at 7:55 p.m. and climbed to 34,000 feet. The mission: to practice celestial navigation and evaluate the technique of the navigator, Lt. John P. Cobb, on a simulated bombing mission over Amarillo, Texas, and Denver, Colorado.

In his seat in the nose of the B-47 Cobb worked with methodical precision. From a folding chair behind Cobb's left shoulder Maj. Joseph B. Maxwell, a senior navigator, observed and graded Cobb's performance. At 10:05 p.m. Cobb had finished the simulated strike on Amarillo and had just given the pilot a heading for Denver, when a series of rumbling, metallic explosions shuddered through the plane.

Up in the cockpit the airplane commander, Maj. James M. Graves, saw fire flickering beneath his left wing, close to the fuselage. The engine must have exploded from oil starvation, he figured. At any second, it would begin flinging its turbine blades like sharp, hot bullets into the fuselage fuel tanks. Certain that they were riding a 200-ton burning bomb he had to get his crew out—*now!*

"Bail out! Bail out!" he ordered.

Cobb swiveled his ejection seat and saw Joe Maxwell pulling on his parachute, which he had removed to get close enough to watch Cobb's work. Reaching to the floor, Cobb pulled a steel column with a D-ring handle up between his knees, braced himself and yanked at the D-ring. A 37-mm charge fired him downward safely out of the bomber.

In that same instant, frigid wind blasted through the open hatch, ripped off Maxwell's oxygen mask, tore off his parachute and knocked him sprawling to the end of a narrow catwalk along the left side of the bomber. As he lay there unconscious, the wind drove loose debris along the catwalk until it nearly covered him.

Meanwhile, copilot Obenauf blew off the long Plexiglas canopy that covered both his cockpit and Graves's. Then pilot Jim Graves tightened his harness and squeezed his ejection trigger. Nothing happened. Again and again Graves pumped at the trigger. The seat would not blow.

No time to fool with it. The two navigators and his copilot were gone by now, he assumed. He had to get out. He dared not go over the side because the knifelike vertical stabilizer might cut him in half. So he ripped his seat harness loose, broke his oxygen connection and struggled down a narrow ladder to the catwalk that led to the navigator's escape hatch. Suddenly he began feeling the effects of anoxia—oxygen starvation: His brain went hazy; his vision blurred. Then he looked back along the catwalk and saw Jim Obenauf climbing down from his cockpit in the rear.

Graves knew he was passing out and he wanted to get out of Obenauf's way, so he groped along the catwalk and dived through the open hatch. A second later Graves was hanging safely in his chute.

Jim Obenauf had gone through the same bail-out procedure and had met the same trouble: His ejection seat would not fire. He had unhooked his oxygen and climbed down the ladder. As he turned to go forward, Obenauf saw something in the rubbish that looked like a leg. He kicked the debris away and went numb with horror at the sight—Joe Maxwell lying unconscious with no oxygen, no parachute. One thing seemed certain: Within five minutes Maxwell would be dead, either from lack of oxygen or from the effects of a midair explosion or a crash.

Obenauf crawled along the pitch-black catwalk, feeling for Maxwell's parachute. He *had* to find it, get Joe into it and throw him out of the plane, *quickly!* Then the cold, opaque fog of anoxia began wrapping itself around him. He grew weak. It was no use. He stood up, peered at Maxwell. He knew no pilot would blame him for leaving now. There wasn't a chance of saving Maxwell; no sense in both of them dying.

Suddenly Obenauf knew what he had to do: On the sheer strength of his will he crawled back into his cockpit. *I can't leave old Max up here!*

He threw himself into the seat, hoping to God it wouldn't eject him. He hooked his mask to the oxygen supply system and looked out. His right wing was now bathed in sparks and sheets of white flame. The right outboard engine had exploded, not the left inboard as they had thought.

Obenauf knocked the airplane off autopilot. He had to get down to low altitude in a hurry. Maxwell's only chance was to breathe the oxygen in a denser atmosphere. Obenauf grabbed his steering column. It was locked, and there was no way to free it once the ejection procedure had been started. It took a sixty-pound pull to overpower the lock and move the control column. But Obenauf made it move.

He peeled the B-47 into a screaming dive. He knew he was making the plane approach its structural limitations, that it might fall apart. But Joe Maxwell was dying.

It was about thirty-two degrees below zero at 34,000 feet, where Obenauf started his dive, and with the cockpit canopy gone, the shrieking 400-knot wind cut deep into his face. It peeled back his eyelids, would not let him blink, dried out his eyes and made them burn until he thought he could stand it no longer. But still he kept diving.

He cut the fuel flow to the crippled engine. At 5,500 feet he leveled the bomber off and switched his radio to Guard Channel, the emergency channel monitored by all ground stations and military aircraft. "This is Air Force jet two-two-seven-eight," he reported. *"Mayday! Mayday! Mayday!"* Instantly, Altus Air Force Base, Altus, Oklahoma, 200 miles away, put a direction finder on Obenauf's voice and gave him a compass heading that would steer him there.

Obenauf's plane had recently been based on Guam, where sand had collected inside it. Now this sand was whipping through the open cockpit, stinging his eyes so he could hardly read his instruments. But somehow he managed to turn the plane until its heading was approximately right. Next Obenauf found a speed where the windblast was less painful: 200 knots. It wasn't good, but he could stand it.

The flames seemed to have died away, but bursts of white sparks still streamed from the engine. He heard a radio voice pleading for him to land at Altus. "Negative!" Obenauf shot back. He was not going to try landing on an unfamiliar field. He would gamble on another 150 miles for a shot at his home field. "I'm going to Dyess! Give me a heading."

Mile by mile, Jim Obenauf fought to keep his crippled bomber on the course for Abilene. A Ground Controlled Intercept station of the Air Defense Command picked him up on its radar and guided him toward the airfield.

When he got near Dyess, visibility was a satisfactory five miles, but with that searing wind, visibility didn't mean much to Obenauf. He could not, however, get down without landing lights—and the switch was on the pilot's control panel in the other cockpit up forward!

Suddenly Obenauf felt something grab his leg and shake it. He looked down. Maxwell, too weak to talk, was on his feet.

As a navigator Maxwell wouldn't know much about the pilot's control panel. But Obenauf needed those lights. Through the intercom he shouted instructions at Maxwell, who staggered forward and pulled himself up the ladder into the pilot's cockpit. The effort was so exhausting that he slumped across the deck, struggling for breath. Except for a few dim glows on the control panel, the cockpit was black as night. He could not find the right switch. He did not dare experiment. Slowly, he made his way back to Obenauf and shook his head helplessly. Obenauf shouted that he *must* have landing lights.

Again, Maxwell made his way into the pilot's cockpit. He lay there in the dark, hoping his eyes would get used to it. But after what seemed a long time he gave up. He climbed down to the catwalk, could go no farther and had to lie down.

Obenauf swore loudly, hoping to shock Maxwell to his feet. Finally the navigator got up. Obenauf remembered a flashlight in his flying suit, handed it to him and shouted the instructions once more. Maxwell went forward, found the switch—and the landing lights went on.

A Ground Controlled Approach operator in a van near the end of the Dyess runway picked Obenauf up on his radar and began talking. Now, all Obenauf had to do was watch his instruments, listen and follow directions. But his instrument panel was a dull blur, and his hands, numb to the elbows now, responded sluggishly. He drifted two degrees off course to the right, then to the left, trying with all his strength to hold the failing bomber where GCA said.

Maj. Doyle Reynolds, chief of flying training at Dyess, sat in a cold sweat in the Dyess tower, watching Obenauf come in. "You're doing fine, Obie," Reynolds said calmly. Obenauf sighed with relief at the sound of Reynolds's voice. If anyone could get him down it would be Reynolds. He had once been Obenauf's instructor and was one of SAC's best.

"Give me your fuel panel configuration," Reynolds said. If he knew what fuel tanks Obenauf had been using, he could figure out where the bomber's center of gravity was; if it had shifted too far back Obenauf might crash.

"I can hardly read it," Obenauf said. "I think I'm going blind." He managed to give Reynolds the fuel readings, then started easing the plane down. It was like walking down strange stairs in the dark. He brought it down a little, leveled it off, then inched it down a little more. Then suddenly he was too high, much too far to the right, and too close to the field to make a major correction.

"Go around! Go around!" barked GCA. But Obenauf kept on coming. He did not have enough life left to try again. He was going down now, to live or die.

There were thirty B-47's tied down beside the runway. Obenauf was headed straight for them.

"It would be better if you could move to the left a little," said Doyle Reynolds calmly.

Obenauf leaned heavily on the control column. The big plane veered sharply. He saw the glow of the lights along both sides of the runway, steered the bomber between them and flew it to the ground.

It was the best landing Obenauf ever made. He chopped his power, worked the foot brakes and hit the lever that dropped a parachute brake. The bomber rolled to a stop.

Joe Maxwell worked feebly at the exit hatch below. Obenauf scrambled down from his cockpit, ripped the hatch open and dropped to the ground. A minute later he was stone-blind. Behind him Maxwell staggered down the ladder into the arms of ambulance attendants.

Obenauf's vision returned after a few hours of rest. By the next day he and Maxwell were able to leave the hospital. They were driven to the Dyess Base Theater, where 800 Air Force men and their families had gathered. Among them was Gen. Thomas S. Power, commander of SAC, who had flown down from his Omaha base after listening in on the tense radio interchange between Obenauf and the men at Dyess.

"Obenauf, in German, means topmost—the best," said General Power. "He's certainly tops in my book, and as long as SAC has men like Lieutenant Obenauf manning its aircraft it will sustain its deterrent posture." Then he pinned the Distinguished Flying Cross on Jim Obenauf's chest.

While a horrified crowd
on the subway platform watched,
the train thundered toward the child.
Could anyone reach her in time?

"There's a Girl on the Tracks!"

BY WARREN R. YOUNG

IT WAS A MOMENT FROZEN in time by terror. Nearly one hundred people waiting on the subway platform at New York City's 86th Street and Lexington Avenue station stood transfixed. A few screamed, but they could barely be heard. For, thundering into the station at thirty miles an hour was a heavily laden rush-hour train—a million pounds of screeching stainless-steel and fateful momentum. And in its path, the onlookers could see a young man, his face pale with concentration, trying to jump up from the tracks four feet below.

With terrible certainty, they could see that he was not likely to make it. The train was hurtling toward him, ponderously swaying within an inch or two of the metal-capped edge of the platform, like a gargantuan sausage slicer. The man's first jump carried him only high enough for his chest to strike the edge of the platform, and he fell back to the track.

Now the train was merely feet away. He gathered himself for one last desperate attempt. Then he felt himself rising, and it seemed just possible after all that at least his torso might get clear. But the last thought he had before the train reached the spot was *There go my legs!*

Less than two minutes earlier, thirty-four-year-old Everett Sanderson, an unemployed musician, had been on his way home after visiting his mother. It was 5:10 p.m., January 16, 1975, and around him swirled the normal evening bustle, as people hurried down from the city's streets or up the stairs from the express train level below. About every two and a half minutes, at this time of day, another local train came through, and one of them had left half a minute before.

At this moment, chance was guiding several strangers—and one particular train—on a path that would soon converge with Everett's. Changing from an express to a local was twenty-year-old Miguel Maisonett, a slender black youth. Miguel was deep in thought about his future. He had just collected his final paycheck as a city health-department rat inspector; his job had been eliminated because of spending cutbacks. Ever since he was fifteen, when he had dropped out of school to support himself and his younger brother (who had continued through high school and was now in college), Miguel had managed; but now jobs were scarce.

Approaching the stairs leading up to the same uptown local platform was transit patrolman Rex Johnson, on his beat. Coming through the turnstile was Mrs. Joanna DeJesus, whose right eye was bandaged from a recent operation. With her were her four-year-old daughter, Michelle, and Margarita Esquilin, Mrs. DeJesus's sister.

Half a mile to the south at 77th Street, in the front cab of his train, sixty-year-old motorman Daniel Miller had just released the brake in response to a green "all-clear-ahead" signal light. Now he swung the master control handle to the "power" position, sending 600 volts of direct current into the forty electric motors that were hooked to the train's forty axles. The seventy-second run through the tunnel to 86th Street had begun.

The DeJesus trio moved through the thickening crowd and stopped about two feet from the bright yellow stripe painted along the platform's steel-capped edge. Just then, Michelle wriggled her hand free from her mother's, hopped toward the edge to look for the train—and slipped and fell onto the tracks. The screams and shouts for help began: "There's a girl on the tracks!" "Somebody get her!" "Save her!" All Mrs. DeJesus could see was the bright red coat and motionless form of her child, face down on the wooden ties with her feet across the nearest rail.

Everett and Miguel, eighty-five feet apart, each stepped to the platform's edge to see what had happened. Everett was about thirty-five feet uptown from the center of the commotion, Miguel fifty feet below. Both could see the helpless figure on the tracks. And both expected somebody in the crowd to jump down and pick up the stunned child.

Fifteen seconds passed. The crowd felt a gush of wind caused by the oncoming train, then heard the first distant grumble as it barreled through the rock-walled tunnel toward them. Down on the tracks, Michelle began to rouse. Her eyes tightly closed, she cried, "Mommy! Mommy!"

The shouts for somebody to save the little girl kept up, but nobody moved. Ten more seconds ticked by—it was almost half a minute since the fall. Then Everett, whose own son was in the custody of his ex-wife, asked himself, "What if it was *my* child down there?" His response was both gallant and foolhardy; he jumped down to the tracks and started running.

Years ago, as an Ohio schoolboy, Everett had played football and basketball and once, at a track meet, had carried off all the awards. But he had never run in conditions like these, dressed in a heavy jacket, down in the trough of a subway—and with a little girl's life at stake.

On the other side of the crowd, Miguel, too, had decided to try to save the girl. Unlike Everett, however, he was thoroughly familiar with the tracks, for as a boy he and his friends, in a daredevil game, used to jump down and run across them between trains. Now, he leaped down and began sprinting.

By the time Miguel had run ten feet, he could hear the sound of the train swelling hugely in the tunnel behind him. He knew that it would reach the station in seconds. But then he saw the other man running toward him, closer to Michelle and with a better chance of reaching her. With an easy vault perfected in the games of his boyhood, Miguel swung his body up onto the platform.

By this time, Officer Johnson was up the stairs and aware of the desperate situation. He knew there was no way to cut off the power from the station, nor any fast way for him to contact the train to stop it. Headlight flashes flickered in the dark tunnel, and the noise level rose. Facing the unseen train and waving his flashlight from side to side, as regulations prescribed for an emergency, the six-foot-three-inch, 200-pound officer began running backward, shouting, "Stand clear! Get back, everybody!" The train would arrive at the station in about ten seconds.

Motorman Miller, at this point, had been pouring power into the 4,000-horsepower electric motors to carry the train up and over a steep little slope in front of the 86th Street station. Because of this incline, Miller could neither see Officer Johnson's warning flashlight nor yet peer into the station to spot any trouble. Near the station entrance, he cut off the power. Normally, the train would be allowed to coast far into the station, then gradually be braked.

Miller's twenty-five years of bringing subway trains into stations had taught him never to be surprised to see objects in his train's path. Usually, they were unimportant. Newspapers blowing along the rails were commonplace. Once in a while, however, an "object" might be human—two or three suicides had jumped to their deaths under his wheels, waiting until the last instant when he could do nothing. And, once, a drunk on the tracks was saved by Miller's quick stop. So now, as always, his right hand was firmly wrapped around the brake lever.

Everett was so busy running that he never saw Miguel hop down and back up, nor did he notice Officer Johnson waving his light. All his thoughts were focused on the girl. She was still twenty feet away when he suddenly felt the asphalt tremble. Two brilliant headlights glared in his eyes as the front of the train, twelve feet tall and nine feet wide, abruptly filled the mouth of the tunnel.

The 240 feet now separating the train from little Michelle looked like far less to Everett as the monster rumbled toward him still going almost thirty miles an hour, or forty-four feet every second. Everett could see the motorman, his expressionless face giving no sign that he saw anybody on the track, looking even more remote because he was so far up—his feet, like those of the people on the platform, were about at Everett's eye level. Everett kept running.

Sometime during the first two seconds after the train entered the station, Motorman Miller spotted the child and the man down on the tracks. He slammed the brake handle into "emergency stop," locking all the train's wheels. Sparks flew like fireworks as they skidded, grinding metal against the rails with a tortured screech. The train slowed immediately, but it would still pass the spot where Michelle lay in only five seconds!

Everett was only a step from Michelle. In the train cab, motorman Miller silently prayed, *Oh, God, I hope I don't hit them!* On the platform, Miguel was also in the path of the train, kneeling and leaning over the edge toward Everett with outstretched arms. With three seconds to go, Everett seized Michelle in his right hand and, possessed of a strength he never knew he had, he hurled her into Miguel's waiting arms. The impact knocked Miguel onto his back, with the child sprawled on his chest, safe at last.

For the first time, Everett recognized his own predicament. The train's speed had by this time been cut in half—to sixteen miles an hour, or some twenty-four feet per second—but it was forty feet away. There were two seconds to go.

Everett placed his hands on the edge of the platform, jumped for his life—and failed. By now, there was a single second left before the train would pass the spot where he was. Everett got ready for one last, desperate jump. Then, with the train so close that its mammoth bulk seemed to be virtually on top of him, he felt himself rising like an elevator. Hands belonging to Officer Johnson, Michelle's Aunt Margarita and Miguel were lifting him by the jacket and his arms. Everett hoped that his torso would clear the train, but he felt sure his legs would be amputated.

As the train passed, motorman Miller lost sight of Everett. With a sinking feeling, he thought the first car must have caught Everett's legs and pulled him under. But he was puzzled by the absence of the familiar, sickening *thud* he had always heard when a train passed over the body of a suicide. For more than three seconds, the train kept skidding. Finally, it stopped, twenty-six feet beyond where Everett and Michelle had been. Miller stepped out on the platform to see what had happened.

A pile of human figures on the platform were struggling to their feet. The three rescuers had tugged so mightily on Everett that some of them fell—with Everett, unharmed, landing among them. (Later, he would find a mark made by the train on the edge of his right shoe.)

For the next few minutes, while motorman Miller and Officer Johnson made sure of the happy outcome, the crowd patted Everett on the back and kept telling him he was a hero. At last, everyone was able to go about his business—Miguel went home in a taxi, Mrs. DeJesus took another cab to a hospital to make sure Michelle was not really hurt, Officer Johnson resumed his beat, and motorman Miller announced that the train would continue its regular run. Everett Sanderson decided to take the train, too, and rode it to his regular stop.

The grateful New York Transit Authority presented Everett and Miguel with medals for civilian heroism, plus a five-year pass for free subway travel for Miguel and a lifetime pass for Everett. In addition, Everett was presented with the prestigious bronze lifesaving medal of the Carnegie Hero Fund Commission and a one-thousand-dollar check.

"I don't know whether this has changed my life," said Everett. "I know it almost ended it. But if I hadn't tried to save that little girl, if I had just stood there like the others, I would have died inside. I would have been no good to myself from then on."

For the young family,
the steps toward disaster were simple enough:
a Saturday outing, a sudden snowstorm,
a missed detour . . .

"What a Crazy Way for Life to End!"

BY TED MORGAN

IN HIS ROOM AT Willamette Falls Community Hospital, Scott McIntire finished five colored-pencil drawings of his frostbitten toes. Soon after, parts of all ten toes were amputated. The drawings were emblems of loss, not only of his toes, but of innocence, an awareness gained at great cost that a man who has done nothing to deserve it can be struck down, and that what we most cherish can turn against us.

Scott McIntire had married Diane Strom in May 1972. Their wedding was held in the Pittock Bird Sanctuary above downtown Portland, Oregon, because the couple shared a love of nature.

When Diane became pregnant, they attended natural-childbirth classes, and Scott was at Diane's side when Emily was born on June 15, 1973.

The first weekend in November, when Emily was four and a half months old, Scott was planning to work at the advertising agency where he was art director. But when he heard on the Saturday morning news that Sunday would be stormy, and when he looked out the window and saw that it was fine and clear, he and Diane decided to head for the hills.

They thought of a place where neither had been, Bagby Hot Springs, about fifty miles southeast of Portland. The water bubbles out of the rock at 137° F., and a trough feeds it into cedar bath stalls with tubs hollowed from big logs. They planned to be back by nightfall.

Thinking that it might get cold, Scott wore a wool shirt and a windbreaker. Diane put on a raincoat over her wool pants, sweater and leather jacket, and Emily was bundled into a fur-lined snowsuit. They took a camera, a blanket, a diaper bag, two pastrami sandwiches, an apple, and a Thermos of hot chocolate. Emily's diet was no problem: Diane was nursing her.

The family left Portland at 12:30 p.m. in their 1966 station wagon. Eight miles past the Ripplebrook ranger station, but still five miles from Bagby, the road was closed off, and a sign detoured them to the springs along a graveled service road.

Reaching Bagby, Scott parked the car, and they hiked a mile and a half uphill to the springs. It began to snow while they were bathing—large soft flakes falling in unhurried silence. It seemed to Scott a comforting sight.

On that same Saturday, Charles Mock, a twenty-three-year-old Forest Service employee, decided to go elk hunting in an area about forty-five miles north of Bagby in the Cascade Range. He packed some dried food, a sleeping bag, an aluminized space blanket, a tarp, an ax, a water bottle, a knife, matches and his rifle. He parked his pickup at the edge of Wahtum Lake and set out onto the forested slope. He was surprised when it began snowing in the afternoon, and immediately made camp.

By the time the McIntires were back at the parking lot, a foot of snow had fallen. "Let's get going," Scott told Diane. "I want to get past that detour before it gets dark." Scott followed the tracks of a

Volkswagen that had left a few minutes ahead of them. The detour sign was by this time covered with snow. Instead of the detour road that would have taken them to the ranger station, the VW, followed by Scott's station wagon, took a logging road that twisted through the forest for twenty miles.

The station wagon started skidding in the snow. Diane drove, and Scott spread the blanket under the rear wheels to give the car traction. It moved along by fits and starts. Scott placed the blanket, ran to catch up, then placed the blanket again. Eventually the car skidded into a ditch. It was now dark, and they realized that they would have to spend the night.

Awakening on Sunday morning, they saw that the car was buried under snow. Sunday was Diane's birthday. She was thirty-one years old. They remarked, half laughing and half worried, that it was some way to spend a birthday. They discussed whether they should wait in the car to be rescued or hike out in the knee-high snow. Scott was convinced that they could not be more than five miles from the ranger station. "We can make it with very little trouble," he told Diane. She agreed, and nursed Emily before leaving the car. Scott pushed through the snow, with Emily on his back. Diane followed.

They could not walk more than fifty feet without stopping to rest. At each turn of the winding road, they thought they would come within sight of the main road back to the ranger station, but instead saw another turn. About ten a.m., after two hours of walking, they stopped and Diane nursed Emily. Diane ate snow. She felt it was the only way to keep up her production of milk. (One sure way to lose body heat is to eat snow. It takes as much heat to turn one ounce of snow to water as it does to heat an ounce of soup at room temperature to boiling.)

Scott and Diane walked for two hours more, then stopped beside a tree, where Diane nursed Emily and ate more snow. She wanted to turn back. Scott was bent on reaching the ranger station. They had gone three miles, he claimed, and could have no more than two to go.

At about three that afternoon, they came to a fork in the road. Scott chose the downhill branch, but after 500 feet they were blocked by a snowbank. "We must have taken the wrong road," he told Diane. They headed back toward the fork. Diane was now walking listlessly, her bare hands dragging. "Where are your gloves?" Scott asked. "I don't know," Diane replied.

It was getting dark. Off the road, Scott spotted a log lying across a dip in the slope. "Let's spend the night here," he said. He shoveled snow out from under the log and they lay down under it with Emily between them. They took turns holding Emily. Diane nursed her. Scott fed snow to Diane. For the first time, they discussed the possibility that they might not get out alive. But Scott was still optimistic. Martha Forster, a friend who had given them directions to Bagby, knew where they were. There was probably a search party out for them already.

When Charles Mock woke up on Sunday morning, his tarp was sagging under the weight of snow. He broke camp, and then it took him six hours to hike the four miles back to his pickup. Unable to move the truck, he spent the rest of the day building a shelter, packing the snow down, setting up his tarp and gathering firewood. "I got myself squared away," he recalls.

Monday morning found Scott and Diane so weak they could barely move. They sat under the log and looked out at the white sky and the falling snow. Emily, like an alarm clock, regulated their dozing. She would start crying, and they would wake and Diane would nurse her. "I can't feed her as much," Diane said. And she ate more snow.

On Monday morning at 9:30, Mrs. Gordon Strom, Diane's mother, called her younger daughter, Susan, in Portland. "I can't seem to reach Scott or Diane," she said. "Something's wrong." Susan was staying with Martha Forster, who had given Scott directions to Bagby. "I bet they got stuck up there," Susan said. "I'll call the forest rangers."

Susan called the Estacada Forest Service immediately. She was told a Sno-Cat was already on its way to Bagby; several persons had been reported missing. "We'll call you when we get a report," the Forest Service said.

At three p.m., the Forest Service called Susan and told her that the Sno-Cat had reached the Bagby parking lot but that the McIntires' station wagon was not there. They advised her to call the Clackamas County sheriff's office. Susan talked to Sgt. Lloyd L. Ryan, who quickly organized a search party, using Ripplebrook ranger station as his base.

Sergeant Ryan called Susan back at five p.m. and told her they were going out that night with four Sno-Cats and ten snowmobiles. Ryan also contacted the Army National Guard in Salem, and Lt. Col. Gale Goyins said he would keep a Huey helicopter on standby, ready to fly as soon as the ceiling lifted.

Charles Mock, warmed by the fire he kept going, was busy all day on Monday. He cleaned the snow from his truck, so it could be seen from the air, and laid out his space blanket for the same reason. He knew he was about thirteen miles from the nearest town and figured he could make it out on snowshoes. He cut four fir saplings, six feet long, and began squaring them up with his ax. . . .

As the Monday hours slipped by, Scott and Diane took a hard look at their chances. "This is a crazy way for it to end," Diane said. Scott was increasingly alarmed by Diane's behavior. She no longer seemed to care about keeping herself warm. She became delirious, and snatched at Emily and Scott with stiff, bent fingers. When Scott tried to talk to her, she replied incoherently.

Scott awoke during the night. Diane lay with her eyes open. He felt her pulse. There was none. He tried to close her eyes. They stayed open. Scott thought: *I've got to hold on. I've got to feed Emily.* He melted snow in his mouth and fed Emily the water mouth-to-mouth. His feet felt like clubs. He tried not to think about Diane.

On Tuesday morning, the search continued. Volunteers, including two Explorer Scout units, came to the Ripplebrook ranger station and joined in the search. There were about a hundred persons involved. It was one of Oregon's biggest rescue operations in years. But they found nothing.

Charles Mock worked on his snowshoes throughout Tuesday, cutting grooves in the tips of the squared saplings and lashing the ends together with rope.

On Wednesday, it was warmer and the weather was clearing. At 1:10 p.m., a private helicopter hired by Scott's boss took off from the ranger station; meanwhile, the National Guard sent its Huey to join the search. Soon the private helicopter radioed the Huey: "We've spotted a rectangular lump in the snow that looks like a car," and gave the map coordinates. The National Guard helicopter found the spot and hovered close enough to verify that it was a car. Leading away from the car was a faint indentation in the snow that could have been a trail. The Huey followed the trail and came upon a log with an arm waving from under it.

Awakened by the sound of a helicopter, Scott began waving frantically. He struggled out from under the log, and by then several men were running toward him.

"I'm Scott McIntire," he told them. "My wife has been dead for two days. The baby is still alive."

"We've been looking for you," Sergeant Ryan said.

Scott entered the emergency room of the Willamette Falls Community Hospital at 3:40 p.m. His temperature was ninety-four degrees, and he was suffering from severe frostbite. Emily was in fine shape; all she had was a diaper rash. Had she been old enough to thaw out her own snow, doctors said, she probably would not have survived. Diane had died, Scott was informed, chiefly because she had eaten snow to nurse her baby. It was only the worst of several mistakes they had made.

On Wednesday morning, Charles Mock finished crafting his snowshoes, cooked and ate what remained of his food and started out. He was able to cover about one mile an hour, and by dark had reached his first road junction. He walked six more miles in the dark before coming to the first house in the village of Dee Flat. It was one a.m. on Thursday. From there he called the Hood River sheriff's office and was taken home.

Entombed in a minisub
at a depth from which no one
had ever been rescued before,
the two chill-racked men
could only wait—and hope

Nightmare
at 260 Fathoms

BY JOSEPH P. BLANK

AFTER ALL THEIR innumerable tests and speculations about emergencies at sea, the submarine pilots, engineers and executives of Vickers Oceanics had concluded that the odds against an accident like the one that occurred at 9:22 a.m. on Wednesday, August 29, 1973, were at least a million to one. And yet it happened.

Eight hours earlier that day, 150 miles southwest of Cork, Ireland, the twenty-foot-long minisub *Pisces III*, manned by pilots Roger

Mallinson, 35, and Roger Chapman, 28, had descended to the bottom of the Atlantic Ocean. Its mission was to bury part of a newly laid transatlantic telephone cable to prevent damage by deep-sea fishing trawls. Using a hydraulically pumped jet of water, the two men furrowed under the cable, which then dropped by its own weight into the trench.

Mallinson, an engineer, and Chapman, a former officer on a British nuclear submarine, made a compatible team. Working side by side in the sub's confined eighty-inch-diameter crew sphere never made them irritable or impatient with each other. They both had the ability to concentrate totally on the job. Mallinson, for instance, who couldn't swim, was hardly even aware of being in depths sometimes approaching half a mile. He used to say, "It is more like working on land and looking into an aquarium."

After trenching three quarters of a mile, Mallinson and Chapman reported by telephone to their support ship, the *Vickers Voyager,* that they were preparing for the thirty-minute ascent to the surface. When the *Pisces III* emerged, a diver in a Gemini (a motor-driven rubber boat) brought a towline to the submarine; then, when the connection was made, the *Voyager* began winching in the *Pisces,* which looked like a small whale on the end of a line.

Suddenly, the diver began to signal frantically. Somehow, incredibly, wave action had flipped the momentarily slack towline around the hatch lock on the sub's rear buoyancy sphere. The hatch pulled off, more than a ton of water poured into the sphere, and the *Pisces III* began to sink.

The sub dropped the length of the 175-foot towline and halted a few moments. Then the line, only one and a quarter inches in diameter and never intended to hold such a load, broke. The sub began its crash dive to the bottom of the sea.

Inside the *Pisces,* Mallinson and Chapman quickly stowed all equipment, turned off the power to eliminate the possibility of fire, placed cushions under their buttocks and curled up to protect themselves. Teeth clenched on rags to prevent tongue-biting, fists tight, they watched the depth gauge intently.

At 1,575 feet, the *Pisces III's* tail hit bottom—the collision was not as stunning as expected—and sank nearly a foot into mud. The two men waited silently for a few minutes, then passed a flashlight beam around the sub's interior. It appeared undamaged. Battery voltage, oxygen and lithium hydroxide, which removes poisonous carbon dioxide from exhaled air, registered at preaccident levels.

Chapman reported their situation to operations controller Ralph Henderson. "Relax," Henderson told them in a voice as casual as if he were ordering lunch. "Maintain atmospheric pressure. No more exertion than necessary.* We'll come down for you as soon as we get another *Pisces* here."

Henderson next radioed the company's headquarters at Barrow on the northwest coast of Britain. Hearing the dismal news, Cmdr. Peter Messervy, Oceanics' general manager, decided to join the *Voyager* and take charge of the rescue operation himself. "The men have sufficient oxygen until Saturday morning or perhaps later," he told Sir Leonard Redshaw, chairman of Vickers, Ltd., the large shipbuilding firm that is the parent company of Vickers Oceanics.

Both men were well aware that, with the *Pisces III* at 1,575 feet, this would be the deepest rescue attempt in sea history. "Time . . ." Redshaw reflected aloud. "The history of submarine tragedies is the running out of time." Then he instructed Messervy: "Get everything you may possibly need—everything. Assume that the odds are against you."

The critical cog in implementing the rescue was the *Voyager*. She had to speed to a port for two waiting subs, the *Pisces II* and the *Pisces V,* which would then descend to the stricken *Pisces III* and, using remote-controlled external arms, attempt to attach lines to hoist the vessel to the surface. But until another ship arrived, the *Voyager* had to remain on station, watching the two buoys that marked the *Pisces III's* position and maintaining voice contact with the trapped men.

The *Pisces II* was surveying a pipeline in the North Sea between Britain and Norway. A fast supply vessel was asked to pick her up and whisk her to the nearest port, where a Hercules air transport waited to fly her to Cork.

---

* The sub's seventy-two-hour oxygen supply—nine hours of which already had been used—was flexible: Excitement and exertion would exhaust it quicker; but if the men remained calm and physically passive, it could last considerably longer.

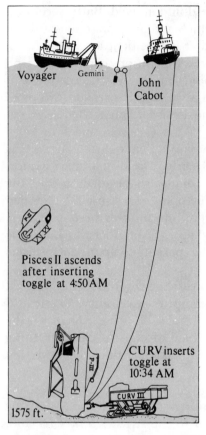

Voyager Gemini John Cabot

Pisces II ascends
after inserting
toggle at 4:50 AM

CURV inserts
toggle at
10:34 AM

CURV III

1575 ft.

By the time the *Pisces II* arrived at the Cork docks, the other sub—the *Pisces V*, owned by a Canadian company—had already arrived by plane from Halifax. And in San Diego, California, the U. S. Navy was preparing still another aid for the flight to Cork—an unmanned sixteen-foot rescue device controlled from the surface called CURV III (Controlled Underwater Recovery Vehicle).

At the Vickers works, engineers, technicians, divers and pilots huddled in conference. Suppose the sub was in an awkward position and a line could not be attached to the regular lifting device. Could the open hatch, the cause of the mishap, also be used to save the situation? Within an hour, engineers had designed a toggle, a contraption with two arms that opened and closed like an umbrella. Closed, it could be slipped through the open hatch. Inside the flooded sphere, the arms would open and lock in position. A line attached to the toggle would then enable the sub to be pulled up. In three hours, Vickers technicians had built two toggles, which were also flown to Cork.

On the floor of the Atlantic, meanwhile, Mallinson and Chapman inventoried their meager nourishment supplies and secured their benches close together to take advantage of each other's body heat. The temperature was about 50° F., but the humidity soon reached ninety-eight percent and both men felt very cold. In the blackness, Chapman reached over and touched Mallinson's hand. "You all right, mate?"

"Yes. Fine."

"If I have to be in a spot like this, I'm glad I'm down here with you."

"That's just the way I feel, too," Mallinson replied.

Throughout the day, Henderson kept the trapped men informed about every phase of the rescue effort. Nine hours after the sinking, he reported that a relief ship had arrived and that he was transferring his communications gear to it so the *Voyager* could depart for Cork. The two pilots felt heartened. Now they could count the hours to rescue: twelve hours for the *Voyager* to reach port, a few hours to load the rescue subs, twelve more for the return trip.

The high humidity had dampened Mallinson and Chapman to the skin, and one marrow-chilling, teeth-chattering shivering bout followed another. Communications between sub and ship were hampered by roaring sounds and the gossipy chattering of porpoises. Henderson didn't tell them that a gale was on the way.

Early on Friday, the *Voyager* returned and moved into position above the stricken sub. At 2:14 a.m., the *Pisces II* began to descend toward the *Pisces III*. Clutched in its external arm was a toggle that pilots Des D'Arcy and Roy Brown were planning to insert in the open sphere. Attached to the toggle, and lightly lashed to the *Pisces II's* side, was a synthetic buoyant line eight inches in circumference.

D'Arcy and Brown had just passed 1,250 feet when they heard the sickening sound of the lashings breaking—the buoyancy of the thick synthetic line had been too strong. In the next second, the pull of the rising line bent the manipulator arm out of commission. As a rescuer, the *Pisces II* was temporarily useless.

On board the *Voyager*, Henderson shook his head in frustration. "We're having difficulty with the *Pisces Two's* manipulator arm," he reported to the sunken sub. "Nothing serious. Will launch *Pisces Five* promptly." The trapped men told themselves that such minor problems ought to be expected and tried to relax.

The *Pisces V*, manned by Canadians, dived with a snap hook and a four-inch line in her manipulator. This time, the plan was to connect the hook to the *Pisces III's* lifting device. For two hours they skimmed over the ocean floor, but their sonar couldn't pick up the target.

Finally, the Canadians decided to surface to have their electronics gear checked. The *Voyager* technicians discovered that the sub's gyro-compass was off by eighty degrees. When this was corrected, the Canadians resumed the search. After two and a half hours, they homed in on the stricken sub. For the trapped men, it was a dramatic moment. Mallinson felt tears running down his face. The ordeal would soon be over.

Within half an hour, the Canadians had connected the snap hook to the *Pisces III's* lifting device. And then misfortune struck again. As the *Pisces V* backed off, the snap hook rolled in the lift attachment and—possibly because it had never been properly closed—came loose. The connection was lost.

Quickly, the Canadians caught hold of the drifting hook and fastened it to the *Pisces III's* starboard propeller guard. But all attempts to forge a link between the end of the line and the lifting device failed, and they eventually had to leave the hook where it was. Although the connection was too flimsy for lifting purposes, it did provide a tangible link between the surface and the sub, and it acted as a guideline for subsequent rescue attempts.

On the surface, technicians worked feverishly on the *Pisces II* while the *Voyager* pitched and rolled in the rising seas. Not a man aboard had slept in nearly sixty hours. Almost numb from fatigue, they moved at half-speed, dropped tools and forgot where they had put down equipment.

More than a quarter-mile below, Mallinson and Chapman waited, shivering, tormented by pounding headaches. The increase of carbon dioxide in the air began to affect them. Chapman became confused about time. Ordinarily very conscientious, Mallinson thought: *I'm not going to work today, and that's that.*

Early Friday night came welcome news from the *Voyager: "Pisces Two* is ready to go. We'll be getting to you soon."

"Very good. We very much appreciate what you're doing." Pause. "No matter what happens." It was the first time that the trapped men had indicated a doubt about the outcome.

Just before eight p.m., the *Pisces II* was pulled into position for her dive. No *Pisces* had ever been launched in such violent seas before, but time was running out. As the sub disappeared beneath the waves, what everyone dreaded happened. D'Arcy and Brown suddenly stiffened in shock. Their water alarm was screeching! *My God,* thought Messervy. *Can we be losing another boat?* The two pilots quickly expelled water in the ballast tanks with forced air to surface, and the *Pisces II* was winched back aboard the *Voyager.*

On the *Voyager,* experts began meticulously checking *Pisces II* to find out what triggered the water alarm. By the early hours of Saturday, the day that the crashed sub *had* to be raised, the cause of the false alarm had been tracked down and righted. The sub was ready for use again.

Messervy decided to send the *Pisces II* down without further delay. At 4:10 a.m., a toggle and a three-and-one-half-inch line grasped in her repaired manipulator arm, she submerged. It took them only fifty minutes to reach the sub and neatly insert the toggle through the hatch. But company policy was to leave nothing to chance. So for two hours the rescue sub tried to transfer the line left hanging to the propeller guard by the Canadians to the *Pisces III's* lifting device. They couldn't do it.

"Come what may, we lift at eleven-thirty," Messervy told the *Voyager* crew. "If CURV can attach a second line by then, fine. If not, we'll go with one line."

At 9:40 Saturday morning, after a series of technical problems had been conquered, CURV descended with a second toggle and a powerful six-inch braided-nylon line.

In fifty minutes, she homed in on the *Pisces III,* then obediently followed her electronic instructions and slipped the toggle into the hatch.

Mallinson and Chapman had been sleeping, but became aware of their imminent rescue with the arrival of CURV. Then, over the radio, they heard that the lift was definitely scheduled for 11:30. The trapped men wanted to believe it, but restrained themselves from becoming excited. There had been too many disappointments.

Meanwhile, operations manager Bob Eastaugh had transferred to CURV's support ship, the *John Cabot.* He reported back that the Canadian cable ship was better equipped for the job of winching the *Pisces III* up from the seabed in the heavy seas that prevailed. As soon as the two toggle lines were connected to an electric winch aboard the *John Cabot,* the order that they had been waiting for came: "Lift!" It was 10:50 a.m.

The position of the *Pisces III,* its stern imbedded in sand, suddenly reversed. It began to be reeled in like a fish with a hook in its tail.

The sea's turbulence made the helpless sub simultaneously bob up and down like a yo-yo and swing like a pendulum. The toggles made a horrible clanging sound, and the trapped men feared the lines wouldn't hold.

The winch halted when the sub was sixty feet from the heavy seas at the surface. Messervy sent down diver Robert Hanley to attach a heavy line to the sub's lifting device so that it could be raised out of the water in a level position. With the line clutched in his hands, Hanley dived within vision range of the *Pisces III*. Carefully timing the sub's erratic movements, he grabbed for it at the height of an arc, rode it like a bucking horse, then managed to secure the line to the lifting point.

In a few minutes, lifting resumed. At 1:17 on Saturday afternoon, the sub was raised clear of the water and the hatch opened. Mallinson and Chapman pulled themselves out—gloriously free of the horror of being entombed for seventy-six hours at a watery depth from which no man had previously been saved.

Actually, they appeared in better physical condition than anyone topside. Their stubble-bearded, gray-faced rescuers were so spent after three sleepless days and nights that they could hardly muster a smile in answer to the rescued pilots' deeply felt "Thank you!" The only sensation the rescuers felt was numb relief. They had been plagued by misfortune, and come close to losing. But they had won.

The young woman
lay critically injured
in the fast lane of the Freeway.
Would no one stop to help?

Rescue
on the Freeway

BY JOSEPH P. BLANK

THAT SUNDAY MORNING—February 23, 1969—was gray and dreary. Clouds drenched Los Angeles with one of the heaviest rains in months. George V. Valdez, 49, was driving north on the eight-lane Golden State Freeway, anxious to reach the hospital where his wife's aged grandmother lay ill.

Valdez made the thirty-five-minute trip to the hospital every Sunday. He also visited the feeble grandmother once or twice during the week, after leaving work as an inspector for a tire company and before going to his part-time second job as a longshoreman. The grandmother spoke no English and never felt really comfortable unless a member of her Mexican-American family was near her. In the Ford camper with Valdez as he drove to the hospital were his mother-in-law and sister-in-law. Traffic was moderately heavy. Despite the downpour, many cars sped past at seventy miles an hour.

As Valdez rounded a gentle curve, he saw, about a quarter of a mile ahead of him, a northbound car suddenly veer into the chain-link fence that divided the north and south lanes. "There's an accident up the road," he remarked to the two women. He began to slow down. He thought it strange that none of the cars ahead of him stopped.

As Valdez reached the scene, he saw that the disabled car, with its entire passenger side torn open, was empty, and he saw two young women. One was sprawled on her right side in the drainage trough near the fence. The other had been projected violently under the fence onto the southbound side of the freeway and was lying there face up, arms extended in a gesture of surrender.

Valdez pulled onto the right-hand shoulder and jumped out of his car. Four lanes of fast traffic separated him from the victims. Not one of the passing northbound cars stopped to help. Drivers and passengers twisted their heads for a quick look at the women and continued on.

His mother-in-law saw him poised to sprint through an opening in traffic and called, "George—your knee!"

"Somebody's got to do *something*," he answered irritably. Valdez had a bad trick knee. It sometimes folded under him without warning, and when that happened he collapsed as if shot.

"Here goes, with God!" he yelled in Spanish; then he ran a jagged course across the four northbound lanes to the fence. He knelt beside Donna Logan, 18. Her nose and mouth lay in the drainage trough's two and a half inches of water. Valdez gently turned her bruised face out of the water. One of her legs must have been broken: The foot was twisted in the wrong direction.

"Help me," she said, partially conscious. "I'm hurting."

"You'll get help," he assured her. He looked through the fence to where Elizabeth Althouse, 20, lay inert in the fast lane of the southbound traffic. Cars bearing down on her squeezed into the adjacent lane to avoid her body. "Take it easy," Valdez said to the first girl. "You're in pretty good shape. But your friend isn't moving. I'll be back in a minute. Don't move. You're safe here."

He vaulted the five-foot fence and ran to Miss Althouse. He saw that her right leg was missing, severed about three inches above the knee. Kneeling in the rain, he held her wrist and put his ear to her mouth. She was breathing. Her pulse was strong. He quickly pulled off his belt and applied it as a tourniquet around her thigh. The girl's head was within two feet of the painted lane line, and he could hear and feel the cars rush by as he worked the tourniquet tight.

The leg, he thought. *Where's the leg?* Still kneeling, he looked around and saw the limb in the most distant southbound lane, about forty feet away. *I have to get that leg. If we can reach a hospital in time, maybe it can be reattached.*

He rose, stood between the young woman's body and the oncoming traffic, and waved. "Stop!" he shouted. "Please! We need help!" Approaching cars were swinging around him. He saw some drivers glare and open their mouths in angry expressions. No one stopped.

He had to get the leg, but he couldn't leave the victim here. He pulled Miss Althouse carefully onto the paved apron alongside the fence. The rain pelted them.

He stood on the painted line between the second and third lanes and frantically waved his suit jacket like a flag. A big semitrailer thundered by and nearly sucked the jacket out of his hands. Cars shot past on both sides. *They won't stop,* he thought. *They won't stop.*

He moved into the second lane, still trying to flag traffic down. Then he quickly hopped to the first lane. There was the leg. He stood over it protectively and, pulling a rain-wet handkerchief from his pocket, he applied a tourniquet to the severed limb, hoping that the retention of fluids might help the doctors in their surgery.

For another minute he fluttered the jacket over his head and, finally, one car drew to a halt in front of him. The driver partially rolled down his window and yelled, "What's the matter?"

"Help me block traffic. A woman lost her leg."

"Whaddya mean, lost her leg? What leg?"

"Down here." Valdez pointed.

The driver fully opened his window and leaned through it. His face turned ashen, and he got sick. Without another word, he gunned his engine, swerved around Valdez and drove off.

Valdez wiped a wet sleeve across his wet face. *Somebody has to stop. Somebody has to help.* Feelings of anger, desperation, frustration and fear churned inside him.

He remained in the center of the lane, waving his jacket. An overhead camper stopped, with a man and a woman in the front seat. "Help me block traffic," Valdez pleaded.

As the driver began leaving the camper, Valdez warned, "Be careful! You'll step on it." The driver looked down at the severed limb, fell back into his seat with an "Oh, my God," and fainted.

Valdez impulsively reached into the cab and pulled out the ignition key. Then, with a towel taken from the camper, he wrapped the severed limb and, carrying it under his arm, stepped into the center of the second lane. The first oncoming car had to stop or run him down. "What's the matter?" the driver demanded.

"Please stay where you are," said Valdez. "We have to get help for that woman over there." He reached into the car and pulled out the keys. Two lanes were blocked.

He moved into the third lane. A car braked to a halt. The driver, glowering with anger, blew his horn furiously. "You're holding up traffic, you SOB!" he screeched. "Who do you think you are?"

Valdez jerked open the door. Something in his face made the driver back away. Valdez removed his ignition key as well, blocking the third lane of traffic.

In the fourth lane, a driver voluntarily stopped his car and ran forward, asking, "Can I help you?" Although all lanes were now corked by stopped cars, some drivers were trying to bypass the jam by drifting down the inside shoulder where the body of the injured girl lay.

"Can you do something about those cars trying to get through?" Valdez replied. The man ran over and stood on the apron, waving cars back.

Valdez knelt by Miss Althouse. Someone handed him an electric extension cord, and he used it to tie a second tourniquet on her thigh.

Several cars had stopped in the northbound lanes now, and a man on the other side of the fence yelled across, "Can I help you, friend?"

"Do you have anything to cover these girls?"

The man got a piece of carpeting, threw it over the fence and climbed after it. He draped it over Miss Althouse's body and head.

"No, no!" Valdez shouted angrily. "She'll suffocate. Hold it over her like a tent."

The man followed instructions for a few minutes, then said, "I can't stand this. I'll leave the carpeting. I'm going." He climbed over the fence and drove away.

After adjusting the carpeting, Valdez went to the fence and spoke to Miss Logan. "Everything'll be all right. An ambulance will be here soon. Don't move."

He was checking Miss Althouse's pulse when a police car sped down a nearby ramp, crossed the four lanes and pulled up. An officer in a yellow slicker stepped out. Valdez asked him, "Please call an ambulance."

"One's coming. It should have been here by now." As the officer absorbed what had happened, his face blanched.

At that moment Miss Althouse, still in deep shock, groaned loudly. "My leg, my leg. It hurts so."

"Your leg is all right," Valdez told her. "What hurts is the tourniquet I put on to stop a little bleeding. I'll loosen it, and it'll feel better." He pressed on her thigh with his thumb to create a new pain sensation. "There. Better?"

"Yeah-h-h."

A fire-department ambulance swung across the freeway. A few minutes later, a wrecker arrived. Valdez and two firemen worked the injured girls onto stretchers. As Valdez helped slide the stretchers into the ambulance, he heard a voice behind him reciting the last rites.

He turned and saw a priest. "What are you doing?" Valdez asked. "Nobody's dying." He felt irritated, and thought, *You're wrong, brother, if you think they're going to die after all the work I did.*

As the ambulance pulled away, Valdez handed the three ignition keys he had removed to a driver standing nearby. He climbed over the fence and went back to his camper, where his mother-in-law and sister-in-law, scared, were saying the Lord's Prayer in loud voices.

"It's over now," he told them. Then he changed into dry trousers and shoes that were in the rear of the camper.

The police car and wrecker moved off the freeway. Valdez pulled onto the freeway and continued north toward the hospital.

"Why didn't they stop?" his mother-in-law asked him. "We were afraid you'd be killed. Why didn't they stop and help you?"

Valdez stared ahead. He thought of his wife and eight-year-old twins at home, and the possibility that he could have been killed. He thought of all the cars that passed him, and all those faces that flashed by—some curious, some impatient, some angry, some indifferent. He shrugged. "It was raining pretty hard," he said. "I guess they didn't want to get wet."

On his return from the visit to the grandmother, Valdez stopped at a service station and called the highway patrol for the name of the hospital where the victims had been taken. He learned that Donna

Logan had a complicated compound fracture of the ankle. Thanks to the lifesaving tourniquets on her thigh, Elizabeth Althouse would survive; and a surgical team was now preparing to attempt to reattach her severed leg. On the following day, Valdez was told that the operation had worked out satisfactorily.

Hospital authorities spread the word of how Valdez had given first aid on the freeway. After it was described in the Los Angeles *Times* and over radio and television, hundreds of letters poured in. The writers thanked George Valdez, and told him that his concern for others, at the risk of his own life, was enough to revive their faith in the human race. This strengthened his own faith. "If so many strangers could think such good thoughts about what happened on that freeway, there must be a lot of wonderful people in this world. Very few of them were on the freeway that Sunday. But maybe at another time, in another place, they *will* be there."

Although Elizabeth Althouse's leg was reattached successfully, as far as bone, muscle and blood circulation were concerned, she never regained control of it or the ability to stand on it. After four months, it was amputated. Today, she walks on an artificial limb. Donna Logan's ankle required a bone graft and treatment for a long time afterward.

In April 1969, the City of Los Angeles officially commended George Valdez for "his heroic effort and uncanny presence of mind in saving the lives of Miss Elizabeth Althouse and Miss Donna Logan." And in August 1969, the Carnegie Hero Fund Commission awarded him its bronze medal.

Strange sources of energy and help
reached out to him the night he was washed overboard
into the cold and stormy waters of Long Island Sound

Who Saved
John Kle?

BY JOHN KLE

IT HAPPENED SO FAST I didn't know what hit me. It was late in the afternoon of June 30, 1975; my friends Peter and Bart and I were sailing on Long Island Sound, plunging along in six-foot seas, surging before a twenty-knot wind, the tail of hurricane Amy. Suddenly a line tangled on the foredeck and, as I went forward to free it, a huge wave hit our stern, slamming our little boat to starboard. I went up in the air and when I came down, there was no deck beneath my feet and I fell straight into the water. I felt the shock of cold water on my flesh. I was not wearing a life jacket and, as the stern of the boat disappeared behind a huge comber downwind, I was filled with fear and the realization that, after twenty years of sailing, I was face to face with death.

I could see Bart and Peter struggling to bring the boat into the wind, but by the time she responded they were eighty yards away and I was just a speck in the angry waves. As I topped each wave, I could see them searching, and I waved my plaid shirt in the air, hoping that they would spot that tiny speck of color in the heavy seas. They beat up toward my left. I could see Bart on the bow searching for me as Peter struggled with the helm. Winds gusting to nearly gale force screamed in my ear, whitecaps slapped me in the face. I think: *They must see me now.* But they don't. The boat disappears from sight. I am alone. I think: *It is my time to die.*

Quickly, I discarded my sneakers and shirt. I remembered a trick from lifesaving class and made a float by tying knots in the legs of my jeans and filling them with air. Two 360-degree turns on the crests of waves revealed that I was near the middle of the Sound, about four miles from Long Island. It was now about 7:30 p.m., with two hours of daylight left. I must make a decision: Which shore? Maybe it is a homing instinct, but I strike out for Long Island, where my wife, Debbie, and I live. The thought of Debbie somehow eases the reality of my situation. Momentarily, fear leaves and confidence enters me as I set to the task: *Save yourself, because no one can find you in this storm.*

The pants float leaks its trapped air, but I manage to refill it twice before abandoning my jeans. Fatigue is setting in. Fear returns. Cold is the enemy. Already her icy fingers grip at my spine. Breaststroke, sidestroke and breaststroke again. At the top of each wave, a whitecap slaps me in the face and I battle the wind. I try to float on my back, but a whitecap washes over my face and I swallow a couple of gulps of water. Salt burns my lungs and my body contracts as I gasp for air. I am drowning; the water I've loved all my life is trying to kill me. *Stay calm, don't fight, work with the elements.*

My body responds, I'm okay. I think of Debbie, and just thinking of her brings new energy. I realize how much I don't want to leave her.

The sun is getting lower in the sky and the light is turning gold. I watch the changing sky while I do the endless sidestroke. This may be my last sunset; I am taken in by its beauty, blown clean by the high winds. The faint noise of a motor comes from somewhere. Turning, I see a small plane directly overhead. I wave, but the pilot doesn't see me.

I have been using the Empire State Building to gauge my progress, and there has been little. *Dear God, I've never asked You for anything before, but please help me now.* This small prayer seems my only hope.

As I keep working, new energy comes—from somewhere. There is perhaps fifteen minutes of light left and still so far to go. But I decide that if I die, it will only be after a fight, after I have given my all.

At dusk, I notice a small object in my path: a float for a lobster pot. It is a small miracle that I have swum straight to this tiny lifesaver. Ten yards to either side and I would have missed it. I grab onto it and take a desperately needed thirty-second rest. The float is not spliced to the line but tied. If only I can untie the knots that hold it captive! My numb fingers work at the knots, stiff with salt water. At last, reluctantly, the knots come apart. The float is mine as night engulfs me.

This tiny friend tucks under my arm like a football and barely floats my chest. Now, I can rest occasionally. I take a bearing from a bright light on Long Island shore—it looks to be about three miles away—and start out again with renewed strength and confidence. I swim endlessly, changing the buoy from side to side. I can rest only for a few seconds before my arms and legs become stiff with cold and fear makes me move on. I have never been so cold. Looking west at the lights of the Empire State Building, I can see that I am making progress, and from her bright lights I feel a new energy fill me. I estimate it is ten p.m.

The blackness is suddenly pierced by the powerful beam of a Coast Guard searchlight. It shoots right over me; then a boat passes no more than a hundred yards away. Looking around the horizon, I see the lights of half a dozen Coast Guard and police boats and three helicopters as they search the waters for me with their powerful lights and dropped flares. I know that Peter and Bart are on one of the boats, and knowing that they are looking gives me additional strength.

Suddenly, the water around me explodes with light from a flare. I turn to wave at a helicopter hovering only seventy-five yards away and swallow the water spewing from a whitecap that hits me in the face. I lose the buoy in a coughing spasm. I cannot breathe. Then my hand retrieves the buoy and gathers it to my chest. *Stay calm. Don't panic.* Once more I can breathe. But leg cramps seize me, and I lose another full minute to the pain. I can feel my neck and lower spine starting to freeze. *Keep moving, or you will die.* Again, from somewhere, energy comes, and my tired legs start to kick. I start a rhythm: two strokes, breathe; two strokes, breathe. I'll hold this pace until the cold wins her battle and my fingers freeze and drop the tiny buoy. Then death. *Oh, God, I don't want to die.* Another surge of energy comes up from some strange, deep place, and it keeps me moving somehow—muscles on automatic. *Debbie, I need you.*

My leg hits ground. I don't have the strength to rejoice but only to keep my forward momentum up the rocky, low-tide beach. I get stiffly to my feet and, clutching the buoy, I stumble toward a nearby house with lights in the windows. I can't feel the ground beneath my feet; I have lost all sense of my body.

My numb hand turns a doorknob; the door is not locked. I go in, out of the killing wind, and call: "Sir, I'm in your living room!" The owner appears, and when he sees my ash-white form, he runs to get blankets. He moves me in front of the stove, feeds me soup. It is now 12:30 a.m. I get my story out through chattering teeth so he can call the police and tell the search boats that I have made it ashore. Soon Debbie arrives and takes me home: home to warmth, love, security, the future.

Shortly after the newspapers reported my story, I received a phone call from Buck, another of my sailing friends. He was very excited as he recounted the following incident:

"On the night you fell in the water, my wife and I were driving past the Empire State Building. We noticed a parking space right in front. Neither of us had ever been to the top of the Empire State, so we parked and went up. It was around ten o'clock. I pointed to the black void of Long Island Sound. 'That's where John and I went sailing last week,' I told Sue. Still talking of you, we put a dime in the binoculars and looked out into the dark sea where you were swimming right then."

As I listened to him, once more I felt myself taking my bearings from the lights of the Empire State Building. I remembered the warmth, strength and guidance those lights had given me. Had I perhaps been feeling the energy Buck and Sue were sending out to me?

A few days later, I received a letter from another close friend, Hitch, who was vacationing in the Caribbean. It was written June 30. He had been sitting on the beach just before writing me and had suddenly been consumed by overpowering thoughts of me. There was no way he could have known that, more than 2,000 miles away, I was fighting for my life. Again, I was transported back to that horrible blackness, to my desperate pleas for help, and to my hopeless feelings and fears, followed by the inexplicable confidence that kept coming back again and again to fight off my terror, and to keep me going. That energy was coming from somewhere: perhaps from that first genuine prayer I'd ever offered, or from those faraway Caribbean waters, or from the top of the Empire State Building, or from Peter and Bart, aboard a search boat—or from my small house in Sea Cliff, where Debbie was waiting.

Was I being tested that night—or protected?

I was still pondering that question when my friend Hitch came to visit us ten days later. He listened quietly to my tale, then went into the kitchen with Debbie to help her with preparations for dinner. A few minutes later he came dashing back into the living room, wild-eyed, with a frightened Debbie in tow.

"Look," he said, "you won't believe this, but the week before you fell in the water, I had a nightmare in which I kept seeing the numbers nine, seven and eight, over and over. They woke me up, and each time I dozed off again they reappeared: nine, seven, eight. The experience frightened me so much that I told my sister about it. She urged me to forget about it, and I did, until just now."

He and Debbie kept staring at me. I asked what this was all about, whereupon Debbie went out to the kitchen and reappeared with the buoy that had saved my life. The small registration numbers carved into that buoy read 978.

To the helpless girl,
it seemed that the car wanted to crush her
beneath its churning wheels

Ordeal
in the Snow

BY CAROLE TAYLOR

IT WAS ALL OVER IN A SECOND—and I was stunned, shocked, disbelieving. *This can't be!* I thought. *This can't have happened!*

But it had. There I was, utterly alone, trapped beneath my small foreign car, its motor running, the rear wheels spinning ever lower in the snow, the upper part of my body terribly cold, my legs burning from the heat of the exhaust, a light snow falling on my face and no one likely to find me for days. . . .

My unbelievable plight began on Tuesday night, February 29,

1972. Tuesday was always a busy day for me at the Montreal General Hospital. My job as a senior medical secretary there included supervision of the Tumour Registry, and about seventy patients were scheduled for examination at the following morning's clinic. I had had to work late that evening to update those patients' charts.

At 11:45, I finally got into my car for the twenty-minute drive to my apartment. The night was very cold—not much above zero— and snow was falling. About a mile from the hospital, I suddenly remembered that I had neglected to stack the next day's charts in alphabetical order, a routine step important to the efficient operation of the clinic.

I turned off the highway and tried to find a shortcut back to the hospital through unfamiliar streets. I found myself on Selby Street. The snow on the street was smooth, without tire tracks, and the way the car bumped along told me that there was just dirt under the snow. Then my headlights picked up the uncompleted construction of the Trans-Canada Highway, and I realized that I was on a dead-end road.

Foolishly, I attempted a U-turn. The car's rear wheels spun in the snow as I tried to go forward up a slight incline, then backward. Just like that I was stuck—but definitely.

I stepped out of the car. It was horribly cold. The only things in sight were the pillars of the highway overpass and a deserted factory, obviously ready for a wrecking crew. Not a light, not a sound. I had no idea in which direction to go for help.

Calm down, I told myself. *Try to think.* Then I remembered a driving trick that my brother had once explained to me. When he was alone and got stuck in snow or mud, he would pull out the manual choke, put the car in forward gear, push it out of the rut, run after it and jump into the driver's seat. It hadn't impressed me at the time, but now I thought it might be the only way out of my predicament.

The rear of the car was facing downhill. I started the engine, pulled the choke, put the car into reverse, left the door open and pushed against the front bumper. The car moved an inch or two, then sank into the snow again.

But the stunt *had* worked, and I felt encouraged. This time I gave a sustained shove with all the strength I could summon. The car lurched, then began rolling backward.

I ran, caught up with it, then passed it so that I could turn and jump into the seat as it came by. Suddenly I slipped on the snow. My legs shot out from under me. The rear wheel on the driver's side ran over my legs, and the bottom of the car pinned me against the ground.

For a moment it didn't seem real. Then I thought, *This time you've really done it.* I tried to jerk, squirm, heave—anything to get out from under that car. It was useless. My right leg was jammed so tightly that I could only move my ankle slightly. My right arm was pinned from the elbow down. I could move my left leg a few inches sideways, and my left arm was free. My back hurt, and any movement intensified the pain.

I lay there, panting. The noise of the running motor seemed terribly loud. The front wheels had turned to the right, and the left wheel was about three feet away, aimed at my head. Any movement of the car would slide it closer. My watch read 12:08.

Someone will come, I thought. *But who? At this time of night, who would have reason to drive up this road that leads nowhere?* Scenes that I had read about flashed through my mind: the boy swimming alone and drowning; the family caught in a fire; the woman found dead, trapped in a car that had gone off the road and into a ravine. *Stop it. Take it easy. Get an idea.* I pushed and pulled and tried to rock the car with my left hand. Useless.

This must be a nightmare. I'll wake up in my warm, cozy bed, and it will all be over. I twisted my head and looked at my watch again. Time was passing. What was happening was all too real.

Now the lower parts of my legs, pressed hard against the car's tail pipe, were burning, and the noise of the motor seemed to be getting louder. *I've got to stop the noise, stop the burning. Maybe, if that noise just stops, I can think of a way out.*

I jammed snow into a hole in the exhaust pipe in the desperate hope of stalling the motor. I succeeded only in burning my hand and hurting my arm. Now agonizing pain was in every part of me. And I knew that, as the rear wheels churned ever deeper, more of the car's weight would press against me.

I had to have relief. Anything! If I was going to die, then the sooner the better. I twisted the upper part of my body in the direction of the exhaust pipe, and took deep breaths, hoping to inhale more of the fumes. Futile. The wind was blowing in the wrong direction, and the effort of keeping my body turned sent excruciating pains through my spine. I fell back, overcome by hopelessness.

Suddenly I was startled out of my misery by a change in the motor's sound. The spinning wheels caught and held, and the car lurched about a foot, moving higher on my body. For a few seconds I felt blessed relief. Then the car settled across my pelvic area as the rear wheels once again spun in the snow.

Pain surged through me. I had no deep religious convictions, but now I found myself praying, really praying, spontaneously and earnestly. I knew that if help ever came, it would be God who sent it. *Please, God, get me out of this. If You do, I'll really believe in You.* Wildly, I began making promise after promise—to be good, to quit smoking. . . . *What am I doing, God, trying to make a deal with You? Just help me, please.*

My watch had stopped at two a.m., and I had only a vague notion of time now. I tried to force myself to sleep, hoping to escape the horrors I was suffering. But sleep would not come above the roaring motor.

I had been moving my left leg regularly to keep it from freezing. I felt it hit something. A rock? A stick? Then I realized that I was kicking my right leg, which now had no feeling. I had been around a hospital long enough to know that if circulation in a limb is cut off for any considerable period, gangrene sets in and the limb has to be amputated. Parts of my back and shoulders were growing numb, too. It seemed to me that the car wanted to bury me alive.

It must have been around three a.m. when I heard the roar of a truck's motor. Soon it was close enough for me to see the red lights that outlined its body. It was useless to yell, so I talked to the truck: "Please, you've got to come closer. Look at my headlights. See me? Come now! I can't wait any longer. Now!"

As the truck's headlights passed out of sight, all my newfound hope faded, too. Whatever strength remained in my body seemed to ooze out of my pores, and sudden, unreasoning terror gripped me. I screamed, "Help! Help me! Selby Street! Selby Street!" As my screams died away into silence, I lay back totally spent.

Then I heard that ominous change in the motor noise again. The car lurched, moved higher on me, settled on my chest. The left wheel was at my armpit. Its next movement would crush my face.

Breathing was almost impossible now, and I was sure that death wasn't far away. I wondered if, when people found me, they would realize what I'd gone through. I couldn't close my eyes, even for a second, because when I did, I kept seeing my head exploding from the weight of the car.

My mind spun in wilder circles all the time. I didn't want to know the moment of death. *Relax,* I told myself. *You're terribly tired. Don't think the motor noise is driving you mad; let it lull you to sleep. If you just fall asleep, it will be all over. God, please help me. Please make me unconscious now and let me die.*

Suddenly I was jerked back to reality by the sound of another motor. I saw the flicker of headlights. They disappeared, then reappeared brighter than before. The car was coming closer! A shiver of fear shook me. I was half-buried in snow and almost completely under the car. The driver might pass without seeing me. Slowly, painfully, I raised my left arm from the elbow and tried to wave.

I heard a car door open and footsteps crunching through the snow. A man's voice said, "Oh, my God!" I looked up at two young policemen. I was no longer alone.

One policeman said, "Keep her talking. I'll radio for help."

The other policeman knelt by my head. "How do you feel?"

I felt paralyzed, and my body hurt terribly. I wanted to say, "Grateful," but I couldn't move my mouth.

Then I heard other vehicles, the quick exchange of words. Four men raised the front of the car while a fifth gently pulled me out by the armpits.

They put me on a stretcher and covered me with blankets. I couldn't stop shivering and shaking. But it was wonderful, so unbelievably wonderful, to have that terrible pressure off me, not to hear that awful motor.

At the hospital, doctors cut off my scorched and torn clothing. My right leg was very swollen and almost completely discolored. At first the doctors thought I might have a fractured pelvis, but, miraculously, no bones were broken.

I was put into a warm bed, but I couldn't sleep. I was afraid to close my eyes, afraid that my safety wasn't real. At seven-thirty in the morning, a nurse came in and asked, "Do you want to call anyone?"

Then I remembered. "Please call Megan Hayes." Megan and I worked together.

When she came on the line, I told her I had been in an accident. "I'm at the hospital, but I won't be in for work. Can you get here right away?"

"I'll be up to see you in a few minutes."

"No, no, Megan, it's not about me. You've got to get here right away to stack the charts in alphabetical order for this morning's clinic."

Later, I learned that I had been found at 4:16 a.m. The two policemen, Vern Wooley and Ron Rollauer, had been patrolling that area for more than a week but had never turned into the dead-end section of Selby Street because it was not in use. On the night of my accident, Officer Rollauer had driven the first half of the night shift, and they had passed by the deserted section of Selby twice. "Then we had our meal at the station house," Officer Wooley explained, "and I took over the driving at four a.m. I had no intention of patrolling that unused stretch. No reason to. As I reached it, though, I just turned in without thinking."

His unconscious impulse will never let me stop wondering.

Was my survival a miracle?
Or did it stem from Andy Mynarski's gallantry?

The
Thirteenth Mission

BY FLIGHT LIEUTENANT GEORGE PATRICK BROPHY, RCAF
as told to David MacDonald

ACCORDING TO OFFICIAL records of the Royal Canadian Air Force, I owe my life to "a miraculous escape." But was it only an amazing twist of fate that saved me from certain death? Or was there something more—another man's incredible courage—that helped me live to tell the tale? Even now, many years later, I still wonder.

That June night in 1944, at 419 Squadron's base in Britain, our seven-man crew was sitting on the grass by our Lancaster bomber, waiting to take off for France. For us, it was a night of mixed omens. A few hours earlier we'd been briefed for a raid on the railway yards at Cambrai—our crew's thirteenth mission. Moreover, we were due on target shortly after midnight, June 13.

Then, as if to compensate, a turret gunner named Andy Mynarski, my closest buddy in the crew, found a four-leaf clover in the grass. Twirling the good-luck token like a tiny propeller, he turned to me. "Here, Pat," he said. "*You* take it."

Minutes later our black, four-engine "Lanc"—*A for Able*—was climbing into the darkness, one of 200 bombers that RCAF 6 Group sent out that night, a week after D day, to pound the German supply lines. I sat alone in the Lanc's Plexiglas-domed rear turret, watching the evening stars pop out. As the "Tail-End Charlie," I was shut off behind the revolving turret's doors, far from all my crewmates. My only contact with them was via the intercom, on which pilot Art deBreyne's voice now crackled briefly: "Estimating eighty minutes more to target."

"Thanks," came Andy Mynarski's reply from the mid-upper turret. "No rush."

In our crew, which had been together for a year, Andy was a relative newcomer. Four months earlier, before our first mission, he'd turned up to replace a gunner who'd gone to the hospital.

At twenty-seven, Andy was a quiet, chunky fellow with a slow, boyish grin. The son of Polish immigrants, he had grown up in Winnipeg and left school at sixteen, when his father died, to help support four kid brothers and sisters. After joining the army in 1941, he'd switched to the RCAF because most of his friends were in it. To Andy, friends were important.

We soon became close chums. Since I was an officer and Andy an NCO, rank kept us in different quarters. But we made light of it. Splitting up on the base after a mission or a pub-crawl in town, I'd clap him on the back and say, "So long, Irish." He'd stiffen, exaggerate a salute and reply with a hint of Polish accent, "Good night, *sir*."

In a tight spot, I could always count on him. Once, on leave in London with Andy and two other crewmates, I got into a late-night scrap and phoned them from a police station. They laughed and said a taste of jail would teach me a lesson. While the others went back to sleep, however, Andy got up to bail me out.

But one thing Andy would not do. Even on practice flights, he would not go into the tail turret. Like most air gunners, he hated its cramped isolation. "Back there," he said, "you're completely cut off."

Back there now, as we crossed the French coast, I saw enemy searchlights sweeping the sky, then lazy puffs of smoke and deceptively pretty sunbursts of sparks. "Light flak below, skipper," I reported.

Suddenly, with a blinding flash, a searchlight caught us. Others quickly converged. "Hang on!" called deBreyne. "We're coned!" He threw the Lanc into a banking dive, then swung upward, trying to squirm away from the deadly glare. Then, just as suddenly, we were in the dark again.

We'd escaped—or had we? The Germans sometimes *let* a bomber shake loose, once their night fighters got a fix on it. It was too soon to tell.

Past the coastal defenses, we began a slow descent. This was to be a low-level raid, from 2,000 feet. We were down to 5,000 feet when I caught a glimpse of a twin-engine fighter. "Bogey astern!" I yelled on the intercom. "Six o'clock!" Instantly, as he'd done to evade the searchlights, deBreyne began to corkscrew. Seconds later I saw a JU-88 streaking up from below. "He's coming under us!"

As I whirled my turret around and opened fire, the white-bellied Junkers flashed by with its cannons blazing. Three sharp explosions rocked our aircraft. Two shots knocked out both port engines and set a wing tank on fire. The third tore into the fuselage, starting another fire between Andy's turret and mine.

We began losing altitude fast. I listened for orders on the intercom, but it was dead. Then a red light flashed in my turret—the signal to bail out. *A for Able* was doomed. For some reason, I glanced at my watch. It was thirteen minutes past midnight, June 13.

While Art deBreyne fought to keep the plane from heeling over in a spiral dive, bomb-aimer Jack Friday tugged at the forward crew's escape hatch. It flew open with a violent blast of air, hit Friday's head and knocked him out. Jack was still unconscious when flight engineer Roy Vigars dropped him through the hole, yanked his D-ring and jumped after him. Navigator Bob Bodie went next, then radio operator Jim Kelly. When pilot Art deBreyne finally jumped—from barely 800 feet—he felt sure that Andy Mynarski and I had both already succeeded in getting out of the rear hatch.

But he was wrong.

To fire, I'd swung my turret to port. Now I had to straighten it out so I could go back into the plane for my parachute and then jump from the rear door. I pressed the rotation pedal. Nothing happened. The hydraulic system had been shattered, locking my turret at such an angle that I couldn't get out. Meanwhile, inside the fuselage, flames were sweeping toward me.

Don't panic, I told myself. *There's still another way.* I managed to open the turret doors a few inches, reached in for my parachute and clipped it on. Then I began hand-cranking the turret to the beam position, where I'd be able to flip right out into the slipstream. To my horror, the rotating gear broke off. Now there was *no* way out. At that moment, imprisoned in a falling plane, I remembered Andy Mynarski's words: "Back there, you're completely cut off."

Then I saw him. Andy had slid down from the mid-upper turret and made his way back to the rear escape hatch, about fifteen feet from me. Just as he was about to jump, he glanced around and spotted me through the Plexiglas part of my turret. One look told him I was trapped.

Instantly, he turned away from the hatch—his doorway to safety—and started toward me. With the aircraft lurching drunkenly, Andy couldn't stay on his feet. He got down on hands and knees and crawled—straight through blazing hydraulic oil. By the time he reached the tail, his flying suit was on fire.

I shook my head—it was hopeless. "Don't try!" I shouted. I waved him away.

Andy didn't seem to notice. Completely ignoring his own plight, he grabbed a fire ax and tried to smash the turret free. It gave slightly, but not enough. Wild with desperation, he tore at the doors with his bare hands—in vain. By now he was a mass of flames below the waist. Seeing him like that, I forgot everything else. Over the roar of wind and the whine of our engines, I screamed and screamed again, "Go back, Andy! Get out!"

Finally, with time running out, he realized that he could do nothing to help me. When I waved him away again, he hung his head and nodded, as though he was ashamed to leave—ashamed that sheer heart and courage hadn't been enough. Even then, Andy didn't turn his back on me. Instead, he crawled backward, through the fire again, never taking his eyes off me. On his face was a look of mute anguish.

When Andy reached the escape hatch again, he stood up. Slowly, as he'd so often done before in happier times together, he came to attention. Standing there in his flaming clothes, a grimly magnificent figure, he *saluted* me!

At the same time, just before he jumped, he said something. And though I couldn't hear, I knew it was "Good night, sir."

I turned, watched him fall away beneath the tail and saw his chute open. *So long, Irish. Good luck.*

Now I was alone. The Lanc was going down less steeply than before, but I knew it would hit the ground in a matter of seconds, with five tons of high explosives barely fifty feet from me. I curled up in the way prescribed for crash landings and waited for death.

Time froze. While I was struggling inside the turret and Andy was fighting to get me out alive, a minute or more had flashed by like a second. Now the last agonizing seconds were like eternity. Prayers and random thoughts raced through my mind. *Hail Mary, full of grace . . . God, I hope Andy got down okay . . . Pray for us sinners . . . "Brophy? Oh, he was shot down over Cambrai."*

Suddenly time caught up. Everything came at once—the dark blur of the ground, the slam of a thousand sledgehammers, the screech of ripping metal. Just as the Lanc went bellying into a field, a thick tree slashed away its flaming port wing, spinning the plane violently to the left—its last dying lurch. *This is it.* But in that instant, at the last possible moment, the whiplash snapped my turret-prison open.

Without knowing it—for I'd blacked out—I was hurled through the air. When I came to a few seconds later, I heard two explosions. Only when I felt the solid, blessed earth tremble under me did I realize that the crash was over, and, somehow, I was alive.

Slowly, fearfully, I moved my arms and legs. Nothing hurt. Then I sat up. I wasn't even scratched! It was as if some gentle, unseen hand had swept me out of that hellish turret, now twisted and blazing a hundred feet away. Incredibly, and luckily for me, only two of the Lanc's twenty bombs had exploded.

But fear and horror had left their mark. For when I hauled off my helmet, most of my hair came with it.

After a night in hiding, I approached a farmer, who turned out to be a Resistance leader. With six other Allied airmen, I was passed through the French underground for eleven weeks, until British troops found us near Lens. All this time I kept seeking word of my crewmates—especially Andy Mynarski.

When I got back to England, on September *13,* I finally found out what had happened. Two of the crew had been taken prisoner; three others had got back via the underground. One of the latter was radio operator Jim Kelly. After his parachute jump, Jim told me, a French farmer hid him in a barn. Soon another Frenchman arrived there. In halting English, he told Jim about a parachutist who had landed alive, only to die of severe burns. Then he held out a flying helmet. Painted across the front was "Andy."

Almost numb with grief, I realized that Jim didn't know—no one else *could* know—why Andy died. I told the story to him, and later to Air Force officials.

The RCAF document describing my escape as "miraculous" went on to say that Andy "must have been fully aware that in trying to free the rear gunner he was almost certain to lose his own life."

With that citation, Andrew Charles Mynarski was posthumously given the Victoria Cross, the British Commonwealth's highest award for valor. His portrait was hung in the National Gallery in Ottawa, and Winnipeg named a junior high school for this quiet young Canadian whose last act was a supreme triumph of the human spirit.

Only the second member of the RCAF to win the Victoria Cross, Andy was one of very few in history whose award was based on the uncorroborated testimony of a single witness. I'll always believe that a divine providence intervened to save me because of what I had seen—so the world might know of a gallant man who laid down his life for a friend.

The tragic, heroic story
of a holocaust that
shouldn't have happened

Skyscraper
on Fire!

BY JAMES H. WINCHESTER

A SECRETARY on the twelfth floor of the new Edifício Joelma was
the first to spot trouble. She saw smoke spiraling down from the
ceiling of her office. It was then 8:50 a.m., on the first day of February 1974.

The twenty-six-floor Edifício Joelma in São Paulo, Brazil's largest
city, had been open for fourteen months. The Crefisul Investment
Bank, in which the First National City Corporation of New York is a
major shareholder, occupied the ground floor and the top fifteen
floors; the ten floors in between were for auto parking. Some 600 of
the bank's 1,032 employees were already in the building, preparing
to start work.

The secretary, alarmed by the smoke now pouring from the ceiling, warned her boss, who tried unsuccessfully to fight the fire with an extinguisher. He then phoned the building's maintenance office. That office dispatched an electrician to investigate.

Already, however, the situation was beyond control. "It was like an explosion," a file clerk said later. "There was only a little smoke, and then suddenly everything was in flames. I never knew fire could travel so fast."

From the ceiling, flames licked at, then ignited, the floor-length drapes. Then, with savage speed they spread to the tinder-dry wood-paneled walls and room dividers, and to the wall-to-wall carpeting. There was no automatic sprinkler system in the building; São Paulo's lax building code didn't require it. Only the building's concrete walls and floors were fire resistant.

Many of the forty people working on the twelfth floor fled down the narrow, open stairs. Others waited for elevators. Few tried to fight the fire. A fire hose on the twelfth floor was never pulled from its cabinet.

On the thirteenth floor, white-haired Rene Contieri, the bank's administrative manager, looked out of a window and saw smoke coming up the side of the building. Dashing downstairs, he met the electrician, who had just stepped off an elevator on the twelfth floor. They could hardly see one another in the dense smoke. Unable to do anything, the electrician headed down the stairs. Contieri stumbled back upstairs to warn his associates. He heard the sirens of fire engines on the street below. They had been alerted by a telephone operator in the hotel across the street. "We need *everything*," the first fireman to arrive radioed headquarters.

On the seventeenth floor, twenty-two-year-old Geni Dias was making coffee for other employees when she smelled something burning. "I thought at first it was the coffee machine," she recalls. It was now 9:15. As smoke and flames increased around her, she ran to the women's rest room. No one else was on the floor. All alone, she began to pray: "God, don't let this be my hour!"

Below, the building's four elevators had been delivering evacuees to the lobby. Now the starter ordered: "No more! The power may go off and leave you stalled." Two of the four women operators defied the starter, shutting the elevator doors in his face when he tried to pull them from their controls. For the next fifteen minutes, both women continued their trips, bringing down as many as twenty-five people each time—although the elevators were designed to carry only fourteen passengers apiece. On her fourth trip, twenty-seven-year-old Helena Carmen Pereira had just reached the blazing twentieth floor when the power did fail. Hours later, firemen found her body near the open door of her elevator.

Zelia da Silva, a twenty-eight-year-old mother of two, reached the twenty-third floor on her third trip. Some twenty-five people pushed into the elevator. The weight was too much. Her car descended at twice its normal speed and smashed to the basement floor with a crunching jolt. The people inside were jammed so tightly that they cushioned one another. No one was seriously hurt. Police pried open the doors and helped them out.

Blocked from going down either the stairs or the elevators, more than 150 employees crawled up the smoke-filled stairs and headed for the roof. At the head of the stairs, they found two windows, one opening onto the roof to the north of a concrete water tower, the other opening to the south. Some climbed through one, some the other. For many, the arbitrary choice spelled the difference between life and death.

Flames coming up the south side of the building, curling over the eighteen-inch-high parapet rimming the roof, roasted nearly sixty people. The one hundred or so who chose the north side, however, were partly protected by the wind, which was blowing from north to south.

By now it was 9:50 a.m. The fire was an hour old. On the twenty-fifth floor, flames began to crawl out to the window ledges where Carlos Alberto Novaes, the bank's thirty-three-year-old planning manager, and three others huddled. Faced with almost certain death, Novaes decided on a thousand-to-one chance. An amateur gymnast, he jumped up and slightly backward, grabbing another ledge two and a half feet above him. His head would have hit the bottom side of the ledge if he had jumped straight upward. Hanging twenty-five stories up, his feet dangling in space, he slowly levered himself up to the ledge just below the parapet of the roof. Then, with the others already there holding on to his legs, he hung head first down the side of the building to grab the wrists of the three men still on the twenty-fifth floor ledge and pulled them up beside him.

Firemen had no ladders tall enough to reach windows above the fifteenth floor. More than forty victims, cornered by smoke and flames, jumped or fell from the roof and windows. As they hurtled down, murmurs of horror rose like a rustling wind from the thousands of spectators gathered below. Said one eyewitness: "The bodies were like bombs falling!"

Fireman Ezequiel Pereira, using a scaling ladder to climb the outside of the building, reached a young woman on the fifteenth floor ledge. Carrying her over his shoulder, he was backing down when a man who had jumped from several floors above dropped right on top of the two, then ricocheted to his death.

"I thought we were *all* goners," the thirty-year-old fireman said later. But somehow he managed to hold both his balance and the woman, and they ultimately reached the street. The woman's back was broken. Paralyzed below the waist, she may never walk again.

On the seventeenth floor, Geni Dias, the young woman who had been making coffee, could no longer stay in the rest room. The heat from the floor was blistering her feet through the soles of her sandals; her hair was smoking. Opening the window, she crawled out on a ledge. "I thought only of death," she says. "I was on the edge of throwing myself to the street when this man's legs appeared before me. Just dropped out of the sky."

Trapped on a window ledge on the twenty-second floor, Celso Bidtinger, a twenty-year-old accountant, had waited until the flames around him subsided. Then, gripping the edge of the ledge, his body swinging in space like a pendulum, he dropped down from floor to floor.

When Geni saw him, she said, "I just grabbed him!"

"We've got to go down," the accountant told her. Hanging by his fingertips again, he dropped to the sixteenth floor. Reaching up, he caught Geni as she followed him. The young man wanted to keep going, but Geni resisted. "I can't do it again. Please don't leave me!"

Holding her tight, Bidtinger stayed. It would be nearly noon when firemen, using a scaling ladder, finally reached the pair and carried them to safety. "All I could do when we got on the ground was hug and kiss that man," says Geni. "It was a miracle!"

By eleven a.m., scores of people were dead on the roof. Survivors tore off their rings and wristwatches and threw them away—they were too hot to endure. Said one who survived the ordeal on the roof: "You could see your skin wrinkle like tissue paper in the heat."

"Oh, my God, I don't want to die!" a woman screamed, and panic started. Shrieks and yelling spread. One man climbed the parapet to jump. "I hit him several times," said Adolfo Cilento Neto, then a member of the bank's budgeting department. "He would just get up and try to jump again. I finally knocked him unconscious. Next day, he thanked me." Said another survivor: "I grabbed the blouse of a girl who was jumping. It tore, and she kept on falling."

Overhead, half a dozen small helicopters had been circling helplessly, unable to approach the top of the blazing building because of the heat and flames. Now one owned by the Pirelli Tire Company came over, carrying Sgt. Carlos Cassaniga, a member of the State Military Police First Battalion, a crack unit that serves as São Paulo's Emergency Squad. The helicopter settled to within eighteen feet of the roof, and Cassaniga, sitting in the open door of the cabin, jumped. He landed heavily, breaking several bones in his right foot.

"It was a real hell on the roof," Cassaniga said afterward. "Nearly everyone was hysterical. My first job was to try to calm them down. One girl was a real help. Though badly burned, she crawled from group to group, soothing them, telling them to hold on because help was on the way, showing them how to breathe shallowly and slowly in the smoke. I never did learn her name, but what a woman!"

The Pirelli helicopter now returned, carrying thirty-nine-year-old Helio Caldas, commander of the São Paulo Fire Brigade's Rescue Company, and a 150-foot coil of one-inch rope. Caldas dropped one end of the line to Sergeant Cassaniga, who made it fast to a support on the roof. The helicopter then landed on the roof of the adjoining twenty-six-storied St. Patrick's apartment building, which was separated from Edifício Joelma by some seventy-five feet. Caldas and others pulled the rope taut and made it fast on the roof of St. Patrick's.

Although most of the flames had by now subsided, the smoke remained blinding. Caldas stood by the rope that was stretched taut across the chasm and calmly announced: "I'm going across."

Swinging and swaying twenty-six stories above the street, pulling himself along with his hands, gripping his legs around the rope for support, Caldas inched across the single strand between the two buildings, unreeling a second coil of line from his belt. When he reached the smoking roof, Cassaniga reached out to grab him. Now the second rope that Caldas had pulled behind him was secured side-by-side with the first, making something like a pair of railroad tracks. Several First Battalion enlisted men worked their way across to join Sergeant Cassaniga and Captain Caldas on the rooftop.

A powerful Brazilian Air Force helicopter, dispatched from its base seventy miles away, now arrived. Hovering low over the roof, it dropped Lt. Luiz Nakaharada, second-in-command of the First Battalion, and a young medical student, Wanderlei Peixoto, who had volunteered to help. As the big helicopter hovered close above their heads, the panic-stricken group became a mob, jumping for its skids, scratching and clawing at each other to try and pull themselves up into the cabin.

The rescuers had to use their fists freely to subdue the most unruly. Gradually order was restored, and the evacuation of the roof, which was to take five and a half hours, was begun. The injured first, then the women, finally the men—eighty-one people in all. Once during this smoky chapter, the rotor blades of the helicopter hit the wall of the rooftop water tank, digging deep furrows into the concrete.

"We just hovered and held our breath as people were lifted up to the cabin," says Maj. Sergio Pradatzky, pilot of the helicopter. "Sometimes we had survivors stacked in there like cordwood."

About eleven a.m., firemen and First Battalion rescue teams began to work their way up inside the building. The heat remained so high that they had to wrap themselves in wet blankets. In one small rest room, six women were found dead, huddled next to each other. In another, two women sprawled, one dead, the other unconscious. Given oxygen, the second woman lived. On another floor were sixteen charred bodies. One was a clerk who had returned to the bank only that week from her honeymoon; another was a young secretary on her first day at work.

Altogether, 188 people died, and another 235 were injured. One quarter of the dead jumped or fell and one third of the victims perished on the roof.

What caused the fire? Investigation showed that six window air-conditioning units on the twelfth floor had not been properly wired. Although the manufacturer required that each unit be provided with its own fuse, only a single heavy-load fuse had been installed in the fuse panel.

In addition, the low quality electric wires leading from the fuse box to the air conditioners had been left spread loose on the false fiber ceiling. While the heavy fuse could bear the load, the wires could not. They overheated and caught fire.

In São Paulo, new fire-protection standards for high-rise buildings—calling for such measures as automatic sprinkler systems, enclosed stairwells and fire-resistant elevator shafts—were proposed and adopted. Said José Roberto Faria Lima, a member of the Brazilian Chamber of Deputies: "Only the heroism of our people prevented more lives lost in Edifício Joelma. Never again should we have to put such bravery to the test."

When the third wave crashed ashore,
it demolished the house and spun its roof out to sea
like a big merry-go-round
with two passengers aboard

Carried to Sea
by a Tidal Wave

BY MARSUE McGINNIS FERNANDEZ

IT WAS DANNY AKIONA who woke us that Monday morning in April 1946, calling from beneath our bedroom window. "Miss Kingseed! Miss Kingseed! You want to see a tidal wave? Come, come quick!"

Helen Kingseed was my roommate. Dottie Drake and Fay Johnson, who also lived with us, were asleep in the bedroom across the hall. The four of us, fresh out of stateside colleges, had come to Laupahoehoe the autumn before to teach. Laupahoehoe, on an eastern point of the big island of Hawaii, looks out across the northern ocean. It was an idyllic spot—our little cottage on the beach, the lazy surf, the eternal spring.

Quickly, Helen and I threw shirts and robes over our pajamas and went outside. Fay and Dottie joined us there. We were just in time to see the ocean suck out swiftly and quietly, baring a sea bottom never before exposed to human sight. It was as if the ocean had taken a deep, belly-filling mouthful of its water. And then, without a sound, without any visible change or warning, the water began to come in again, steadily, without surf or breakers.

We were awed and silent, but Danny was excited. "Watch it!" he shouted. "It's coming in now—big water!" It came, and it kept coming. It crawled past the usual high-tide marks and almost up to us. It hung there, lapping at our feet for a few seconds, and then it began to recede.

So this is all there is to a tidal wave, I thought. Then I heard Danny shout, "Here's another one!" Along the horizon a second wave was building up. As the five of us watched it, Fred Kruse, a Hawaiian who taught history at the high school, splashed by with five boys. I shall never forget his beaming smile. "Good fun," he called to us.

The wave reached the beach and began to come in, but it was small and we were rather disappointed. Helen turned to go into the cottage. "The show's over," she said.

"I wish a really big one had come," I answered.

Dottie and Helen went inside, but Fay and I lingered a moment on the porch. Then we both saw it at the same time. The ocean drew out once more, fast this time, with a vast, deep sigh. The deep pool just off the rocks, where we had gone swimming, drained suddenly dry. A tremendous wall of water was gathering out to the left of the lighthouse. For the first time I felt fear, an almost paralyzing fear.

Fay and I ran back into the house, slamming the door behind us. Running into the kitchen, we met Dottie and Helen. The four of us hesitated for a moment at the back door, all with the same thought: Should we risk the dash across fifty yards of lawn to the hillside beyond?

Then it struck. There was a roar like all the winds in the world. I looked back to see brown water fighting at the windows, heard the crash of shattering glass as the windows burst in and the sharp cracking of parting timbers. The four of us clung to the door frame as the cottage began to tilt and move. "It's going to tear the cottage down," Helen said. She spoke calmly, and there was more wonder than fear in her voice. No one screamed; we just braced our feet against what suddenly became nothing, and then the four of us were thrown into the water. Helen, struggling to keep her head above water, sank right in front of me. I reached down and caught her under the armpit, but the rushing water jerked her from my grasp and she was gone.

In the first rush of water the cottage was demolished and swept away, leaving the roof turning like a big merry-go-round. Fay and I caught its edge and crawled up to the ridge. There was a shudder and the wave began to draw out. We had a sensation of great speed as the roof, swaying from side to side, was swept out toward the open sea. We saw Mr. Ferdun's tan car, which had been in the garage in back of our cottage, turning end over end in the turbulent water.

Suddenly our roof-raft tilted and stopped. It had caught on a jagged rock and the sea was drawing out from under it. Fay looked at me and said, "I don't have any clothes on." I looked at myself. All that remained of mine were my checked shirt and pajama top.

Then we saw Dottie's head bobbing among the debris at the far corner of the roof. She was clutching the roof with both hands; her eyes were glazed with fear and panic. I started to inch down toward her, but her hands slipped off the edge and she sank.

"We are going to be killed," said Fay, again quietly.

"We've got to get to shore—the water is sucking out!" I shouted to her. We crawled down the roof together and dropped into the water, now only knee-deep. The bottom was rocky and uneven. Fay could not swim, and we held hands, hard and tight and desperately as we struggled forward. It wasn't far now. "We'll make it, we'll make it," I kept repeating. "Hang on, we're going to make it!"

And then another wave hit us. Fay's hand was snatched from mine as I was swept head over heels toward the jagged, knife-sharp rocks near the point. Giving up all thought of survival, I completely relaxed and became as limp as seaweed. This saved my life.

Instinctively, I held my breath. As my body was dashed against the rocks, it seemed that I could hear the breaking of my bones and the tearing of my flesh. I waited for death, and as I waited I had clear thoughts I remember well.

I thought of my brother who had survived three years of war, while I, a sheltered schoolteacher, was about to die by violence. I thought of Leabert Fernandez, a local doctor I had met at a school party just after we got to Hawaii. We had seen a good deal of each other and had a date for that very evening. We both knew we were in love. And now all this was gone. Then, as my lungs were bursting, I thought of the untold millions who had died through all the centuries before me as I was about to die. The finality of death—how well you understand when it is your own death!

Then I became dimly aware of a frothy white mass of bubbles; the darkness was shot with faint streaks of light. My bursting lungs could hold out no longer. I took a deep breath—of fresh, pure air! Miraculously, I was on top of the water! As I gulped down the life-giving air, I began to take stock. I moved my arms first, surprised that they were still attached. Then I tried my legs; they were still part of me too, and I could move them. I could see. But I couldn't hear; the pressure on my ears had temporarily dulled my hearing. I was in a frenzied, tossing, but soundless sea.

I began to swim, an awkward and halting stroke indeed, but it carried me to calmer waters, beyond the rocks. I was surprised that I could float so easily until I discovered that I was clinging to a piece of debris, a painted green board about as long and wide as my body. I raised myself out of the water as much as I could and shouted, "Help!" My hearing was coming back, and my own voice frightened me—hoarse and cracked. Then I saw the distant shore, and the tossing water between, and knew that no one could hear me. I could see automobiles moving leisurely along the coast road.

When I noticed several boards still nailed together floating toward me I swam to them and tried to climb aboard. The raft would accommodate only half of me, but I draped myself across it and felt more secure, for I was higher out of the water. I kept thinking of the dangers from below—barracuda, moray eels, stingrays—and *sharks!* But I calmed this fear with a little reasoning. In an ocean churned by a tidal wave most fish would surely keep close to the protection of the bottom. As my panic left me, I looked around—and it was then that I saw the others.

On the crest of a particularly high wave I counted seven heads. Some were clinging to remains of broken buildings; two were holding onto an uprooted lauhala tree. "Hey!" I yelled. But they didn't shout back—they just stared as if in a coma. They were all children.

Later I looked down from the top of a big swell and saw a small boy clinging to a large log. He began to struggle toward me and I toward him.

"What's your name?" I asked.

"Thomas Fujimoto—you're Miss McGinniss?"

"Yes," I said, and we drifted close enough to touch each other, separated only by his log and my raft. I tried for modesty's sake to keep most of me under the water. "Where were you when the wave came?"

"In the school washroom," he answered. So the wave had got up that far; that accounted for all the children I had seen. "Hang on!" I advised as we drifted apart.

Time had little meaning now, for I began to feel acute physical distress. My left hip was raw, from the Laupahoehoe rocks. I could feel cuts and bruises all over. I had bitten through my lower lip and couldn't close my mouth without pain. I was getting colder. A stiff wind was blowing, and a cold drizzle had started.

My raft was beginning to fall apart when I spotted another, larger one coming toward me. Finally it drifted within swimming distance, and I caught it. This one was big enough for me to lie down on, but I had to balance myself just right or be flipped over and dunked. It seemed to me I climbed aboard that thing a thousand times.

Now I began to hear planes overhead. I knelt on the raft and waved. This usually caused my raft to take a nose dive, dumping me into the water. I would climb aboard again, rebalance myself and wait hopefully for the next plane.

To pass the time I made a mental list of the unusual things that floated by. I counted eight dead chickens, our neighbor Mr. Nakano's, no doubt. Then there was Fay's fiber purse, which she had carried the first time I ever saw her. A moment later my own lauhala purse went drifting by. It had been in the tightly closed bottom drawer of my dresser. Then there was Mrs. Nakano's photograph that Mr. Nakano displayed on the shelf in his living room, a sodden book titled *Literature and Life* and Dottie's orange-crate chest, still with its cover of tapa paper.

The current was carrying me around a point, parallel to the coast. Laupahoehoe had disappeared long ago and now the Ookala sugar mill was coming into view. Seeing the workers' houses, I began to shout again. But it was growing late. People would be sitting down to supper with those they loved, while I was alone here, forgotten and doomed.

Then another plane flew over me, this time so low that I could see the pilot. I waved vigorously, took the inevitable spill and climbed back aboard the raft. But I didn't care. He had spotted me.

He made a long circle, came back and dropped a bundle. I reached the yellow package in a few strokes. Stenciled on it in large black letters were the simple instructions: TO INFLATE, UNSNAP AND PULL HANDLE. That's all there was to it. Swish! Like magic, the raft inflated, and I climbed aboard.

I lay in the bottom and relaxed; for the first time since I had come up for air I could rest. There was no fear of falling off, no balancing, no waving or shouting. I was in heaven.

It was then I saw the little boat coming directly toward me, so close I wondered why I hadn't seen it before. The man foremost in the bow was Leabert Fernandez. "This can't be," I thought. "It's too much like a storybook." But it was indeed Leabert. As soon as he heard about the wave, he had rushed to the shore, found a boat and was now looking for survivors. He was in swimming trunks and he looked wonderfully strong and secure and familiar. He leaned far over and held the raft fast to the boat as the waves dashed the two craft up and down.

"Are you all right?" he asked. I could not answer. "Marsue! Can you climb into the boat?"

I found my voice. "I haven't any clothes on."

"Never mind," he said, and he climbed into the raft, wrapped me in a blanket, and lifted me into the boat.

Also aboard were two schoolboys, one huddled in the bottom, looking more dead than alive; the other was sitting up facing the stern, his head bandaged. His face was rigid and his eyes expressionless, that same look I had seen on those other childish faces bobbing up and down among the wreckage.

There was a quiet and sad-faced crowd waiting on the shore. Waiting for Dottie and Helen and Fay and Thomas Fujimoto and

169 others who would never come home. I was lifted out and Leabert carried me to his car. The two boys were put in the backseat, and we started for the hospital.

There, covered with blankets and surrounded with hot-water bottles, I still shivered. My lips stayed blue for hours, but finally I fell asleep and slept the clock around. When I woke, Leabert was sitting beside my bed. For a long time neither of us spoke. Finally, very gently, he said, "Marsue, will you marry me?" I couldn't kiss him, for I had four stitches in my lower lip. But we have lived very, very happily ever after.

How a tugboat skipper
and his five-man crew
helped avert what might have been
the most devastating explosion
in the history of shipping

Trouble off
Bergen Point!

BY THOMAS GALLAGHER

FOR CAPT. GEORGE SAHLBERG, master of the tugboat *Julia C. Moran,* June 16, 1966, began routinely enough. He and his five-man crew towed a fuel barge past the Statue of Liberty to a ship anchored in New York Harbor. With two Moran Company sister tugs, they butted an ocean liner into her berth in the Hudson River. Then they cruised over to Brooklyn where they jockeyed a pile-driving rig into position alongside a pier that was being repaired.

At two p.m., sky clear, waters calm, and a light breeze from the south, they were tied up at the Moran yard on Staten Island, awaiting orders. Sahlberg, a stocky man with a weather-worn face after thirty years as a Moran tugboat captain, kept his engine idling. "In this business, you never know."

Fifteen minutes later, over his shortwave radio, crackled the order that turned the day into one that Sahlberg would never forget: "Proceed to Bergen Point. There's been some trouble." Then silence.

From the dispatcher's tone of voice, Sahlberg knew the problem was serious. The confined waters off Bergen Point were among the most dangerous in New York Harbor. Tankers two city blocks long

often passed within yards of each other on their way through the Kill Van Kull, a narrow channel separating Staten Island from Bayonne, New Jersey.

"Hey, Inge!" Sahlberg bellowed to his mate. "Trouble off Bergen Point. Let's get going!"

As the snub-nosed *Julia* set out toward the Kill Van Kull, Inge Nordberg and deckhand Jerry Thorpe laid out extra heaving lines. Chief engineer Richard Decker and oiler George Hudson unlimbered fire hoses, extinguishers and additional towing gear. Even Frank Oliveiras, the cook, lent a hand.

The high pilothouse provided Sahlberg with an unobstructed view as he swung around a point of land. Dead ahead, just off Bergen Point, he saw two huge tankers lying at right angles to each other, so close that Sahlberg knew they had collided in midchannel. Although their own tugs lay nearby, the *Julia* was the first rescue vessel on the scene.

"No fire," Inge said to Sahlberg.

Each knew what the other was thinking. Earlier that morning, going through the Kill, they had passed one of the tankers, the 575-foot-long *Texaco Massachusetts*. She had been discharging a cargo of high-octane gasoline, which meant that the air in her now-empty tanks was heavy with explosive gasoline fumes. This made her even more dangerous than when she was fully loaded; now she was, in fact, a 16,500-ton floating bomb. And she lay only 200 yards from the Texaco tank farm at the tip of Bergen Point, where 37.8 million gallons of highly flammable petroleum products were stored.

Sahlberg didn't know it, but the other tanker, the 11,252-ton *Alva Cape,* was loaded with 4.2 million gallons of naphtha, a lethally volatile petroleum solvent. Nor could he see the thirty-foot gash in her starboard bow, the thousands of gallons of naphtha gushing from her forward compartment, and the deadly spread of it over the water surrounding the ships.

But aboard the tug *Latin American,* tied to the *Texaco Massachusetts* just 150 feet from the flowing naphtha, the crew saw the danger and struggled desperately to slack off their towline. They didn't make it. The naphtha vapors, sucked into the tug's engine room through a ventilator, were ignited by a spark from the generator. The tug exploded, sending fire and debris in every direction. A huge, mushroom-shaped incandescence lit the area as the vapors hovering about the ships and pouring from the *Alva Cape* also caught fire.

To Sahlberg, now within 500 yards of the dreadful scene, it looked like the beginning of the end of the Port of New York. The *Alva Cape,* a roaring inferno, was aligning herself with the current, swinging clockwise on her anchor. In five minutes she would fetch up alongside the *Texas Massachusetts.* If the *Texaco Massachusetts* blew up, tons of hot metal would fly onto the Texaco tank farm at Bergen Point.

Once the Texaco tanks went, the flames would quickly spread to the Ross Oil Terminal tanks only a few blocks away, then to the adjacent Humble Oil Company tanks, and then to the Bayonne Industries tanks. In all, twenty-six terminals and refineries, holding billions of gallons of flammable chemicals and petroleum products, radiated outward from the collision area. If the fire spread, the entire harbor and every ship in it would be endangered. The Statue of Liberty would be engulfed in flames. Every window in downtown New York would be smashed as the petroleum tanks exploded. On the New Jersey side, Newark, Bayonne, Elizabeth, Gulfport, Carteret and Perth Amboy would have to be evacuated—and, with the tide coming in, the fiery oil on the water would be carried to Manhattan itself.

Had Sahlberg veered the *Julia* away from such a prospect, no one would have blamed him. But he could see crewmen aboard the blazing *Alva Cape*, some diving overboard with clothes aflame. To reach Bergen Point, they would have to swim around their flaming ship and through the burning naphtha. The *Julia*, lying only 200 yards from them now, was their only chance.

Sahlberg didn't hesitate. "Get ambulances and doctors to the yard," he radioed his dispatcher. "We're going to pick up survivors."

He made his approach from windward, to keep the smoke blowing away from the *Julia*. Soon the water around the tug was alive with men screaming to be hauled aboard. But ahead of them two frenzied survivors were in a life-and-death race with a wall of flame rolling toward them like ocean surf. "They're in the most danger," Sahlberg said to his crew. "We have to get to them first."

The *Julia* was so close to the blazing *Alva Cape* that its crew could hear the crackle of the flames and the dull thud of paint blisters bursting along the waterline. Tensely, Nordberg and Thorpe waited on deck, heaving lines poised. Both threw perfect shots that landed inches from the two men in the water. Desperately, the men clutched and held on. But then another terrible thing happened.

The second of the attending tugs, the *Esso Vermont*, only a hundred yards from the *Alva Cape*, exploded, killing her entire crew. White flames shot out in all directions, and now the *Julia* herself was engulfed in fire. "Don't haul those men in yet!" Sahlberg shouted. "I'll back out and we'll pull them after us."

Slowly, to avoid running over any of the survivors he had passed by earlier, he drew the two men back from the sea of flame. Clear of the inferno, the men were quickly hauled in and wrapped in blankets.

Every second counted now. The screaming men around the tug had to be pulled aboard before the flaming naphtha reached them. As Sahlberg maneuvered his tug among the bobbing heads and outstretched arms, Nordberg and Thorpe, at the bow, heaved their lines to those farthest away. The engineer, oiler and cook concentrated on those close enough to be pulled aboard by hand.

Up in the pilothouse, Sahlberg saw the burning *Alva Cape* swinging closer and closer to the *Texaco Massachusetts*. It was time to run for it. He radioed his dispatcher: "We're on our way to the yard. Twenty-three survivors."

Minutes later, the survivors were taken off the tug to the waiting ambulances. Then Sahlberg and his men sped back to Bergen Point. Three fireboats had arrived, as well as two Coast Guard boats and five other Moran tugs. As the fireboats played long parabolas of water and foam against the *Alva Cape*, the blazing tanker swung parallel—and ever closer—to the *Texaco Massachusetts*. For the second time that day, Sahlberg saw what needed doing and didn't hesitate. Coordinating the *Julia's* efforts with those of the other Moran tugs, he moved in for the most urgent task of all: towing the *Texaco Massachusetts* away from the *Alva Cape* before the *Alva Cape* exploded.

It would not be easy. The *Texaco Massachusetts* had been abandoned, so no one was aboard to operate her anchor windlass. If the tugs attempted to move her away, her dragging anchor would cut the main cable carrying power and telephone lines between Staten Island and New Jersey.

While two tugs maneuvered under the bow of the tanker, Sahlberg drew the *Julia* close to her starboard side. From there, Nordberg scrambled up the tug's boarding ladder to the tanker's upper deck. Knee-deep in fire-fighting foam, he pulled aboard a heavy hawser from the *Julia* and made it fast. Next the *Susan Moran* pulled alongside, and again Nordberg, with brute strength alone, pulled her line up and made it fast, too. Meanwhile, other Moran men had climbed aboard. Discovering that there was still power on the ship, they started the anchor windlass and raised the anchor just clear of the water.

With U. S. Coast Guard vessels leading the way, the hot, smoking ship was towed at a dirge pace to an anchorage off Brooklyn. There the tug crews freed their lines and chugged back to their routine chores. Later, they learned that the fire aboard the ill-fated *Alva Cape* had been brought under control.

When Sahlberg returned to his home in Brielle, New Jersey, that evening, he was embarrassed to find himself hailed as a hero. A modest man, he insisted that he had done no more than anyone else. But the facts proved otherwise. Thirty-three men had died in the disaster. Of the seventy-seven who were rescued, the *Julia* had saved twenty-three. Moreover, she had led the effort to tow the *Texaco Massachusetts* away from the inferno, thus averting what might have been the most devastating explosion in the history of shipping.

Four months later, New York's Mayor John Lindsay presented Sahlberg with the Greater Times Square Committee's first Good Citizenship Award, in recognition of his "leadership and courage." The following month, the U. S. Department of Commerce honored the *Julia C. Moran* with a Gallant Ship Award, the highest honor the government can bestow on a merchant ship. It was accompanied by a Merchant Marine Distinguished Service Medal for Capt. George Sahlberg, and unit citations, ribbon bars and meritorious-service medals for each of his crew. Before the year was over, Sahlberg received the greatest honor of all: the American Bureau of Shipping Valor Medal, presented only three times since its creation in 1928 and never before to a tugboat captain.

George Sahlberg was retired and living in a seaside cottage in Manasquan, New Jersey, when this was written. Occasionally, sitting on the porch of his cottage, he showed the Valor Medal to a friend. Of all the rooms he had, he preferred the porch, because from it he could see his fishing boat swaying in the inlet a few yards offshore, and watch as his grandchildren danced with joy every time they netted a crab.

To plucky Marg Laidlaw,
swallowed by waves of snow,
the silence and loneliness were like the grave itself.
Then, along came Zacho,
the best avalanche dog in all Italy

A Brush
With White Death

BY FRANCIS SCHELL

SNOW HAD COME DOWN heavily in the Italian north throughout the winter of 1971–72. By early March, the villagers of Macugnaga were warily eyeing the Alpine slopes for avalanches triggered by spring thaws. One house and three ski tows had already been crushed. Then the snow changed to rain, and all the ski lifts in the area were closed because of the growing threat of avalanches.

On Saturday, March 11, it was still raining. Access to the village was blocked to car traffic by slides. Impatient with two days of enforced inactivity, Margaret and Ernest John Laidlaw from Toronto, in Macugnaga for a skiing vacation, decided to move on in search of sunnier slopes.

About eleven a.m., they hoisted their packs on their backs, shouldered their skis and set out in the winter drizzle for the village of Ceppo Morelli, seven miles away. There they could take a bus to the nearest railroad station.

Both seasoned athletes, Marg and Ernie set a brisk pace on skis and on foot. They reached the tunnel at the base of the 10,000-foot Battel peak by noon, only to find that it had been blocked by an avalanche. There, they met three Italian nurses from Como—Vanna Rizzi, her younger sister, and a friend. In a mixture of French, Italian and gestures, they agreed that in order to rejoin the road on the other side of the tunnel—some 250 yards away—it

would be necessary for them to walk right over the avalanche field, following footprints presumably made earlier by road crews.

Marg and Ernie were reluctant and wanted to turn back, but when they saw the nurses proceeding safely, they decided to risk it. Ernie had walked and skied over avalanche fields before. If the girls could make it, so could they.

He carefully picked his way across, with Marg following about twenty-five yards behind. Suddenly she heard her husband shout. Marg looked up and instantly saw the danger. Sweeping toward her at hurricane speed were waves of thundering snow. She tossed away her skis and tried to free herself from her backpack as she stumbled into a run. It was too late. Vanna Rizzi, some distance away, saw Marg's red-parkaed figure being swallowed by the racing snow as she tried to hold on to a broken scrub birch.

A second avalanche came down, then a third covering the entire area with a craggy mass of icy boulders. Ernie calmed the now near-hysterical nurses and sent them racing off to summon help.

Among the first to get the news was Renato Cresta, a thirty-five-year-old former army captain. A volunteer member of the National Alpine Rescue Squad, Cresta was responsible for the Macugnaga avalanche area. He scooped up his gear—probing rods, paper flags, megaphone—summoned some men and raced to the tunnel. There he immediately posted lookouts with walkie-talkies on the opposite slope to watch the heights for any new snow movement. Some fifteen men lined up elbow to elbow about where Marg had disappeared and began probing with their twelve-foot metal rods. With Cresta directing operations by megaphone, the men would advance one step, then push the rods into the snow. Each area probed was then marked off with flags.

Soon an avalanche dog arrived—one of fifty-four specially trained animals available for avalanche rescues. In twenty minutes an avalanche dog can search an area that would take twenty men ten hours to explore. Everyone was cleared from the field while the dog smelled about. He found nothing—and to Cresta the dog seemed distracted and uninspired. *If only it were Zacho!* Renato thought. Zacho belonged to his good friend Alberto Borgna, and Renato believed him to be the best avalanche dog in Italy. But Borgna lived about 200 miles away.

When the men could no longer see up the mountain, the search had to be called off. It was an anguished moment for Ernie, but Cresta held out hope for the next day: He would call Borgna and urge him to bring his dog.

On Sunday, drizzle alternated with snow. Even the church bells sounded doleful. Several new slides up the road prevented the early arrival of the rescuers and probing didn't get underway until eight-thirty. Ernie worked steadily with forty volunteers all day, clinging to the hope of the other dog that Renato had promised him would come. What he did not know then was that Borgna had been delayed—first by avalanches in his own region, then by trouble with his car along the way.

At six-thirty p.m., the drenched volunteers had to stop, for heavy fog made further searching impossible. Those who could agreed to resume early Monday. By then Borgna and his dog would surely be there—the one thought that would get Ernie through another impossible night.

When the first wave of snow washed over her, Marg tried to "swim" as near to the surface as possible, using a kind of breast-stroke to stay upright. One rough tumble, however, and she found herself buried under the snow in almost total darkness.

Her first thought was: *I'm going to suffocate!* But after a few minutes she was able to take stock of her situation. She could move her right arm in what seemed to be a small cavity in front of her face, but the left one was twisted awkwardly and immobile. Her legs—one bent at the knee and slightly twisted, the other straight out—were solidly wedged in. She had on heavy knee-length woolen socks, thick gabardine knickers, her red parka and under it a warm Icelandic ski sweater. But with trepidation she remembered that she had removed her black leather ski mitts and asked Ernie to put them in her rucksack. Now her hands were bare, and the sack was lodged above and in front of her head.

It was imperative, she knew, to avoid panic, to keep busy and do everything she could to attract attention. She burrowed her right hand into a position where she could scrape away the icy chunks holding her left. It took what seemed like hours of patient chipping, twisting and pulling, but at last her left hand was free.

Now she could attend to a vital problem: She was wearing contact lenses and knew that if she fell asleep or became unconscious they could cause a serious eye inflammation. With fingers cramped from the cold she got first one lens out, then the other. They disappeared in the snow.

Marg now tried to scrape more space around her, perhaps even worm her way out. With only her bare hands? She remembered a plastic name tag on her rucksack. Wriggle, wrench, twist, turn—at last she had it. She began enlarging the space around her face, and gradually a kind of small cavern emerged, allowing her to move her shoulders slightly.

Exhausted, she put her hands under her sweater and rested. After a while, she reached for her scraper, but couldn't find it. Disaster! But, then she remembered that tucked inside her parka was a small plastic purse with a sturdy metal frame. She continued scraping with that, trying to free her legs so that she'd have more leverage. Finally she could move them up and down, but her feet would not budge. And the rucksack blocked any forward movement. At frequent intervals she stopped to rest until the cold became unbearable, then she began again.

Suddenly, she heard voices—even footsteps—above her. She began shouting in every language she could remember: "Help!" *Aiuto! Au secours!*" (She didn't know that snow is one of nature's poorest sound conductors.) Again and again she cried out. The steps and voices ebbed and flowed nearby, then faded away for good. The silence was excruciating, the loneliness overwhelming. Marg felt overcome with horror at the sound of her own voice screaming.

It was no use. Perhaps, after all, falling asleep in the snow was not such a bad way of dying.

Her thoughts turned to Ernie, and she wondered if he was all right. When she had last seen him hurrying toward her, he had seemed beyond the path of the avalanche; but perhaps not. She thought of her family and friends, of the cross-country skiing trip she and Ernie had planned back home for the coming Easter.

It was the end of the third day, according to Marg's calculations, when she finally lost consciousness.

Alberto Borgna, one of Italy's most accomplished avalanche-rescue experts, arrived in Ceppo Morelli with his dog Zacho on Sunday night. He had raised Zacho from a puppy, and his meticulous training had won the big German shepherd a number of first prizes at avalanche-dog field trials. They had by now shared many real rescue missions, too, but had never yet recovered someone alive from under an avalanche.

At six forty-five the next morning, they went to the search site. While Ernie was left on the road to watch for new avalanches—and also to spare him in case Marg's body was discovered—Borgna and Zacho started their routine. First, he walked Zacho about to relax him. Then he pulled on a special orange parka that he wore only on rescue operations, an instant reminder to Zacho of what the outing was about. He knelt down to encourage the dog and let him loose.

Closely sniffing the ground, Zacho systematically zigzagged over the area. After a while the boulders in his way made Zacho's search erratic and Borgna put him on a long leash. They now covered the lower half of the territory worked over by the probers on Sunday. Nothing.

After twenty minutes Borgna made Zacho stop and rest. Then they resumed the search and covered the upper half of the area, again with no results.

Cresta, who had been keeping out of the way, now came up. "What do we do?" he asked.

"Go back to the village and rest," said Borgna. "The dog can only work effectively half an hour at a stretch before his attention wanders."

While they were talking, Zacho had climbed uphill, in the opposite direction from the search area, as far as his long leash would let him, to about fifty feet from the road. All of a sudden he stopped, sniffing repeatedly. Then he took one or two steps and began pawing away at the snow with unaccustomed frenzy.

Borgna nudged his friend. "He must have found something," he said. *"Good dog, Zacho. Go! Go!"* he encouraged the dog.

Once, twice, three times, Borgna probed around the spot. He moved a bit higher and probed again. The fourth time something blocked his rod. He began digging, with Zacho tensely watching each shovelful of snow removed.

About three feet down, a dull gray-green patch of material came to light, part of a rucksack. Lifting more of the snow away, Borgna soon saw a red-clad shoulder and then a lock of hair. Marg was lying face down. Borgna now slipped his arm into the hole to ascertain Marg's position. Bending over her, he heard a soft, plaintive moan. She was breathing!

"She's alive!" Borgna yelled for all to hear. Cresta joined him at once. Ernie bounded down from the road, and together the three rushed to remove the snow. Soon Marg's back was visible, and peering down more closely, Borgna could see a slight trickle of saliva flowing from her lips, forming tiny air bubbles. Gradually they freed Marg's torso, and Borgna gave her heart massage. He also covered her eyes to protect them against the light. The hard snow then literally had to be cut away from around her feet. At last she was free—a frozen mass, her hands showing frostbite, her face deathly white but with no trace of a bluish tint, the sure sign of oxygen deprivation.

Marg's stiff body was loaded onto a road-crew minibus and driven to a nearby hotel. Under Borgna's expert direction, lukewarm water bottles were placed on her stomach, she was wrapped in warmed blankets and towels and gently massaged. By the time a doctor arrived, Marg's heartbeat was near normal.

Why had she survived her ordeal? "Because I was excessively lucky," said Marg modestly later. "Because she is a strong girl with a great will to live," explained Ernie, "and because she was dressed warmly for any emergency." "Because she was in top physical condition with a remarkably robust heart," say the doctors. The avalanche experts add: "Fortunately, the chunky snow contained enough trapped air." And she had not been taken by the full force of the avalanche—but rather quickly shouldered aside under a mere five feet of snow.

One week from the day of the accident, Marg was sitting beside Ernie in a plane bound for home. Back in Toronto, Marg Laidlaw received extensive skin grafts on her right hand, left elbow and both knees. A compressed nerve in one leg left her with a temporary limp and recurring pain. But three months after the accident she was back at work, and she was able to spend a weekend canoeing and camping with her husband.

Sometimes human warmth
is the only solace for a frozen spirit

The Trail

BY STEPHEN A. CRANE

FOR THE FIRST THREE DAYS of my hike through New Mexico's Pecos Wilderness area, a snow fell, heavily powdering the trees with a blanket of white. The third afternoon I made camp on Truchas Peak. Next morning, I awoke to a sun shining so sharply against the new snow that it was difficult to see even with goggles. But it felt good hiking into the sun in the cold morning air.

I remembered the trail better than I thought I would. I had hiked through these mountains five years before with Joni, my wife. I did not believe I would remember the twisting and bending of the trail as it slowly made its way through the valley and along the crest of the mountains. But I did, clearly and distinctly—as if the five long years since Joni's death had been erased.

We had walked this trail in the early spring with the hills, valley and upper mountains just beginning to blossom after a long winter. Now, in mid-April 1975, I hiked alone, with the mountains frozen solid and the streams we once swam in still locked in the coldness of winter. There was a chill deep inside me—a chill much worse than the physical cold.

The day's hike of more than twenty miles was hard, hampered by four-foot drifts and a strong wind. Near sundown, I entered a deep canyon. I pitched my dome tent and put my pack inside. Exhausted, I stood in the waning light watching the final rays of the sun trace their way up the canyon's side. In the sudden silence and darkness I felt totally alone—not lonely or afraid, just completely alone.

I removed my snowshoes and climbed into the tent. After dinner I fell asleep.

It was a blessing to sleep after so many nights spent shuffling aimlessly through the home Joni and I had built—hours spent trying to read or watch television, hoping that soon I would be able to sleep, only to find myself watching the colorless light of early morning filling the house.

I awoke the fifth day just before dawn to find the floor of the tent frozen solid against the snow-packed ground. But the cold didn't bother me—it seemed almost natural. Five years of no warmth is long enough to get used to the cold, to become a part of it and, maybe, even to feel some comfort in its consistency, its damnable permanence.

As the first ray of light descended on the opposite side of the canyon, I took down the tent, tied my boots into my snowshoes and began to walk. The canyon floor was now filled with clear bright sunlight. But far in the distance, large white clouds were pushing in from the north. Even while I stood there, I could watch them cover the sky with billowing intensity until they became so dark it was impossible to see the tips of the trees. I was not worried; I had plenty of food, and if the weather got too bad I could just settle down and wait it out.

I headed toward the storm, remembering the spring of the third year Joni and I were married, and the vacation we had spent in Wyoming taking pictures for a tourist agency. We had backpacked about thirty miles into the Tetons and set up a base from which we would take short hikes each day to get the pictures we needed. On the fourth day, at nightfall, a violent storm came up, and the whipping wind and hail destroyed our tent in minutes. With our heads wrapped in our jackets to protect us from the hail, we had run to a cave a mile from our camp. Joni fell at one point, and I swept her up and carried her. She seemed weightless to me.

We slept that night in the cave wrapped in each other's arms. The temperature dropped way below freezing, but I was warm just feeling her breath sweet and warm against my cheek. There is a mystery of love, a mystery that not only can endure all but can prevail over all; I was warm then, warm and needing nothing more. Two springs later, a drunk lost control of his car in a supermarket parking lot in Sacramento, California. I had been cold ever since.

The trail crossed a valley and, just as I started along the winding path up the side of the next mountain, the wind began to blow hard from the north. The clouds had covered the sky completely, and the wind swept the blowing powder hard against me until it began to freeze to my face. The cold that had been living inside me for so long finally began to grip me with the same freezing hand that had gripped the stream. It froze me motionless and quiet inside.

I knew that I should stop, but I didn't; I just continued letting the snow slowly cover and mat my face in a shield of coldness. I climbed slowly to a spot on top of the mountain where Joni and I had stood hand-in-hand looking down into the valleys, marveling at the mystery of life, at the beauty of nature and the wonder of God. But now I stood there alone, with the snow blowing so hard that it prevented me from seeing anything—my only sensation the ever-enveloping coldness. As I started down the mountain, I cried—not hard or even making a sound—but I felt the tears while I thought of her breath warm against my cheek in that cave.

Although I couldn't see, I could tell I was heading down the mountain. I continued for hours, not knowing if I was on the trail or not. I fell once, lying in the snow for a long time, feeling a strange peace. I now know that it was just an abandonment, a letting go and giving up. I wanted it to surround me and become fused to me. But I rose again, not knowing why, to continue against the hard blowing wind and freezing snow.

As the trail was beginning to climb again, I heard a sound. I thought it was just the wind, but then I heard it a second time— weak, childlike and helpless. I stopped and listened but could not hear anything. Just as I was about to go on I heard it once more. I dropped my pack and tried to run, but even my snowshoes sank deep into the snow. I yelled into the howling wind and heard it again—a faint, almost inaudible, cry.

After a long time, I found a boy no older than twelve, lying beside an overturned snowmobile, bleeding from the head. The blood had filtered deeply through the snow, and he was motionless, looking up at me, his eyes already glazed. I knelt beside him and brushed the snow away from his face. "I'll be back. I'll get my pack and be back," I told him.

Somehow I found my way to my pack and back to the boy without any trouble. I got the tent up, then carried him inside to my sleeping bag. His head had stopped bleeding, but his face had a gray, lifeless cast and his fingers were deep blue from frostbite. I threw my coat over him and, after starting the small stove to warm the tent, took an extra shirt I had and cut it to make a bandage for his head. I spent hours rubbing his hands and feet, trying to get his blood moving freely. Slowly a little color began to return to his face; his breathing grew deeper, and he slept for a long time.

About midnight, the stove ran out of gas, and an hour later the boy awoke crying, saying he was cold. His voice was weak and thin. I pulled off my sweater and wrapped it around him. He slept quietly for an hour, then began to shiver. I lay down beside him with my arms wrapped around him. As I listened to his breathing, I began to feel warm. I slept for a few minutes and dreamed of Joni, of us wrapped in each other's arms in that cave.

Before I was totally awake, I thought it was Joni lying asleep beside me. I wanted to cry, but I lighted a candle and looked at the boy. He was still pale, but his color was better and his breathing stronger. He opened his eyes and stared at me; he wasn't frightened and seemed to know where he was. He shut his eyes again before speaking: "You saved my life."

I blew out the candle and thought for a long time. I felt ashamed about the day before, when I had fallen and almost given up. I wanted to tell the boy that he had saved my life, too. I sat there for a long time, confused and afraid.

Toward dawn, I began to feel a little better. The snow was still falling hard outside with a strong wind. I fell asleep and woke as the sun began to rise. The storm had passed. The forest was quiet, except for the breathing of the boy.

I climbed out of the tent and watched the sun slowly rise behind the trees. Suddenly, a large bird took to the air, making the silhouette of a cross as it spread its wings and flew toward the sun. For a moment I felt a warmth run through me—not a violent heat, but gentle, soothing warmth that slowly began to jar me free from the cold and loneliness I had known for the last five years. And then, as I watched the bird cutting across the sky with its great wings spread flat against the sun, I prayed. My sadness didn't totally pass, but it slowly began to dissolve and melt away, as the snow would shortly.

The snowmobile would not start, but the boy was weightless as I carried him the ten miles to the highway. I knew that he was going to be all right.

ILLUSTRATION CREDITS

Pages 10-11: © Four by Five, Inc. Pages 154-155: Joan Kramer and Associates. Page 184: Richard Hamond. Pages 292-293: © Ernest Braun/The Image Bank. Pages 396, 398, 420: United Press International. Page 399: Wide World Photos, Inc. Pages 414, 415: *San Francisco Chronicle*. Pages 432-433: Glenn Kirkpatrick/FPG.

ACKNOWLEDGMENTS

THE RESCUE ON STATION CHARLIE, by Capt. Paul B. Cronk, was condensed from *The Atlantic Monthly*, July 1950. Copyright © 1950 by The Atlantic Monthly Co., Boston. CAR ON THE TRACK!, by Evan McLeod Wylie, was condensed from *Yankee*, November 1978. Copyright © 1978 by Yankee Publishing, Inc., Dublin, NH. ORDEAL IN WHISKEY-ECHO, by Richard Hamond, originally appeared in the Australian edition of *Reader's Digest*, April 1970, published by Reader's Digest Services Pty. Ltd. THE INCREDIBLE SURVIVAL OF DEMI MCCLURE, by Lt. Col. David G. Simons with Don A. Schanche, was condensed from *Man High* by David G. Simons and Don A. Schanche, copyright © 1960 by David G. Simons and Don A. Schanche. Reprinted by permission of Doubleday & Co., Inc., New York, and Sidgwick and Jackson Ltd., London. THE NIGHT MY NUMBER CAME UP, by Air Marshal Sir Victor Goddard, was condensed from *The Saturday Evening Post*, May 26, 1951, copyright © 1951 by The Curtis Publishing Co., Philadelphia. THE TORNADO AND THE SERMON, by Allen Rankin, also appeared in *Christian Herald*, November 1973. "A PILOT IS DOWN!", by Richard Armstrong, was condensed from "It's Great To Be Alive," *The Saturday Evening Post*, June 4, 1966, copyright © 1966 by The Curtis Publishing Co., Philadelphia. GRANPA AND THE ATLANTIC OCEAN, by David O. Woodbury, was condensed from *Down East, The Magazine of Maine*, August 1961, copyright © 1961 by Down East Enterprise, Inc., Camden, ME. NIGHTMARE IN THE JUNGLE, by Juliane Koepcke, copyright © 1972 by Stern/Gruner & Jahr AG & Co., Hamburg, Germany. ONLY ONE CAME BACK, by Øystein Molstad-Andresen, copyright © 1973 by Gyldendal Norsk Forlag, Oslo, Norway. A TOWN'S RACE AGAINST DEATH, by Claus Gaedemann, originally appeared in the Australian edition of *Reader's Digest*, February 1975, published by Reader's Digest Services Pty. Ltd. I FELL INTO A THUNDERSTORM, by Lt. Col. William H. Rankin, was condensed from *The Man Who Rode the Thunder*, by Lt. Col. William H. Rankin, U.S.M.C. ©1960 by Prentice-Hall, Inc. Published by Prentice-Hall, Inc., Englewood Cliffs, NJ. THE TOWN THAT WOULDN'T DIE, by Gerald Moore, also appeared in *The Saturday Evening Post*, December 1975. HOW ICELAND FOUGHT THE FIERY MOUNTAIN, by Paul Henissart, originally appeared in the British edition of *Reader's Digest*, January 1974, published by The Reader's Digest Association Ltd. THE BOY WHO CAME BACK TO LIFE, by Sidney Katz, originally appeared in the Canadian edition of *Reader's Digest*, November 1976, published by The Reader's Digest Association (Canada) Ltd. CASE OF THE DEADLY HOT PEPPERS, by Al Stark, was condensed from *Michigan: The Magazine of the Detroit News*, May 22, 1977, copyright © 1977 by The Evening News Assn., Detroit. TWO SURVIVED, by Guy Pearce Jones, copyright © 1941 by Guy Pearce Jones, © renewed 1968 by Guy Pearce Jones. Reprinted by permission of Harold Matson Co., Inc., New York. EMERGENCY AT WAITANGI, by Maurice Shadbolt, originally appeared in the South African edition of *Reader's Digest*, May 1979, published by The Reader's Digest Association South Africa (Pty.) Ltd. THE MAN IN THE BURNING BOMBER, by John G. Hubbell, also appeared in *True* magazine, September 1958. "WHAT A CRAZY WAY FOR LIFE TO END!", by Ted Morgan, was condensed from *Esquire*, November 1974, copyright © 1974 by Esquire, Inc., New York. A BRUSH WITH WHITE DEATH, by Francis Schell, originally appeared in the Canadian edition of *Reader's Digest*, February 1973, published by The Reader's Digest Association (Canada) Ltd.

The quotation on page 293 from *The Old Man and the Sea*, by Ernest Hemingway, is reprinted with the permission of Charles Scribner's Sons, New York. Copyright 1952 Ernest Hemingway, copyright renewed 1980 by Mary Hemingway. The quotation on page 433 is from *The Faulkner Reader*, copyright © 1954 by William Faulkner. Published by Random House, Inc., New York.